T0318191

SUCCESS IN AGRICULTURAL TRANSFORMATION

Lifting and keeping millions out of poverty requires that smallholder agriculture be productive and profitable in the developing world. Do we know how to make this happen? Researchers and practitioners debate how best to do so. The prevailing methodology, which claims causality from measures of statistical significance, is inductive and yields contradictory results. In this book, instead of correlations, Isabelle Tsakok looks for patterns common to cases of successful agricultural transformation and then tests them against other cases. She hypothesizes that five conditions are necessary to achieve success. She concludes that government investment in and delivery of public goods and services sustained over decades is essential to meeting these conditions and thus successfully transforming poverty-ridden agricultures. No amount of foreign aid can substitute for such sustained government commitment. The single most important threat to government commitment is subservience to the rich and powerful minority.

Isabelle Tsakok has worked on issues of economic development, particularly for agriculture and rural areas, for more than 25 years, primarily as a staff member at the World Bank and, since retirement, off and on as a consultant. Her professional activities focus on the policy and institutional and incentive environments for agriculture, agro-business, and rural development in open, market-oriented, and transition economies. Dr. Tsakok has been involved in agricultural policy analysis, program and project formulation and evaluation, and research and training activities throughout the developing world, primarily in Africa, Asia, the Middle East, and Latin America. She is the author of *Agricultural Price Policy: A Practitioner's Guide to Partial-Equilibrium Analysis* (1990), a manual widely used by development practitioners. Dr. Tsakok also developed the policy simulation game "Exaction" with Professor Graham Chapman (1982–83), then at Cambridge University. She received her Ph.D. in economics from Harvard University.

Success in Agricultural Transformation

What It Means and What Makes It Happen

ISABELLE TSAKOK

CAMBRIDGE UNIVERSITY PRESS

CAMBRIDGE
UNIVERSITY PRESS

Shaftesbury Road, Cambridge CB2 8EA, United Kingdom

One Liberty Plaza, 20th Floor, New York, NY 10006, USA

477 Williamstown Road, Port Melbourne, VIC 3207, Australia

314–321, 3rd Floor, Plot 3, Splendor Forum, Jasola District Centre, New Delhi – 110025, India

103 Penang Road, #05–06/07, Visioncrest Commercial, Singapore 238467

Cambridge University Press is part of Cambridge University Press & Assessment, a department of the University of Cambridge.

We share the University's mission to contribute to society through the pursuit of education, learning and research at the highest international levels of excellence.

www.cambridge.org
Information on this title: www.cambridge.org/9780521717694

© Isabelle Tsakok 2011

First published 2011

A catalogue record for this publication is available from the British Library

Library of Congress Cataloging-in-Publication data
Tsakok, Isabelle.
Success in agricultural transformation : what it means and what makes it happen / Isabelle Tsakok.
p. cm.
Includes bibliographical references and index.
ISBN 978-0-521-71769-4 (pbk.)
1. Agriculture – Economic aspects. 2. Agricultural productivity.
3. Agriculture and state. I. Title.
HD1415.T73 2011
338.1–dc22 2011001822

ISBN 978-0-521-88894-3 Hardback
ISBN 978-0-521-71769-4 Paperback

In Memory of Bruce L. Gardner (1942–2008)
Mentor and friend: Simply the best

Contents

Figures and Table

Preface

I wrote this book because Bruce Gardner wanted me to write it. I kept telling him that I was tired of writing World Bank reports that nobody reads and that governments consider a nuisance. I finally agreed to write the book, provided that he agreed to write it with me. He did, but tragically passed away on March 14, 2008, well before we finished writing. Despite this immeasurable loss, this book is truly a joint product.

The book grew out of discussions Bruce and I had had since September 2001. Soon after I retired from the World Bank in July 2001, I went to see Bruce with one burning question: Why is it that our operations at the Bank to develop smallholder agriculture fail so often? We put in so much effort; we consult the people on the ground as well as their governments; we draw on the best experts. Seemingly, we come on the development scene with tremendous intellectual and financial advantages. But despite these, more often than not, we fail. Why is it that so often our recommendations on how to develop agriculture and reduce rural poverty don't work?

Bruce Gardner said he did not know the answer. We need to do research, he said. I listened in disbelief. I was convinced he would know, since like the entire profession, I regarded him highly – he had written so extensively and had real-world experience working with governments. He was without any doubt an expert's expert. And so began nearly seven wonderful years of working together, digging into this messy subject called promoting agricultural development and reducing rural poverty.

Our very different backgrounds added to the intensity of the research. Bruce was from one of the most powerful countries today, the United States of America, whereas I was from the tiny island of Mauritius, which most educated people have never heard of. He was from a farm family. I was from a Chinese refugee family whose ancestors had long fled the farm. He was an academic. I was a development practitioner. The work was exciting, as we had no sacred cows to protect, no deadlines to meet, and no bosses to please. We tried to meet once every month, although we were often not able to do so in view of Bruce's very busy schedule and my periodic World Bank missions. We called our research *What Works: Why and Why Not?*

I had gone to Bruce because he had impressed me earlier. I first met him when he gave an oral presentation of his review of the World Bank report I task-managed on Morocco rural development (1996–97). Completing this report was a bittersweet experience for the team. Bitter, because the government of the Kingdom of Morocco objected to the report as being much too critical and as its title emphasized the inconvenient fact that there were two Moroccos: the rural and poor – the forgotten half – and the urban and favored half. In its wisdom, Bank managers of the region decided not to publish the report. But the experience was also sweet, because the report was praised as a model by the office of then-Bank president James D. Wolfensohn. From that experience, I was reminded again that politics is definitely in command at the World Bank. At the end of Bruce's presentation, I remember thinking to myself that I would like to work with this person some day, as I found his review both insightful and balanced – and it had none of the nastiness that unfortunately mars too many reviews. So I called him when I was about to retire. By the end of our first meeting, I was delighted when he said he wanted to work with me on a subject we both loved, searching for the answers to my question.

From the very start, we decided to look for patterns in cases of success. These patterns would provide a clue as to what was going on and thus serve as a guide in our search for the essential missing links in cases of failure. Understanding the wellsprings and contribution of agricultural development is an old quest. So as not to be deluged by the voluminous literature grappling with similar issues of agricultural development, we wanted to reformulate alternative views in such a way that we could assess the conditions under which they hold up and where they break down and why.

We started our research with three clear cases of success: England in the 18th and 19th centuries; Japan under the Meiji rule (1868–1912) and after WWII; and the United States in the 19th and 20th centuries. Analyzing these and other developing countries such as the Republic of Korea and Taiwan, China, we identified a pattern upon which we developed a testable hypothesis. That was in March 2002. I was happy we had identified a pattern but wondered whether we should go on, because the conditions we identified were "obvious." I was hesitant about stopping, however, since we still did not know how good the answer to our question was. We had not yet tested our hypothesis by looking at the experience of other countries. It was at that point that Bruce urged that we continue and even write a book together.

Bruce wrote in an email to me on March 7, 2002: "It is obvious that those things ought to make a difference, but it is far from obvious that those are the main things and that other things that people have suggested are less important or unimportant. Showing convincingly that your factors really are key, and not other factors, and that a country needs all five, would be an enormous contribution."

How could we show that countries need all five conditions? Specifically, how could we test our hypothesis? Thus began the second stage of our research. We first needed a methodology that did not have the pitfalls of the current econometric approach. As all agricultural economists know, Bruce was a highly accomplished econometrician. Yet he became dissatisfied with econometrics as a tool for settling policy controversies. In 2007 he argued that "[a] natural way to try to assess agriculture as a cause of growth is through econometric investigation of cross-sectional data for a panel of countries, or possibly regions within a country. However this approach is fraught with difficulties that have so far precluded definitive findings. Most notably, the criteria of statistical significance have not provided answers as durable as the confidence intervals on estimated coefficients would lead one to expect." He therefore categorically rejected the idea that the econometric approach was capable of establishing causality (Tsakok and Gardner, 2007: 1145).[1] Already in 2002, in a review of the state of agricultural economics, he wrote: "What is striking though is how seldom econometric studies have been decisive in determining the state of scholarly opinion and in contrast how much of the work that these chapters discuss derives from ideas, inferences, models and observations that have not been confirmed, refuted, or even seriously confronted with statistical data ... and it is striking after reading the chapters ... that descriptive analysis really doesn't have much less to offer than the large investments in more formally worked-out analyses have achieved" (Gardner and Rausser, eds., 2002: 2241, 2243).

---

[1] Isabelle Tsakok and Bruce Gardner, "Agriculture in Economic Development: Primary Engine of Growth or Chicken and Egg?" *American Journal of Agricultural Economics* 89 (Number 5, 2007): 1145–51.

Instead of trying to confirm hypotheses, we would test them by looking for evidence that might refute them. Thus, as we stated in our book proposal (December 2006) to Cambridge University Press, "Our approach is directed more centrally at refutation of key hypotheses (following the Popperian idea that outcomes inconsistent with a hypothesis constitute more powerful evidence against the hypothesis than positive statistical correlations can generate in favor of the hypothesis)."

While at the London School of Economics and Political Science, I had the good fortune to attend the Popper seminars on scientific method, the methodology of social sciences, and the open society and its enemies. Popper's lectures were always packed, intellectual confrontation always intense. Every lecture was a debate. I found the debates on the irrefutability of Marxism and the problem of induction particularly pertinent to what was going on at that time. That was the period of weekly anti–Vietnam War demonstrations and of university student takeovers of buildings. The Marxists were particularly vocal. Popper demolished their claims by showing that they found confirming evidence of class struggle and the impending collapse of capitalism everywhere. Popper (1963: 37) called it their "soothsaying practice."[2] No evidence could ever refute their claims. The irrefutability of their claims, which they considered to be a strength of their position, was in fact their weakness. Moreover, they generalized from single events that always "proved" their point about the demise of the entire capitalist system.

Theory can never emerge from facts by a logical or mathematical algorithm, Popper (1953/1974: 102) argued. "There is neither a psychological nor a logical induction. Only the falsity of a theory can be inferred from empirical evidence and this inference is purely a deductive one."[3] Little did I realize then that these hotly contested points would prove so valuable in later years in my work as a development practitioner.

Popper had, however, never made clear how new, testable social science theories would look. And economists had not followed his advice

---

[2] Sir Karl Popper, 1963. *Conjectures and Refutations: The Growth of Scientific Knowledge.* London: Routledge and Kegan Paul.

[3] Sir Karl Popper, 1953, 1974. "The Problem of Induction." Reprinted in David Miller, ed., 1983. *A Pocket Popper*: 101–17. Fontana Paperbacks.

and looked for testable hypotheses. Instead they had looked for correlations, and confirmation of those correlations. The result has been a mass of conflicting correlation data, from which not much could be concluded – the situation Bruce lamented. William Berkson (1989), a student of Popper, suggested to me that instead of looking for testable singular predictions of events, I look for patterns that could be tested across different times and societies.[4] So this is the Popperian methodology I adopted. And Bruce was convinced that, given the poor results of normal approaches, it was worth trying.

Once we had decided on the methodology, we reformulated prevailing views on the primary importance of agriculture in the transformation of entire economies, putting them in testable form. Then we looked for cases that might refute them. We also formulated our own hypotheses so as to make them testable. For each of the five conditions, we first had to satisfy ourselves that their existence or non-existence could be ascertained in the real world of available data. Once we were satisfied that sufficient data existed for our purpose, the research then consisted primarily of developing case studies that could potentially refute positions taken or turn out to be consistent with them. Following Popper, positions or hypotheses that could stand up to testing and not be refuted would be accepted as established (until their possible refutation some day). No hypotheses can be proved; rather, the best we can do is to have testable hypotheses that withstand attempted refutation by empirical data.

Except for the case of the United States, I did most of the actual research and writing, and produced a dozen or so research notes. We discussed these in depth every time we met. And only when we were both satisfied with each note did we move on to the next. After several years of such collaboration, Bruce felt we had the building blocks for a book and decided that we should write a book proposal.

We believe our answers can and should be improved upon. If Bruce and I had had more time to work together, we would have devised further tests of our hypotheses, combining both case studies and econometrics. The goal of the next step of our research would have been twofold. The first would have been the challenge of strengthening and refining our hypotheses, so that they could explain more facts of

---

[4] William Berkson, "Testability in the Social Sciences," *Phil. Soc. Sci.* 19 (1989) 157–71.

economic development. The second challenge would have been methodological – to test the scope and limits of Popper's methodology of
social sciences.

As I said in the beginning of this preface, I would not have written this book without Bruce Gardner. However, I had to complete it
without him. I wanted to complete it despite the inevitable pain of
not having Bruce to work with, because by the time we started work
on the proposal, I totally agreed with Bruce, who felt strongly that we
had an important message. The message is that much of smallholder
agriculture remains mired in low productivity and poverty primarily
because of bad governments. The five conditions cannot be created and
maintained without good government. It is not just a matter of transparency and low levels of corruption; not just a matter of creating these
conditions until the next election. Not one government, but a long
succession of governments, has to be committed. Decades of investment in public goods and services, and their proper operation and
maintenance, are required for successful agricultural transformation.
Successful agricultural transformation requires a shared vision and a
long-term approach.

I write this preface with sadness and joy – sadness because Bruce is
no longer with us and joy because he would have been so happy that
the first stage of our joint work is seeing the light of day.

Isabelle Tsakok
November 15, 2010

Acknowledgments

I would not have been able to complete this book without the unwavering support of family and friends. My husband, William Berkson, never doubted that I could finish the book, even during the darkest days. I am grateful to the World Bank for making its wealth of data and analysis easily accessible. Particularly stimulating were discussions on the struggles for development with friends met at or still at the World Bank, and on China with Tang Zhong of Renmin University of China. As a visiting scholar at the Department of Agriculture and Resource Economics, University of Maryland, I was granted access by Lars Olson, chair of the department, to the University of Maryland's libraries while completing the book. I am deeply appreciative. Liesl Koch and Katherine Faulker continued to assist me even after the passing away of Bruce Gardner, when they had no obligation to assist. Their warm friendship and practical help mean everything to me. Liu Xiangping, then a doctoral candidate, was ever so forthcoming and clear in discussing methodological econometrics issues with me. The librarians at the Joint International Monetary Fund/World Bank library always did their best to give me the fullest access possible. Thank you, Sue Borlo, Rebecca West, Naseem Mohammed, and Chet Nunoo-Quarcoo. Juan Feng assisted me with the Excel charts despite her hectic schedule. Constantly busy Syviengxay Creger and Marie-Francoise How Yew Kin, longtime friends since we worked together on North Africa, were always so helpful. Last but certainly not least, I would like to thank Luis Constantino, World Bank sector manager, who made it possible for me to obtain more generous library access.

Summary

Without transforming its agriculture, no country with a major agriculture sector has been able to become a wealthy industrialized economy. What, then, has been the role of agriculture in the industrial transformation of economies? Despite a large area of consensus among researchers, many answers remain controversial.

Research during the earlier decades centered around the support of one or the other of two polar views using a combination of case studies and relatively simple one- or two-sector modeling of a nation's economy. The polar views are that investment in agriculture is essential to achieve industrialization and that agricultural development can be bypassed altogether. During later decades, the case for or against the critical importance of agricultural development has centered on econometric cross-country studies looking for correlations in the data that support one or the other of the polar views. The problem is that positive correlations can be found for both polar views. Evidently, a more complex mechanism is involved in successful development.

This book is the result not of the search for correlations, but of the effort to identify conditions that are common to all successful agricultural transformation. It tests these conditions by looking at experience worldwide. The five conditions that survive these tests are the following:

1. A stable framework of macroeconomic and political stability. The central and local governments are able to enforce peace and order.
2. An effective technology-transfer system. Research and extension messages reach the majority of farmers.
3. Access to lucrative markets. The majority of farmers face expanding markets of paying customers. To them, investing in agricultural and rural production is good business.
4. An ownership system, including a system of usufruct rights, that rewards individual initiative and toil. It is feasible for farm/rural families to gain monetarily from risk taking and hard work.

5. Employment-creating non-agricultural sectors. As agriculture becomes more productive, it must shed labor, which unless absorbed in non-farm jobs that pay as well as agriculture would simply constitute exporting farm poverty to other sectors.

While these may seem obvious as stated, what is not obvious is how some governments have been able to maintain them over decades. How governments have succeeded in maintaining them has varied from country to country. However, there is a common thread. Underlying all five conditions is *sustained government investment in and delivery of public goods and services over decades.*

The main policy implication, then, is that success in agricultural transformation requires decades of government investment in and delivery of public goods and services.[1] Such investment creates a stable environment within which market opportunities flourish and are accessible to all. And it enables generations of farmers, in particular the majority of smallholders, to invest in the productivity of their farms and profit from such investment. It also enables farm and rural households to diversify their risks and returns by including non-farm incomes and opportunities in their portfolio. In short, creating an environment to sustain agricultural transformation requires strong, development-minded, and competent governments to take charge.

This book does not advocate laissez-faire market orientation in which governments are weak and allow only the rich and powerful to access opportunities and gain. It does not advocate the other extreme either – government ownership of the factors of production and a monopoly over decision making – for agricultural growth requires decentralized, knowledgeable, resilient, and motivated decision makers to be in charge. The right- and left-wing diagnoses have both been simplistic and their policy prescriptions off the mark.

This book does, however, advocate a more egalitarian distribution of income and opportunity, for concentration of wealth and political power historically does undermine governments' ability to govern for the prosperity of all. Farmers, not governments, produce and sell. However, only governments can create the environment that enables

---

[1] The actual delivery can be operated by the private sector, but the government is responsible for its financing and making sure it operates efficiently (World Bank: *World Development Report*, 2004).

the majority to do so profitably. To achieve success in agricultural transformation, development-minded governments must be in the driver's
seat – not foreign aid with its legion of experts or free markets serving
only a minority of powerful elites. Sustained government investment
over decades in public goods and services such as education, infrastructure, agricultural research and extension, and markets is the path
to successful agricultural transformation.

Introduction

In this rapidly globalizing world, possibly the most fundamental problem facing us all is the continuing prevalence of poverty in so many countries while only a minority of industrialized countries enjoy wealth. The World Bank estimates that more than half of the world's poor live in rural areas, the majority of them subsistence farmers. "More than half a century of persistent efforts by the World Bank and others have not altered the stubborn reality of rural poverty, and the gap between the rich and poor is widening. Most of the world's poorest people still live in rural areas and this will continue in the foreseeable future" (World Bank, 2002a).[1]

Can success in agricultural transformation make a major contribution to solving this problem, and if so, how? This is one of at least two major questions regarding agricultural policy today. A second one concerns agricultural protection in rich industrialized countries. Such protection has major implications for agricultural development in developing countries. While we do not focus on agricultural policy in rich countries, we do address it insofar as it affects agricultural development in developing countries.

To answer these questions, the book addresses an old debate: How critical is the role of agriculture in economic development? Since England's agricultural and industrial revolutions in the 18th and 19th centuries, the world has witnessed the spread of sustained and transformative rises in income and consumption in only a minority of countries. These are primarily the industrialized economies of Western Europe,

---

[1] Throughout we use the internationally accepted poverty level of two dollars per day. Extreme poverty is at one dollar per day. According to the 2008 World Development Report on agriculture, 75 percent of the world's poor still live in rural areas. The September 2008 update on the Millennium Development Goals (MDGs) indicates that, despite progress, the world population suffering from extreme poverty remains substantial; it declined from 41.8 percent in 1990 (1.8 billion) to 25.7 percent in 2005 (1.4 billion).

North America, Australia, and New Zealand.[2] In the 1980s, there was economic convergence among some countries of Western Europe, such as Ireland, Portugal, and Greece, and since WWII between the West and a minority of rapidly developing countries mainly in East and Southeast Asia – for example, Japan; the Republic of Korea; Taiwan, China; Malaysia; and Singapore. However, there has been widening economic divergence between this minority of industrialized and rapidly industrializing countries and most of the developing world.[3]

A striking similarity among the countries where economic development has lagged is the economic predominance and slow growth of their agricultural sectors, low rates of increase of rural household incomes, and the prevalence of poverty in rural areas. It is equally notable that in the minority of economies that did develop agriculture, the entire economy thrived.

Is this an accident? Or is there a causal link between success in agricultural transformation to broader-based growth in rural areas and the overall economy? Or instead, do the same underlying causes that enable agriculture to thrive also promote broad-based overall economic growth?

These are old questions. Indeed, debates concerning the productive role of agriculture date back to the physiocrats in 18th-century France. Among development economists, there are two polar views regarding the centrality of agriculture's role in building the wealth of a nation. At one pole, there is a large literature arguing that agricultural development is necessary for the overall economic transformation of a country (Eicher and Staatz, eds., 1998). The contribution of agriculture in terms of food, fiber, raw materials, labor, and financial surplus (including foreign exchange) to invest is essential to jump-start the process of industrialization in its early stages, during which, by definition, the industrial sector is small. At the other pole is the view that economies can bypass this process of agricultural development and instead invest in building an industrial base (while extracting

[2] This group of countries is commonly referred to as the West or the Western world because these countries share a common European (Anglo-Saxon, Romance, etc.) cultural heritage. Unlike high-income industrialized economies, New Zealand is high income but with agriculture still its most important tradable sector.
[3] "The average income in the richest 20 countries is already 37 times that in the poorest countries.... Both the gap between rich and poor countries and the people living on fragile lands have doubled in the past 40 years" (World Bank, 2003c).

agricultural surplus for industrial investment). The latter view, popular in the 1950s, has recently gained adherents, even among macroeconomists. Many believe "resources devoted to slow growing agriculture as wasted" (Timmer, July 2005).

The pro-agriculture view argued by Johnston and Mellor (1961), among others, emphasized the five potential contributions of agriculture to the structural transformation of an economy and the critical importance of investing in agriculture in order to generate a surplus for industrialization. This view did not, however, explicitly claim that rural poverty would be significantly reduced in the process, although rural poverty reduction was implied. Johnston and Mellor did advocate a unimodal land distribution (land fairly equally divided among the majority of farmers), which would make possible an equitable distribution of the benefits of agricultural development. Kuznets (1968) argued that a revolution in agricultural productivity is indispensable for modern economic growth.

The pro-agriculture view defended agriculture's role in response to the position of the early development economists (Rosenstein-Rodan, 1943; Lewis, 1954; Hirschman, 1958; Fei and Ranis, 1964). They treated agriculture as a passive sector with weak links to non-agriculture, a resource reservoir from which to extract labor and other resources to invest in industry, considered to be the leading sector. Agriculture could be exploited, but it was not necessary to invest in the sector for it to contribute to economic growth. In the Lewis model, expansion of a two-sector economy is fueled by unlimited supplies of rural labor. Expansion of the capitalist sector would continue until capitalist and rural wages were equal. This anti-agriculture view was reinforced by Prebisch (1959), who argued that agriculture faces secularly declining terms of trade. Thus, for different reasons, investing in agriculture was a bad development strategy. We label this anti-agriculture view the "squeeze agriculture" development strategy. The entire import-substitution industrialization (ISI) strategy, popular among developing countries in the 1950s, is predicated on the belief that investing in agriculture is a bad strategy.

The key difference between these polar views was whether or not they asserted that it was necessary to invest in the agricultural sector for it to play a key development role. Both agreed that the sector was necessary to generate the surplus needed by industry in its early stages but disagreed on the importance of agricultural invest-ments to generate such surplus. A more recent (mid-1980s) version of this anti-agriculture view is based on trade: World cereals prices have fallen by 50 percent over a span of some four decades – from around USD 300 per metric ton (in USD 1990 prices) in 1960 to around USD 150 per metric ton in 2005. This secular decline in real cereals prices, combined with agricultural price subsidies in mem-ber countries of the Organisation for Economic Co-operation and Development (OECD) – an estimated USD 360 billion per year – removes much of the rationale for investing in agriculture (Ashley and Simon, 2001: 405). Whether the food crisis caused by the spectacular rise in cereals prices of early 2008 will actually rekindle and sustain interest among donors in investing in the sector remains to be seen (Slayton and Timmer, 2008).[4]

In sum, the measure of agriculture's contribution to overall eco-nomic development in increasingly urban economies and whether it is necessary to invest in the sector to generate that contribution is still in doubt among many academics, policy makers, and development practitioners.

What the Book Does and Does Not Address and How it is Organized

This book revisits this old but still unresolved debate. Drawing upon selected historical and post-WWII country experiences, it seeks to answer two main questions:

1. In a world of widespread rural poverty and highly unequal develop-ment, does success in agricultural transformation matter?
2. If it does, in what ways does it matter, and how can such transfor-mation be brought about?

Part One deals with what success in agricultural transformation means, and Part Two with what makes it happen. To address the first issue, the book evaluates the evidence on the role of successful agricultural transformation in promoting industrialization and general economic

---

[4] Rice prices rose to $1,100 per ton in April 2008, from $375 per ton in December 2007. Over a longer period, real (in constant 2007 dollars) rice prices declined from $2,500 per ton (1974) to $200 per ton (2002) (Timmer, 2007: 51).

growth, assessing as definitively as possible the relative accuracy of the polar views. To address the second, it discusses the literature and country evidence on causes and consequences of sustained increases in agricultural productivity and broad-based growth.

This book, however, does not address two major agriculture-related concerns. The first is how to achieve environmentally sustainable agricultural development. Environmental sustainability deals in part with the selection of agricultural technologies and is without doubt essential for long-term agricultural and overall economic development, but it is not the focus of this book. With the reality of climate change, the specific steps governments should consider to facilitate agriculture's adaptation constitute a major subject that deserves at least a book by itself. The arguments here regarding the importance of achieving success in agricultural transformation and the public foundations of achieving such success are not affected by considerations of environmental sustainability in the context of climate change. Successful agricultural transformation in the years to come must be environmentally sustainable and adjust to climate change. The second concern is the multi-functionality of agriculture – for example, agriculture as the repository of bio-diversity and recreational activities. The argument is that as a sector that fulfills several critical public sector roles, it should be supported. Again, the arguments made here are not affected by considerations of multi-functionality. Environmental sustainability and multi-functionality are both important concerns, but they are not the focus of this book.[5]

The book is organized in two parts. Part One reviews the evidence on the role of sustained agricultural development in promoting overall growth, raising rural incomes, and reducing rural poverty. It also compares the approach of the book with that of several other studies that set out to evaluate the contribution of the sector to economic development and poverty reduction. Part Two proposes a hypothesis about what makes success in agricultural transformation happen and systematically tests it using evidence from both economic history and more recent post-WWII worldwide experiences. The hypothesis proposes

---

[5] McCalla (2000: 2–5) discusses the three major challenges of agriculture in the 21st century. These are global food security, poverty reduction, and sustainable natural resource management.

five conditions that must be maintained for decades for agricultural transformation to materialize. The hypothesis itself draws upon patterns identified in successful agricultures.

Throughout, the book is structured so as to highlight "main messages" and thus facilitate selective reading by the busy reader.

The Meaning of "Success in Agricultural Transformation"

"Success in agricultural transformation" refers to two simultaneous developments:

1. Increases in productivity (output per unit of input, variously defined) sustained over two to three decades at least; and
2. Sustained increases in income for the majority of farm/rural households.

Quantitatively, and at macro and sector levels, the process of agricultural transformation is characterized by (a) a declining share of agriculture to gross domestic product (GDP); (b) a declining share of agricultural employment to total employment;[6] (c) positive growth in productivity sustained over several decades; and (d) steady income increases over several decades for at least 50 percent of rural households.[7]

Thus cases of agricultural development where only a minority of rural households participate in and benefit from economic growth are ruled out as being "successfully transformed." It follows that the growth of dualistic agricultures is ruled out as being successfully transformed, because only a minority of rural households benefit. The concept of successful agricultural transformation used here goes beyond the concept of sustained agricultural growth in that it has a distributional component, namely broad-based income growth and rural poverty reduction. The book takes an inclusive view of successful agricultural transformation.[8] This view borrows from Sen's (2000) *Development*

---

[6] When the absolute number of people employed in agriculture declines, Tomich, Kilby, and Johnston (1995: box 1.1) call it the "structural turning point."

[7] The exact length of time it takes varies among countries, as historical experience indicates. See country cases discussed in this book. However, it is always "long." Also see Timmer (2007: 26). Timmer (1988) characterizes this long process in terms of different stages.

[8] Timmer (2009: 4–6, fig. 1–1) characterizes the successful process in similar terms, consistent with what is described here. Quantitatively, the process has four main features: a falling share in economic output and employment; a rising share of urban economic output in industry

as Freedom. For Sen, development is not just increases in income and productivity, but more fundamentally, the expansion of human capabilities, enabling the enrichment of human lives. People have greater freedom to choose the lives they want to live. Likewise, success in agricultural transformation transforms human lives. Such success is both the means to transforming the daily lives of millions of smallholders and poor people and an end in itself. My view of agricultural transformation therefore goes beyond the instrumental view of Johnston and Mellor (1961) stressing the material contribution of agricultural development to industrialization.

Empirically, productivity increases are measured by total factor productivity (TFP) growth or best proxies thereof.[9] For increases in the income of rural households, the book uses movements in median household incomes or best proxies thereof.[10] The concept of successful transformation in this book thus has both efficiency and distributional dimensions: sustained and widespread productivity gains in agriculture and substantial income gains for poor households, which constitute the bulk of the rural population.

In the book, the term "agriculture" refers to the crop, livestock, and forestry sub-sectors.[11] The term "rural" is notorious for its ambiguity, as the concept varies among countries, and sometimes even within the same country over time.[12] For the purposes of data collection, we have no option but to accept (as does the World Bank) the definition of "rural" adopted by a given country government, even if the definitions

---

and services; the migration of rural workers to urban settings; and a demographic transition in birthrates and death rates.

[9] TFP growth refers to the output growth not accounted for by input growth. Appendix B presents a glossary of commonly used economic terms.

[10] The best proxies are often per capita income levels and their rates of increase over time and a measure indicative of the country's income distribution.

[11] As in many works on agriculture, this book does not deal with the fishing sub-sector.

[12] The term "rural" is obvious to the layperson, but its administrative/operational definition varies by country, and within a given country, over time. Census criteria take various cutoff points between rural and urban. For example, in Mexico the cutoff point is a locality with more or less than 2,500 inhabitants. In other countries the cutoff point may vary between 5,000 and 10,000. The World Bank accepts each country's definition, even though there is no consistent definition of "rural" across countries. There is really no choice but to accept the country's definition. Another example is China, where the concept of what constitutes "rural" has changed. "Rural" population is the population not included in towns. What constitutes a "town" changed in 1964 and 1984.

differ across countries. What is common in the various definitions is that "rural" is a multi-dimensional concept that refers to areas where population density, and the availability and quality of public infrastructure and services, are lower than in urban areas. However, at the end of the day, the administrative demarcation of rural versus urban is arbitrary. The practical implication of this arbitrariness is that it is poverty reduction that matters for this book, not whether the poverty is rural or urban. After all, the rural poor crowd cities and are then counted as urban. It is the stagnation of the agriculture and rural sector and the despair of agriculture/rural households that are the problem, wherever they are.

Methodological Approach of the Book: Testing Theories by Seeking Refutations, Not Confirmations

The book uses economic history and quantitative analysis in the following ways. First, it documents the ways in which successful agricultural transformation has enabled countries to promote industrial wealth and raise the income levels of the majority of poor households, in particular, rural households. Second, it identifies patterns and regularities in historical and post-WWII data. Using insights gained from these patterns and regularities, it formulates hypotheses that, it is hoped, can constitute a fruitful start for further research. On the basis of these empirical patterns, it hypothesizes that five conditions must be met for achieving success in agricultural transformation. Third, it tests this hypothesis by seeking instances that could refute the five conditions.

This approach stands in sharp contrast to the more common approach, which involves a search for supporting or confirming instances using regression analysis and computable general equilibrium (CGE) modeling. Instead, in the present approach, testable hypotheses are developed to explain well-known events in agricultural development.[13] To assess the relative accuracy of competing universal hypotheses on growth and development, one tests them by seeking to refute them. This is counterintuitive to the prevailing practice, which is to find confirmations, based on an inductive use of econometric

---

[13] On testability in the social sciences within the Popperian approach, see Berkson (1989).

measures of statistical significance. Currently, the approach is to get theory to emerge from evidence by using regression. Regressions are run on a number of variables in the data, usually in the hope or expectation that some of the variables are a cause of the others. When it is found that a correlation exists, the "null hypothesis" is refuted, and a theory of a causal relationship is confirmed. This theory is then advanced. It is important to recognize that even though logically speaking a "null hypothesis" is an alternative theory, it is extremely weak in giving us any guidance on where to test further, as it contains no theory of causation.[14]

It is no wonder that this approach has led to contradictory claims, as evidenced by several recent studies, including those on agriculture's role in promoting pro-poor growth.[15] Within this confirmation-cum-inductive-inference approach, there is no independently replicable way to resolve contradictions. Specifically, the book considers the validity of claims made in several recent studies regarding the importance of growth of the primary sector or of agriculture in promoting income growth and in reducing poverty – for example, studies on India (Ravallion and Datt 1994; Beesly, Burgess, and Esteve-Volart 2004), China (Ravallion and Chen, 2004), Indonesia (Timmer, September 2004), and worldwide cross-country regressions by the World Bank (January 2005). Using econometric methods, these studies derive statistically significant coefficients and quantify various elasticity estimates – for example, the elasticity of poverty with respect to growth, cross-sector growth elasticity, and elasticity of connection. Then they proceed to infer causality from growth to poverty reduction and make judgments about the relative quantitative role of primary or agricultural growth within this causal structure.

In his recent review of these studies, Timmer (July 2005: 11–12) writes, "What are we to make of all this confusion?"[16] Timmer proposes

---

[14] This same point is made by Meehl (1978: 817) and is discussed in Freedman (1991: 310). See Appendix A.

[15] According to one definition (Martin Ravallion, 2004, of the World Bank), growth is pro-poor if it reduces poverty. This happens when the distribution of growth reduces poverty and average living standards rise. According to a second definition (Baulch and McCullock, 2000; Kakwani and Pernia, 2000), growth is "pro-poor" when poverty falls more than it would have if all incomes had grown at the same rate – in other words, when growth disproportionately benefits the poor.

[16] The countries discussed are India, Bangladesh, Indonesia, Japan, the Republic of Korea, Taiwan, China, and the People's Republic of China.

"enforcing common data, definitions and methodologies [that] would help clarify the different cases considerably."The answer here is: change the method.

The approach of this book is directed more centrally at the refutation of key hypotheses. In this, it follows the Popperian idea that outcomes inconsistent with a hypothesis constitute more powerful evidence against the hypothesis than positive statistical correlations can generate in favor of the hypothesis. The focus on potential and actual refutations is the hallmark of Popper's methodology and stands in sharp contrast to the current inductive approach that seeks confirmations (Popper, 1961: 134). Popper makes use of a well-known logical principle, namely the asymmetry between confirmation and refutation: Countless clear confirmations cannot establish the truth of a universal claim, but one clear refutation can refute a universal claim. Thus, finding another white swan cannot prove that all swans are white, but finding one black swan can demolish the universal claim that all swans are white. In our case, for example, the finding that the surplus food, raw materials, and investible wealth generated by England's agricultural revolution (the white swan) were essential to the success of England's industrial revolution cannot prove the universal claim that agricultural development is an essential condition of successful industrialization (all swans are white). The successful industrialization of the United States is a refutation of such a universal claim. It constitutes the black swan.[17] The methodological approach of the book is discussed more fully in Appendix A.[18]

[17] Nassim Nicholas Taleb, author of *The Black Swan: The Impact of the Highly Improbable*, refers to Popper's technique of using falsifications to distinguish between science and non-science (Taleb, 2007: 56–58). In his section entitled "Negative Empiricism," he argues that "we can get closer to the truth by negative instances, not by verification! Contrary to conventional wisdom our body of knowledge does not increase from a series of confirmatory observations, like the turkey's." Taleb uses the existence of black swans, events of low predictability but with high impact, or the non-occurrence of highly probable events to question how we go about dealing with risk, uncertainty, and outliers. Of particular interest to social scientists, he lambasts portfolio managers in the way they measure "risk." Thus, "(we will see how they dress up the intellectual fraud with mathematics). This problem is endemic in social matters" (2007: xviii).
[18] Tsakok and Gardner described their research methodology in a paper presented at the American Agricultural Economics Association annual conference in Portland, Oregon, July 2007 (Tsakok and Gardner, 2007: 1145–51).

Audience for the Book

This book is intended for development professionals and anyone interested in promoting agricultural development so that it can contribute substantially to the reduction of widespread rural poverty.

Given the potentially broad readership, the book does not assume the reader is familiar with technical economic jargon. It presents the arguments in plain English; however, when that is not possible, it explains the technical jargon in plain English in Appendix B. The prospective audience includes the following:

- Faculty members and students in undergraduate-level courses in economic development who can use this book as a primary or supplementary text.
- Staff members at aid agencies, non-governmental organizations (NGOs), and other civil society organizations who are concerned not only with bringing immediate relief, but helping the rural poor develop longer-term solutions to their chronic problem of deprivation.
- Development practitioners who, on a day-to-day basis, grapple with how best to expand the meager asset base of poor rural households and improve their access to higher-productivity jobs in agriculture and elsewhere. The practical question often is: Given the constraints of the situation and the tools at hand, what factors should be given priority?
- Policy makers of national governments in central and sector ministries and their staff, who can shape and implement policy and mobilize public resources.
- Those in the general public who are interested in one of the most important achievements of humankind, a productive agriculture that has saved millions from the devastation of the Malthusian Law of Population.[19]

---

[19] Thomas R. Malthus states in the first edition of his "Essay on the Principle of Population" (1798): "Population when unchecked increases in a geometrical ratio. Subsistence only increases in an arithmetical ratio. A slight acquaintance with numbers will show the immensity of the first power in comparison of the second.... And, that the superior power of population cannot be checked without producing misery or vice, the ample portion of these two bitter ingredients in the cup of human life, and the continuance of the physical causes that seemed to have produced them bear too convincing a testimony."

Indeed, success in agricultural transformation has done more: It has transformed the lives of millions for the better.

What countries have defeated Malthus's grim predictions and how?[20] This book is a search for those enduring conditions which have made successful agricultural transformation happen.

---

[20] Giovanni Federico (2005) discusses the economic history of agriculture from 1800 to 2000.

PART ONE

THE MANY FACES OF AGRICULTURAL TRANSFORMATION IN AN INDUSTRIALIZING WORLD AND WHAT IT MEANS

Introduction to Part One

Summary. The two polar views regarding the centrality of agriculture's contribution to building the industrial wealth of a nation are refuted in a variety of country contexts. They have to be substantially qualified as follows:

First, there is strong but not universal support for the pro-agriculture view. The centrality of agriculture's contribution depends largely on what other opportunities the country could exploit to earn or attract foreign exchange and other funds to invest – for example, trade in mineral exports, foreign direct investment (FDI), aid, and remittances. In most cases where agriculture made substantial contributions to the economy, it did so following major investments by private and public sectors and major institutional changes. Moreover, decades of agricultural development does not necessarily by itself reduce rural poverty, for much depends on the prevailing income and land distribution, as well as the functioning of rural labor markets, among other things.

Second, success in agricultural transformation (sustained productivity and broad-based income increases) itself is furthered by (a) sustained industrialization within an expanding overall economy and (b) well-functioning rural labor markets to raise the wages and incomes of rural households. Thus agriculture's successful transformation itself depends on its integration into the wider national and international economies. Sustained agricultural productivity is an important part of the transformation story, but it is not the whole story, for there is a close interdependence between sustained agricultural development and poverty reduction, on one hand, and sustained industrialization, on the other. The causality is two-way. There can be a virtuous circle of growth and transformation between the two sectors.

Third, where agriculture is important – it contributes to some 10 percent or more of GDP or 10 percent or more of employment – there is no evidence that a country can successfully bypass promoting agricultural productivity growth and yet succeed in solving its twin problems of sustained industrial growth and rural poverty reduction. Quite the contrary has been the case. Extracting agricultural surplus without reinvesting in the sector has undermined not only agricultural development (as is to be expected), but also the country's entire development and therefore its poverty reduction agenda.

Main questions asked and coverage of review: This book assesses what has been the contribution of agriculture to overall economic development and rural poverty reduction in widely differing country contexts and time periods. It then compares the evidence with the claims of the polar views. Does the evidence support, undermine, or modify the claims? Chapter I analyzes the role of agriculture in the earlier developmental stages of three major industrialized economies today: England in the 18th and 19th centuries, Japan since the Meiji Restoration in 1868 until the 1960s, and the United States from the mid-19th to the 20th century. These three countries are of particular interest because England was the first country to experience both agricultural and industrial revolutions; Japan was the first non-Western country to industrialize, and the United States, a major industrialized country today, was a country with abundant rural labor (CARL) in the early stages of its industrialization in the mid-19th century (Tomich et al., 1995: 67–77). Chapter II reviews selected post-WWII experiences of long-term (three decades and longer) agricultural development in a range of developing economies. It excludes economies where agriculture has always been unimportant – for example, oil-exporting economies such as Saudi Arabia and city-states such as Singapore.

I

The Industrialized World

Success in Agricultural Transformation in England, Japan, and the United States

I.I. England's Agriculture in the 18th and 19th Centuries

Summary. The agricultural revolution in the 18th and 19th centuries in England is the first known case of successful agricultural transformation. England's experience is both good and bad news for those who argue that agricultural development is necessary at the early stages of industrialization.

The good news is that agriculture's contribution was substantial and timely. Economic historians argue that, without such contribution, England's industrial revolution might well have been aborted. Counterfactuals are hard to prove. The counterclaim, however – that England's agricultural development could have been bypassed – has no supporting evidence.

The bad news is that agricultural development alone did not immediately generate substantial benefits for poor rural households. The poor had to wait for decades after the start of the agricultural and industrial revolutions and after massive emigration to the New World tightened labor markets, thus enabling their wages to rise.

The core of the revolution. That there was an agricultural revolution is not debated among economic historians. What is still debated is its precise timing and distinguishing features. There is a consensus that the core of the revolution was "an increase in cereal yields per acre that is the amount of grain that could be produced from a given area and sown with a particular crop" (Overton, 1998: 1). Increases in output were brought about by increases in productivity instead of area expansion. Economic historians agree that the revolution consisted of a set of agricultural practices that enabled farmers to break the closed circuit that prevented increases in output other than by extending cultivated area. Before the agricultural revolution, increases in output required increases in area or a reduction in fallow. After the revolution, instead of fallow, farmers adopted new crop rotations whereby they planted fodder crops, which enabled them to keep more animals, obtain more dung, increase the fertility of the soil, and increase output.

Two main concepts of the revolution. The debate is not whether there was an agricultural revolution but (a) what range of changes should be considered critical and (b) how far back in time one should date the start of the revolution. Broadly, there are two concepts of what changes constituted the revolution. One concept focuses on farming techniques only, the cows and ploughs concept. The other, broader concept includes institutional changes, in particular social and economic relationships or institutions within farming and the spread of market development. The debate about what constitutes an agricultural revolution or transformation is still with us today, as the assessment of more recent country cases will show.

The narrow concept. The main changes identified by the "cows and ploughs" concept were (a) the introduction of nutritious fodder crops, in particular turnip and clover, and the adoption of a four-course rotation system of wheat–turnips–barley or oats–clover or rye-grass (the so-called Norfolk four-course rotation); (b) the reduction of bare fallows due to the four-course rotation system; (c) the use of mechanical seed drills instead of broadcasting seed and the increasing use of agricultural machinery – for example, threshers and reapers; (d) the marling of light soils and the draining of heavy clay soils; and (e) the improvement of livestock breeds.

The broader concept. The institutional changes referred to in the broader concept of the agricultural revolution include (a) the removal of common property rights as more and more commons became private property through enclosure mandated by successive acts of Parliament (this process accelerated between 1790 and 1820) and the consolidation of small farms into large farms (Overton, 1998: 148–49);[1] and (b) the geographical expansion of markets as different methods of

---

[1] There is debate among economic historians concerning which period had the highest rate of enclosures. Note that the enclosure movement was a violation of common property rights, giving land that the poor used to the rich. In today's terms, the enclosure movement would be considered a reverse land reform.

transport improved, with improvements in systems of market information and the development of the daily mail (1840), and as the medieval
system of industrial/commercial regulations was being dismantled in
favor of competition;[2] (c) the prevalence of a tripartite landlord–tenant
farmer–laborer structure of a commercialized agriculture within which
the landlord–tenant farmer relationship had responsibilities clearly
delineated and which imparted security of tenure (even if there was no
legal sanction); (d) a fluidity between country and town people, namely
the landed gentry and the urban business community, which benefited
estate management through the infusion of both capital and business
ideas (Chambers and Mingay, 1966: 200); and (e) the institution of
agricultural societies.

*Alternative periods given for the agricultural revolution, either preceding
or simultaneous with the industrial revolution.* Since economic historians
debate about the range of changes that constitute the agricultural revolution in England, they disagree about the start and end dates of this
revolution. The alternative dates include the following periods: 1560–
1673, 1650–1750, 1750–1850 (Overton, 1998: 6–7), and 1650–1880
(Chambers and Mingay, 1966). It is notable that the periods for the
transformation stretch over decades, over a century at least. This long
period is of note particularly when the book considers post-WWII
experiences. For our purpose here, what is important is that the period
of the agricultural revolution either preceded or was simultaneous with
the industrial revolution, the beginning of which is dated from the
mid-18th to the early 19th century.

*Impact on agricultural output and productivity, employment, and income
of the rural poor.* The question is: What was the main contribution
of the agricultural revolution to the industrial revolution and to the
incomes of poor rural households? The three figures below show sustained productivity and production increases in English agriculture
(1700–1850), selected key structural changes in that period, and data
on increases in prices and wages of agricultural labor. The main story
they tell is that the agricultural revolution was significant in terms of
agricultural production and productivity increases, and that it had an

---

[2] Adam Smith (1723–1790) published *An Inquiry into the Nature and Causes of the Wealth of
Nations* in 1776.

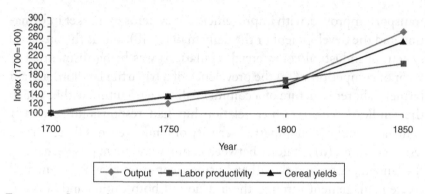

Figure 1.1. Sustained productivity and production increases in English agriculture (1700–1850).
Source: Overton (1998: table 3.11).

impact on the structure of the economy, among other things, but the beneficial impact on rural poverty reduction came only after a long lag. In fact, in the earlier years and for decades, real wages declined! Since available quantitative data do not fully answer the question asked, the book also draws upon the writings of major thinkers of that period.

Quantitative data on agricultural output and agriculture's changing role in the economy. The data presented in Figure 1.1 shows sustained agricultural production and productivity increases between 1700 and 1850. These sustained increases in agriculture inevitably altered the structure of the English economy and the contribution of agriculture within it. In 1700, agriculture dominated the economy, and the landed aristocracy dominated political life. As shown in Figure 1.2, agriculture's contribution was estimated to be around 43 percent of GDP in 1700. But by 1880, its contribution had declined to 10 percent. Roughly 75 percent of the entire English population was directly or indirectly dependent on agriculture in 1700. By the late 19th century, the urban population predominated predominated.

Did household incomes increase for the rural poor during the agricultural revolution? It is difficult to grasp the whole picture of the impact on the incomes of poor rural households, because systematic data were not collected then. From the piecemeal evidence available, the picture

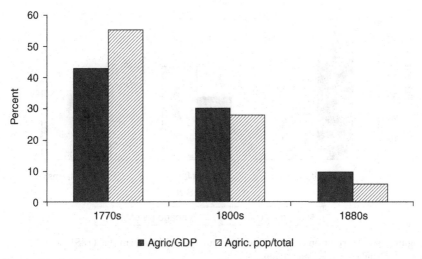

Figure 1.2. Selected key structural changes in England (1700–1880).
Sources: Agriculture: Chambers and Mingay (1966); agricultural population: Mingay (1996).

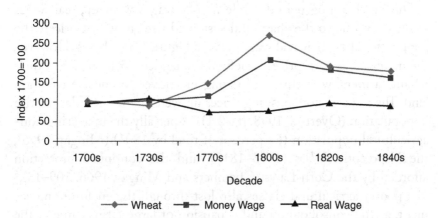

Figure 1.3. Wheat prices, agricultural money, and real wages, 10-year averages (1700–49 = 100). The corn laws were repealed in 1846.
Source: Overton (1998: table 3.1).

is mixed until around the mid-19th century (Overton, 1998: 70).[3] As shown in Figure 1.3, we have agricultural wage data, but these are not the income levels for rural households. From agricultural wage data alone, we can see that the rural poor suffered real wage decreases for a long time, at least until the mid-19th century.

[3] Comprehensive, nation-wide agricultural statistics were not collected in England until 1866.

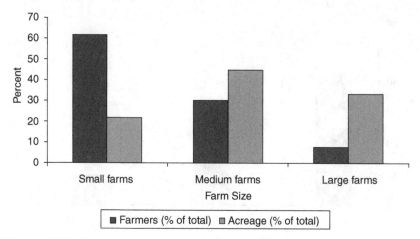

Figure 1.4. Distribution of farmers and agricultural land by farm size (1851).
Source: Chambers and Mingay (1966).

During this long period, while money wages went up, real wages went down due to the sharp and sustained rises in wheat prices. The poor suffered as their real wages fell, as Figure 1.3 – shows. However, the increases in corn prices benefited the landed aristocracy and their tenant-farmers, who thus had strong incentives to enclose common land. The main factors pushing prices up were the unprecedented rise in population (Overton, 1998: fig. 3.1),[4] especially the increasing non-agricultural population (64 percent of total by 1801) (Mingay, 1996); the Napoleonic Wars (1793–1815); and the continued protection afforded by the Corn Laws (Chambers and Mingay, 1966: 109–13).[5] The poorer agricultural classes also lost through the enclosure movement, as the consolidation and expansion of large farms came at the expense of small farms (a small farm is 100 acres or fewer). By the 1850s, small farms were a minority. Medium to large farmers constituted 38 percent of farmers but controlled 78 percent of total land (see Figure 1.4). Also, by then, around 75–80 percent of land was controlled by landlords who leased their land to tenants and who were responsible for much of the capital investment in land (Overton, 1998: 195, 204).

[4] Population rose from 6 million in the 1740s to 8.7 million in 1800 and to 16.7 million in 1851. According to Gregory King, a late 17th century statistician, he expected England's population to grow from 5.5 million in 1700 to 6.42 million in 1800 and to 7.35 million in 1900. He assumed static agricultural technology.
[5] There was also a succession of very poor harvests from the late 1780s to 1800.

Agriculture had become fully commercialized. There was increased agricultural investment, which gradually included the purchase of industrially manufactured farm implements. The expansion of export and re-export trades generated much wealth, which was reinvested in agricultural land by the successful merchant class (Jones, 1974: 88). A virtuous circle of agricultural and industrial integration and expansion had set in. The laboring class would benefit from such integration but only in the long term (around the mid-19th century).

Demand-pull from expanding industry. Agricultural wage (nominal and real) and farm size distribution data, however important, tell only part of the story. The other part is the increasing integration of agriculture and the rural economy into the expanding industrial sector – for example, increasing employment opportunities in textile mills and the expanding railway, road, and canal systems. The economic fate of agricultural and rural households very much depended on the rising industrial demand for labor. Industrial expansion reduced surplus agricultural labor by the mid-19th century, leading to a sustained though slow improvement in wages and the living conditions of laborers (Mingay, 1977: 52–53). In the 18th century, most labor was not mobile.[6] So the beneficiaries of increased industrial demand for labor in the 18th century and the earlier decades of the 19th century were mainly in the Midlands and the north, and around London. In the south, however, with as yet little pull from industrial growth, agricultural wages were much lower. In southern England, laborers' wages often had to be supplemented by poor rates (Mingay, 1977: 52, 213–15). Comparing the middle of the 19th with the middle of the 18th century, average nominal agricultural wages had risen by 66 percent in the north but by only 14 percent in the south. During the mid-19th century, the tightening of labor markets was also aided by the great waves of emigration. In his lectures, Toynbee (1884: sec. 6) noted that some 3 million people were estimated to have left since 1846.

Biomedical measures of differential social impact of the agricultural and industrial revolutions. As pointed out by Fogel (2004: 36), income measures often do not tell the whole story of the welfare impact of socio-

---

[6] Low mobility was partly due to poor transport, and partly also to the Law of Settlement which restricted laborers to their parish which was responsible for doling out poor relief.

economic changes. For example, data on the gap in stature between upper and lower classes in Great Britain in the 19th century show that the gap apparently increased between the end of the Napoleonic Wars (1815) and the beginning of the 20th century, whereas calculations based on income distributions suggest that income inequality remained constant during much of the 19th century. Furthermore, data show that the life expectancy of the lower classes remained constant or declined in some localities, but the gap in life expectancy between the upper and lower classes increased by about 10 years from the beginning of the industrial revolution to the end of the 19th century. Thus biomedical evidence reinforces the conclusion that the poor (rural and urban) did not benefit from both revolutions until decades after their onset and that the disparity between rich and poor increased during those decades.

Greater income and wealth but greater disparity in their distribution and a substantial lag in improvement for the laboring class. By late 19th century, England, the birthplace of both the agricultural and industrial revolutions, emerged as a world leader and a great colonial power. England had indeed made a great leap, but it took at least a century. The extent to which the poor classes (rural and urban) benefited from these revolutions, especially before the mid-19th century, has been a subject of great controversy. Economic historians and many famous writers have documented the tremendous wealth creation of certain classes and contrasted it with the growth in pauperism.[7] William Blake's "dark Satanic mills" crystallized the gloom of this difficult period for the working classes.[8] Toynbee (1884: sec. 14) noted that the condition of the working classes had improved since 1846 because demand for labor had increased, as labor was being employed more regularly than in the preceding century, and because of free trade. Using data on weekly cash wages of agricultural laborers from 1824 to 1907, Mingay (1972: 25–60; table 1) pointed out that the gap between agricultural and urban wages tended to widen down to 1850, but from then on, the gap narrowed as intensified migration, expanded employment in the railways and drainage works, and the growth of manufacturing

---

[7] Some of the famous writers are: William Blake (1757–1829); Charles Dickens (1812–1870); John Stuart Mill (1806–1873); and Karl Marx (1818–1883).

[8] The poem is "Milton: And did Those Feet in Ancient Time?"

contributed to the prosperity of the mid-Victorian boom. Writing in 1969, Sir John Hicks pointed out "that there is no doubt that industrialism, in the end, has been highly favorable to the real wage of labour. Real wages have risen enormously in all industrialized countries, over the last century.... The important question was why it was so long delayed; whether there was a small rise, or an actual fall, in the general level of wages in England between (say) 1780 and 1840 leaves the issue untouched. It is the lag in wages behind industrialization which ... has to be explained" (Hicks, 1969: 148). The poor had to wait (Hartwell et al., 1972: vii).

Continuing controversy over timing of gains in real wages in pre-industrial England. Unlike other economic historians to date, Clark argues that real wages of the laboring class (e.g., builders, carpenters) rose steadily around the 1640s, well before the onset of the industrial revolution in the mid-18th century. He also argues that his "new series suggest that the classic Industrial Revolution of the eighteenth century was much more favorable to workers' real earnings than other recent studies suggest" (Clark, 2005: 1308–19).[9] However, in Clark's series, real wages were depressed around the 1770s–1810s due to heavy indirect taxation to pay for the Napoleonic Wars and fight the American Revolution as well as due to disruptions in trade during this turbulent period. Furthermore, it was not until the 1820s that real wages were higher than the levels of the mid-18th century. Thus, even if Clark's claim is correct, there is still a long pause in real wage increases after the onset of the agricultural and industrial revolutions. Furthermore, he provides no evidence to counteract Mingay's claims of the widening gap between urban and rural wages until around 1850.

Similar experiences of agricultural transformation in Western Europe. Economic historians point out that higher agricultural productivity made possible the entire economic transformation not only of England but of Western Europe, for it supplied the food, labor, raw materials, and surplus funds required by industry, as well as a market for industrial goods. According to Slicher Van Bath (1963), England and the Low Countries had the highest yields and experienced the highest

[9] A prior real wage series was from Henry Phelps Brown and Sheila Hopkins (1962). The series ran from 1264–1954.

yield increases in this early period. In these countries, seed/yield ratios between 1500 and 1820 increased from 7.4 to 11.1. Between 1880 and 1930, wheat yields continued to increase by roughly 20 percent (Grigg, 1992: tables 4.1–4.3). They point out that for the first time in the history of humankind, the high birthrate in Western Europe between 1750 and 1850 was accompanied not by famine but by a major expansion in production. The key developments historians point to are as follows:

- In England, sustained population growth from around 1740 to 1840 was unprecedented. The English population never exceeded a total of around 5 to 6 million before the 18th century. However, from around 1780 and into the 19th century, England's population grew at more than 1 percent per annum. Total population rose from 8.7 million in 1800 to 16.7 million in 1851 (and 30 million by 1901) (Overton, 1998: 8, 65, 69, fig. 3.1).
- The rural population of the Western world is estimated to have doubled between 1750 and 1890.

Western civilization in the 18th century was unique in that it escaped the dire consequences of the Malthusian Law of Population, whereby population grows at a geometric rate while food supply grows at an arithmetic rate. How? Sustained increases in agricultural productivity warded off diminishing returns of a stagnant technology. In fact, the whole century from 1750 to 1850 is regarded as a time of agricultural boom in Western Europe (Slicher Van Bath, 1963: 221). According to Thomas R. Malthus (1766–1834) the excess of population growth over food supply is brought back into balance by a higher death rate, inflicted upon humanity through various calamities – for example, war, famine, and disease – unleashed as the pressure for food intensifies (Malthus, 1798).[10] Diminishing returns in agriculture would not only set the limit on population growth, but also undermine the maintenance of social peace and stability, and the accumulation of surplus and wealth (Rostow, 1999: 69–72).

Fundamental structural changes entailed by the agricultural revolution in Western Europe as well. As in England, the economies of Western

---

[10] Malthus published six editions from 1798 to 1826.

Europe underwent fundamental structural changes following the agricultural revolution. There was a steady decline in the share of the population and workforce that was entirely dependent on agriculture for a living. The decline set in at different times in different countries. It started the earliest in England around the 1720s, in much of Western Europe around the 1850s–1890s (depending on the country), and in Mediterranean Europe as late as the 1950s. The agricultural population declined from more than 70 percent of the total population in the earlier years. By the end of WWII, agriculture's share had fallen to well below 10 percent of total population in much of the Western world (Grigg, 1992: figs. 3.1–3.3).

How necessary was the contribution of the agricultural revolution to England's industrialization? The evidence is strong that the agricultural revolution made a major contribution to the growth of industrial wealth in England by enabling England to maintain social and political stability while undergoing radical socio-economic changes in an otherwise turbulent time. In particular, agricultural productivity growth (a) fed an increasing labor force, (b) generated financial resources for non-agricultural investment, and (c) expanded rural purchasing power for industrial commodities. Not only did England escape the Malthusian Law of Population, but building on the peace and social stability that had been made possible, it went on to become a great world power. But how "necessary" was the contribution? Evidence to date supports the argument that "there are no examples of industrialization and growth in any of the major economies of the world which were not preceded or accompanied by an agricultural transformation" (Jones, 1974: xi). In this context, E. L. Jones refers to "Napoleon's dictum that an army marches on its stomach applies *a fortiori* to a nation" (Jones, 1974: xi, 97). England had both an agricultural and an industrial revolution; it was the first country to have had both and to have averted the Malthusian Law of Population. England's experience thus refutes the polar anti-agriculture claim that a country can bypass agricultural development and still achieve industrialization. England's historic experience, however, does not confirm the polar pro-agriculture claim, namely that agricultural development is always necessary for successful industrialization. Finding a white swan does not prove that all swans are white.

I.II. Japan's Agriculture from the Meiji Restoration (1868–1912) to the 1960s, When Its Industrialization Took Off

Summary: The farsighted modernization policies of the Meiji rulers laid the foundations for success in the transformation of Japanese agriculture. In addition to an increased supply of food and labor, there was a net outflow of financial resources from agriculture to finance investment in non-agriculture even though the government was making major investments in agriculture. Also, during the Meiji period, substantial savings by landlords were transferred by banks to invest in small-scale industry. The misguided economic policy of the inter-war years (1920–40), among other things, and the two world wars severely disrupted Japan's agricultural transformation. Following its defeat by the Allies in 1945 and at the end of their occupation in April 1952, the government of Japan succeeded in mobilizing the nation for its industrialization and export push, thus making Japan the first non-Western nation to become an industrial power. It became an OECD member on April 28, 1964.

Did the rural poor benefit from the agricultural transformation? Fragmentary evidence from the Meiji period indicate substantial income benefits to agriculture, but their distribution is not known, as data are not available and land was very unequally distributed. During the decade after WWII, high agricultural and overall economic growth rates and a successful land reform raised farm wages and rural incomes. However, despite these improvements, the rural–urban income gap became a thorny political issue, a major determinant of agricultural protectionist policies starting in the 1960s.

The pro-agriculture view is correct in that sustained agricultural production and productivity growth made a substantial contribution in the critical early stages of industrialization. However, the extent to which agricultural transformation was translated into broad-based rural income growth, including poverty reduction, depended in part upon non-agricultural factors, in particular the structure of land distribution (which was highly skewed before the land reform undertaken after WWII) and the extent to which an overall growing economy succeeded in tightening labor markets and wages (which accelerated rural–urban migration in the 1950s). Although Japan became an OECD country in the 1960s (April 28, 1964), the disparity between rural and urban incomes has persisted as an important political issue.

Westernization as the way to regain national independence. Japan was the first non-Western nation to successfully industrialize. Researchers date the beginning of its break from a traditional low-productivity economy to the Meiji period (1868–1912). They emphasize the strong progressive nature of the Meiji government in promoting broad-based development. Like other subjugated Asian nations of the period, Japan was forced to sign unequal treaties. The Meiji rulers were determined to end this subordinate status, close the technological and economic gap between Japan and the Western powers, and regain its independence through Westernization. The Meiji rulers sought to break down rigid class divisions prevalent in Tokugawa Japan, promote democracy, and allow religious freedom. Before 1868, prior to the Meiji Restoration, Japan was feudal under Tokugawa rule for some three hundred years. After this long feudal period, it is no surprise that the Meiji reforms met with strong opposition in the first decade of Meiji rule, as the rulers had to quell some two hundred peasant uprisings and four samurai revolts (Tomich et al., 1995: 99).

Fundamental reforms in agriculture and the rest of the economy. Japanese agriculture benefited from this modernization drive. The reform of the land tax (1873–76) was a major reform measure, as it promoted incentives to increase farm investment and productivity and to commercialize agriculture. Predictable tax rates were levied on individual parcels of land instead of on villages as entities (Jansen and Rozman, eds., 1986: 18). At an aggregate level, the real tax burden is estimated to have fallen during the Meiji period (Yamamura, 1986: 382–99, 393).[11] The government also promoted yield-increasing agricultural innovations. It sought Western advice (e.g., from the German scientist Justus Liebig) on plant nutrition. The use of chemical fertilizers began to spread as early as 1880. Furthermore, the prevalence of peace and freedom of movement under the Meiji rulers enabled proven techniques developed by small farmers to spread throughout Japan as government invested heavily in transportation and communication. Agriculture was already dominated by small-scale farmers by then. Researchers

---

[11] The land tax was levied in cash on the real value of the land which was measured by its productivity. The tax rate which was fixed was lowered from 3 percent to 2.5 percent of the assessed base in 1876.

at the experiment stations directed the extension activities of farmers' associations. Public investment, legislation, and local institutional
innovations jointly improved land infrastructure. Irrigation expanded;
water control and drainage improved. Other than agricultural innovations, the government made education compulsory in the early 1870s.
This policy built on the Tokugawa *terakoya* education system, a private school system that had spread throughout Japan. The legacy of
this system is a high literacy level (Minami, 1994: 15). However, a
major difference under the Meiji rulers was that it promoted technical
education as an important pro-modernization factor. According to the
Education Code of 1872, "[K]nowledge may be regarded as a capital
for raising one's self." This was an important break from tradition, as
the purpose of education in the Confucian tradition was "to make [the
student] virtuous by teaching him the wisdom of gods or sages and so
forming his character" (Tomich et al., 1995: 93). The Meiji government
also instituted basic public institutions such as the central bank (1882),
the police, and postal services.

Importance, structure, and performance of agriculture. Japan's agricultural
transformation started in the late 19th century under the Meiji rulers. In the 1880s, agriculture, the dominant sector, offered employment to nearly 75 percent of the total labor force. The combined share
of agriculture, forestry, and fishery in the GDP fell from 45 percent
in 1888 to 18 percent in 1938 (Minami, 1994: 16). A century later,
agriculture's employment contribution was of minor importance. By
1955, the size of the agricultural force peaked and then fell rapidly. In
the 1950s, annual farm output growth averaged 4.4 percent and gross
value added grew at around 4.0 percent per year. In 1960, agriculture
accounted for 30 percent of employment, but by 1985, its contribution
had shrunk to around 8 percent of GDP (Tomich et al., 1995: box
3.6). Over the entire period, productivity rose, but the progress of
Japanese agriculture was severely interrupted during the interwar
(1920–40) years.

Figure 1.5 gives selected agricultural growth rates in output and
productivity. Annual average growth rates during the pre-war period
(1880–1935, 1876–1938) were roughly half of those of the post-war
period (1945–65, 1947–69). Excluding the inter-war years (1920–40)
and years of devastation from war (1935–47), the growth of agricultural

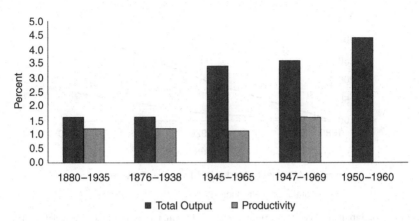

Figure 1.5. Japan: selected agricultural growth rates (percent, per year, 1880–1969). *Sources*: Yamada, Saburo and Yujiro Hayami (1979); Tomich, Thomas P., Peter Kilby, and Bruce, F. Johnston (1995).

output and productivity was sustained. During those difficult inter-war years, growth in output and productivity stagnated. The sustained increase under Meiji rule (up to 1912) was a sharp departure from the nearly three hundred years of stagnation and serfdom during the Tokugawa period (1603–1867). During this long period, there was peace but no freedom of communication or movement among villages and no freedom of choice. Figure 1.6 sets out the sustained produc-tivity increase following the Meiji Restoration. In a little less than a century and after suffering from more than a decade of war, Japan's agriculture was successfully transformed.

Spread of yield-increasing agricultural techniques. The fundamental insti-tutional and infrastructural reforms implemented by the Meiji rulers created supportive incentive for adopting yield-increasing agricultural techniques. The freedom of movement alone spread the use of pre-Meiji high-yielding, fertilizer-responsive crop varieties throughout Japan. Research stations experimented with improving rice varieties by pure line selection and then artificial cross-breeding. Over time, selection and breeding of high-yield, fertilizer-responsive rice varieties fostered a "fertilizer-responsive rice culture" (Tomich et al., 1995: 78). There was also a silk revolution; for example, improved techniques of fertilization, the development of hybrids between Chinese and Japanese silkworms less susceptible to disease and capable of spinning larger cocoons, and

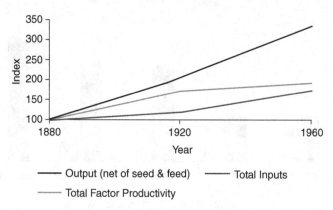

Figure 1.6. Japan: indices of output, input, and total factor productivity (1880 = 100, 1880–1960).
Source: Tomich, Thomas P., Kilby, Peter, and Johnston, Bruce, F. (1995).

progress in the hatching and rearing of silkworms contributed to a seventeenth-fold increase in the output of raw silk between 1880s and 1930s. The yield of raw silk per metric ton of cocoons rose from about 75 kg to almost 140 kg between 1908–12 and 1938–42 (Tomich, et al., 1995: 78–79).

Agriculture's financial contribution to the economy. Agricultural productivity increased, including that in sericulture, which was an important earner of foreign exchange, as silk and silk fabrics averaged 42 percent of merchandise export between 1868 and 1930. In the absence of foreign loans, export surpluses, largely originating in agriculture, were required to purchase foreign capital goods for the modernization of Japan's industry (Okhawa and Rosovksy, 1967: 307). Agriculture's rising productivity and surplus financed investments in manufacturing and other non-farm sectors, such as transport. The land tax was an important vehicle for transferring resources for investment in non-agriculture. From 1883 to 1887, agriculture paid taxes equal to 20 percent of net national product, while non-agriculture's share was only 2 percent (Minami, 1994: 72). Agriculture contributed 80 percent of the tax revenues in 1888–92 and around 40 percent between 1918 and 1922 (Tomich et al., 1995: 80). Other than the official flows, private savings (deposits from farmers and from big landlords in cooperatives and other institutions) were also important contributors to non-farm growth, as they financed the launching of many small-scale factories.

Japan's pre-WWII period of modern economic growth, from 1868 to 1940. Japan's pre-war rate of growth was substantial, with GNP growth at around 3 percent per year. This period can be divided into distinct stages. During the initial stage, until 1900, Japan exploited its traditional agriculture to generate exports and revenues for the government. Between 1878 and 1900, light industry (e.g., food processing, textiles) accounted for nearly 70 percent of total manufacturing output. Its contribution to economic growth was substantial, around 75 percent. A large number of the companies were small (with 5–49 employees) located in rural areas. These rural non-farm companies were a major source of employment and income for farmers (Minami, 1994: 95–96, 123, 126). Labor-intensive rural non-farm activities also generated substantial surplus funds, including foreign exchange earnings. These funds were used to invest in infrastructure, such as railroads and ports, and to import technology to develop industries such as cotton textile manufacture and manufacture items related to military needs. The next phase lasted until the Great Depression. This period included the boom period of WWI (1914–19) and the difficult years of adjustment of the 1920s. Cotton textiles became the most important industry. In the 1930s, Japan (unlike many other countries) experienced rapid growth, at 5 percent per year. In response to the militarist ambitions of the government, heavy industry – for example, chemicals, metals, and machinery – was developed (Patrick and Rosovsky, eds., 1976: 8–9). In pre-war Japan, the land/labor ratio in agriculture rose because expanding labor demand for non-agriculture absorbed surplus agricultural labor (Minami, 1994: 75). By the dawn of the 20th century, Japan had already started its period of modern economic growth.

Years of economy-wide stagnation and unrest. However, from 1920 to 1940, Japanese agriculture stagnated. Ironically, a major reason cited is the collapse in rice prices as Japan flooded the domestic market with rice extracted from its colonies. Following the rice riots of 1918, Japan aggressively used its colonies – Korea (1910–45) and Taiwan, China (1895–1945) – to extract rice (and sugar from Taiwan) to satisfy its growing urban demand. During this 20-year period, the non-farm sector was also stagnant, due to tight monetary policies that slowed down the growth of the labor-intensive non-farm sector and foreign exchange policies, which consistently overvalued Japan's exchange rate (1920–32), thus reducing the competitiveness of Japanese exports. Thus the development of agriculture was profoundly affected by interventions well beyond agriculture – in this case tight monetary policies and overvalued foreign exchange rates. Agricultural production fluctuated widely in the 1920s, and the rate of growth of agricultural output and productivity on average stagnated (Patrick, 1971: 215–19).

An alternative view of agricultural stagnation during 1920 to 1940. Instead of the factors cited, Loren Brandt (1993) argued that the period of stagnation was due to increasing labor shortage in Japanese agriculture and limited substitutability between labor and other farm inputs. In Brandt's view, such labor shortage explains the paradox of agricultural stagnation despite substantial investments in yield-increasing farm technologies. This labor shortage in turn resulted from demand-pull generated by the growing non-primary sector, in particular cotton textiles, which contributed to half of foreign exchange earnings. Thus, in her view, Japan's industrialization process had already started in these early years, as labor demand generated by this growth had already started pulling away farm labor. Another way of looking at the same development is that Japan's agriculture-financed industrialization had already started, as argued by Minami. Moreover, even if one argues that agriculture in those early years (1920–40) was already a protected, uncompetitive sector, then its drag on industrialization was short-lived, as the outcome of WWII (1939–45) dramatically changed world dynamics.

The post-war period until the end of the Allied occupation on April 28, 1952. Japan surrendered to the Allies on August 15, 1945. Despite their defeat, the Japanese greeted the occupiers with calm and cooperation. There was no resistance. The Americans imposed economic reforms aimed at establishing a competitive economy with a more egalitarian income distribution. Ownership of land, farmed by tenants, 45 percent of total, was redistributed to the tenants. Land reform had been planned by the Japanese authorities long before WWII. When the Allied occupation ended in 1952, per capita GNP was only USD 188. Although it was poor like many other developing countries, Japan was distinguished from those countries by certain features, including significant infrastructural and institutional investments in agriculture, a highly literate and skilled labor force, and substantial managerial and engineering skills.

Economic performance after the Allied occupation until the early 1970s. In the 1950s, there was still considerable uncertainty and gloom. However, by 1959, people were talking of the "Jimmu Boom" to refer to the greatest expansion since the reign of Japan's first mythical emperor. From 1959 to the early 1970s, agriculture grew at around 4 percent per year, while the Japanese economy grew at an average annual rate of 10.8 percent (Patrick and Rosovsky, eds., 1976: 12–13) During this period, Japan's government gave priority to basic industries, such as steel, electric power, and chemicals. During this entire period, Japan's exports grew at twice the rate of world trade.

Did incomes increase for the majority of farm households during the Meiji period of agricultural transformation? Fragmentary data suggest that during the Meiji era, incomes of farm families increased due to increased productivity, mainly in grain and sericulture. The silk-producing areas of eastern Japan benefited much more than western Japan, which specialized in cotton instead. It is estimated that Japan's real income increased by as much as 65 percent as a result of Japan's entering world trade, with agricultural exports being major (Saito, 1971: 400–20). There was also increasing labor demand from industrial development, which raised wages. There was, however, an increase in tenancy rates and more unequal income distribution as the commercialization of agriculture proceeded. There are some data on the Yamaguchi prefecture during 1922–39 which show that income distribution was very unequal, with a Gini coefficient of 0.5 (Minami, 1994: 223). It is believed that discontent arising out of very unequal distributions in rural areas contributed to social instability and the rise of militarism. However, without more representative or nation-wide evidence, it is not possible to ascertain whether the majority of farm households (as opposed to only the big landlords) benefited from the agricultural transformation.

Agriculture and rural incomes in a rapidly industrializing Japan. After WWII, Japan under Allied occupation undertook a successful land reform (1946–47). The size distribution of land into operational units did not change much, but landownership changed dramatically.

Landlords who did not live in the countryside could not own land. Those who did live in the countryside could rent out (except for land-lords on the island of Hokkaido) a maximum of one *chobu* (roughly a hectare). The maximum landlords could retain was four *chobu*. Reform greatly increased purchasing power among most of the rural population, as former tenants, now owners, did not have to make large rental pay-ments. Per capita GDP growth between 1960 and 1985 was 3 percent per year (World Bank, 1993a: fig. 2). In the mid-1950s, farm–urban labor migration was already high, estimated to be 4 percent per year (Yamada and Hayami, 1979: 56). In 1960, the share of agriculture in GDP, which was 14 percent, declined to 3 percent in 1985. Part-time farming prevailed by the mid-1990s. Despite the rapid integration of farm labor in the non-agriculture labor markets, the income differen-tial between farm and non-farm households widened, increasing pres-sure for protectionism to boost farm incomes. By the 1960s, agriculture policy became primarily an income support rather than a production-promoting policy. The Agricultural Basic Law of 1961 enshrined the restrictions and price support policies that protect agriculture. Like other countries with support policies, Japan accumulated rice surplus, which absorbed substantial government resources. By 2001, the share of agriculture dwindled to 1 percent of the GDP, but the cost of its protection remained high (World Bank, 2004a: 118). Thus agriculture in Japan is no longer an important productive sector supporting the rise of a major world power and its rapid industrialization as it was in the crucial earlier period of Meiji rule.

How necessary was the contribution of the agricultural transformation to Japan's industrialization? Japan's experience supports but qualifies the pro-agriculture view. It supports it because Japan's agriculture made major contributions in terms of food, labor, raw materials, foreign exchange earnings, financial transfers (private and public) to Japan's early and post-WWII industrialization drives. Its long-term transfor-mation, begun under the fundamental reforms of the Meiji rulers, gen-erated sustained productivity and output increases (interrupted during the inter-war years). Japan's colonial policy (which laid the basis for agricultural transformations in its colonies) enabled it to tap addi-tional agricultural resources from Korea (1910–45) and Taiwan, China (1895–1945) to promote its industrialization and militarist ambitions.

The post-WWII land reform successfully redistributed wealth in the countryside, as 45 percent of farmers were tenants.

Japan's experience qualifies the pro-agriculture position because broad-based rural income gains materialized after the land reform and after the industrial takeoff raised the demand for and wages of rural labor. Sustained agricultural output and productivity growth were not sufficient for broad-based rural income gains. The disparity of rural and urban incomes is, however, still an issue that the Agricultural Basic Law of 1961 was intended to resolve. Japan's meteoric rise as an industrial power from around the late 1950s to the 1970s is a refutation of the view that a country can do without high-productivity agriculture on the road to industrialization.

I.III. American Agriculture from the Mid-19th to the 20th Century

Summary. American agriculture today is an economic powerhouse after a century of territorial expansion in the 19th century followed by sustained productivity growth in the 20th century. Given that the United States was still a CARL at the time of the American Civil War (1861–65), how necessary a contribution was this growth to the industrialization of America, now a superpower?[12] Our analysis suggests that the contribution was significant but not necessary.

The development of American agriculture has been nurtured by the leadership ever since the founding fathers (Gardner, 2002: 176).[13] Thus, by the end of the 19th century, many of the institutional and infrastructural foundations of a commercial agriculture had already been laid. The two revolutions in agriculture – the first with the rapid adoption of horsepower in late 19th century, the second with the application of mechanical power, chemical fertilizers, pesticides, herbicides, and hybrid seeds in the early 20th century (Hurt, 1994: 379) – overlapped with the rise of industrial America, the period that historians date from around 1874–1900. During the late 19th century and into

---

[12] At the time of the War of American Independence (1775–83), 95 percent of the population was in farming. A CARL is a Country with Abundant Rural labor. This term is from Tomich, Kilby, and Johnston (1995: 67). In 1850, 55 percent of the labor force was in agriculture; by 1900, 40 percent.

[13] "It will not be doubted that with reference to either the individual or national welfare agriculture is of primary importance" George Washington in his annual message to Congress in 1796.

the 20th, American agriculture was transformed, productivity growth was sustained, farm families enjoyed rising incomes, and urban consumers enjoyed lower and more stable real food prices.

Over time, farms have become larger and the disparity among farms in terms of acreage and sales value has increased. Despite that, the disparity in terms of income distribution among farm families has decreased. Success in agricultural transformation in terms of broad-based poverty reduction and income increases of most farm households did not take place until the 1990s, when the development of a dynamic non-farm sector in a growing overall macroeconomy tightened rural labor markets and raised farm family earnings.

The American case does not support either the pro- or the anti-agriculture view. Massive U.S. investment in modern infrastructure and industry was largely foreign funded (not countries as nations, because the investment [financial and sweat equity] came from private citizens, a great surge of European immigrants [among them bankers and venture capitalists]. U.S. government also invested in railroads and canals, etc.) Moreover, agriculture was not overlooked by the substantial investments in modern public transport and communications. Such investments greatly expanded market access for agriculture's products and services, thus promoting its sustained development. Agricultural productivity growth did contribute to the overall economic transformation, mainly through export earnings and urban food supply. As in the case of the other open economies analyzed here, American industrial transformation could draw upon non-agricultural and foreign sources for investment finance. Finally, the American case also supports the finding that the broad-based improvement of farm household incomes depended on farm families' expanded access to non-farm jobs generated by a growing national economy rather than on sustained agricultural productivity growth alone.

From a CARL to an industrial superpower. It might be thought that the transformation of the United States from a subsistence economy with little or no economic growth to one with sustained increases in real income had already happened when the United States gained independence in the 1780s, as records of colonial America indicate that many individuals were prosperous. Yet until 1830 more than 90 percent of the population lived on farms, and neither the data available nor narratives of the times indicate substantial productivity growth in agriculture. A common view among historians describes "eighteenth and early nineteenth century farmers in New England as trapped by poor husbandry in chronically low-yield, subsistence agriculture" (Rothenberg, 1995: 71). Nonetheless, as Rothenberg documents, farming in New England underwent a transition from subsistence to a commercial market economy starting in 1750. The plantation economy of the South was from the beginning oriented to commercial exports. It is apparent that the economic transformation of the United States and the accompanying international political recognition occurred during the 19th century. In 1814, the British invaded and burned the government buildings of Washington, D.C., with relative ease. A hundred years later, the United States was economically the most powerful nation in the world.

What was the role of agriculture in achieving this transformation? There are different views on the role of agriculture in achieving this transformation. The standard histories of the economic development of the United States recognize the centrality of agriculture as the 19th century began. With more than 90 percent of the population living on farms, growth of agricultural production would seem essential for growth of the economy. North (1961, 1966) developed the case that the opening up of commercial markets for agricultural commodities "has been the prime influence inducing economic growth, the development of external economies, urbanization, and eventually industrial development" (1966: 259). This argument hypothesizes a different causal path from the more common mechanisms postulated for agriculture as an engine of growth. That story is roughly as follows: Scientists, engineers, and innovative farmers, in both the private and public sectors, apply their knowledge to problems of agriculture; informal dissemination and, later, extension services place new knowledge widely in farmers' hands; and with sufficient property rights and price incentives to call forth the necessary investment, farmers adopt new technology and generate more output and income from their resources. Most of the gains drive down prices, but nonetheless this is the paradigm of growth. It is true that the American consumer has benefited substantially from these sustained productivity increases (as well as developments in refrigeration and marketing improvements), as real food prices declined by 35 percent from 1913 to 1996 (Gardner, 2002: 141, fig. 5.5).[14] When agriculture is the predominant sector of an economy or becomes a paradigm for other sectors, agriculture becomes an engine of overall economic development. North's argument pushes causality one step back to the opening of markets (which itself may be attributable to technological innovation in transportation and institutional innovation that allow for secure long-distant transactions and trade).[15] Yet despite the advocacy of North, other sources of growth are more prominently treated by historians. The spread of population into the Midwest early in the 19th century and of farming and ranching into the Plains and far West in the second half of the century are obviously important aspects of the economic development of the United States, and are seen by economic historians generally as major elements of the expansion in the size and scope of the nation. Yet the growth of real output and income per person, the central indicators of economic growth, are more commonly associated with innovations and investment in manufacturing, transportation, finance, and trade.

What are the facts on accelerated and sustained income growth? Figure 1.7 – shows the continuous rise for two centuries in real GDP per person as the United States became increasingly urbanized. If the 1800–2000 time span is divided into four 50-year periods, it can be seen that the rate of growth of real GDP per person was 0.7 percent annually during 1800–50 and 1.7, 2.0, and 2.2 percent during the succeeding three periods. It is noteworthy that the growth rate almost tripled during 1850–2000 as compared with 1800–50.[16] As of 1850, the non-farm population still accounted for less than 20 percent of the United States total. Both the transformation of agriculture and the acceleration of overall economic growth came later. The period

---

[14] Transporting refrigerated meats on railroad cars in the United States started in the late 1870s.

[15] North widens his argument too: "Whether we look at Denmark between 1865 and 1900, the Pacific Northwest between 1880 and 1920, the Canadian economy between 1900 and 1913, or indeed any of a myriad of possible illustrations, it has been the expansion of one or more agricultural expansions which has been the prime mover in initiating expansion" (1961: 260).

[16] The source of these data is *Historical Statistics of the United States*, 2000 edition, Volume 3, Table Ca-C. The data sources are notably weaker for the early period, but there is no reason to believe the estimates are biased either positively or negatively for 1800–1850 as compared to later years.

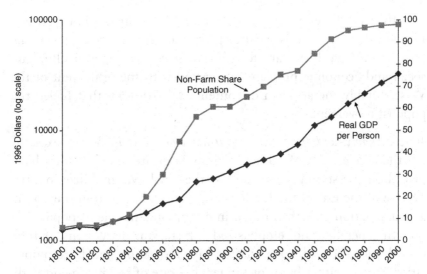

Figure 1.7. United States: real GDP and non-farm share of the population (1800–2000).
Source: Historical Statistics of the United States.

after the Civil War is the time when we see both accelerated GDP growth and a sharp increase in the non-farm share of the American population.

Given these basic facts of America's socio-economic transformation, this book addresses two questions:

1. What was the contribution of agriculture to this transformation?
2. What were the causes of agriculture's successful transformation?

Throughout, the book reviews and assesses the extensive work of both economic historians and economists addressing these and closely related questions. The book also presents its own empirical analyses.

Was improved agricultural technology or investment in agriculture responsible for the increased and sustained rate of growth? The Homestead Act of 1862 is a well-known element of the westward expansion during the post–Civil War period. It capped a period of distribution of uncultivated federal lands at favorable prices by giving 160 acres of Great Plains prairie to individuals who promised to cultivate the land. These developments were unquestionably central to the geographical expansion of the American economy, and hence of its aggregate size. But evidence that agricultural growth was a causal factor in the accelerated growth of GDP per person after the mid-19th century is not apparent. Besides, that hypothesis has not gained adherents among economic historians. What historians focus on most concerning agriculture are social and economic problems associated with the settlement of the West, notably the agrarian discontent of 1870–1900 that fueled the populist movement.

Were economy-wide and trade-related factors responsible? In explaining the acceleration of economic growth, greater emphasis has been placed on the stimulus provided by the Civil War mobilization, the decline of the export market for cotton and tobacco from the South, and population growth through immigration. The role of population growth generally is not emphasized in historians' discussions, and the data do not show obvious relationships indicating that faster population growth either helps or hinders the rate of real income growth. The 19th-century picture shows the rate of increase of real income per person increasing as the rate of population growth slows over the 19th century (see Figure 1.8). However, it is not seriously suggested that the slower growth at the beginning of the century was attributable to decreasing marginal returns, as more people were added to a fixed resource base.

Was expansion in nation-wide infrastructure and market access for agriculture responsible? The causal factors that get the most attention are matters of technology and large-scale investment – for example, canals, exemplified by the opening of the Erie Canal in the 1830s; later the development of railroads, culminating in the transcontinental railway completed in the 1870s; and a series of industrial innovations, which, financed by venture capitalists and banks that were unrestrained by regulations or scruples, created great industries in steel, shipping, machinery, and building materials. The building of this modern transport infrastructure, funded largely by foreign sources pivotal in expanding agricultural markets and raising prices. In the mid-1800s, American farmers and politicians fully appreciated the importance of accessing markets – domestic urban and export markets – for the continued growth and profitability of American agriculture. The proportion of agricultural output sold in the growing urban markets rose from 20 percent in 1840 to 40 percent by 1870. Agricultural export earnings

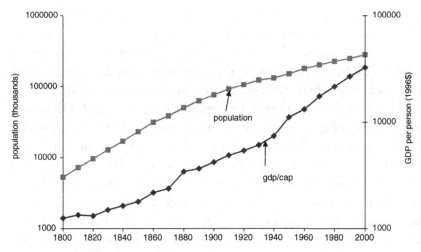

Figure 1.8. United States: real GDP per person and population (1800–2000).
Source: Historical Statistics of the United States.

contributed to 83 and 81 percent of total merchandise export earnings in 1820 and 1870, respectively (Tomich et al., 1995: 70–71). This view, emphasizing the critical importance of modern transport and communications infrastructure and access to expanding markets, is similar to that of North (1961, 1966).

Is the American value system responsible? A more fundamental view put forward is that none of these particular factors matter, and indeed the data are not reliable enough to sort out periods of growth acceleration or decline with precision. The solid evidence is of a general trend of real output growth of income per person over the century as a whole. The causal factors behind that growth are said to be basic characteristics of the American people and institutions. Krooss (1966) is an economic historian who goes even further; he considers political institutions to be key, but not themselves fundamental causes because they are endogenous – created as part of the process. What he sees as fundamental is the "American value system" (Krooss, 1966: 51–52), where "the great desideratum was material prosperity" and an "obsession with success," being "always stalwart champions of the entrepreneurial frame of mind, with its admonitions to work productively, to make a profit, and to plow it back" (Krooss, 1966: 54).

Is agriculture responsible by virtue of its size and comparative advantage?
With respect to agriculture in the overall growth context, the situation is reminiscent of the tension highlighted in the classic text of Mellor (1966): At the early stages of economic development, agriculture uses such a high fraction of an economy's resources that almost by definition some change in farming must occur to get GDP growth started; but at the same time, it is almost a truism that at a high level of income per capita, the predominance of consumption and hence production must become non-agricultural, so that sector must grow the fastest – notwithstanding the possibility that a country could have a strong international comparative advantage in agriculture and so produce much more in agriculture than it consumes. Mellor (1966: 19–20) cites Canada, Australia, New Zealand, and Denmark as examples. One might say that overall economic growth could be fueled in part by agriculture, but if so this is just a fortunate accident of soil or climate and not essential for a poor country to move to the path of sustained economic growth.

Is total factor productivity growth in American agriculture responsible? In the American case, Mundlak (2005) mobilizes evidence consistent with the idea that agriculture made a contribution to U.S. economic growth, but not a large contribution. He estimates that the inputs of land, labor, and capital all grew at an annual rate of about 2 percent over the whole period from 1800 to 1900, but relatively faster, at almost 3 percent annually, for all three input categories during 1800–40 (Mundlak, 2005: fig. 1). Total factor productivity growth was, however, much slower: 0.2 percent annually in 1800–40, 0.56 percent in 1840–80, and 0.15 percent in 1880–1900.[17] The increases in inputs helped in the growth of aggregate output, but productivity growth at the rates cited indicate only a modest contribution to output per capita, since the increases in output did not do much more than pay for the additional inputs. These estimates provide the basis for a quantitative assessment of agriculture's place in the overall picture. As Mundlak's analysis indicates, agriculture's role is positive but modest. The contribution is not sufficient to explain the nation's transformation from economically almost negligible to economically predominant over the course of the 19th century.

---

[17] Tomich, Kilby, and Johnston (1995: 71) make a similar point. "It was not until the 1930s that increases in yield per acre began to make a significant contribution to productivity growth."

Agriculture's relative contribution to the early stages of American transfor-mation in the 19th century – positive but not crucial: When historians consider, as they typically do, the fundamental causes of the changes in investment and technological change, agriculture's role is again some-what attenuated. Mechanical innovations such as the cotton gin, the steel-moldboard plow, the reaper, and barbed wire are recognized as innovations that made a real difference in agricultural productivity; but what get more attention are railroads, industrial and chemical innova-tions, and communications technology like the telegraph. Still more fundamental to innovations in all sectors are Americans' willingness to take risks, their love of money, and their entrepreneurial spirit, as well as the laws of the United States and (lack of) state regulation. But these have no particular agricultural content. Indeed, although agriculture grew in the 19th century and was home to some notable innovations, as mentioned earlier, it can be argued that the successful transformation of American agriculture in terms of sustained produc-tivity growth did not occur until the earlier part of the 20th century. Nevertheless, agriculture did contribute to America's overall economic transformation – for example, through total factor productivity growth and in terms of export earnings and increased urban food supply. The minimum that can be said is that agriculture did not act as a drag on the overall dynamism of the economy. Moreover, agriculture sub-stantially benefited from developments in transport and communica-tions, increasing the integration of the sector into the national and international economy, so that it became highly commercialized and productive.

Contending hypotheses on the successful transformation of American agri-culture in the 20th century: The aspect of agricultural transformation that is the source of agriculture's contribution to overall growth is productivity growth. The main acceleration of productivity growth did not occur until the 1930s (see Figure 1.9). However, Tomich et al. (1995: 101) place the turning point in the structural transformation of American agriculture at 1910. Their main criterion is the share of the labor force in agriculture.[18] Figure 1.9 shows the sustained accel-erated growth of total factor productivity from 1940 to 1980. One

---

[18] The structural turning point for agriculture is when the absolute size of the agricultural labor force peaks and then declines (Tomich, Kilby, and Johnston, 1995: Box 1.1).

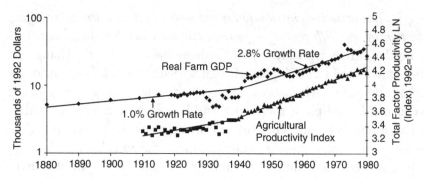

Figure 1.9. Total factor productivity growth and real farm GDP per person in U.S. agriculture (1880–1980).
Source: Gardner (2002).

question is: What caused the acceleration and the sustained high rate of growth that followed? And how are productivity and farm income growth related? Did productivity growth cause farm income growth? Or did farm incomes grow despite productivity growth? Are trends in both the result of common causal factors? Could the relationship between productivity and income have gone either way depending on conditioning factors such as commodity policies and the international market situation? Many theories, both simple and complicated, have been advanced. The following is a sample of contending hypotheses:

> The effectiveness of technological changes after World War II was testimony to the value of the research programs carried on primarily by the Department of Agriculture and the state agricultural colleges and experiment stations, as well as by industry. Furthermore, the information had reached the farmers. (Rasmussen, 1962: 590)

> Developments since 1940 are of a wholly different order from all that has gone before.... [They are] the payoff on ... [1] the expansion of a commercially minded farm population ... [2] the development of the institutions and attitudes from which scientific agriculture could grow ... and [3] the raising of productivity and national wealth to levels at which capital formation – in the soil, in equipment, in ideas, and in the training of human beings – could proceed. (Parker, 1972: 373)

> Specialization, large-scale operations, and improved financial, insurance, and transportation facilities have contributed in a quite direct

> way to farm productivity. These direct sources of rising productivity can ultimately be viewed as the result of non-conventional inputs ... [education and research]. (Tweeten, 1971: 134)

> This [efficiency of post-WWII farming] is largely because our farmers have had an optimum combination of free incentive, adequate capital, and a long period of sound technological training. (Henry A. Wallace, quoted in Knoblauch, 1962: 598)

These writers focused on the acceleration of productivity growth that occurred after 1940. This change, called a revolution in U.S. farming by some scholars, became quantifiable only as the data on inputs and outputs in agriculture were developed and refined by economists at the United States Department of Agriculture's (USDA) Bureau of Economic Analysis and elsewhere beginning in the late 1940s.[19]

Hypotheses emphasizing the "demand-side" causes of the transformation. The break in the productivity trend after the mid-1930s provides fodder for explanatory work, in that one can then look for what causal factors changed at that time. Several researchers have attempted to explain this phenomenon. Rasmussen (1962: 579) points to "the strength of and variations in demand for farm products," noting that prices of farm products doubled in 1939–45, as they had in ushering in a period of agricultural expansion in 1861–65. But this appears too transitory an impetus for a new trend that has lasted so long (and the length of which Rasmussen could not have known at the time he wrote). A related general idea is that what changed after 1940 was not so much the availability of and knowledge about technological innovations as the economic environment in which they would be used. A classic study of the adoption of hybrid corn by Zvi Griliches (1957) established the connection between the profitability of a technological innovation and the extent of its use by farmers. Profitability can be

---

[19] See Barton and Cooper, 1948; Kendrick and Jones, 1951; Johnson and Nottenburg, 1951; Schultz, 1953, Ch. 7. The issue of whether technological change in U.S. agriculture was revolutionary or evolutionary was debated by economic historians in 1940–60, with good points made on both sides (see Rasmussen, 1962, for a brief review). Only in retrospect has it become clear how sharp and lasting was the break in productivity growth that occurred during the 1930s. One who saw this early was T.W. Schultz: "With knowledge already at hand, it would appear that the recent surge forward is still in its early stages because it will take years, perhaps decades, to put into practice in all parts of agriculture what is already known." (Schultz, 1953: 112).

the result of favorable prices as well as reduced costs from a technical advance. In agricultural commodity markets, there did occur a long-lasting change intended to influence the overall profitability of farming, the set of commodity support policies introduced with the New Deal farm programs of the 1930s. Willard Cochrane and Mary Ryan put the case thus:

> What did the price and income support programs have to do with these gains in agricultural productivity? They had a lot to do with it. They provided the stable prices, hence price insurance, to induce the alert and aggressive farmers to invest in new and improved technologies and capital items, and the reasonably acceptable farm incomes and asset positions to induce lenders to assume the risk of making farm production loans. (Cochrane and Ryan, 1976: 373)

Sally Clarke (1994) made a variant of this hypothesis the focus of her book. She concentrates mainly on farmers' investments in tractors in the Midwest in the 1930s, concluding that "farmers' willingness to invest turned in large part on the long-term changes initiated by the New Deal farm policy" (1994: 200). However, the New Deal also introduced a variety of regulatory requirements and action-specific subsidies that arguably retarded the adoption of new technology, and while market sources of instability were reduced, uncertainties associated with the policies themselves were increased.[20]

Hypotheses emphasizing the "supply-side" causes of the transformation. A case may also be made for the "supply-side" view that the key factor was the availability of a continuing stream of better and more applicable new technology after 1940. An acceleration in productivity growth around 1940 could be explained by the acceleration of agricultural research that took place between 1910 and 1930, with long lags for developing commercially viable new technology from this research. Public spending on agricultural research tripled between the decade of 1900–1909 and the 1910s, and tripled again between the 1910s and the 1920s. Agricultural extension efforts under both federal

---

[20] For a review of conceptual and empirical literature on policy and technology adoption, see Sunding and Zilberman (2001). They cite evidence, for example, that irrigation subsidies retarded the adoption of water-saving technology. But their review did not uncover evidence that would either support or refute the specific Cochrane-Clarke assertions.

and state support also grew rapidly (Alston and Pardey, 1996: 34, 54). Ronald Mighell (1955) presents the view of U.S. government analysts based primarily on the agriculture census data (1950). He clearly sees an acceleration of productivity growth in the mid-1930s (Mighell, 1955: 5), and while this event is linked to agricultural research and education, he does not even mention a possible connection with New Deal commodity support policies.

Methodological concerns raised by econometric attempts at quantifying the contribution of different causal factors. To explain U.S. agricultural transformation, several researchers have used econometric approaches to quantify the relative importance of selected causal factors. As routinely pointed out in econometrics textbooks, econometric techniques can identify potentially important correlations for which the causality still needs to be established by independent testing of the theory or theories. However, even if one were to accept the researchers' claim on causality, one could question their specification, as their empirical results sometimes contradict each other and sometimes are simply counterintuitive. For example, Wallace Huffman and Robert Evenson (1993) attempt to sort out the effects of research, farmers' schooling, and commodity supports using a multivariate econometric model, mainly with state-level data from 1950 to 1982. They find that while they cannot reject the hypothesis that price supports led to increased productivity, about 95 percent of the growth in productivity that they can explain is attributable to lagged effects of research and extension, with only about 5 percent attributable to commodity programs.[21] Munisamy Gopinath and Terry Roe (1997) investigated the same subject with a different statistical approach derived from USDA data, 1949–91. They found that public spending on agricultural research is

[21] A more extensive body of research examines the role of agricultural price policies as they affect productivity outside the United States, primarily in developing countries. T.W. Schultz (1979) argued that under pricing agricultural products retarded adoption of new technology and agricultural research efforts in many developing countries. Mundlak (1988) and Fulghiniti and Perrin (1993) provided evidence that less taxation of agriculture would increase productivity in such countries. On the other hand, Kalaitzandonakes (1994) provides reasons for doubting that price support promotes innovation, and argues that support may reduce competitiveness. The empirical evidence in support of this comes from New Zealand where liberalization that reduced agricultural support is estimated to have increased productivity growth.

the most important factor contributing to productivity growth and that growth in purchased input use and labor quality have also played a significant role. But other factors, notably private sector research and development, public infrastructure, and the scale of agricultural output, were estimated to have little or no importance in productivity growth. They reported no attempts to examine the role of commodity policy. Gopinath and Roe found no effect of private sector research or of "learning by doing," as an earlier study by Y. Luh and Spiro Stefanou (1993) had done.

The challenge of assessing the relative importance of different policy instruments. Given that the aforementioned econometric approaches have not been able to resolve the question of the causal importance and relative merits of different policy instruments in promoting sustained growth, the challenge remains to get as good an assessment as possible of the roles of particular policy variables, especially public investment in research, extension, and education, and commodity support programs. For practical purposes, it is tempting to lump many factors together, as indeed action-oriented observers who lack patience with scholarly dissection of the subject have done. For example, Lee Iacocca, "the straight-shooting businessman who brought Chrysler back from the brink,"[22] wrote about post-WWII agricultural productivity growth as follows:

> There is more going on here than good climate, rich soil, and hard-working farmers. We had all those things fifty years ago, and all we got were dust bowls and disasters. The difference lies in a wide range of government-sponsored projects. There are federal research projects; county agents to educate people; state experimental farms; rural electrification and irrigation projects such as the TVA; crop insurance; export credits; price supports; acreage controls.... With all that government help (or, some would say, interference) we've created a miracle. Our agricultural industrial policy has made us the envy of the world. (Iacocca, 1986: 348)

Could the United States have done better if it had fine-tuned its policies and been more selective? For example, what if the United States government had left the research, education, and infrastructure

---

[22] Taken from the back cover of Iacocca's (1986) memoir.

investments in place but had not spent the roughly $500 billion (in 1992 dollars) on commodity support programs in the past 50 years?

Did the New Deal commodity programs encouraging increased private farm investment promote sustained productivity growth? This causal link still has to be established with respect to capital investment data. One hypothesis is that the commodity programs generally made farmers more production-oriented and optimistic, as well as raising farm incomes, and productivity increased in response to this. But more consideration has to be given to the mechanism of such an effect. It is not enough that farmers attempted to produce more by applying more inputs (and in fact, although there was an increase in input use in the late 1930s, the aggregate agricultural input index was the same in 1930 and 1940). For productivity to grow, output has to increase more than proportionally with inputs. David Orden, Robert Paarlberg, and Terry Roe (1999) argue that even if the programs did stimulate output and investment, increases in them have not been responsible for post-WWII productivity growth. Even in 1947, the capital stock in agriculture had only just recovered to its level of 1930. But by 1980, the capital stock had tripled. These considerations cast doubt on the idea that the New Deal programs fostered productivity growth by stimulating investment during the late 1930s.

What do the data on net investment in agriculture suggest about the causal link between commodity programs and sustained productivity growth? The data indicate the ill effects of the long period of unfavorable economic conditions in agriculture, with net investment by farmers being negative throughout the 1920s and 1930s. The economic meaning is that the farm community was to some extent living off its capital stock, or "eating the seed corn," by letting its capital stock depreciate. In this context, the increase in investment at the end of the 1930s and early 1940s is really quite modest. The takeoff in net investment did not occur until
· 1946, after which the rise was spectacular. The timing is suggestive in two important ways. First, since overall productivity growth began to accelerate about 1940 and had definitely begun its permanently faster growth before 1945, it is a mistake to tie the acceleration of productivity growth to farmers' investment in capital equipment. Second, while the New Deal programs undoubtedly gave farmers reasons for being less pessimistic, the

investment data do not indicate a real switch to ebullient willingness to invest any time in the 1930s and early 1940s. Wartime restrictions helped keep a lid on some investment until 1945, but even so the facts of overall investment limited the extent to which underlying optimism could be converted into productivity-increasing new equipment.

Productivity growth continued despite a decline in prices and in commodity program support. Why? While much of the discussion has focused on the acceleration of productivity growth in the late 1930s, a second surprising event in the 20th-century history of farm productivity is also worth detailed discussion: namely, the fact that agricultural productivity (both output per worker and total factor productivity) kept increasing at an undiminished rate, while U.S. manufacturing and overall productivity slowed down after the mid-1970s. The productivity slowdown has been attributed to a number of factors, of which the most widely agreed upon appears to be the rapid rise in the cost of energy following the OPEC oil marketing strategy change of 1972. Agriculture was cushioned from the immediate impact of energy price increases because farm output prices soared at the same time. But by 1978, grain prices had collapsed and farmers were marching on Washington in a show of political discontent unique in the second half of the century. Economic problems in agriculture only deepened with the wave of farm business failures that characterized the "farm crisis" of the mid-1980s. Commodity program spending and financial assistance responded with massive assistance to agriculture, but by the mid-1990s, the federal government's role in agriculture was waning, and farmland prices had still not returned to the levels of 1981 in nominal, much less real, terms. Agricultural productivity continued to grow at the accelerated 1940–70 pace. Why? This subject has been investigated to a much lesser extent than the post-1940 acceleration, but the data suggest the science-and-research hypothesis as perhaps the most plausible reason. Not only was support for commodity programs dwindling over the last decade of the century, but net investment ceased after 1980 and the farm capital stock declined, and the decline in farm numbers that may have fostered increased efficiency of labor use slowed down. Growing concerns about the environment as well as input costs led to the reduced use of chemical inputs after 1980. These inputs appeared to have generated increased output value far in excess of their cost. In the face of these obstacles, improved technology and improvements in farmers' knowledge and ability to put that technology to work appear to be the most likely remaining factors explaining the continued agricultural productivity growth.

Did the majority of farm families benefit from the sustained agricultural growth? One of the two major components of successful agricultural transformation is the sustained income increases of the majority of rural/farm households. This section addresses this question by looking at different indicators and reviewing the characteristics of the American farm population. One indicator is the movement of real farm wage rates. A long-term economic change about 1940 was the rise in real farm wage rates as the general economy emerged from the Great Depression, and especially as labor markets tightened during WWII. One of the sharpest changes of trend in relative prices was the rise in farm relative to non-farm wage rates that began in 1941. A possible reason is that the economic development of agriculture was fostered by economic progress in the non-farm industries of the United States, which was reflected in rising real wage rates throughout the economy. The key developments in the farm sector according to this view were those that resulted in closer, more rapid, and cheaper connections between rural and urban America – improved roads, electronic communications, consolidated schooling, and better education. T. W. Schultz (1953) gave oxygen to this view with his reasoning based on the relatively rapid economic progress in the 1930s and 1940s of rural areas that were located near cities as compared with more remote areas. According to this view, farm wage rates benefit from the increasing integration into the labor market of farm families in a growing non-farm economy.

Does technological progress necessarily benefit farmers monetarily? While farmers have seen the benefits of technological progress in their individual operations, some farm organizations as well as agricultural economists have been skeptical about the benefits to farmers as a group when a large number or all of them adopt new technology. Economists have provided analytical support for such skepticism. There are two kinds of concern: a distributional worry and one related to aggregate farm income. The distributional worry is that only the early adopters of new technology will gain. The idea is that the aggressive, low-cost farmers expand output and this drives down prices, so that farmers who stay with older technology can no longer cover costs. Their incomes fall. The concern about aggregate farm income is a longer-run consequence. As the high-cost producers are squeezed out and their farms are taken over by more aggressive, growing farm enterprises, the whole sector finds itself with output increasing and prices falling so far as to just cover the new, lower costs (or with overshooting of output, not covering costs for the sector as a whole). Thus only buyers of farm products are sure to gain.

Summary of the situation for farm productivity and farmers' incomes. It remains an empirical question how productivity growth in U.S. agriculture during the 20th century, and particularly since 1940, has affected both aggregate net farm income and the inequality of income distribution among farmers. In considering factors that determine the incomes of farm families, it is important to place the discussion in the context of the broad socio-economic developments that the farm and rural population underwent over much of the 20th century. The overall picture is that of an agriculture increasingly integrated into the broader national and global economy; a sector exhibiting greater equality in income distribution despite increasing concentration in terms of land distribution and sales value; and a drastically reduced farming population, more and more dependent on non-farm sources of income for sustained and significant increases in incomes. Specifically, there are eight important developments:

1. The farm population shrank from 30 million in 1900 to 4.5 million by 1990 (less than 2 percent of total population) and 2.5 million by 2000. Part-time farming now prevails.[23]
2. The rural non-farm population in 1900 was 16 million; by 1990, it had increased to 47 million, far surpassing the farm population.
3. There has been substantial out-migration since the 1920s, but especially between 1940 and 1980, so that by 1997, the average age of farm operators was 54.

---

[23] In 1900, total U.S. population was estimated at (million): 76, rural at 46; of which farm at 30. Thus rural non-farm population was 21 percent and farm population nearly 40 percent of total (Gardner, 2002: 92–93, fig. 4.1a and 4.1b). The urban: rural ratio was around 40:60. In other words, U.S. population was primarily rural, at 60 percent.

4. The number of farms declined from roughly 6 million in 1910 to around 2 million in the 1990s, with the number of small farms increasing.[24] Most farms are still family-owned. In 1997, individual and family-owned farms accounted for 86 percent of all farms; partnership and family-held ones for 12.9 percent; and corporation-held (not family) ones for 0.4 percent. There is increasing involvement of non-farm people in agriculture – for example, corporations and production contractors, as in the broiler sub-sector.

5. An estimated 1.5 million of these farms are small-scale and depend entirely on off-farm sources of income to remain economically viable. In 1997, the USDA estimated that 85 percent of the average farm household's income came from off- or non-farm sources.

6. There has been increasing land concentration, and large farms dominate in terms of acreage and sales value. In 1992, the largest 10 percent of farms accounted for 76 percent of total farm acreage and 70 percent of all sales value. The largest 20 percent of all farms accounted for 87 percent of total acreage and 85 percent of sales value. The smallest 50 percent of farms had only 4 percent of total farm acreage and around 2 percent of total sales value in 1992.

7. Despite this increasing land concentration and inequality in sales value, the distribution of farm household incomes in 1990 was more equitable than in 1950. Over this 40-year period, median real household income of farm households grew at an annual rate of 3.3 percent and at 5.8 percent per year in the 1960s. The Gini index of farm household income was 0.5 in 1950 and 0.4 in 1990.

8. Poverty among farm households has fallen significantly. In 1965, poverty incidence among farm families was estimated to be 31

---

[24] "Small" and "large" are defined by value of annual sales, not just by acreage. The "small" farm averages less than USD 50,000 in annual sales and has on average 187 acres. Its net farm income is however negative, a loss of USD 1,600 annually. A total of 1.5 million U.S. farms fall in this category. The second farm category has annual sales between USD 50,000 to 100,000, and averages 719 acres. This is the smallest category considered commercially viable. The third category has annual sales of USD 100,000 to 250,000 and averages 1,186 acres. The fourth category, the "large" farm has USD 250,000 and more in annual sales and averages 1,834 acres. This farm category has been growing the fastest.

percent versus 15 percent for non-farm families. By 1991 (in
the last survey to identify farm families as a separate group), the
respective incidences were 10.1 and 11.5 percent. Poverty incidence was actually lower among farm than non-farm families.
In yet another measure of poverty that combined measures of
income, consumption, and net worth (1998), only 1 percent of
farm households were classified as poor. Rural poverty among
the non-farm population was more prevalent than among farm
families.[25]

How did farm households benefit from the agricultural transformation?
The benefit came from several factors, in particular from the integration of labor markets. We do see an increasing trend in real returns
to farming since 1940, the same period over which the rate of productivity growth increased. But over this same period, we also have
the growth of governmental support for farm commodities. And other
factors also have to be considered as explanations for the time path of
farm income. The increasing importance of off-farm employment by
farm household members and the rise in farm household income associated with that employment suggest that integration of the farm and
non-farm labor markets may have a lot to do with farm income trends
since 1940. The case of cotton in the South as analyzed by Richard Day
(1967), as well as labor migration more broadly, suggests that the pull
of off-farm labor demand as well as the push of technology-generated
labor redundancy was important. It is possible that, by the 1990s, earnings of comparable labor would have been the same in farming and
in non-farmwork, regardless of changes in agricultural technology.
According to this view, technical progress affects the size of the agricultural labor force but not, in the long run, the earnings of people
employed in farming; and differences in labor earnings depend on people's time spent working and their qualitative characteristics (e.g., age,
education, experience). This view we call the "integrated labor market
view." It implies that the growth in farm household labor income relative to that of non-farm households since 1930s is attributable to

[25] The definition of "rural" is a residual. "Urban" is defined as towns with more than 2,500 people. So, rural refers to towns with less than 2,500 people (Gardner, 2002: chapter 3 on Farms,
especially p. 71, tables 3.1, 3.2, 3.4, figs. 3.9, 3.16, 3.17; chapter 4 on Farm Communities,
especially pp. 92–93, 103–106, fig. 4.1a.).

non-agriculture developments: improvement in the education and other income-generating attributes of farm people. A variant of the integrated labor market view is a more historically nuanced hypothesis that labor market integration emerged only gradually after WWII. So what we observe in the household income data since 1940 is not only an improvement in farm people's earning capacities, but also the correction of a persistent labor market disequilibrium that appeared in U.S. agriculture after WWI, leaving too many workers in agriculture. This disequilibrium may have been caused in part by technological changes in farming, but the remedy was not.

Higher farm household wealth through increased property values. Even if the integrated market view is correct, it is not the whole story for farm income because it omits farmers' returns from their investments in farming and from land. Since 1950, there has been a trend of increasing real rental value and price of farmland. That trend is not a matter of adjustment to disequilibrium. Land rent is rather a residual, reflecting the demand for land's services in the face of a largely fixed supply. It is true that land can shift from farm to non-farm use and has done so dramatically in suburban areas. But in fact the acreage of land in farms and in crops has not changed greatly, and has even increased slightly this century. In 1910, the United States had 880 million acres in farms and 310 million acres of cropland. In 1997, there were 970 million acres in farms and 338 million acres used for crops (with an additional 56 million acres idled, mostly under government programs). So the increase in returns to land must be attributable to an increasing demand for agricultural land services, and this could be attributable to technological change, to commodity programs, or to other factors in the demand for farm commodities (such as foreign demand for U.S. farm products).

Higher farm household incomes through capital market integration. With respect to farmers' returns to investment in equipment and other non-land capital, the picture is perhaps even more bifurcated between short-run and long-run considerations than for labor. In the short run, one finds evidence at farm sales and junkyards everywhere that new technology constantly creates obsolescent and nearly valueless capital goods. This does not necessarily imply a low return to investment in those goods, for they may have reached the end of their expected life anyway. But it is a reasonable hypothesis that farmers have often found themselves in a fixed-investment trap that has lowered their returns considerably. At the same time, a long-run view of investment in agriculture lends itself to an integrated-market hypothesis even more strongly for capital markets than for labor markets. In the long run, the rate of return to investment in agriculture should not be expected to depart much from the rate of return to non-farm investments of comparable risk. Interest rates for borrowing are set in a national capital market, and the terms on which farmers can obtain funds are close to the same as those for non-farm businesses; and the opportunity returns for farmers' investments include a range of off-farm investments that potential farm investments must compete with in the farmer's decision making. Increases in farmers' incomes relative to non-farmers' that are attributable to capital market developments must stem from an economy-wide increase in returns to investment coupled with farm households earning a larger share of their income from non-labor sources than non-farm households do.

Are higher farm household incomes primarily through the operation of non-economic factors? Historians have unearthed further evidence on what was taking place during the period when U.S. agriculture entered its period of strong and sustained productivity growth. This evidence, which has been largely neglected by economists, includes facts about farmers' attitudes and preferences, the intellectual and exemplary contributions of visionary individuals, and the establishment of institutions and forms of economic organization conducive to growth. The idea of the farmer as an ignorant, intellectually ossified follower of traditional practice and fearful of change, and constitutionally unable to forgo consumption in order to invest, was an influential view in the first half of the 20th century. According to this view, investment in new technology would require a cultural transformation. Griliches (1957) disputes this. He brilliantly showed that profitability was sufficient to explain the pattern of adoption of hybrid corn. But rural sociologists also staked a claim to cultural/social explanations such as community leadership and informational networks (e.g., Ryan and Gross, 1943; Havens and Rogers, 1961). Danbom (1979) describes the efforts by many promoters of progress in agriculture, notably President Theodore Roosevelt in the first decades of the 20th century, to instill in farm people a mentality conducive to commercialization of their enterprises, investment, and adoption of innovative technology. Broader modes of thought are, of course, not new in the theory of development. Hagen's ideas (1962) exemplify thinking in the 1950s according to which obstacles to development are largely traditional rural village institutions and/or inside the heads of the villagers. Thus "economic theory has rather little to offer" and "both the barriers to growth and the causes of growth seem to be largely internal rather than external" (Hagen, quoted in Stevens and Jabara, 1988: 94). This view is the opposite of Griliches's hypothesis that inputs from outside of agriculture are key and that, if profitable, they will be adopted. The non-economic approach lost luster with the perceived failure of U.S. community development schemes. And since the 1950s, new varieties and other innovations have been almost universally adopted, apparently without need of cultural or psychological transformation in rural communities.

The greater importance of the non-farm labor market than farm productivity in raising farm household incomes. Gardner (2002) undertook an analysis of U.S. state and county data on farm sales, value added, farmland prices, and, most important, farm family income. The hypothesis is that the growth of agriculture as a sector of the economy is promoted by investment, farm productivity improvement, and governmental support of agricultural research. These variables are, of course, not independent of one another, and it is not claimed that any one of them is more important than another as a separable cause of growth. Other variables that were considered likely to enhance agricultural growth, notably farmers' schooling, regional and commodity specialization measures, and government commodity support programs, turn out not to be consistently significant. The growth of real farm family incomes, from farm and off-farm sources together, is more directly important from the viewpoint of people's welfare. The surprising finding with respect to causes of family income growth is how little any agriculturally specific variables explain differences among counties. This is true even of the areas that are most heavily dependent on agriculture. Instead, farm family income growth is explained mainly by the relationship of farm to non-farm family earnings. This relationship is taken to be attributable principally to labor market adjustments. Incomes in areas where farm family income was relatively low as a fraction of non-farm incomes in 1960 rose significantly faster than incomes in counties where farm and non-farm incomes were close, and farm incomes consistently rose together with non-farm incomes. These results strongly indicate that the economic story is one of integration of factor markets, with adjustment to an initial state of disequilibrium created by technological progress reducing the demand for labor in agriculture. Thus causes of sustained productivity increases are different from causes of broad-based improved incomes of farm families.

Which of the polar views does the U.S. case support, undermine, or modify? On the basis of estimates of total factor productivity growth, agriculture's role as a causal factor during the early stages of America's industrial transformation in the 19th century is judged to be significant but not crucial. Thus the U.S. case does not support the pro-agriculture view. However, it does not support the anti-agriculture view either. The massive investments in America's modern infrastructure and industries were financed largely by foreign capital and waves of immigration; and agriculture was not bypassed by the public investments in modern transport and communications infrastructure, and in research and extension institutions. The contribution of an increasingly productive agriculture mainly entailed merchandise export earnings and an expanding urban food supply. Agriculture's role in the 20th century is different in that its productivity growth was larger in the 20th than in the 19th century, so that its contribution to overall growth is larger. However, since agriculture started off the 20th century with only about a quarter of the labor force in farming, a given boost in agricultural productivity gave a smaller boost to overall productivity growth. The nature of agriculture's role also changed, in that as the farm labor force declined from about 14 million in 1940 to 2.5 million in 2000, the movement of workers to non-farm employment provided the kind of support to the non-farm economy during the peak years of out-migration, from 1940 to 1970, that immigrant labor is said to provide today. The growing urban consumer population also benefited as real food prices became more stable and declined significantly. Overall the contribution of agricultural growth to national economic transformation is best characterized as significant but not crucial for the 20th century, as it was for the 19th. As industry did well, so did the incomes of the greatly reduced number of farm families who could increasingly access well-paying non-farm jobs. In sum, the industrialization of the United States, one of the most powerful economies today, both benefited from and contributed to the successful transformation of its agriculture. It was a synergistic causal interaction.

II
The Developing World

Contribution of Agriculture to a Country's
Drive for Industrialization and Improved
Well-Being for All

Introduction

Summary. In reviewing the variety of country experiences, we find that most of them support, but some undermine or modify, the pro-agriculture position. Most cases support the pro-agriculture position that sustained agricultural development makes a major positive difference. However, the polar view is refuted. Agriculture is not the major contributor in countries where trade, aid, remittances, foreign direct investment, and so on can provide the main sources of foreign exchange and investment. However, even in these cases, investing in agriculture was rightly deemed necessary so that agricultural backwardness would not constitute a bottleneck to overall growth and broad-based development. The "squeeze agriculture" position is convincingly refuted, as China's repeated attempts to squeeze agriculture before 1979 amply show. To date, there is no successful case of the "squeeze agriculture" approach. This approach has exacerbated rural poverty and urban squalor, thus undermining instead of building broad-based and sustainable industrialization and wealth.

Main questions asked and coverage of review. For more than half a century since the end of WWII, country after country has been striving to achieve industrialization and, with it, increased wealth and improved well-being. Most have not considered successful agricultural transformation an integral component of their strategies. This chapter examines the strategy applied to and the performance of agriculture, first in relatively few highly performing but very different countries so as to better assess the role of agricultural development in the industrial rise of such economies.

For the first set of high-growth countries, we assess whether their experiences support, undermine, or modify the polar views on agriculture's contribution. Specifically, among these highly performing countries, in which agriculture contributed to at least 10 percent of GDP at the early stages of their industrialization, what was the developmental role of agriculture, if any? If we conclude that they have succeeded in their industrialization drive without successfully transforming their agriculture, then that would weaken the pro-agriculture position.

For the second set of less industrialized countries with substantial rates of rural poverty, the search is for any combination of the following:

1. Sustained high output and productivity growth in agriculture with persistent high rates of rural poverty and mediocre overall economic growth; or, alternatively,
2. Stagnant low-productivity agriculture with high rates of overall economic growth and low (or lower) rates of rural poverty.

The existence of either combination would undermine or refute the claim of agriculture's substantial contribution to overall growth and poverty reduction. Likewise, the non-existence of either combination would undermine or refute the anti-agriculture view.

Countries chosen and rationale for choice. Two sets of countries at different stages of economic development have been selected for analysis in this chapter. The first set comprises economies that have been widely recognized as high performers in terms of sustained economic growth, rapid structural transformation, and broad-based rural income growth and poverty reduction. The second set comprises major developing economies with the following:

1. Substantial agricultural sectors that over the past four to five decades have made substantial progress toward their agricultural transformation and poverty reduction but still have high rates of poverty and destitution (some 10 percent of the rural population) – for example, India, China, and Indonesia.
2. A high degree of inequality in terms of access to land and/or income-earning opportunities and a major focus on reducing rural poverty – for example, Malaysia, Tunisia, Brazil, and Chile. What was the contribution of sustained agricultural growth to reducing poverty in an unequal setting? Though very different, all

these economies also had an important agriculture sector (contributing to 10 percent of GDP or more) during the initial years of their economic transformation.

The selection purposely includes countries characterized by wide differences in historical and cultural heritage, as well as in resource endowments, so as to help identify the distinctive elements of agriculture's contribution, positive or negative, to industrialization and poverty reduction in a wide variety of cultural and policy contexts.

In Section C, the chapter compares the methodological approach taken here for evaluating the contribution of agriculture to overall economic development and broad-based poverty reduction with those of several recent studies addressing the same question. Section D summarizes the main conclusions from these tests.

Approach to each country case. This chapter briefly describes the country context in terms of major socio-political and economic events that affect the kinds of economic policy adopted and economic performance realized. It also includes the socio-political and policy context, since it is critical to better understand the aspirations and actions of governments and their people. The focus is on overall economic performance and selected aspects of social progress, in particular on rural income gains and poverty reduction. Within this context, the chapter discusses the importance, structure, and performance of agriculture over several decades. The time period of the analysis is mainly post-WWII; however, earlier decades are also included, depending, in part, on data availability. The basic question is: What is the evidence that sustained agricultural development (sustained growth in productivity and production), in particular success in long-term agricultural transformation, was necessary for overall economic growth and transformation?

Organization of chapter. This chapter has four sections[1]

Section A: In the first set, the countries chosen and approximate periods are as follows: Europe: Ireland (1960–1990s) and Portugal (1960–1990s); East Asia: the Republic of Korea (1920–1990s) and Taiwan, China (1910–69).

---

[1] Unless otherwise noted, the GNI data for all country cases discussed is from the World Bank: World Development Indicators, September 2010.

Section B: In the second set, the countries are India (1947–1990s), the People's Republic of China (1949–1990s), Indonesia (1960s–early 2000s), Malaysia (1957–1990s), Tunisia (1960–1990s), Brazil (1950s–1990s), and Chile (1950–1990s).

Each country case is unique, with a distinctive combination of constraints, opportunities, assets, and challenges. Despite such wide differences, what do their experiences teach development practitioners about agriculture's contribution? In particular, the chapter tries to identify a common pattern in the evidence supporting or undermining the claim regarding the substantial nature of agriculture's contribution and regarding the need to invest in agriculture and the rural areas for it to contribute fully.

Section C: This section compares the methodological approach here with the inductive approach commonly used.

Section D: This section summarizes main insights from the tests.

SECTION A
Countries Widely Recognized as Having Been High Performers

II.I. Ireland – GNI per capita: USD 44,310 (2009)

Brief background. Ireland is no longer considered part of the developing world.[2] In less than two generations (1960–2000), Ireland went from being considered a poor, backward agricultural region of Great Britain to a developed industrial country of the European economy, often referred to as a "Celtic Tiger." At independence (December 6, 1921), its GDP per capita was a little more than half of Britain's (Kennedy, 1998). In the 25 years after independence (1921–46), Ireland went through a difficult period that can be divided into three sub-periods. It went through a civil war until August 1923. In the first decade after independence, the government of Ireland focused on agriculture, which was the biggest sector. However, prices collapsed following the boom after WWI and agriculture did poorly. The second period started in 1932 when the new government of Fianna Fail took over (March 1932–February 1948). It adopted nationalist and protectionist policies and engaged in an economic war with Britain. This economic war, which lasted until 1938, originated over the payment of land annuities. During this period, Ireland was hit by worldwide depression. The third period encompassed the war years and lasted until 1946. Both agriculture and industry were hard hit by shortages, as Ireland was forced to be self-sufficient. Since it remained neutral during the war, it did not receive substantial Marshall aid. For a decade after the end of WWII, economic performance was dismal, with terms of trade deteriorating and the government adopting a highly deflationary budget.

Substantial improvements in the 1960s. By 1960, Irish GDP per capita was still half of Britain's (Kennedy, 1998). Nevertheless, important steps were being taken toward an increasingly outward-oriented economy, with particular emphasis on attracting foreign investments. The period from 1958 to 1972 saw sustained growth as terms of trade improved, the government adopted expansionary fiscal policies, and a Free Trade Area Agreement with Britain (AIFTA) was signed (1965). A national agricultural institute for research and extension

---

[2] World Bank: World Development Indicators, September 09/2010.

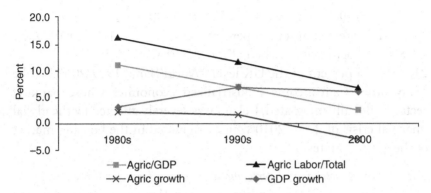

Figure 2.1. Ireland: selected key economic indicators (percent, annual averages, 1980s–2000s).
Source: World Development Indicators.

was created in 1958. Free secondary education was instituted in 1968. Agricultural (in particular livestock) and manufactured exports grew. This first period of sustained growth is labeled Ireland's "first golden age" (MacSharry and White, 2000: ch. 2, 54). By 1972, Ireland was no longer a primarily agricultural country (Kennedy, Giblin, and McHugh, 1988: 33–71).

Mixed performance after EU accession in 1973. Much was expected from the European Union's accession in 1973. The earlier years following accession were good. Total transfers (agriculture subsidies and structural funds) accounted for 5 percent of GDP in 1986 and 4 percent of GDP by the late 1990s (MacSharry and White, 2000: ch. 2, 89). However, economic performance was dismal in the late 1970s. Ireland suffered from the two oil crises of 1973 and 1979, a public deficit that exceeded 10 percent of GDP, and stagnant to negative employment growth. Economic gloom prevailed in much of the 1980s.

High-growth performance, especially after the mid-1990s until 2007–2010. The transformation of the Irish economy of the 1990s has been attributed to the 1987 reforms, which reversed the rising public debt of 1974–86, held labor costs down, and reduced taxes. This created an environment that attracted foreign direct investment, in particular American investments in the information and communications technology sector. In 1960, Irish GDP per capita, which was 60 percent of EU-15 average GDP per capita, rose to 85 percent of EU-15 average by 1996 (MacSharry and White, 2000: ch. 2, 85, chart 2–19). Irish GDP grew at around 9 percent per year from 1995 to 1999. By 1998, GDP per capita reached USD 18,340, while the UK's was USD 21,400 – 86 percent of the UK level (World Bank, 1999/2000).[3] Like many other high-income industrialized economies whose banking sector is globally integrated, Ireland was severely affected by the global financial crisis of 2007–2010 which originated in the housing market of the United States.

Importance, structure, and performance of agriculture until the 1960s. At independence (1921), agriculture was a major sector. It contributed around 33 percent of GDP, 50 percent of employment, and 75 percent of merchandise exports (Kennedy et al., 1988: 202). Livestock was the main export. Up to EU accession (1973), the main market for Irish agriculture was Britain. Britain subsidized its own producers, and the market was static. Furthermore, Irish exports faced quantitative restrictions, and prices were low. From 1912, the eve of the WWI, to 1960, agricultural output was fairly stagnant.

Agriculture's growth performance in the 1960s and early 1970s. The 1960s and early 1970s was a growth period for agriculture, as agriculture benefited from substantial government subsidies (particularly in butter and milk) and as terms of trade improved, including in the important British market. This was also a period of high overall economic growth, from virtually zero to 4 percent a year (MacSharry and White, 2000: ch. 2, 54). During this period, there was greater polarization in agriculture, as growth was concentrated on the larger farms. The number of small farms declined. For the remaining small farms, economic viability depended increasingly on availability of off-farm employment and income. This trend continued. By 2000, in some 45 percent of farm households, one operator or spouse had non-farm income and employment (Phelan, Frawley, and Wallace, 2002). Researchers argue that the pattern of land tenure and transfer was not conducive to improving efficiency because it contributed to the advanced age structure of the farming population and, given the low level of education, was largely responsible for the low level of farm management (Kennedy et al., 1988: 223).

[3] Selected World Development Indicators, table 1.

Agriculture's relative lackluster performance in the 1990s. From 1990 to 2000, agriculture's contribution to GDP and to employment declined further, from 10.1 to 3.5 percent and from 14.2 to 7.3 percent, respectively (see Figure 2.1). Over the same period, overall GDP almost doubled. Gross agricultural output (GAO), which grew at an average annual rate of 2.3 percent in the 1980s, slowed down to 0.6 percent in the 1990s. The rate of technical change also slowed down considerably in the 1990s. The slowdown is attributed to the production quotas, especially after the MacSharry Common Agricultural Policy (CAP) reforms of 1992. When the GAO is adjusted for production subsidies and market transfers, agriculture's contribution at world market prices was only 2.1 percent in 1996 and 1.0 percent in 2000. Harte argues that Irish agriculture is "hopelessly under-productive and so dependent on consumer and tax-payer transfers" (2002: fig. 13, table 1, p. 4). Similar concerns about a slowdown in productivity changes in Irish agriculture are expressed elsewhere. During 1984–98, there was technical change as measured by changes in best practice; however, it continued at a declining rate. On average, farms achieved 65 percent of the efficiency level of best-practice farms. Moreover, the average level of farm efficiency had been decreasing by 0.4 percent per year during this period (O'Neill, Leavy, and Matthews, 2000: 1).

Which of the polar views does the Ireland case support, undermine, or modify? The case of Ireland does not support the pro-agriculture view. During the decade of fundamental macroeconomic reforms of 1987 and of high growth from the mid-1990s on, agricultural growth was far less and slowing down. Besides, agriculture has been a major recipient of funds under the EU accession policy, not a generator of surplus being invested in non-agriculture. The overall economy responded to the fundamental macroeconomic reforms that made Ireland attractive to FDI. The sustained dynamism took place largely in the 1990s. Except for bouts of growth, agriculture has for a long time also been a low-productivity, stagnant sector. Productivity increased after accession, but the rate of increase decreased in the 1990s. Agriculture is being transformed, and there have been productivity increases, but it cannot be said to be a success story yet. Indeed, researchers are concerned that its productivity growth slowed down in the 1990s and is in fact regressing in some sectors, such as in beef and sheep farms.

The most that can be said about the contribution of agriculture is that it did not act as a constraint on overall economic growth and dynamism.

II.II. Portugal – GNI per capita: USD 20,940 (2009)

Brief background. For a long time, Portugal was viewed as a Third World country in Europe.[4] Portugal became a member of the European Free Trade Association (EFTA) in 1961 and joined the European Community (EC) in January 1986. As a member of the EFTA, Portugal adopted an export-oriented strategy of industrialization, unlike many developing countries that adopted import-substitution strategies. With respect to the EC, Portugal negotiated a transitional period for agriculture that exempted it from the Common Agricultural Policy (CAP) until 1991 with the simultaneous setting up of a development fund for agriculture with a budget of ECU 700 million for 10 years (Programa Especifico de Desenvolvimento da Agricultura Portuguesa, PEDAP, 1986–96). The transition period was extended to 2001 because of fears that the backward nature of Portuguese agriculture would require a longer adjustment time. Since 1960, Portugal has experienced major ups and downs, as discussed later.

Spurts of short-lived growth until the mid-1970s. Between 1960 and 1973, the eve of the revolution against the Salazarist regime in 1974, the overall economy experienced high growth – an average annual growth rate of around 7 percent – fueled by a high rate of emigration and the remittances it generated and an influx of foreign direct investment (FDI). Industrial sector annual growth averaged 9 percent, but agricultural growth was barely 2 percent. This industrial wealth was, however, highly concentrated both economically (40 families) and geographically (Corkill, 1993: 17–28). This high-growth period was short-lived, and Portugal was still viewed as part of the Third World.

---

[4] World Bank: World Development Indicators, September, 2010. Portugal is a high-income country. World Bank income GNI groupings (2008) are (USD), calculated using the World Bank Atlas Method: high: 11,906 and above; upper middle: 3,856 to less than 11,905; lower middle: 976 to less than 3,855; low: less than 975.

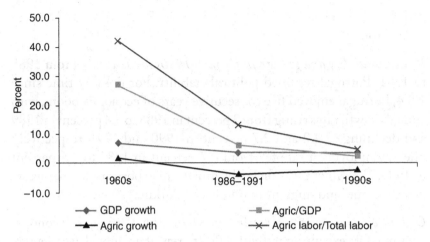

Figure 2.2. Portugal: selected key economic indicators (percent, annual averages, 1960s–1990s).

Sources and Notes:

GDP growth: 1960s, 1986–91 – David Corkill. 1993. *The Portuguese Economy since 1974*. Edinburgh University Press. Pp 17–28, 117–126. 1990s – Economic Survey of Portugal: Policy Brief. OECD Observer. April 2001. Table: Macro performance at a glance 1996–2000.

Agric growth: David Corkill. 1993. *The Portuguese Economy since 1974*. Edinburgh University Press. Pp 17–28. 1986–95, and 1995–2001 respectively: decline in agricultural output. Communication from the Commission to the Council and the European Parliament: Report on the situation in Portuguese Agriculture, Brussels 19/6/2003. COM (2003) 359 final. Para 3.1, 3.3; section 4–6.

Agric/GDP, Agric labor/total labor: 1960s – V. Xavier Pintado. July 1964. *Structure and Growth of the Portuguese Economy*. European Free Trade Association. Table II. Mid 1980s – David Corkill. 1993. *The Portuguese Economy since 1974*. Edinburgh University Press. Table 3.2. 1990s – Nelly Jazra Bandarra. Janvier 2002. "Les Perspectives du Développement Rural au Portugal". *Revue du Marche Commun et de l'Union Européenne*. No. 454, Pp 44, 46, Tableau 1 & 2. Agro-industry contributed another 5.4 percent of GDP (1998).

The 1975–1985 period was a decade of crises.

Years of crisis from the mid-1970s to the mid-1980s. In 1975–76, Portugal plunged into a crisis. There were dramatic events in close succession, including the change of regime in 1974; the oil crisis of 1973–74; the loss of African colonies in the mid-1970s; the return of refugees from the lost colonies; the return of migrants from the recession in the mid-1970s Europe; the de facto agrarian reform of 1974 (however, agricultural land distribution remains highly skewed)[5];

---

[5] Holdings of less than 2 ha represented 54 percent of all holdings in 2000 and occupied 6 percent of total utilizable agricultural area (UAA), while 1.4 percent of holdings of more than 100 ha per holding occupied 53 percent of total UAA. Communication from the Commission to the Council and the European Parliament: Report on the Situation in Portuguese Agriculture, Brussels, June 19, 2003. COM (2003) 359 final, para 2.3.

and the nationalization of many industries. Political instability prevailed from 1974 to 1985.[6]

Political stability and growth in the mid-1980s to the 1990s. From 1985 to 1991, Portugal regained political stability. For the first time since 1974, Portugal enjoyed five consecutive years of economic boom, with annual growth rates rising from 3 percent in 1985 to 5.4 percent in 1989 and declining to 4.2 and 2.7 percent in 1990 and 1991, respectively. The unemployment rate fell from 8.7 percent in 1985 to 4.5 percent in 1991. The growth was fueled by growth in exports, tourism, investment income, and migrant remittances (Corkill, 1993: 117–26).

Overall economic performance in the 1990s. The Portuguese economy continued its expansion in the 1990s. It grew at an annual average rate of around 3.0 –3.5 percent in the second half of the 1990s. In fact, its annual growth rate was well above the average annual of the Euro-area of around 1.5–2.5 percent. The unemployment rate had declined from around 7 percent in 1996 to 4 percent in 2000. This growth was fueled by stronger demand from Portugal's EU partners. The current account deficit, however, also continued to widen, reaching 10 percent of GDP in 2000 (*OECD Observer*, April 2001).[7]

Importance, structure, and performance of agriculture by EC accession (1986). In 1900, the share of agriculture in GDP was 42 percent; by 1920, it was 31 percent of total (Lains, 2003: 6). In the 1960s, Portugal had several features common to a developing country (see Figure 2.2). In 1961, agriculture contributed 27 percent of GDP and 42 percent of total employment. The GNP per capita was USD 301 and the illiteracy rate was 41 percent (Pintado, 1964: table 2). This 1961 GNP per capita level was only 32 percent of Germany's and 63 percent of Spain's (Da Silva Lopes, 1993: 7). Portuguese agriculture was characterized by low productivity – land and labor, low levels of investment, extensive methods of production, highly fragmented farms in the north, and high land concentration in the south.

A significant reduction in the relative size of agriculture by the late 1990s. By the mid-1980s, the importance of agriculture had declined

---

[6] The African colonies were Guinea Bissau, Mozambique, Cape Verde and Sao Tome, and Angola.

[7] Table: Macro performance at a glance 1996–2000.

substantially, but it was still important. It accounted for around 6 percent of GDP and 13 percent of total employment. There are, however, other estimates of its contribution (Corkill, 1974: 3.2)[8] (see Figure 2.2). Its share of GDP was nearly halved, from 5.1 percent in 1990 to around 2.8 percent in 2001. Its contribution to total employment decreased to 8 percent of total by 2000.[9] So, from 1960–2000, Portuguese agriculture exhibited a classic feature of agriculture in high-income countries as its share of GDP declined from 27 to around 3 percent.

Impact of accession policies on agriculture. Agriculture was profoundly affected by the accession policies. These policies consisted of investments to finance structural changes in processing and commercialization, technology transfer, and the delivery of rural services, among others. Accession also meant, however, a decline in real output prices for most commodities.[10] Between 1985 and 1989, farm family incomes fell substantially (Avillez in Da Silva Lopes, 1993: table 2.6). Real prices for cereals, milk, and meat decreased further with the reform of CAP in 1992 and the Agenda 2000. These price cuts were compensated for by direct payments.

Was Portuguese agriculture successfully transformed by the 1990s? Some 15 years after accession, Portuguese agriculture still could not be considered successfully transformed, although there were major improvements in the competitiveness and quality of outputs such as olives, wine, and fruits. During the 1990s, there has also been a major shift from arable crop to animal production. Between 1990 and 2001, crop production decreased by 0.3 percent per year, while final animal production increased by 1.5 percent per year. This shift has been a positive development, as it has been a shift from commodities with very low productivity to extensive animal rearing, an activity that corresponds more closely to the comparative advantage of the less favored areas. However, over the 1986–95 period, Portuguese agricultural output decreased in real terms at a rate of 3.1 percent per year. The rate of

[8] For example, two other estimates are 12 percent of national income and 25 percent of total employment (Pearson et al.: 1987) and 6.7 percent of GDP and 20 percent of total employment (Da Silva Lopes, 1993: table 1.2).

[9] Communication from the Commission to the Council and the European Parliament: Report on the Situation in Portuguese Agriculture, Brussels, June 19, 2003. COM (2003) 359 final, para 2.1, 2.4.

[10] These are potatoes, white *vinho verde*, rice, and sunflowers (Pearson et al.: 1987: 26).

decline slowed between 1995 and 2000 to 1.6 percent per year, which
was less than the average rate of decline of EU agriculture at 2.2 percent per year. Productivity as measured by agricultural output per labor
unit was only about 28 percent of the EU average. There still is substantial underemployment in Portuguese agriculture despite the fact
that overall unemployment has declined to some 4 percent by 2000,
and the agricultural labor force has been decreasing by 2.4 percent per
year between 1995 and 2000. (For the rest of the EU-15, the rate of
decline was 3.1 percent per year for this period.)[11]

*More than 15 years required for the successful transformation of Portugal's
agriculture.* The EU Commission has decided that further assistance
for structural improvements is necessary. A major program of rural
development was undertaken (2000–2006). Priority improvements are
in the area of increasing labor productivity and the competitiveness
of small family farms (in particular) and of processing and marketing.
Priority commodities are olives, fruits, wine, dairy products, and meat
production. It is clear that the successful transformation of Portuguese
agriculture will require much more than 15 years.

*Which of the polar views does the Portugal case support, undermine, or
modify?* As in the Irish case, the pro-agriculture view is refuted. Over
a period of nearly two generations (40 years), Portugal went from
the status of a developing country to that of a high-income country,
yet agriculture's development was not a necessary contributor. Thus
Portugal's transformation into an industrial economy does not support
the claim of the centrality of agricultural transformation for building
the industrial wealth of a nation. Instead, it shows the key importance
of trade and the influx of foreign resources for financing investment
and growth. Portugal has for a long period been an open economy.
Even during its years of turmoil in the 1970s and up to 1985, the
influx of remittances, FDI, and tourism fueled what turned out to be
short-lived growth. Portugal's agriculture, however, did not constrain

---

[11] Communication from the Commission to the Council and the European Parliament: Report
on the Situation in Portuguese Agriculture, Brussels, June 19, 2003. COM (2003) 359 final,
para 3.1, 3.3; secs. 4–6. Politically, a major positive development is the impressive and steady
growth of real agricultural income per unit of labor. Agricultural output per hectare of
Utilizable Agricultural Area UAA was about 75 percent of the average EU level (Euro 1,642
per ha UAA vs. Euro 2,205 per ha UAA).

the growth of the overall economy because Portugal received substantial agricultural investments financed mainly by the EU to raise agricultural productivity. Although agriculture had not been successfully transformed by the time Portugal became industrialized, its productivity improved in major areas. Although the Portugal case does not support the pro-agriculture view, its experiences do not support the anti-agriculture view either, since the sector was neither exploited to provide resources for investment elsewhere, nor ignored in the drive for industrialization.

Summary. In both Ireland and Portugal, successful agricultural transformation was not necessary for overall economic transformation. In recent decades (1990s on), agriculture is being transformed, as it has been benefiting from access to an expanded EU market, institutional restructuring, and substantial EU support funds. Investment in agriculture has promoted productivity growth in some agricultural subsectors. The transformation of agriculture and the national economy have proceeded in parallel in Portugal and Ireland, with agriculture benefiting from its integration into an expanding non-agriculture sector and not being a constraint to overall growth and development.

II.III. The Republic of Korea – GNI per capita: USD 19,830 (2009)

Brief background. The Republic of Korea (henceforth, referred to as Korea or South Korea) is well known for at least three things: (a) its sustained high economic growth under an export-oriented strategy; (b) the controversy about whether this spectacular growth was due to a "laissez-faire" or "state-led" development approach, a controversy also referred to as neoclassical versus revisionist (World Bank, 1993a: 9); and (c) the controversy regarding the role of agriculture in this remarkable growth performance. The main question addressed here is: Was Korea's rapid industrialization agriculture-led?

Remarkable growth performance for decades. Korea has been one of the fastest-growing economies during the post-WWII period. It maintained an average annual growth rate of 9–10 percent for nearly three decades, from the early 1960s to the late 1990s, up to the outbreak of the Asian financial crisis starting in late 1997. Per capita annual income grew from less than USD 100 in 1962 to nearly USD 10,000 in the late 1990s (World Bank, Feb. 1999: 14). High growth has picked up again in recent years (e.g., 7 percent in 2002), but there are still major financial problems that can undermine sustained robust recovery (World Bank, Oct 2003b). Despite these recent problems, Korea has been transformed in less than two generations.

Stark difference at the dawn of the 21st century between North and South Korea. This transformation has been dramatic, as is evident when one compares the two Koreas. The Korean peninsula was partitioned in 1945. In 1948, the Republic of Korea was created in the south, and the Democratic People's Republic of Korea in the north. In the earlier years, North Korea was said to be doing much better than South Korea. However, after more than half a century, the south has become a member of the club of rich nations, the OECD (December 12, 1996), while deprivation is widespread in the north, as there have been persistent rumors of food shortages (Eberstadt, 1996: 131, 156).

Difficult early years as Japan's colony and following the devastation of war. Korea was a Japanese colony from 1910 to 1945.[12] After years of occupation and war, Korea in the 1950s was one of the poorest countries. After partition, Korea had to absorb millions of refugees from the north. From 1940 to 1960, its population is estimated to have grown from 16 to about 25 million. Despite substantial U.S. aid, its economy stagnated until the 1960s. In these early years, agriculture and the rural population were important. Agriculture contributed to around 46 percent of GDP, with the share of the farm population constituting some 61 percent of total population. It had the structure of a typical developing country (Eberstadt, 1996: 145).

Interventionist Korean governments with a strong commitment to development. To promote their export-led industrialization strategies, successive South Korean governments have been highly committed to development (World Bank, Feb. 1999: 25).[13] The priority sectors were industry, with an emphasis on manufactured exports in the 1960s

---

[12] The Japanese invasion of Manchuria and the Sino-Japanese War started in 1937.
[13] The World Bank staff speaks of high government commitment within a remarkable partnership.

and 1970s, and heavy industry, chemicals, and transport in the 1980s. Exporters benefited from subsidized credit from the nationalized banking system. The exchange rate was kept low relative to competitors. The power of labor unions was curbed to maintain moderate wage increases. As in other high-growth East and Southeast Asian economies, Korea's development strategy emphasized macroeconomic stability, high savings and investment rates, export orientation, heavy investment in human capital, and a private business-friendly environment.[14] Policy was state-led but pro–private sector.

Salient features of Korea's economic transformation. Rapid development started under the export orientation strategy of General Park Chung Hee (1961–79). This strategy was continued into the 1980s and 1990s. From 1962 to 1994, a high GDP growth of around 10 percent was fueled by an annual export growth that averaged 20 percent, while investments exceeded 30 percent of GDP (World Bank, Feb. 1999: 14). Export growth is estimated to have declined to an average of around 16 percent per year between 1992 and 2002.[15] Unlike Hong Kong, Taiwan, China, and Singapore, Korea borrowed heavily from abroad. Korea's total debt was 0.525 of GNP while total debt was 142 percent of exported goods and services during 1985–86 (World Bank, 1993a: table 3.3).[16]

Major improvements in rural well-being. Sustained high growth was accompanied by major socio-economic changes. In the 1930s, around 75 percent of the population of Korea was agricultural. Less than 50 percent of the rural population was literate. Rural infant mortality was 160.9 per 1,000 live births in 1944 (Ban, Moon, and Perkins, 1980: 298, 310–13). Today, 83 percent (1996–2002 data) of the total population (of 47.6 million people) is urban. Illiteracy has virtually disappeared. Illiteracy is estimated to be 2 percent for the general population and 3 percent for females. Infant mortality at the national level is 5 per 1,000

---

[14] The period analyzed is 1965–90. The high-growth economies are Japan, Hong Kong, Singapore, Taiwan, Indonesia, Malaysia, and Thailand.

[15] World Bank, "Korea at a Glance," September 2, 2003. www.worldbank.org.

[16] There seems to be some disagreement as to whether the Korean savings rate was high. According to Eberstadt (1996: 151–52, 96, 97), the household savings rate was low, but business and government savings rates "compare with or exceed, those of other rapidly growing export-oriented economies."

live births.[17] The land reform of 1949–50 was also a major boost to broad-based rural income and wealth distribution.

The ups and downs of Korea's remarkable economic transformation. Average annual GDP growth was high for decades: around 9 percent from 1963 to 1990; on a per capita basis, it was around 7 percent (OECD, 1999: 22). During the later period, from 1982 to 1992, the growth rate was also around 9 percent; and from 1992 to 2002, it was 5 percent. In per capita terms, the growth rate was 7.8 and 4.4 percent, respectively.[18] These averages mask major highs and lows. The highs have been around 12 percent, as in the late 1970s and late 1980s, and the lows as in the early 1980s and late 1990s: –2 percent in 1980 and –5.8 in 1998 (World Bank, Feb. 1999: 14, 32–33). The late 1970s was also marked by traumatic national events.[19] Figure 2.3 presents selected growth rates and ratios since WWII. The high-growth performance as of the mid-1960s contrasts with the early post-WWII period, during which Korea's growth was low despite (some may say, because of) substantial aid. During 1946 to late 1961, Korea received substantial U.S. aid, in the form of direct grants. The aid of USD 5 billion was substantial, as GNP in 1953 was estimated to be USD 2 billion (Eberstadt, 1996: 145–46)!

The sustained high GDP and export growth rates are truly remarkable, especially when one considers the nearly half a century of very difficult economic and political conditions. A comparison of these post-WWII growth rates clearly shows that, as of the 1960s, overall GDP growth far surpassed agriculture growth during this period. As the notes in the Appendix C tables make clear, the estimates are taken from different sources and constructed using different methods. They are not strictly comparable, but they correctly capture the major trends.

Importance, structure, and performance of agriculture. Over the course of the 20th century, the share of agriculture shrank from nearly 50 percent of GDP to 4 percent of GDP by 2002 (Ban et al., 1980: table 2).[20]

[17] World Bank, "Korea at a Glance," September 2, 2003. www.worldbank.org.
[18] World Bank, "Korea at a Glance," September 2, 2003.
[19] There were the assassination of General Park in 1979; a brief period of political uncertainty and social unrest; high inflation, unemployment, external debt, and current account deficits; and the second oil price shock (OECD, 1999: 22). Also in World Bank (2000a: table 1.1).
[20] Also in World Bank, "Korea at a Glance," September 2, 2003. For 2007, AG/GDP shrank to 3 percent (World Development Indicators, 2007).

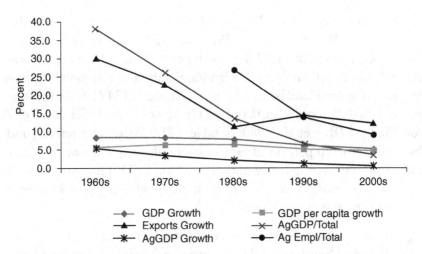

Figure 2.3. The Republic of Korea: selected growth rates and ratios (annual averages, 1960s–2000s).
Source: World Development Indicators, respective years.
Note: The Japanese invasion of Manchuria and the Sino-Japanese war started in 1937. The war continued until 1945. The partition between north and south was in 1948. The Korean War lasted from 1950–53. Therefore Korea was under foreign domination followed by war from 1910–1953, nearly half a century.

So did its share of employment. Thus, by the close of the 20th century, some 11 percent of the labor force was producing less than 5 percent of the GDP. A large proportion of the labor force was, however, not full-time farmers (OECD, 1999: 29). The population, primarily rural at the end of WWII, is now predominantly urban (Ban et al., 1980: 298).[21] The high rate of emigration of farm labor and the widespread literacy of such labor into industrial Korea has been one of agriculture's important contributions to Korea's economic transformation.

Equitable land distribution in land-scarce smallholder agriculture. The government of Korea and the U.S. government successfully carried out land reform, launched by the Land Reform Act of 1949–50. The percentage of owner-families rose from around 14 percent in 1945 to nearly 70 percent in 1965. The upper limit allowed for each landowner was around 3 hectares (ha). The land reform was successful because not only land redistribution, but also income-earning opportunities, were broad-based. The way land reform and complementary policies were implemented leveled the playing field in agriculture. Moreover,

---

[21] Also in World Bank, "Korea at a Glance," September 2, 2003.

there is no evidence that this small farm size undermined productivity increases (Ban et al., 1980: 297, table 120). Korean agriculture is land-scarce, and until the high growth performance of the mid-1960s, it was labor-abundant. Its arable land/agricultural population ratio was the lowest among land-scarce countries. It was 0.134 (1968–70) compared with 0.258 for Japan, 0.164 for China, 0.442 for India, and 0.417 for Thailand (Ban et al., 1980: 5, table 4.7).[22] After land reform, and by 1965, some 70 percent of farm households were full owners, while only 7 percent were pure tenants (Ban et al., 1980: 120). Korean land reform is considered one of the most thoroughgoing and successful land reforms ever undertaken.

Agricultural policy – from agricultural taxation to subsidization. As in most East and Southeast Asian countries, achieving rice or food grain self-sufficiency was a major objective of agricultural policy. Under Japanese rule, promoting rice production and its exports to Japan was the prime objective. In independent Korea, food security and rice self-sufficiency remained a major objective, which, however, did not translate into government support in the earlier years. After the Korean War (1950–53), with abundant American aid under US PL480 and with an export-led industrialization strategy in place, agricultural development and investment were of low priority in the first Five-Year Plan (1961–66). During this plan period, rice farmers received well below world market prices. However, the 1971 elections clearly showed that rural discontent with the government of Korea's policy was widespread. It is believed that due to this widespread discontent, the government reversed its policy of discrimination to that of heavy subsidization of the sector (Eberstadt, 1996: 148–49). This policy of heavy protection is still in force. Indeed, the estimate of the Producer Subsidy Equivalent (PSE; these are transfers as a percentage of the value of the production) was 97 percent in 1997, with transfers to rice accounting for nearly three-quarters of total PSE (OECD, 1999: 72–73). Since the 1970s, agricultural policy has been largely an income support policy.

Agricultural investment under Japanese rule (1910–45). During the colonial period, the Japanese invested substantially in agriculture, primarily

---

[22] The comparable U.S. land/man ratio was 21.475.

because they wanted to increase Korea's rice production to satisfy Japan's growing demand. They completed a cadastral survey by 1918. This survey became the basis for their land taxation and for their system of private property rights (which replaced the feudal system). Instead of being serfs, the majority of Korean farmers became tenants of a minority of Japanese (who owned most of the land) and Korean landlords. The Japanese authorities set rental and tax rates and collected the taxes from the landlords. The Japanese authorities also converted land to paddy, founded research and extension services, and introduced new seed technologies, responsive to chemical fertilizer.

Controversial impact of Japanese colonial policy on agricultural output and productivity growth. Researchers disagree as to whether "Korea took off in the postwar era without any prior investment in agriculture" (Kang and Ramachandran, 1999: 783). Ban (1979) argued that although there was accelerated growth of agriculture in the 1930s, "total productivity remained almost constant over the 1918–41 period." Why there was no net improvement in productivity remains a puzzle. Estimates of partial land and labor productivities, however, showed some growth (Ban, 1979: 100, 111). As shown in Figures 2.3, 2.4, and 2.5, agricultural growth and productivity did accelerate during the post-war period, but they were nowhere near the high growth rates of non-agriculture.

Ban et al. (1980: 5) argue that "[a] Korean agricultural revolution did not precede or lead development in the other sectors in the economy. There were no substantial net flows of savings or tax dollars from the rural to the urban sector.... For the most part, however, it was agriculture that benefited from the industrial and export boom rather than reverse." They pointed out that although Korea's agricultural growth rates during 1952–71 of between 3 and 4 percent were not as spectacular as its non-agriculture growth rates, they were comparable to the overall Asian growth rate average (all of Asia was around 3.5 percent from 1952 to 1971), and it was higher than that of the land-rich regions of Africa and Latin America (Ban et al., 1980: table 3).[23] Kang and Ramachandran disagreed. They argued that "[a]n agricultural revolution did take place in colonial Korea, and it was the direct result of the Japanese colonial policy to modernize Korean agriculture" (Kang and Ramachandran, 1999: 797). They pointed out that there were

---

[23] The growth rate was measured by the FAO method, using 1965 constant prices.

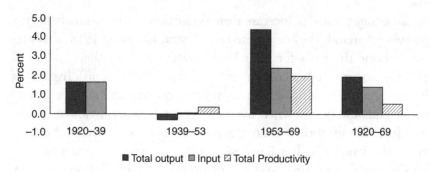

Figure 2.4. Korean agriculture: output, input, and productivity growth rates (percent per year, 1920–69).

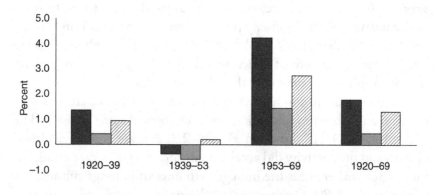

Figure 2.5. Korean agriculture: gross value-added, input, and productivity growth rates (percent per year, 1920–69).

Sources and Notes: Ban, Sung Hwan. 1979 "Agricultural Growth in Korea, 1918–1971." In Hayami, Yujiro, Vernon M. Ruttan, Herman M. Southworth, eds., 1979. *Agricultural Growth in Japan, Taiwan, Korea, and the Philippines*. Published for the East-West Center by the University Press of Hawaii, Honolulu. Tables 4.1, 4.5 a, 4.5 b.

Note that the tables are based on two different measures of total productivity: one on a total output basis and the other, on a gross value-added basis. See Annex C, Table C10.

substantial investments in the agricultural sector prior to the industrialization takeoff of the 1960s. The Japanese successfully pursued a policy of land intensification. Between 1910 and 1938, the annual growth rate of irrigated area was approximately 18 percent; that of fertilizer consumption, roughly 22 percent per year; and that of the multiple cropping index, 1.28 percent (Ramachandran, 1995: 371). They argued that continued investments in irrigation and rural infrastructure, and

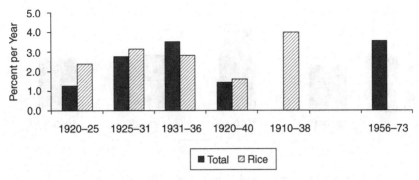

Figure 2.6. Korea: agricultural growth rates (1920–73).

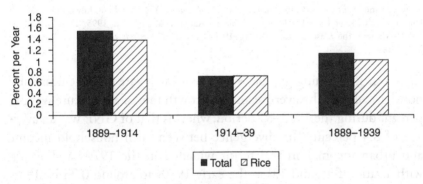

Figure 2.7. Japan: agricultural growth rates (1889–1939).

increased use of chemical fertilizers and high-yielding seed varieties, in the context of fundamental institutional changes transformed Korean agriculture from a feudal to a capitalistic agriculture. To support their arguments, Kang and Ramachandran (1999) showed that output growth in colonial Korea was well above Japan's, though below that of Taiwan, China. See Figures 2.6, 2.7, and 2.8.

As shown in Appendix table C12, growth rates of Korean rice production and exports to Japan were high, at 4.0 and 15.5 percent per year (Ramachandran, 1995), respectively, over the 1910–38 period. These high export growth rates were the very reason Japan invested in Korean agriculture.

Low agricultural performance relative to non-agriculture post-WWII. From 1954 to 1961, agriculture grew at an annual rate of 4.1 percent, while GNP grew at an annual rate of 4.8 percent. After 1960, however,

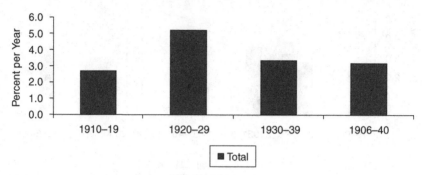

Figure 2.8. Taiwan, China: agricultural growth rates (1910–40).
Sources and Notes: For 1920 to 1940, and 1956–73: Table 1, pp 786 in Kang, Kenneth, and Vijaya Ramachandran. "Economic Transformation in Korea: Rapid Growth without an Agricultural Transformation?" *Economic Development and Cultural Change*, Vol. 47, No. 4, July 1999: 783–802. University of Chicago Press. For 1910–38: Table 1 in Ramachandran, Vijaya. 1995. "Does Agriculture Really Matter? The Case of Korea, 1910–1970." *Journal of East Asian Economics*, Vol. 6, No. 3: 367–384.

there was a widening gap between the growth rate of agriculture and non-agriculture. The average annual growth rate of agriculture was 3.7 percent during the 1962–81 period, whereas that of GNP was an average of 8.4 percent. The divergence between farm household income and urban incomes in real terms widened in the 1970s and 1980s, with a ratio of around 1.0 in the early 1970s to around 0.75 by 1985. There has been increasing emphasis on developing off-farm incomes. The ratio of out-migrants to total farm household population rose from 1.7 percent in the late 1950s to 5.0 percent in the 1970s (Chung, 1990: 141). The sector was relatively neglected in terms of public fiscal investments in that early period. During the 1962–80 period, only 17.3 percent of government investments were allocated to agriculture (Chung, 1990: 138, 142).

Agricultural contribution to non-agriculture. Other than a steady flow of young, able-bodied, educated labor to expanding industry, the other major contribution came in the form of farm household savings and government tax revenues in the early years of Korea's industrialization. Farm household savings as a proportion of total domestic savings, though high, declined from 32–42 percent in the 1963–64 period to 8.3 percent in the 1977–82 period. Agricultural land tax revenues were some 40 percent of total government revenues in the early 1960s, decreasing to 10 percent after 1970. So agriculture's financial contribution (private and public) was significant mainly in the earlier years of the 1960s (Chung, 1990: 145–46). The Korean economy, however, did not rely on agriculture for its major staples, as it received abundant supplies of American surplus products from the early 1950s until 1960. Its consumer product industries of textiles, sugar, and flour became dependent on these cheap supplies. Under PL480, substantial amounts of concessionary food grains were imported.

Is the disagreement semantic or substantial? Both groups of researchers agree that there were major institutional changes and investment expenditures in the agriculture of colonial Korea. Both agree that total productivity during 1918–41 remained almost constant. They both consider important the reform from a feudal to a private property rights/ownership system of a capitalistic agriculture; the expansion of irrigation and rural infrastructure; the setting up of research and extension services; the introduction of high-yielding, fertilizer-responsive paddy varieties; and the increased use of modern non-farm inputs, especially chemical fertilizer. Their growth rate estimates until the mid-1970s are comparable, as they send similar messages (they are not exactly the same because the two groups refer to different sub-periods and use different methods). Both agree that there was some sustained productivity growth in colonial Korea. Their message, that there were sub-periods of substantial positive and negative growth in the pre-WWII period, is similar. However, one group refers to the pre-war performance as an "agricultural revolution" whereas the other does not. One group emphasizes the substantial investments undertaken before the industrial takeoff; the other group emphasizes the beneficial post-war inter-sector interactions for agriculture's growth. Is the disagreement mainly one of semantics? It seems so. This disagreement emphasizes the importance of agreeing on what is meant by "agricultural revolution." If the existence of (a) substantial investments in physical infrastructure, (b) major institutional changes and adoption of new agricultural techniques, and (c) sustained growth and productivity increases over decades (even if the latter is interrupted for long periods as in Japan during the inter-war years) constitute an "agricultural revolution," then Korean agriculture, like Japanese agriculture, has undergone such a revolution. Note that the concept of what constitutes an "agricultural revolution" is still debated among economic historians, as in the case of England two centuries ago!

Did Post-WWII agricultural growth benefit from high non-farm growth? "Agriculture has been the major beneficiary of Korean economic growth, but not the major cause of that growth" (Ban et al., 1980: 31). Available evidence supports this viewpoint. However, it does not follow that Korean agriculture did not undergo a revolution and was not transformed or did not contribute to overall development. As already noted, there were substantial public investments and major institutional changes in agriculture during the pre-industrial takeoff period, first under Japanese rule, followed by land reform (1949–50) under the U.S. occupation, and even during early post-WWII. For example, land under irrigation increased by about 85 percent from 1954 to 1970 (Ramachandran, 1995: 377). The substantial rise in the number of irrigation associations and farmers' cooperatives enabled President Park to build his New Community Movement (*Saemaul Undung*, 1971) on these associations to promote agricultural productivity (through services such as research, extension, and input distribution, including credit) and rural welfare (through education). The agricultural output growth of post-WWII until the 1970s was sustained at between 3 and 4 percent per year, an estimate consistent with the estimate by Kang and Ramachandran, at 3.5 percent per year during that period. Estimates for annual productivity growth were above 1 for two sub-periods (1920–69 at 1.32 and 1946–73 at 1.23). The agricultural land tax was substantial up to the 1960s. These are not characteristic of a stagnant agriculture. In fact, Korea is considered one of the most advanced farming nations. For example, its rice yields (4,550 kg/ha, 1970) compare well with those of Taiwan (4,160 kg/ha, 1970) and Japan (5,640 kg/ha, 1970) (Ban et al., 1980: table 4).

Which of the polar views does the Korean case support, undermine, or modify? Both polar views are undermined. The Korean case undermines the argument that successful agricultural transformation is necessary for overall economic transformation. Korea's experience resembles that of Portugal and Ireland. All three economies are dynamic, small, trade-dependent economies. They did not have to rely on domestic agricultural expansion to generate the resources needed for industrial investment and expansion. They could draw upon other sources. In all three cases, the huge influx of foreign resources (including aid) loosened the stranglehold of a sluggish agriculture on overall economic growth. Domestic macroeconomic management created a stable and competitive environment. The huge influx of foreign exchange was made possible by aid, then by manufactured exports in the case of Korea and by remittances, EU accession, FDI, and tourism receipts in the case of Portugal and Ireland.

Why was Korean agriculture not a bottleneck to overall growth? To say that agricultural transformation was not necessary is not to say that its development made no contribution. In the case of Korea, the minimum that can be said is that the agricultural growth achieved meant that it did not constrain overall growth, for two main reasons. First, there was sustained growth in output and productivity. Although agriculture did not grow as fast as the manufacturing sector, it was not stagnant either. Second, in the earlier years, there was a substantial supply of subsidized grain (wheat, rice, barley) imports under the US PL480 aid (1955 until 1969). PL480 grain contributed to the Korean governments' ability to control inflation and keep food prices stable by subsidizing growing urban demand. The government did not have to tax farmers through low procurement prices as in the earlier years. Without PL480, the taxation might have been more severe or more prolonged. This in turn might have provoked political instability and undermined sustained industrialization.

Summary. In the post-WWII period, Korea underwent rapid economic transformation, but successful agricultural transformation was not a condition. The sector's contribution to overall fast growth was largely through labor migration and less through the transfer of financial resources or cheap food (although grain was taxed in the 1960s). The sector's sustained post-war output and productivity growth benefited from its access to expanding urban markets and farmers' freedom to invest in cash crops instead of being forced to produce grain for grain self-sufficiency reasons. The growth benefits were widespread because of a successful land reform, widespread education, and the government's ability to deliver basic public goods and services in rural areas as of the 1970s.

II.IV. Taiwan, China – GNI per capita: 17,294 (2007 USD)

Brief background. Taiwan, China is well known for its post-WWII economic transformation. Within a span of some three decades (early 1950s–1980s), it was transformed from a poor developing country to a high-growth industrializing economy.[24] Taiwan not only had sustained high growth but also an equitable distribution of the socio-economic benefits of such growth. Taiwan's experience is a counterexample of the Kuznets thesis that inequality must worsen in the early stages of economic development. Equity improved with growth! After decades of sustained high growth, the Gini coefficient for income stood at 0.28 (1972) (Fei et al., 1979: fig. 1.10, table 3.2). Policies on expanding education and health services in rural areas improved equitable access to expanding opportunities. All socio-economic indicators improved dramatically over the 1950s–1970s. Sustained high growth and broad-based socio-economic development changed the face of Taiwan over a period of several decades. GDP per capita grew at an average annual rate of nearly 4 percent (1960–85) (World Bank, 1993a: 131–34, 154–55). The government went from import substitution in the 1950s to export promotion thereafter. Thus, in one generation, Taiwan achieved what is still a distant dream for many developing countries. What role did agriculture play in this remarkable performance?

Productivity-increasing investments under Japanese rule (1895–1945). Taiwan was under Japanese colonial rule from 1895 to 1945. With the objective of using Taiwan as its supplier of rice and sugar (the same as extracting rice exports from Korea), Japan invested heavily in agricultural research institutions and rural infrastructure, including irrigation. The Japanese colonial administration spent an average of 25 percent of its government expenditures on rural infrastructure, such as roads, railroads, ports, and irrigation systems. By the 1920s, access to inexpensive transport throughout the island was achieved (Tomich et al.,

---

[24] Taiwan Statistical Data Book,. http://www.cepd.govtw/encontent/m1.aspx?sNo= 0001453&key=&ex=%20&ic=&cd=, Taiwan Economic Statistics, vol. 6, no. 5, May 2008. GNP per capita, USD current prices. Also for some earlier years, in Taiwan Statistical Website,. http://www.dgbas.gov.tw/dgbas03/english/, section entitled: "Key Economic and Social Indicators." The World Bank has no GNI data on Taiwan, China, as it is treated as a province of the People's Republic of China.

1995: 320–25). Ho argues that before the 1920s, overall agricultural productivity in Taiwan agriculture remained virtually unchanged. But such productivity increased rapidly thereafter. Better sugarcane and rice seed varieties were successfully introduced. Taiwan's agricultural surplus is estimated to have accounted for more than 70 percent of total agricultural production between 1936 and 1940 (Ho, 1978: table 4.3, 66).

Successful land reform in the early post-WWII period. A hallmark of Taiwan's successful land reform (1949–53) was that it was firmly within the framework of private property rights. Another important feature was that the concept of land reform was confined not only to the redistribution of land but also to the creation of an environment in which opportunities would also increase and be redistributed. The land reform succeeded in bringing about a unimodal agrarian structure and was complemented by government putting in place institutions and incentives that enabled/encouraged the myriad smallholders to achieve high levels of productivity and income. In 1953, the Gini coefficient was about 0.56 (comparable to Latin American levels, e.g., Brazil at 0.59 in the 1980s) (World Bank, July 2002a: 5); by 1964, it was 0.33 (Kuo et al., 1981: 44).

Substantial American aid during the difficult early years after WWII. Right after WWII, per capita income was around USD 70 (Kuo et al., 1981: 7). The pressure on resources was intense, with an influx of 1.6 million refugees from the People's Republic of China. Population was growing at an annual rate of 3.4 percent (Shen, 1964: 33). During these early years, the government devoted a considerable amount of budgetary resources to maintaining a big military capability. It was in this very difficult context and after the Korean War (1950–53) that U.S. commodity and military aid was expanded. The commodity aid was funneled through the China–United States Joint Commission for Rural Reconstruction (JCRR). From 1951 to 1965, U.S. aid funneled through JCRR totaled around USD 213 million, or 22.5 percent of total American aid. This was substantial, as it amounted to 59 percent of net domestic capital formation in agriculture (Wu, 1994: 153).[25]

---

[25] Total U.S. aid from 1951 to 1965 was more than USD 4 billion. The non-military aid amounted to around USD 1.421 billion, equivalent to more than 6 percent of GNP (Li, Ranis, and Fei, 1988: 51, 55–58).

The effective management of U.S. aid. The JCRR is a rare example of an effective institutional structure for managing aid. It was a semi-autonomous institution, well funded, and staffed by experts of both nationalities, Chinese and American. It designed the overall strategy for transforming rural Taiwan, as well as formulated and implemented yearly plans (Wu, 1994: 152). All projects had a 40 percent contribution from the local sponsoring agencies or project teams. This 40 percent was a minimum, as it excluded contribution in the form of manual labor, office space, land, and other facilities. An estimated 95 percent of farmers benefited from JCRR programs (Shen, 1964: 40). The JCRR worked closely with a wide range of local-level organizations – farmers' associations, fishermen's associations, farm irrigation associations, local governments, local universities, and the provincial departments of agriculture. The JCRR financed not only projects but also research and extension (in agriculture and fisheries). The JCRR had sustained financial and political support from the highest levels. It combined central direction with decentralized implementation. It combined world-class technical expertise with detailed local knowledge. It structured its technical and financial support so that the project could draw upon the best combination of knowledge – technical expertise and local savoir faire, and all involved had incentives to achieve lasting results, not just maximize aid. The agricultural and rural aid was only one component of a larger aid package. This larger package financed around 50 percent of government investment in public infrastructure, in particular the road and power network.

From import substitution to export promotion within an interventionist approach. In the 1950s, the government pursued an import-substitution strategy with extensive quantitative restrictions and high tariffs. Overall growth averaged 9 percent in the early 1950s, but declined to around 6.5 percent in the late 1950s (Figure 2.9.). The import substitution penalized exports and contributed to a growing trade deficit (much of it paid for by American aid). The government decided that this approach was unsustainable and switched to vigorous export promotion. (See Figure 2.9.)

In the 1960s, Taiwan unified its exchange rates, reduced tariffs and quantitative controls, and developed export processing zones. Like other East Asian governments, it did not, however, adopt a laissez-faire approach. Instead it picked winners. Following recommendations from the Stanford Research Institute (which it paid to identify

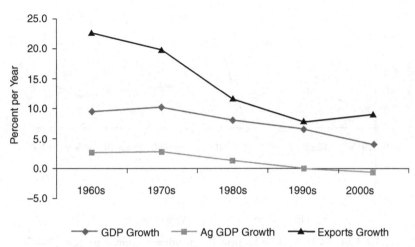

Figure 2.9. Selected growth rates in Taiwan, China (1960s–2000s).
Source: World Development Indicators, respective years.

promising industries), it picked a range of light manufacturing industries, electrical machinery, and textiles to promote. Food processing
was very important in the earlier years, until around 1970. The transition from an import-substituting to an export-promoting strategy had
a dramatic impact. Exports grew at an annual rate of 12 percent per
year between 1953 and 1962. However, this rate jumped to 28 percent
per year between 1963 and 1972. Industrial expansion grew at between
16 and 20 percent per year during the late 1960s and early 1970s, and
the share of industrial exports grew close to 50 percent by 1973 (Ranis,
1996: 19).

*Replacement of official American aid by private resource flow by the
1970s.* By the 1970s, FDI replaced American aid as the main source
of foreign capital. From a newly independent colony struggling to
survive, Taiwan had become an attractive place for foreigners to
invest (initially mainly overseas Chinese, then increasingly Americans
and Japanese). Taiwan had export processing zones with cheap but
healthy, efficient, and well-educated laborers, an absence of militant
trade union activity, and well-developed infrastructure, in particular
adequate transport and electricity connections. The government continued to invest substantially in higher education, including technical education and in research and development for industry (Ranis,
1996: 25–34).

The Developing World

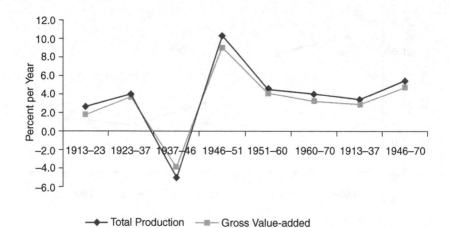

Figure 2.10. Taiwan, China: selected agricultural growth rates (percent per year, 1913–70).

Sources and Notes: Lee, Teng-Hui, and Chen Yueh-Eh "Agricultural Growth in Taiwan, 1911–1972." In Hayami, Yujiro, Vernon M Ruttan, Herman M. Southworth, eds. 1979. *Agricultural Growth in Japan, Taiwan, Korea, and the Philippines*. Published for the East–West Center by the University Press of Hawaii, Honolulu. Table 3.1 Output is total production minus agricultural intermediate inputs; gross value added is output minus non-farm current inputs.

Importance, structure, and performance of agriculture. The transformation of Taiwan's agriculture had already started under Japanese rule. As in Korea, the Japanese developed agriculture through substantial investments in irrigation infrastructure, road and other rural infrastructure, and the introduction of new rice varieties – ponlai – and of fertilizer and other modern inputs (see Figure 2.10).

In 1951, agriculture was a major sector, as it accounted for 33 percent of total GDP (Shen, 1964: table 14.1) and absorbed around 68 percent of the labor force.[26] Researchers estimated that by 1964, the farm workforce peaked at 1.8 million and then started to decline, falling below 50 percent of total. Tomich et al. (1995: 319–20) call this the structural transformation turning point. During the immediate post-war decade, there were substantial increases in crop yields and in multiple cropping.

The increasing importance of rural non-farm activities. By the 1960s, after a decade of sustained agricultural growth, rural non-farm or off-farm activity became increasingly important. The agricultural census of 1960

[26] By 1996, agriculture was around 2 percent of GDP (Taiwan Economic Statistics, vol. 6, no. 5, May 2008).

found that less than 50 percent of all cultivating farm households were fully engaged in the operation of their farms. Indeed, more than 40 percent of the cultivating farm families with less than 0.5 ha of land considered farming a sideline occupation (Ho, 1978: 156–57, table 9.5). By the late 1960s, rural–urban migration and off-farm occupation had depleted Taiwan agriculture's surplus labor. The 1970s thus marked the beginning of mechanized agriculture in Taiwan. In April 1980, the government undertook the second stage of the Agricultural Land Reform Program and established the Farm Mechanization Fund to encourage farm size expansion to 15–20 ha, land consolidation, and farm mechanization. A major objective was to accelerate the transfer of farm labor to rural non-farm activities. Under the Accelerated Rural Development Program (ARDP), labor-intensive industries (e.g., food processing, textiles) were encouraged to establish new plants in rural areas. By 1986, farmers allocated an average of only 36 percent of their time to farming; the remainder was allocated to rural industries (Calkins, Wen, and Tuan, 1992: 112–13).

Contribution of agriculture since Japanese rule. During the pre-WWII period of 1913–37, the rate of growth of productivity on a gross-value-added basis averaged 1.4 percent per year; for the post-war period 1946–70, it averaged 3.2 percent (Lee and Chen, 1979: table 3.4b). Labor productivity in agriculture is estimated to have grown by an annual rate of 3.6 percent between 1953 and 1968, and 4.2 percent between 1968 and 1978 (Kuo et al., 1981: table 2.4). Total agricultural productivity grew steadily from 1950 to 1966 (Ranis, 1996: 25–34). The post-war growth rate was around 5 percent per year. This sustained growth in productivity generated a surplus that was taxed and transferred outside the sector. The outflow was estimated at 30 percent of the value of agricultural product from 1911 to 1915, at 22 percent from 1950 to 1955, and at 14 percent from 1966 to 1969. The net outflow of funds was in the form of land rent, interest payments, and taxes (Lee, 1995: 328). Agriculture was the major contributor to exports in the earlier years. Its share declined from 92 percent in 1955 to 22 percent in 1970. The structure of agricultural exports also changed during this period: from sugar and rice, which accounted for around 75 percent of total in 1955, to higher-value crops, such as pineapples, mushrooms, asparagus, and processed food exports, which dominated agricultural

exports in the late 1960s. The dramatic change in the structure of agricultural exports also reflected the high rate of technical change. By the
1970s, total exports were dominated by industrial exports (Tomich et
al., 1995: 320). In 1960, agricultural exports contributed to some 59
percent of total; but by 1994, it contributed only 3 percent of total
(Ranis, 1996: table 5).

*Which of the polar views does the Taiwan case support, undermine, or
modify?* The Taiwan case supports but qualifies the argument that
successful agricultural transformation was necessary for its overall
economic transformation, since agriculture did make a substantial contribution but by no means was the only source of investable surplus.
During the colonial period, agriculture generated substantial net surplus. During this period, it had begun its transformation from a backward to a highly productive, commercialized agriculture. After the end
of WWII, it made a critical contribution largely until the 1960s, before
the expanding non-farm sector had access to other major non-farm
sources of investable surplus. Even during this critical period, however, agriculture was not the only source of finance. Taiwan received
a substantial amount of U.S. aid until 1965. As of the 1960s, its successful export growth generated its own foreign exchange surplus.
Furthermore, Taiwan's macroeconomic and trade strategy succeeded
in attracting substantial FDI.

*Two-way causality between agricultural and non-agricultural trans-
formation.* There was a virtuous circle between high-productivity
growth and trade not only for agriculture but also for industry. Taiwan
is a good example of a country where agricultural and rural transformation has been successful in both senses: productivity and broad-based
income increases. There was also a substantial transfer of agricultural
surplus to the growing non-farm economy in the earlier years up to
the 1960s, after which period non-farm exports took off. Sustained
high agricultural productivity enabled Taiwan's agricultural exports to
be competitive. However, the competitiveness also benefited from the
government's export-oriented strategy. The agricultural surplus greatly
contributed to the expansion of the non-farm sector in the earlier years.
In classic fashion, agriculture supplied food, finance, exportable surplus,
and a youthful and educated labor force to the growing non-farm sector.
Ranis characterized Taiwan's development success "as a consequence of

the mutually beneficial interactions between its export performance and domestic growth ... during the 1950s and the early 1960s, Taiwan's processed food exports boomed as a result of domestically generated agricultural productivity growth" (Ranis, 1996: abstract).

Summary. Taiwan, China's case supports but qualifies the strong argument that successful agricultural transformation is necessary for successful overall economic transformation.[27] There was a virtuous circle between high-productivity agricultural growth, competitiveness of agricultural exports, and overall export-driven growth. Agriculture's contribution, however, was not the only factor promoting Taiwan's economic transformation, as Taiwan received substantial aid and, in later years, FDI. In addition to the rate of growth, the broad-based nature of the benefits of agriculture's growth was important. Increased rural incomes and employment were widespread, and the non-farm population had access to affordable basic food. The broad-based nature of these benefits strengthened political stability, which in turn increased the economy's resilience to shocks (the first oil price shock was in 1973). Taiwan's experience shows that it is not only agricultural growth that matters, but also the nature of that growth, in particular the simultaneous improvements in social well-being that are realized.

---

[27] The word "transformation" is used instead of "sustained high or accelerated growth in output and productivity" because there is a change in structure of production as well as increases in the levels of production. There are both quantitative and qualitative changes. We try to capture the same idea as the quality of growth, not just its level.

SECTION B
Selected Developing Countries with Substantial but Uneven
Progress toward Industrial Status and Broad-Based Wealth

Introduction

This second set of countries made substantial but (in some cases) very uneven progress toward achieving their industrialization goal, developing their agriculture sectors, and reducing rural poverty. To assess agriculture's contribution over several decades of development, we look for any of the two following scenarios. Do we find a combination of

1. Sustained high output and productivity growth in agriculture co-existing with persistent high rates of rural poverty and mediocre overall economic growth, or
2. Stagnant low-productivity agriculture co-existing with high rates of overall economic growth and low(er) rates of rural poverty?

Either scenario or combination would undermine the claim of agriculture's substantial contribution to growth and poverty reduction, whereas the non-existence of either would strengthen the claim. Why? Because the existence of either of these scenarios would imply that sustained agricultural growth made virtually no difference to overall growth and poverty reduction.

The chapter identifies associations and patterns, for these can be suggestive of underlying causal chains. However, the essential methodological difference between the use of associations here and that of regression analysis is that the purpose is to test hypotheses. The search is for potential refutations of hypotheses and not for their confirmations. Evidence can refute a claim but cannot confirm it, even though it may be consistent with the claim. In the latter case, the evidence is supportive but still not conclusive. For empirical evidence to scientifically refute one claim and support a rival claim, independent tests and crucial experiments are needed. We present the methodology of research of this book more fully in Appendix A.

The way associations are used here is schematically presented in the following tabulation:

Agricultural development, overall growth, and rural poverty reduction:
which combinations do we find over decades of development?

	Economy doing well, widespread rural poverty decreasing	Economy not doing well, rural poverty widespread
Agriculture doing well, sustained output and productivity growth	Pro-Ag 1	Anti-Ag 1
Agriculture not doing well, stagnant output and productivity growth	Anti-Ag 2	Pro-Ag 2

Combinations Pro-Ag 1 and Pro-Ag 2 would refute the anti-agriculture view. Their existence would be consistent with the pro-agriculture view, although the consistency would not by itself prove the correctness of the causal claim of the pro-agriculture view.

Combinations Anti-Ag 1 and Anti-Ag 2 would refute the pro-agriculture view. Their existence would be consistent with the anti-agriculture view, although the consistency would not by itself prove the correctness of the causal claim of the anti-agriculture view.

II.V. India – GNI per capita: USD 1,180 (2009)

Introduction. Does the performance of India's agriculture over the past five decades or so support or refute the claim of the pro-agriculture viewpoint? Which of the four combinations have prevailed? India's experience with agricultural and economy-wide development and poverty reduction provides fertile ground for addressing this question, given that India is a major agricultural country with a large population and that many of its people are still struggling to ensure basic food security. A comparison of the agricultural growth and poverty reduction performance of the richest state, Punjab, with two of the poorest states, Bihar and Orissa, also provides a test of the different claims.

Brief Background. At independence in 1947, India was and today still is a low-income country. India has made steady progress on many fronts since independence, but it has still not achieved middle-income and industrialized country status. Though the incidence of poverty has declined, it is still high. In 2000, the incidence of poverty was estimated to be around 29 percent, somewhat less than a third of its population of around 1.03 billion people (World Bank, Dec. 2003).[28] Today, 75 percent of India's poor are still rural (World Bank, Dec. 2003: 73, table 1).

Major socio-economic problems inherited by independent India. India was under British rule from 1857 to 1947, for almost a century. It is estimated that British India grew at less than 0.5 percent per year (Myers, 1996: 168). The economy was primarily agricultural, with large inequalities in resource endowments and income distribution among and within regions and states. The population was and still is primarily rural, at a rural/urban ratio of 66:44 in the 2001–2006 period. Poverty was widespread, especially in rural areas, with about 50 percent of the total population estimated to be poor in the early 1950s (Sury, 2001: table 1.2). Social indicators inevitably reflected characteristics of widespread poverty, for example, an 84 percent illiteracy rate and 27 per 1,000 mortality (Quibria, 1994: 192). Newly independent India faced major developmental challenges.

Long-standing land-related issues. India also inherited difficult distribution and administration issues. According to the ninth Five-Year Plan (1997–2002), the situation had not significantly improved. "Despite attempts at land reforms over successive Plan periods, the basic character of the agrarian economy has not undergone any structural change. The pattern of land distribution is highly skewed, with a high concentration of land in the hands of a few land owners on the one hand and the growing number of marginal and sub-marginal farmers on the other" (Sury, 2001: 155). The World Bank, however, argues that land distribution is less skewed in 1999–2000 compared with 1971–72. This distribution does not take into account the quality of land on farms of

---

[28] Also in *Little Data Book* (World Bank, 2003a: 109). The estimate of 29 percent is still controversial. The government of India's official estimates of national poverty incidence is 26 percent (a fall from 36 percent in 1993–94 to 26 percent in 1999–2000). If one uses the international standard of USD 1 per day, poverty incidence for 1997 is 44 percent. It is not clear that the estimate of around 50 percent poverty incidence at the time of independence was based on a dollar per day standard. However, no matter what the line, the number of poor is in the millions. The estimate of India's population in 2007 was 1.123 billion.

different sizes. Moreover, there are still many issues of land legislation and administration that inhibit the efficient functioning of land rental markets, the formation of long-term tenancy contracts, and the proper functioning of land administration (World Bank, July 2003: fig. 5.3, 82–84). The World Bank also points out that high levels of implementation (in the 1970s and 1980s), for example, in West Bengal, are associated with higher rates of income and asset growth and of the educational attainment of children, than in states with low levels of implementation effort, such as Madhya Pradesh (World Bank, 2007a: table 11).

Long-term developmental goals within an interventionist, import-substitution strategy until the late 1980s. Through successive five-year plans (the first was in 1951–56) Indian planners had the same objectives, namely economic growth, social justice, self-reliance, poverty reduction, industrialization, and productivity improvement. Achieving self-sufficiency in grains (mainly wheat and rice) was an overriding national objective. Like most developing countries, India adopted an inward-looking, import-substitution, industrialization-first strategy (ISI).[29] It espoused a centrally planned approach, seeking to control the private sector through myriad licenses. Its emphasis on self-reliance and import substitution contributed to a stagnation in exports well into the 1980s. The complex industrial licensing system and restrictions on capital flows reduced competition. In combination with the high trade barriers, they generated monopoly rents and stifled growth (World Bank, 2001b: 1).

Steady but modest per capita growth performance until the late 1980s. India's economy-wide annual (GNP/GDP/NNP) growth rates averaged 4–6 percent from 1950 up to 1989. NNP per capita grew at a little more than 1 percent per year over roughly the same period (Chacko, 1997: 61) (see Figure 2.11 for selected average annual growth rates).

Growth performance improved in the 1980s, but it was not sustainable as it relied on deficit financing. The 1991 macroeconomic and balance of payments crises (annual GNP per capita growth of –1.8 percent in 1991) spurred the government of India to undertake reforms. It

---

[29] India did not undertake economic reforms to liberalize and improve trade openness and market orientation until the late 1990s.

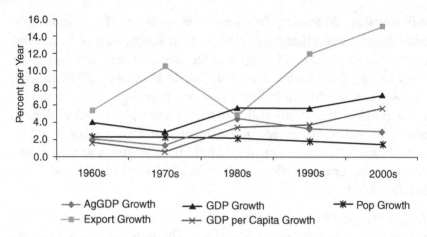

Figure 2.11. India: selected average annual growth rates (1960s–2000s).
Sources: Annual growth of AgGDP, Exports, GDP, GDP/Capita, population growth: WDI respective years.

launched far-reaching economic reforms dismantling much of industrial licensing, and liberalized the foreign trade and exchange system (World Bank, 2001b: 2–3). The GDP growth rate rose to 6–7 percent per year in the 1990s until 1997. The agriculture growth rate also rose from 3–4 percent per year in the 1980s to 5–6 percent per year until 1997. A more disaggregated look at GDP and agriculture GDP growth rates for the 1980s and 1990s is presented in Figure 2.12.

Importance of agriculture and the primary sector. Agriculture was and remains an important sector in India. As happened elsewhere, the primary sector, comprising agriculture, fishery, mining, and quarrying, has shrunk considerably. Agriculture's contribution to employment has remained important, however, declining gradually from around 70 percent in the early years to 67 percent in the 1990s (Dasgupta, 1978: 11, table 2.1b). This is indicative of significant surplus labor in agriculture.

Performance of irrigated and rain-fed agriculture. India is a vast country with much variation in its agricultural production systems and growth performance. For example, irrigated agriculture is important in the northern states (Punjab, Haryana, and Uttar Pradesh). Green Revolution technology benefited primarily irrigated rice and wheat

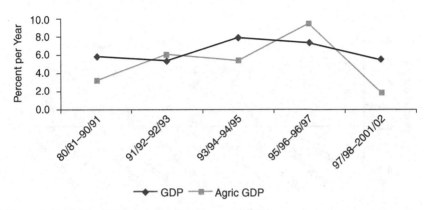

Figure 2.12. India: GDP and agriculture annual GDP growth rates (percent per year, 1980–2002).
Sources: World Bank. 2002. *India: Evaluating Bank Assistance for the Agricultural and Rural Development – A Country Assistance Evaluation.* Operations Evaluations Department; Working Paper Series. Table 1.1. The source for the period of 1997/98 to 2001/02 is World Bank. July 2003. *Sustaining Reform, Reducing Poverty.* Table 5.1.

cultivation.[30] By 1992–93, around 49 percent of rice and 85 percent of wheat was irrigated (World Bank, August 1999: table 1.3). However, large parts of peninsular and western India (Andhra Pradesh, Madhya Pradesh, Gujarat, Haryana, Karnataka, Maharashtra, Tamil Nadu, and Uttar Pradesh) are characterized as semi-arid tropics (SAT), areas where irrigation accounts for less than 50 percent of net cropped area. SAT areas are characterized by long dry seasons, and inadequate and unpredictable rainfall. By the late 1990s, SAT comprised three-fifths of net cropped area. This high percentage of rain-fed agriculture explains the sharp year-to-year fluctuations in agricultural performance (World Bank, 2002a: 1.3) (see Figure 2.13).

---

[30] The impact that Green Revolution technologies can have on farming and farmers' decision making is brought to life in the Green Revolution Game, a sophisticated gaming simulation of the drama of rural development and technological change in agriculture, based on original fieldwork in India. It is not a computer simulation. It is available as a kit, which provides all the materials necessary for an enactment of the simulation. The kit is durable and reusable. The simulation is for up to 24–30 players and lasts an entire day. It may release a full range of emotions in players, including anger and apprehension, as well as altruism and confidence. It provides insights into the interconnectedness of technical, environmental, sociological, and economic aspects of change, as well as into personal psychology. The game must be managed by a trained manager (preferably two) or a manager who has thoroughly acquainted her- or himself with the kit and undertaken some small trial runs (Chapman, 1982).

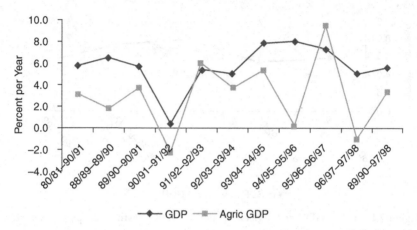

Figure 2.13. India: selected annual growth rates of GDP and agricultural GDP (1980–98).

Source: World Bank. 2002. India: Evaluating Bank Assistance for the Agricultural and Rural Development – A Country Assistance Evaluation. Operations Evaluations Department; Working Paper Series. Table 1.1. An alternative set of estimates of annual agricultural growth are: for 1982–92 at 3.0 percent; 1992–2002 at 3.0 percent. World Bank. India at a glance (08/25/2003).

In the early years of the Green Revolution (1960s), irrigated rice and wheat were the main beneficiaries. More recently, the widespread adoption of improved technologies across regions and crops in the 1980s was a major factor in the acceleration of growth in the 1980s. Technological change is estimated to have contributed to around a third to a half of output growth, depending on the commodity and geographical coverage. At sector level, estimates of growth of total factor productivity rose from 1.37 percent in the 1970s to 1.99 percent in the 1980s but dropped to –0.59 percent from 1990–95. The Indian government's expenditures on agricultural technology, irrigation, rural infrastructure, and education contributed to this growth (World Bank, June 1999: paras 2.5–2.7, table 2.3). The deceleration in the 1990s has been attributed to, among other things, a decline in these public investments, a rise in natural resource degradation, and continuing constraints of a highly regulated market. Despite the positive productivity developments in the 1980s, large parts of Indian agriculture are said to be dominated by traditional, low-productivity, subsistence cultivation methods. However, no quantitative assessments of the extent of subsistence farming are given (Sury, 2001: 146–48).

Achieving food grain self-sufficiency after decades of growth. A major achievement of India's agricultural policy by the 1990s was the attainment of food grain self-sufficiency. Ensuring affordable grain helped the poor. The grain sector, dominated by rice and wheat, occupies some 40 percent of cultivated area and contributes about 26 percent of the agricultural GDP (World Bank, August 1999: para 1). India's food grain production has increased fourfold, from about 51 million tons in 1950–51 to some 200 million tons in 2000–2001. However, due to continuing high population growth, the increase in per capita availability of food grains per day has been modest: from 395 grams in 1951 to 466 grams per day in 2000. According to the Planning Commission, just to keep pace with the rising population, India must produce 100 million more tons by 2011–12 (World Bank, August 1999: para 1). This increase has to be achieved mainly through productivity increases rather than area expansion, as the potential for the latter is virtually exhausted. Moreover, the man/land ratio (per ha) is low, around 0.33 in 2000.[31]

Key features of India's agricultural subsidies and market interventions until the early 2000s. The benefits and costs of India's interventionist agricultural and food grain policies are still being debated. The Targeted Public Distribution System (introduced in 1997) supplies rice, wheat, and sugar nationally, and other commodities such as edible oils and coarse grains in some states, at subsidized prices. Major benefits include the following. Producers get minimum support prices, thus reducing uncertainty. In addition, these benefits have contributed to political stability and to poverty reduction. The subsidies have also contributed to the adoption of improved technologies and to increased productivity. Yields on major crops such as rice, wheat, sugarcane, and cotton

[31] The goal of food grain self-sufficiency is a priority in much of the developing world, as the subsequent case studies will show. The concept of food security is different and broader and has very different policy implications. Timmer has written extensively on food security, especially in Asia and on rice. The following is a U.S. government definition referred to in one of his most recent papers (Timmer 2010:3): "Food security exists when all people at all times have physical and economic access to sufficient food to meet their dietary needs for a productive and healthy life. Food security has three dimensions: availability of sufficient quantities of food of appropriate quality, supplied through domestic production or imports; access by households and individuals to adequate resources to acquire appropriate foods for a nutritious diet; and utilization of food through adequate diet, water, sanitation, and health care." It is striking that many countries still focus on food grain self-sufficiency as a priority goal. The case of Singapore clearly shows that food grain self-sufficiency is not necessary to be food secure. There are, however, many deep structural and historical reasons that so many countries still cling to the food grain self-sufficiency concept and approach. The goal of food security will remain one major challenge for global agriculture in the 21st century. The other two challenges are poverty reduction and sustainable natural resource management (McCalla, 2000: 2).

have increased significantly (Sury, 2001: 149).[32] There have also been substantial production increases and yield improvements in rain-fed crops, such as oilseeds (e.g., soybean and sunflower, rapeseed-mustard seed) and cotton, of which 70 percent of production is rain-fed (World Bank, June 1999: annexes 4 and 5). However, to support the system of pricing and distribution, private trade is restricted, and many controls exist on marketing, small-scale reservation (only small-scale units are allowed to operate), and so on. As a result of these many controls, processing and marketing efficiencies are low – for example, in sugar, oilseeds, and cotton. The subsidies are also costly, crowd out other needed public investments, and allegedly benefit primarily the large farmers, the better-off group in rural society.

The high variation in state-level agricultural performance: Punjab versus Bihar and Orissa. How beneficial agricultural growth has been to broad-based income growth and poverty reduction can vary sharply among states, as a comparison of the richest and poorest states shows. Punjab is one of the richest states in India, and it is the state where the Green Revolution took off in the mid-1960s. From 1967–68 to 1987–88, Punjab recorded high annual growth rates of 4.9 percent in wheat, 15.6 percent in rice, and 6.6 percent in food grains (Bhalla, 1995: 67–112, 94–95). There was also high growth in other sub-sectors as well, in particular when incomes rose and demand increased for livestock products. These high growth rates were partly the result of substantial state investments in public irrigation and rural infrastructure. More recent growth rates for the sector as a whole are lower and set out in Figure 2.14. This is in contrast to the non–Green Revolution states of Bihar and Orissa, where agricultural growth rates have been way below those of the Punjab. Bihar, Orissa, Madhya Pradesh, and Uttar Pradesh are the poorest Indian states. They are home to more than half of India's poor, more than two-thirds of whom are rural (World Bank, July 2003: box 1). Bihar, a primarily agricultural state, is one of the poorest states. The latest rural poverty estimate (1999–2000) for Bihar is around

---

[32] For example, yield increases from 1960–61 to 1997–98 were: for rice, from 10.1 to 18.9 quintals (87 percent); for wheat, from 8.5 to 24.7 quintals (1.91 percent); for sugarcane, from 46 to 70 tons (52 percent); and for cotton, from 125 to 213 kg (70 percent). However, yield increases are considered low by international standards (e.g., sugar and cotton).

40 percent versus the all-India average of around 29 percent (World Bank, 2005a: table 1.3). Agriculture employs 80 percent of Bihar's labor force and contributes to 40 percent of GDP (World Bank, 2005b: executive summary, 2). While Orissa has only 3.7 percent of India's population, it has more than 5 percent of India's poor. Around 47 percent of its population of 35 million lives under the poverty line (World Bank, September 2003). The state is also primarily agricultural and rural. Bihar and Orissa have some of the lowest agriculture growth rates in the 1990s (Figure 2.14).

While the Green Revolution techniques have reached these states by now, their agricultures did not get the boost from the Green Revolution that the agricultures of Punjab and Haryana did. Their low agriculture growth rates (even negative for Bihar in the 1990s) persist. Take, for example, rice, the main crop, in Orissa. In the 1990s, the trend rate of growth in production and productivity was negative: −1.3 percent per year for production and −1.4 percent per year for yield (Ahluwalia, 2003: table 2).

A comparison of selected state-level poverty rates. In comparing the poverty levels between selected non–Green Revolution and Green Revolution states, it is clear that the poverty levels in the former are significantly higher than in the latter. See Figure 2.15 which presents headcount ratios based on the official government methodology and adjusted estimates. Detailed estimates are also presented in Appendix Table C19.

What do these comparisons show? These comparisons strengthen the pro-agriculture view regarding the important contributions of a high-productivity, high-growth agriculture to overall development. Punjab has high agriculture growth rates and low poverty incidence rates. Bihar and Orissa suffer from persistent low agriculture growth rates and high poverty incidence rates.

Did the Green Revolution in Punjab spur its industrialization, income increases, and poverty reduction? The answer is a qualified yes. It is a yes because high agricultural growth from the mid-1960s to the mid-1980s did stimulate growth in other sectors. By the 1990s, agriculture still accounted for about 40 percent of the state domestic product and around 40 percent of the state total labor force (World Bank, September

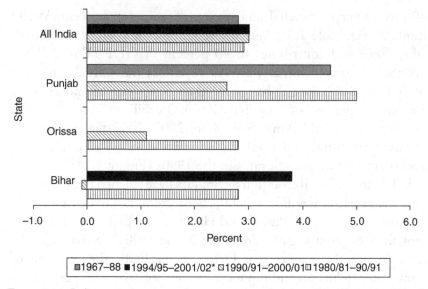

Figure 2.14. India: agriculture growth rates at selected state and at the national level (percent per year, 1967–2001).

Sources and Notes:

Bihar and Orissa: 1980/81–2000/01, 1994/95–2001/02: World Bank. 2005 *India: Bihar: Towards a Development Strategy*. Tab. 2.1. "Orissa SAL: Note on Agriculture Growth Issues" by Deepak Ahluwalia, March 2003; Table 1.

Punjab: 1967–88: Bhalla, G.S. 1995. "Agricultural Growth and Industrial Development in Punjab." In Mellor, John W., ed. *Agriculture on the Road to Industrialization*. Published for the International Policy Research Institute by the Johns Hopkins University Press. pp 67–112. Table 3.1. 1980–2001: "Orissa SAL: Note on Agriculture Growth Issues" by Deepak Ahluwalia, March 2003; Table 1. 1990/91–2000/01: World Bank. Rural Development Unit. South Asia Region. September 2003. *India: Revitalizing Punjab Agriculture*. Executive Summary. Para 3.

All India: 1967–88: Bhalla, G.S., 1995. "Agricultural Growth and Industrial Development in Punjab." In Mellor, John W., ed. 1995. *Agriculture on the Road to Industrialization*. Published for the International Food Policy Research Institute by the Johns Hopkins University Press. pp 67–112. Table 3.1. 1980–2000/01: "Orissa SAL: Note on Agriculture Growth Issues" by Deepak Ahluwalia, March 2003; Table 1. 1994/95–2001/02: World Bank. 2005. *India: Bihar: Towards a Development Strategy*. Tab. 2.1.

The growth rates are of Gross State Domestic Product (GSDP). Bihar split into two states in 1993/94, Jharkand and Bihar. 1994/95 is the first year for which data for divided Bihar is available.

2003, paras 1.2–1.3). The growth of manufacturing averaged 6.9 percent between 1978–79 and 1985–86, whereas the all-India rate was 6.2 percent per year (Bhalla, 1995: 67–112). However, the answer is a qualified yes because the non-agricultural growth rate fell far short of the levels achieved in Taiwan, South Korea, and Japan, whose economies were transformed in two decades. Researchers and practitioners

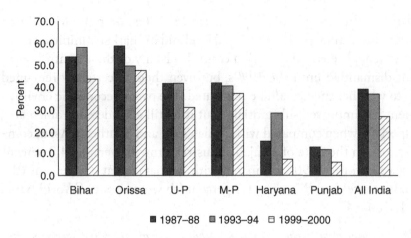

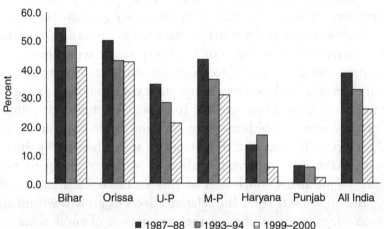

Figure 2.15. India: poverty incidence – selected state-specific rural headcount ratios, official methodology, and adjusted estimates (1987–2000).

Source and Note: Deaton, Angus and Dreze, Jean "Poverty and Inequality in India: A Re-examination." *Economic and Political Weekly*. pp 3729–3748. September 7, 2002. Table 2-a

U-P is Uttar Pradesh, M-P is Madhya Pradesh

Note that the estimate by the World Bank is 29 percent (2000). World Bank. India Country Brief (posted 20/12/03 on www. worldbank.org) and Little Data Book, 2003, p 109. There is a controversy with respect to the extent of poverty reduction. The controversy centers around the use of price indices and the non-comparability between the data of the 50th and 55 th round of the National Sample Survey Organization (NSSO) of India. For more discussion, see World Bank *Development Challenges and Poverty in Bihar*, p 4.

attribute this disappointing performance to the government's inward-orientation strategy at the national level and its market-inhibiting measures (e.g., licenses and myriad controls). Many of these controls were not dismantled until the 1990s, but even then, uncertainty remained as to whether they would be reinstated. The overall economic environment has improved substantially, but it is still considered problematic, especially when compared with India's East and Southeast Asian competitors. In the state of Punjab, industrial growth averaged 4.8 percent per year in the 1990s, compared with Karnataka's at 8.5 percent (the highest rate) and Bihar's at 1.2 percent (the lowest rate) (World Bank, July 2003: 4).

The debate about the relative importance of primary-sector versus non-primary-sector growth in promoting income growth and poverty reduction. Two groups of researchers have made contradictory claims about the relative importance of rural or primary sector growth to poverty reduction. According to Ravallion and Datt (1996), rural and primary sector growth is a more important contributor to rural poverty reduction than urban growth. To quote, "We find that primary and tertiary sector growth was poverty reducing in both urban and rural sectors.... By contrast, the secondary sector had no significant impact on the rate of poverty reduction in either urban or rural areas.... [T]he main conclusion of this article holds that, if anything, the opposite is true: The relative effects of growth within and between each sector reinforced the importance of rural economic growth to national poverty reduction in India" (Ravallion and Datt, 1996: 17, 19).

However, according to Beesly et al. (2004: 20–21), "Contrary to previous evidence from Ravallion and Datt (1996), the results [in table 10] suggest that the biggest contribution to poverty reduction has come from the secondary and tertiary sectors, while the primary sector has only had significant contribution in a few states (namely, Assam, Bihar, Gujarat, Punjab, and West Bengal)."

What are we to make of these contrary claims, covering approximately the same periods (1951–91 and 1965–94, respectively) and based on regression analysis? Both claims cannot at the same time be true. Both are based on extensive econometric research and offer important insights into the workings of the Indian economy.

However, they wrongly infer theoretical significance from statistical significance. They both interpret the correlations as confirmations of their claims. As Popper pointed out, correlations can refute claims but cannot confirm them. Therefore, confirmations based on statistical correlations do not prove anything. At best, confirming instances using regression analysis can serve as valuable insights into the workings of the system in which we are interested. They are not by themselves statements with explanatory power. For a fuller discussion of the methodology of research in this book, see Appendix A. The researchers did identify what they consider to be important factors, but unfortunately, neither group of researchers used insights from their regression results to develop independently testable hypotheses on what the underlying causal mechanisms may be. For example, at the end of the Ravallion–Datt (1996) paper, the authors identify what causes may be at work: "India's development strategy (starting from the Second Plan in 1950s) emphasized capital-intensive industrialization concentrated in urban areas in a largely closed economy." This is an important insight that could be developed into an independently refutable theory with explanatory power. But it was not used as such. Thus their claims about relative sector contributions cannot be empirically generalized.

Does the India case support the pro-agriculture position? Yes, it does; the case of India illustrates our combination Pro-Ag 2, which refutes the anti-agriculture view that agricultural development does not matter. It supports the pro-agriculture position because over a span of more than five decades, its development experience contained no combination of (a) sustained high output and productivity growth in agriculture co-existing with persistent high rates of rural poverty and mediocre overall economic growth; or (b) stagnant low-productivity agriculture co-existing with high rates of overall economic growth and low rates of rural poverty. Instead, at the national level, there was persistent (decades of) low annual agricultural growth (until the 1990s), barely keeping up with the annual population growth rate (averaging 2 percent until the early 2000s), slow reduction of poverty, and low annual increases in NNP per capita. A fundamental reason was the continued mediocre performance of agriculture, a major sector (in a fairly closed economy), in terms of its contribution to GDP, income, and employment. Briefly, to recapitulate, the overall growth picture at the national level since 1950–51 is that of a slow-growing agriculture. Average annual growth rates were 2–3 percent up to the 1970s, 3–4 percent in the 1980s, and 3–4 percent again in the 1990s until 1997, with some years rising to 6 and 9 percent and then declining below 2 percent after 1997. An alternative World Bank estimate puts the annual average growth at 3 percent from 1982 to 2002. During this long period, average GDP growth performance was also slow – averaging 3–4 percent until 1980, 5–6 percent in the 1980s, 6–7 percent in the 1990s until 1997, and declining to 4–5 percent since then. The annual rate of reduction of poverty incidence for 1960–2000 is estimated to be –0.65 percent (linear) and –1.43 percent (log-linear) (Ravallion and Datt, 1996: table 2). At the state level, in Punjab, a state considered a leading agricultural state (until the 1990s), there has been substantial poverty reduction (the lowest poverty rate of all states), whereas in Bihar and Orissa, with stagnant agricultures, poverty rates have remained high and are the highest in India.

II.VI. The People's Republic of China – GNI per capita: USD 3,590 (2009)

Introduction. The question addressed is the same as before, but the answer may be totally different. Why? Though China and India share important similarities, they have important differences too. China, like India, is a lower-middle-income country with a large population, and many of its people are very poor.[33] Also, like India, achieving food self-sufficiency has been a matter of utmost national importance for China. However, China has chosen a different development path. The comparison thus promises to be a good test of the pro- and anti-agriculture hypotheses.

Brief background. China and India are often compared. They are both populous nations, still largely agricultural, each with a very distinctive culture and civilization, with the majority of their populations at low incomes. At the start of the post-WWII period, they had similar

---

[33] World Bank, World Development Indicators, 2010. The World Bank's income categories (GNI 2008) are as follows: low income, USD 975 or less; lower middle income, USD 976–3,855; upper middle income, USD 3,856–11,905; and high income, USD 11,906 and up.

economic structures, with a dominant agriculture (roughly 60 percent
of GNP). Per capita GNP was very low: RMB 66.1 (Lin, Cai, and
Li, 1996: 21).[34] For decades, they both adopted centralized planning
and inward-oriented developmental approaches. For a long period
(1949–79), poverty was extensive in China: After three decades of such
strategy, more than half of the population was still poor (Ravallion
and Chen, 2004: table 4).[35] Since 1979, under the leadership of Deng
Xiaoping (1904–1997), China has dramatically reoriented its policy
and strategy: from Soviet-style central planning to market-orientation
and from import-substitution to export orientation. Although the
reforms were fundamental, they were implemented in a piecemeal and
incremental fashion. As the Chinese leadership put it, the approach was
"crossing the river by feeling the stones" (Lin et al., 1999: 166). Despite
sustained high growth since the agricultural reforms of 1979,[36] China
is still a predominantly rural and low-middle-income country where
the urban/rural population ratio is 42:58.[37] Since the reforms started,
three developments have been of note: (a) the pace of China's economic transformation, including the high level of FDI; (b) the rapid (if
geographically uneven) rate of poverty reduction; and (c) the increase
in income inequality. How important was agricultural performance in
achieving such rapid overall growth, poverty reduction, and structural
transformation?

*The Great Leap Forward Strategy in a highly centralized and closed econ-
omy (1949–79).* Under this strategy, the Chinese economy built a
substantial industrial base but at a high cost, in terms of increasing inefficiency and substantial forgone consumption (Dernberger,
1999: 46–47). The nationalist objective, to catch up with the West,
was to be achieved, in large part, by squeezing agriculture and transferring the surplus to industry, considered the leading sector. Armed
with such a strategy, China was to accomplish a great leap forward

---

[34] RMB is renminbi, the Chinese currency.
[35] The incidence using the headcount index is 52.84 (1981) at the national level. The rural
poverty line is at Y 850 per person per year (2002); the urban poverty line is at Y 1,200 per
person per year.
[36] Strictly speaking, the reforms started at the end of 1978.
[37] The People's Republic of China is the most populous nation, at 1,324.8 million people
(2008). The urban/rural population ratio (2002–2008) is 40:60; the numbers are roughly 530
million/794 million (World Bank, "China at a Glance," December 9, 2009).

from a backward agricultural economy into an industrialized power. During those Cold War years, such a great leap had tremendous political appeal. As a member of the Communist bloc, China was politically and economically isolated from Western countries and was de facto closed. In the early 1950s, agriculture with its extensive surplus labor was the dominant sector, accounting for 60 percent of total output value. Yet like India and many other developing countries, China adopted the autarkic import-substitution industry-first strategy. Such a strategy had a strong nationalistic appeal, but it violated all tenets of comparative advantage. To accommodate the demands for capital in a capital-scarce economy, key macro and sector prices were distorted – for example, low interest rate, overvalued foreign exchange rate, low prices for agricultural products such as raw materials into heavy industry, and basic necessities for urban labor. By severely distorting resource allocation, pricing policy was a major mechanism that the government used for extracting and transferring agricultural surplus.

Socio-economic performance under the Great Leap Forward Strategy. China did not leap forward. She hobbled. The overall growth rates were high according to some scholars – 6.0–7.0 percent per year – but these high growth rates did not mean that China's economic development was efficient with broad-based benefits for the average consumer. Lin et al. (1999: 64) show that the high aggregate growth was driven mainly by industry growing at 11 percent per year, with heavy industry growing the fastest at 15.3 percent per year. China developed an extensive industrial base, but low production efficiency prevailed, as an international comparison of China's consumption of inputs per unit of GDP clearly showed. For example, the share of working capital in total capital was 33 percent in China (1981) versus 28 percent in India (1979), 29 percent in the Soviet Union (1972), and 7 percent in Korea (1963). Factors including protection from imports, lack of competition, lack of enterprise autonomy, and the then-prevailing attitude of "eating from the big pot of the state" all combined to reduce efficiency and incentives. Much of China's state-owned enterprise sector is still problematic today (Minami, 1994). This emphasis on heavy industry stands in stark contrast to the industrialization experiences of Japan, South Korea, and Taiwan, China all of which developed light (consumer-oriented, mainly agro-related) manufacturing exports in the early stages of their industrialization to earn foreign exchange for financing their industrial investment. Like industry, agriculture also did not do well. Its average annual growth from 1952 to 1980 was around 3 percent (Lin et al., 1999: 63–64, 81). Averages are not very meaningful, for during this period the economy twice underwent major political and economic shocks. The Great Leap Forward movement launched in 1958–60 saw widespread famine. The Great Proletarian Cultural Revolution (1966–76) was a decade of intense turmoil. Moreover, the government exacted a very high rate of accumulation, between 25 and 30 percent of total social output value. GNP per capita, which stood at USD 52 in 1952, was only USD 210 in 1975 (Lin et al., 1999: 62). One bright spot in the development of rural areas was the extensive commune-run network of basic health care clinics and public education establishments. For example, China was famous for its barefoot doctors, who assisted rural residents in far-flung regions. The liberation of women was also a major achievement of far-reaching importance. Women had more opportunities than in traditional feudal China. However, growth in personal income and consumption was suppressed to make way for a high savings and investment rate. As China scholars have repeatedly pointed out, these vast resources were very inefficiently used. The annual growth rate of total factor productivity in China during 1952–81 was only 0.5 percent, well below the levels of 19 other developing countries, according to Lin et al, and stagnant and even negative, according to the World Bank. Such was the economic performance of a strategy relying on self-reliance and self-sufficiency.

The substantial but declining "peasant burden" during the 1949–79 period of collective agriculture. Farmers of 40 centuries, Chinese farmers have been paying a variety of taxes, official and unofficial, and since 1949, through administrative, price, and other compulsory marketing mechanisms. One such tax is well known: the ancient agricultural tax, which dates back to the Shang dynasty (1600–1066 BC).[38] In 1958, the agricultural tax rate was fixed at 15.5 percent of grain yield (the actual rate applied was lower, at 12.5 percent). One estimate of the total "peasant

---

[38] Different dates are given for the Shang Dynasty: 1766–1122 BC, 1766–1050 BC, 1600–1046 BC, or 1566–1046 BC. The ancient tax was abolished effective January 1, 2006.

burden" (the collection of taxes, levies, and charges) shows that farmers contributed to 39 percent of total taxes in 1950, decreasing to 4.8 percent by 1980[39] (Aubert and Li, 2002). Some authors point to the relative high price of industrial products in the 1950s, the "price scissors" phenomenon. The unfavorable price ratio was primarily for purchased consumer, not producer, goods. According to Perkins and Yusuf (1984), there was a 47 percent markup on retail consumer sales prices in rural areas. Still other Chinese economists refer to the "unequal exchange" from the 1950s to the 1970s, in the sense that the terms of trade deteriorated for agriculture over these three decades (Nolan, 1988: 62–63). Prices were slanted in favor of industry and urban dwellers, subsidizing their food, housing, and other needs. Very little was reinvested in agriculture in return. Another estimate of agriculture's financial contribution in the 1950s is 16 percent of funds for state investment in industry, national defense, and general government administration. This contribution fell to less than 6 percent by the late 1970s. Heavy industry received the lion's share of public capital construction investment – from 34 percent in 1952 to 51 percent in 1965 and 40 percent in 1981. The respective shares for agriculture were 13, 14, and 7 percent (Perkins and Yusuf, 1984: 19). The main capital investments in rural areas were primarily in the form of labor-intensive mobilization drives for constructing irrigation works. China expanded its irrigated area from 20 million ha in 1952 (19 percent of arable area) to 43 million ha in 1975 (43 percent of arable area) (Nolan, 1988: 56). Strong urban bias in supporting both investment and consumption persisted into the late 1980s (Johnson, 1992: 25–38).

Sustained high growth rates since 1979. The economy and society proved to be resilient, however, for the situation improved dramatically under the series of fundamental reforms to increase market orientation and to promote private incentives. Researchers agree that China's sustained growth performance after the 1979 reforms was one of the highest worldwide, although exact estimates differ somewhat. According to one estimate, from 1978 to 1992, annual GDP growth rate averaged 8.8 percent. The growth rate of exports was even more impressive: from around 3 percent per year (1965–75) to

---

[39] It is not clear whether the taxes refer only to the central government or to all government taxes. This marks a milestone in agricultural policy and agriculture's role in the economy.

14 percent (1982–92).[40] According to another estimate, the average rate was 9.7 percent from 1982 to 1992. Furthermore, from 1992 to 2002, the annual GDP growth rate averaged 9.0 percent.[41] Since then, annual growth has remained high, at above 7 percent despite the world recession in 2001–2002 (OECD, 2002: 15). These different estimates clearly show that estimating China's GDP growth rate is tricky. Note that there are two other, lower estimates of GDP. For 1978–95, these are 8.0 and 6.8 percent per year (Chai, 2000b: 512–19, box 1.1). Even these lower estimates are high when compared with the high growth of East Asian economies. In addition to sustained high growth rates, China has been a recipient of some of the highest inflows of FDI. In 10 years, FDI grew from around USD 430 million in 1982 to USD 49.3 billion in 2002 (which is around 4 percent of China's GNI).[42] Selected growth rates are given in Figure 2.16.

The Household Responsibility System, a bold local initiative that spread. These fundamental reforms started at the micro level. Three decades after the successful Communist takeover in 1949, and after the two dramatic and destabilizing social experiments (the Great Leap Forward and the Cultural Revolution), the Household Responsibility System (HRS) was tried in Anhui province (1978) by a small number of production teams. This system spread rapidly even though it was prohibited (until late 1981) by the central government. Under the HRS, households became responsible for production and they, not the collective, were entitled to the profits. By 1981, 45 percent of production teams had adopted the system; by 1983, 98 percent (Lin, 2000: 120). In fact, China had returned to the system of small family farms prevalent elsewhere in East Asia. This reform – a return to institutions based on private incentives – not only successfully promoted dynamic growth in agriculture but also greatly facilitated reforms in other sectors.

Basic differences in the incentive environment for farmers following official endorsement of the HRS. The most important difference was the way

---

[40] Another important indicator is the ratio of exports of goods and services to GDP. Thus for 2003: 34.2 percent; for 2004: 39.7 percent (World Bank, "China at a Glance," September 8, 2005). For 2007: 39.7; for 2008: 36.8. World Bank. "China at a Glance," December 9, 2009. These high ratios clearly show that China's growth is export-driven.

[41] World Bank, "China at a Glance," August 29, 2003.

[42] World Bank, "China at a Glance," August 29, 2003. China's GNI is estimated to be USD 1,219.1 billion (2002).

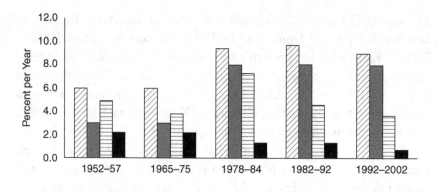

☑ GDP   ■ GDP/capita   ⊟ Agricultural GDP   ■ Population

Figure 2.16. China: selected growth rates since the 1950s (percent per year, 1952–2002).
Sources and Notes:

GDP: China experienced sharp ups and downs during the earlier period of 1952–78. The Great leap Forward (1958–60) experienced negative growth of up to -30 percent and during the Cultural Revolution (1967–77), negative growth of up to -10 percent. Source: "Understanding the Present," pp 512–519 in Chai, Joseph, C.H., ed. 2000. *The Economic Development of Modern China. Volume III: Reforms and the Opening Up Since 1979.* An Elgar Reference Collection. Cheltenham, UK. Northampton, MA, USA. pp 513–514, Figure 1.3. For the pre-reform period, Thomas G. Rawski states that "...specialists now agree that China's economy has experienced substantial growth over the last three decades. Estimates of annual GDP growth cluster around 6–7 %..." in Rawski, Thomas G. "Economic Growth and Employment in China." *World Development*, 7, No. 8/9, August-September 1979: 767–782. These rates are much higher than the rates from Perkins (1994, pp 42, footnote 1), who put it at around 4.8 percent for 1952–78. For 1978–95: the annual rate is 9.4 percent. Source: "Understanding the Present", pp 512–519 in Chai, Joseph, C.H., ed. 2000. *The Economic Development of Modern China. Volume III: Reforms and the Opening up Since 1979.* An Elgar Reference Collection. Cheltenham, UK. Northampton, MA, USA. Table 1.1. For 1982–2002: China at a glance (08/29/2003). From 1997–2007, average annual growth: 9.5 percent. Source: World Bank. China at a glance (09/24/08). From 1998–2009, 9.9 percent per year. China at a glance (12/09/09).

GDP per capita: For 1950–78: 3.0 percent and for 1978–95: 8.0 percent annual growth rate: "Understanding the Present", pp 512–519 in Chai, Joseph, C.H., ed. 2000. *The Economic Development of Modern China. Volume III: Reforms and the Opening up Since 1979.* An Elgar Reference Collection. Cheltenham, UK. Northampton, MA, USA. pp 512, Figure 1.1. For 1982–2002: China at a glance (08/29/2003). 1997–2007: 8.7 percent per year. Source : World Bank. China at a glance. 09/24/08.

Agric. GDP: For 1952–57, 1965–75: Perkins, Dwight and Yusuf. 1984. Shahid. *Rural Development in China.* A World Bank Publication. Johns Hopkins University Press. Table 3–3. An alternative estimate for 1952–78 is 2.9 percent, for 1978–1984 is 7.7 percent, and for 1984–87 is 4.1 percent. Source: Lin, Justin Yifu. "Rural Reforms and Agricultural Growth in China" pp 117–134 in Chai, Joseph, C.H., ed. 2000. *The Economic Development of Modern China. Volume III: Reforms and the Opening up Since 1979.* An Elgar Reference Collection. Cheltenham, UK. Northampton, MA, USA. Table 1. For 1978–84: Perkins, Dwight. "Completing China's Move to the Market". Table 1, in chapter 2 in Chai, Joseph, C.H., ed. 2000. *The Economic Development of Modern China. Volume III: Reforms and the Opening up Since 1979.* An Elgar Reference Collection. Cheltenham, UK. Northampton, MA, USA. Still another estimate for 1952–78 is 1.9 percent, for 1978–87 is 6 percent, for 1984–87 is 3.4 percent.

remuneration was linked to work. The basic production and income-sharing unit in China's collective agriculture consisted of a group of 25–30 neighbors in the same village. This production team reserved 5–10 percent of collective land for the private use of individual house-holds to grow vegetables, rear pigs, and so on. The production team also had the right to control part of its surplus. However, close monitoring of labor was problematic. Pay was not closely related to effort expended. In fact, pay was based on age and gender. Thus the incentive to work was poor and the free-rider problem pervasive. The HRS solved this problem by decentralizing decision making on resource allocation. This basic improvement of the incentive system at the micro level was strengthened by sector-level measures, such as government raising the purchase prices of most agricultural products, re-establishing rural markets in a way that lowered transactions costs, and liberalizing labor mobility into rural non-farm enterprises (Ho, 1994: 26–27). In sharp contrast to the Great Leap Forward strategy of the first 30 years, the spread of reforms of the incentive and marketing systems actually enabled China to leap forward. The transformation of the entire economy started in agriculture, but not in the manner envisaged by the founders of new China.

Importance, structure, and performance of agriculture. Agriculture was and remains a major sector despite its declining relative contribution to the overall economy. In line with its declining importance, agriculture's

(Figure 2.16. source continued)

Source: Lardy, Nicholas "Chinese Agricultural Development under Reform and Future Prospects" pp 21–35 in Tso, T.C., ed. 1990. *Agricultural Reform and Development in China – Achievements, Current Status, and Future Outlook. Sixth Colloquium Proceedings*, IDEALS, Inc. pp 22, Table 1. For 1982–2002: China at a glance (08/29/2003). 1997–2007: 3.7 percent. Source : World Bank. China at a glance. 09/24/08. For 1998–2008: 3.9 percent per year. China at a glance. 12/09/09.

Population growth rates: yearly average at 2.2 percent between 1957 and 1975. Source: Rawski, Thomas G. "Economic Growth and Employment in China" pp 769 in *World Development*, 7, No. 8/9, (August–September 1979): 767–782. The one-child policy was instituted in the late 1970s. By the late 1970s, the rate declined to less than 1.4 percent. Source: Perkins, Dwight and Yusuf. 1984. Shahid. *Rural Development in China*. A: World Bank Publication. Johns Hopkins University Press. pp 31. The annual growth rate during 1996–2002 period averaged 0.8 percent. Source: China at a glance (08/29/2003). 2000–2007: 0.6 percent per year. Source: China at a glance (09/24/2008)

These growth rate figures are country-wide averages. The growth rates in coastal provinces were higher. For example, the coastal provinces grew at 9.7 percent per year between 1978 and 1995. There are two alternative estimates of China's GDP growth rate from 1978–95 in Chai, pp 513, Box 1.1. These are 8.0 and 6.8 percent.

contribution to rural household incomes has also declined, from around 66 percent in 1985 to around 48 percent by 2000. Agriculture in China includes crops (by the late 1990s more than 50 percent of total), livestock (30 percent), fisheries (less than 10 percent), and forestry (around 3 percent). Among crops, the major category is grain (rice, wheat, corn, potatoes, coarse grains, and soybeans), accounting for around 80 percent of sown acreage by 1981. Policy has focused on achieving grain self-sufficiency. Cash crops (e.g., horticulture, cotton) accounted for around 12 percent (Perkins and Yusuf, 1984: table 3–6). Some China scholars estimate that during the earlier (and at times, tumultuous) years of collective agriculture, the annual growth averaged only 2–3 percent. Agricultural growth rose dramatically in the post-reform period, to average 3–4 percent per year in the 1990s. TFP also increased rapidly during the early years of the reform period but then tapered off (Nyberg and Rozelle, 1999: 75). For the subsequent 1988–96 period, the different estimates of annual agricultural productivity growth are controversial. They range from 5.6 percent using national data, to 6.7 percent using provincial (Jiangsu) data, to 1.9 percent using household data (Rozelle and Sumner, 2003: 240).[43]

A land- and water-scarce, labor-abundant agriculture. Like India's agriculture, China's is land- and water- scarce and labor-abundant. China has only 7 percent of the world's cultivated land, but it has to feed more than a billion people (some 21 percent of the world's population in 2002). As scarce as cultivable land is, water is agriculture's most limiting resource, especially in northern China. In 1996, out of a total of 95.5 million ha of cultivated land, some 50 million ha (or 52 percent) were irrigated. However, since cropping intensities on irrigated land (at 203 percent) are much higher than on rain-fed land (at 114 percent), 66 percent of *sown* area is irrigated (World Bank, May 1999: para 8.21).

Drastic socialist experiments to develop agriculture. Developing such a land- and water-scarce agriculture to adequately feed and clothe its teeming millions and generate a surplus for industrialization has been a central challenge for China's leadership. As already described, different variants of collectivization and mass labor mobilization were

---

[43] Carter, Chen, and Chu (Rozelle and Sumner, eds., 2003: 240) argue that the only plausible estimates are those from household data, because there were reduced investment and rising farm input prices during that period.

tried until 1978. The official line was that collectivization was to promote rapid agricultural growth by mobilizing devotion for the collective and the motherland and without diverting resources from industry (a Chinese variant of the "squeeze agriculture" position). The Great Leap Forward movement, launched in 1958, however, proved to be a dramatic failure of Chairman Mao's approach (1949–76), according to which China could rely on mass labor mobilization to promote sustained output and productivity growth. During the Readjustment Period of 1961–66, there was renewed emphasis on price and material incentives. However, this approach was again overturned. The Cultural Revolution (1966–76), though not targeted solely to agriculture, proved to be extremely disruptive throughout the economy.

Macro and agricultural policy before 1979. Like most developing countries, China espoused the ISI. It wanted to "catch up" with the powerful industrialized nations. Agriculture was to play a supportive role; it was to help achieve self-sufficiency in major food/fiber products. China believed that such self-sufficiency would also be instrumental in achieving national security. To generate the surplus, it taxed agriculture in order to invest in industry using a variety of socialist institutions. In particular, it taxed agriculture through collectivization, centralized planning, price fixing, domestic state procurement and marketing, and control of foreign trade. These were to transfer agricultural surplus to government and industry. To promote production, the government emphasized the use of modern inputs, notably of fertilizer and high-yielding varieties; investment in research and the spread of extension; and the development of small-scale rural industries to supply modern inputs. This policy of collectivization and resource extraction did not work.

Agricultural price policy after 1979. The official approval of the HRS in 1983 opened doors to reforms in other major areas. As mentioned earlier, other than making households responsible for and therefore the main beneficiaries of output sales, the 1979 rural reforms also consisted of (a) substantial increases in quota and above-quota prices for grain, oil crops, cotton, sugar, and pork; and (b) substantial increases in the role of markets (in other words, reduction of state intervention operations) for guiding production decisions. The implicit taxation of the main crops (grain, including soybean), however, continued until

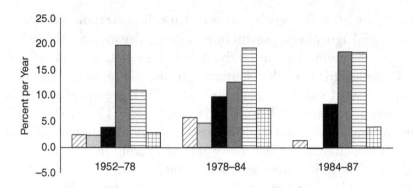

☑ Crops ☐ Cotton ■ Animal husbandry ▤ Fishery ⊟ Sidelines ☐ Agricultural growth

Figure 2.17. China: average growth rates in main subsectors of agriculture (percent per year, 1952–87).

Source and Note: Lin, Justin Yifu. "Rural Reforms and Agricultural Growth in China" pp 117–134 in Chai, Joseph, C.H., ed. 2000. *The Economic Development of Modern China. Volume III: Reforms and the Opening up Since 1979*. An Elgar Reference Collection. Cheltenham, UK. Northampton, MA, USA. Table 1. For the subsequent period, 1987–97: 4.4 percent per year, and 1997–2007: 3.7 percent. *Source*: World Bank. China at a glance (09/24/2008).

In 1952, the weights (in percent) of the sub-sectors in 1952 were: crops: 83.1; animal husbandry: 11.5; fishery: 0.3; forestry: 0.7; sidelines: 4.4. In 1987, the weights were: crops: 60.7; animal husbandry: 22.3; fishery: 4.7; forestry: 4.8; and sidelines: 7.0. Outputs from village-run enterprises were excluded.

1997 and then these crops were implicitly subsidized from 1998 to 1999 (Kwiecinski and Li, 2002: 33–51, box fig. 1).[44]

Agricultural performance before and after the 1979 reforms. The reforms made a huge difference to agricultural growth right after the reforms as Figure 2.17 shows. Lin finds that of the total output growth between 1978 and 1984, increased inputs accounted for 45.6 percent of this growth; productivity growth accounts for another 48.6 percent, of which institutional changes alone accounted for 46.9 percent.

The yearly average agricultural GDP growth declined to 4.6 percent from 1982 to 1992 and to 3.7 percent from 1992 to 2002. Beyond the immediate post-reform period, the increases in growth rates were most pronounced in sub-sectors without any government controls.

Productivity performance before and after the 1979 reforms. The rate of adoption of these more productive technologies was high. Even during

[44] The implicit tax/subsidy is calculated as the difference between the prices of the state procurement system and domestic market prices.

the pre-reform period, grain yields were high by international comparisons. The annual growth rate in grain yields averaged 2.7 percent
during this period (Perkins and Yusuf, 1984: table 3–10). The first
decade into the reforms (1977–87) witnessed sharp increases in TFP.
With 1952 = 100, the index rose from 75 in 1977 to 133 in 1987
(Tomich et al., 1995: fig. 9.3). China scholars attribute these high rates
of return – a 20 percent growth in agricultural productivity (between
1965 and 1994) – to agricultural research and development (World
Bank, 1997a: 15). Researchers argue that productivity growth in rice,
wheat, and maize (for the 1984–95 period) is attributable primarily to
research investments. They also attribute the slowing of growth in the
late 1990s to the substantial decline in public support for research and
development. Of grave concern to researchers is that research funds
per scientist declined by 25–30 percent in the 1990s (World Bank,
May 1999: paras 18, 9.6–9.7).

Dynamic growth of the rural non-farm sector. An outstanding feature
of China's vigorous agricultural growth is its linkage with the rural
non-farm (RNF) sector. Rural industry, notably from the Town and
Village Enterprises (TVE), now contribute more than 50 percent of
total household income (Kwiecinski and Li, 2002: table 2). By the mid-
1990s, the RNF sector contributed to 25 percent of China's exports
(Nyberg and Rozelle, 1999: 87). The yearly growth of the TVEs averaged 24 percent between 1985 and 1995 (compare with agriculture's
growth rate, which was around 4 percent). Thus, unlike the situation
in most countries, a large share of industrial output is being produced
in rural areas employing 25 percent of the rural labor force (World
Bank, May 1999: paras 1.7, 2.17). The explosive growth of TVEs has
also greatly benefited local governments, as they generated one of
the major sources of local government extra-budget revenues. TVEs
existed before the market-oriented reforms, but they were run like by
collectives and constituted roughly 8 percent of gross industrial output
(Zhu, 2001: 267–79). Today, TVEs face a competitive market. They
must purchase and sell at market prices. Unlike state-owned enterprises, they do not get low-interest loans or any price subsidies. TVEs
are able to exploit local comparative advantages, in particular abundant literate labor. The high growth of primary agriculture has generated both the raw materials and the rural purchasing power that
TVEs need to thrive. Rural households benefited from agricultural

and RNF sector growth, but those living in the coastal provinces (e.g., Jiangsu, Zhejiang, Shantong, Fujian, and Guangdong) near urban centers benefited much more, such that, over the decades, the disparity among rural households between the lower two quintiles and the top two quintiles widened. The main factor causing this widening disparity was greater access to non-farm sources of incomes. Rural poverty reduction in provinces/regions with better access to non-farm sources of incomes has been more pronounced than in the interior provinces/regions (Tang Zhong, 2002: table 6, 7).

Substantial poverty reduction since the reforms of 1979. According to China's poverty line of 0.66 USD per day (in 1985 constant purchasing parity dollars), the latest national poverty rate is 5 percent, down from around 33 percent in 1970 (World Bank, 2003a: 64). At this national poverty level, the reduction in poverty went from 260 million in 1978 to 34 million in 1999 (Kwiecinski and Li, 2002: 34–35, table 1). According to the international poverty line of one dollar per day, the decline, though less, is still substantial and remarkable. At a dollar per day poverty line, China reduced poverty by some 400 million people during the post-1979 reform period (World Bank, October 2003: ii). Poverty incidence fell from 49 percent in 1981 to 6.9 percent in 2002, an estimated absolute decline from about 490 to 88 million over the same period (World Bank, 2004c: Shanghai Conf.). By the late 1990s, urban poverty virtually disappeared. Therefore, poverty is now primarily rural and a problem in remote areas, with harsh natural resource environments. By the end of 1998, rural poverty still afflicted about 11.5 percent of the rural population, or some 106 million people, a very large number (World Bank, 2001a: xiii). In the 1990s, to further reduce rural poverty in poor regions and counties, the government launched the 8–7 National Poverty Reduction Program for 1994–2000. Based on lessons learned from this program, it launched the New Century Rural Poverty Alleviation Plan (2001–2010).[45]

Increase in income inequality since the reforms. Income inequality has risen between the coastal and inland regions, and among the better- and

---

[45] The official Chinese statement of the government's continuing work to reduce poverty, especially in the central and western regions of China, can be found at http://qa.china-embassy. org/eng/zt/zfbps/t18987.htm. Despite substantial progress since the reforms of 1979, much work remains.

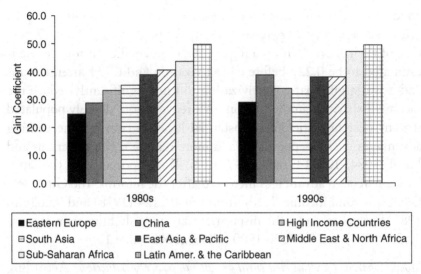

Figure 2.18. Worldwide comparisons of income inequality, Gini coefficient (1980s, 1990s). *Source:* "Overview," In Chai, Joseph, C.H., ed. 2000. *The Economic Development of Modern China. Volume III: Reforms and the Opening up Since 1979:* 549–553. An Elgar Reference Collection. Cheltenham, UK. Northampton, MA, USA.

worse-resource-endowed rural regions. The urban/rural per capita income ratio is one of the largest in the world. The ratio fluctuated between 1.83 in 1983 to 2.86 in 1994 and 2.79 in 2000. The Gini coefficient for rural incomes rose from 0.24 in the early 1980s to 0.35 in 1999. Average income per rural resident in the east is almost double the level in the west (Kwiecinski and Li, 2002: 36, 34). Compared with that of other countries and regions in the world, China's higher Gini coefficient is now similar to that of the United States and close to the East Asian average. The Gini coefficient is above that of South Asia but well below that of sub-Saharan Africa and the Latin America and Caribbean region (see Figure 2.18).

Rising income inequality in a socialist economy? The rise in income inequality is a major concern for the central government because rising inequality can be politically destabilizing. The Communist leadership is also perfectly aware that, in Taiwan, China equity improved with income growth. Moreover, a battle cry of the Communist Party in the 1940s was the building of an egalitarian society. Data on the distribution of rural income before and after land reform (in the late 1940s and early 1950s) show that the land reform had a significant effect in reducing income disparities. The share of the poorest 20 percent rose by nearly 90 percent. The top 20 percent lost about 17 percent of their share. Within a region, the Gini coefficient for income is estimated to be 0.227 before collectivization and 0.211 after. Perkins and Yusuf argue that collectivization did not significantly reduce the income disparities among regions. Moreover, more densely populated regions near big cities had substantial location cum income-earning advantages over less populated and more remote regions (Perkins and Yusuf, 1984: 108–14, tables 6–1, 6–2). The importance of the latter location-related advantages increased after the reforms. The Gini coefficient for rural income distribution was 0.2124 (1978) and 0.2636 in 1985. For urban areas, the disparities narrowed slightly: estimates are 0.186 (1977) and 0.180 in 1990 (Chai, 2000a: table 10).

How important was agricultural growth to poverty reduction? According to Ravallion and Chen (2004: abstract, 12, 13, 26, tables 7, 8), agricultural and rural growth were very important for poverty reduction in China (1980–2000). Ravallion and Datt (1994), in their paper on India's growth and poverty reduction experience, reject the null hypothesis that sectoral composition of growth does not matter and then argue that the statistically significant regression estimates show that "rural economic growth was far more important to national poverty reduction than urban economic growth; agriculture played a far more important role than the secondary and tertiary sectors of GDP." The authors regress the rate of poverty reduction on the rate of growth in household mean income. They obtain the elasticity of poverty reduction to growth of more than 3 for the headcount index. They decompose the growth rates by rural and urban income components. They also decompose GDP into "primary" (mainly agriculture), "secondary" (manufacturing and construction), and "tertiary" (services and trade). They find that "the sectoral composition of growth matters to the rate of poverty reduction. The primary sector has a far higher impact (by a factor of about four) than either the secondary or tertiary sector." Using province-level data and regressing rural poverty reduction on rural income growth, the authors obtain the statistically significant coefficient of −1.58. Their claim may be substantially correct, but methodologically it is invalid as it is based on measures of statistical significance. Statistical significance does not imply causal significance. This basic point is often ignored, though it is routinely pointed out in econometrics textbooks. For example, "a statistical relationship, however strong and suggestive, can never establish causal connection: our ideas of causation must come from outside, ultimately from some theory or other" (Kendall and Stuart, 1961: 279).

Does the China case support the pro-agriculture position? The case of China supports the pro-agriculture position. It illustrates the combination Pro-AG 2 before 1979 (agriculture and economy not doing well) and Pro-Ag 1 (agriculture and economy doing well) after 1979. The China case refutes the anti-agriculture view. We found no combination of (a) sustained high output and productivity growth in agriculture co-existing with persistent high rates of rural poverty and mediocre overall economic growth or (b) stagnant low productivity agriculture co-existing with high rates of overall economic growth and low(er) rates of rural poverty. That no such combination existed is true of the three first decades (1949–79) of central planning as well as for the subsequent post-1979 reform years (1980–2002). In the earlier decades during which collective agriculture was severely taxed to promote industrialization, the entire economy did poorly. The high growth rates of heavy industry were achieved at the cost of massive distortions in resource allocation and meager improvements in the standard of the living of the people (Lin et al., 1999: 65–75).[46] The "squeeze agriculture" approach did not work. After the adoption of the HRS-energized private agriculture, the high growth performance of agriculture was followed by the sustained high performance of non-agriculture, with substantial reductions in poverty. The China experience, however, also qualifies the pro-agriculture position in three ways:

1. While there were improved price incentives, the major boost to growth in the early years was institutional (HRS), not increased hardware investment per se. There was no major program of rural public investment at the time of reform.

---

[46] Perkins (1986: 9, 23, 45–47) makes the same point. China's high growth rates of the earlier years were due almost entirely to increases in capital and labor, not to productivity increases.

2. The contribution of agricultural growth to overall growth was not just in terms of resource transfers but, more important, in the virtuous circle of growth initiated between agriculture and non-agriculture, thus validating the switch to a more market- and export-oriented strategy. After the first decade or so of high agricultural growth, the overall performance of the Chinese economy was such as to attract large amounts of FDI, thus fueling further growth. Thus, over time, agriculture's contribution to GDP became less important.

3. The continued transformation of agriculture and broad-based improvements in rural well-being still require demand-pull for rural labor from a growing non-farm sector and substantial public investments in rural areas to improve access to basic public goods and services, such as roads and communications and marketing infrastructure, schools, clinics, and agricultural research and extension.

In sum, the contribution of sustained agricultural output and productivity growth has been necessary but definitely not sufficient. The focus of the current five-year plan (2006–2010) is to promote broad-based rural development and reduce increasing income inequality through major public investments in rural infrastructure and the delivery of basic social services.

II.VII. Indonesia – GNI per capita: USD 2,230 (2009)

Introduction. Like India and China, Indonesia is a populous Asian country with an important agriculture and with high levels of poverty. Indeed, Gunnar Myrdal in his *Asian Drama* held out no hope for Indonesia: "As things look at the beginning of 1966, there seems to be little prospect of rapid economic growth in Indonesia" (Myrdal, 1968: 489). Myrdal has been proved wrong. Indonesia has made tremendous progress. What, if any, was the contribution of agriculture to its development? Whose claims is correct, the pro- or anti-agriculture camp?

Brief background. Indonesia is well known for being an oil-exporting country that invested substantially in smallholder agriculture; attained rice self-sufficiency by 1984; maintained three decades of political

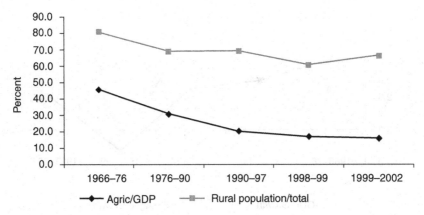

Figure 2.19. Indonesia: agricultural contribution to GDP and population (1966–2002).

and economic stability after the tumultuous Sukarno years (until the 1997–98 Asian financial crisis); substantially raised indicators of socio-economic well-being; and reduced rural poverty. It is primarily a lower-middle-income country, but it has made tremendous progress. In the early years, Indonesia was plagued by political upheavals; regional, ethnic and religious divisions; and a structure of wealth distribution that was divisive, as it heavily favored the Dutch and Chinese minorities. Even granted the difficult years of the financial crisis and the recent slow recovery, Myrdal has been proved wrong. What did Myrdal miss?

Figures 2.19, 2.20, and 2.21 – show that progress on major fronts was substantive, though uneven, for Indonesia, an important agricultural country with a major rural population. The development events of note are the growth rates of agriculture and of the economy over decades, the extent of poverty and its reduction, and the deep crisis of 1997–99.

From independence (1945) to political stability (mid-1960s). Indonesia won its independence from Holland in 1945. It did not achieve peace until 1949, however. It also did not gain political and price stability until much later, when hyper-inflation was brought under control under General Suharto's stabilization program of 1966–68. Under President Sukarno (1958–65), resources to address continuing domestic upheavals fueled increasing deficits and mounting inflation. With macro and political stability restored, Indonesia turned its attention to long-term development issues.

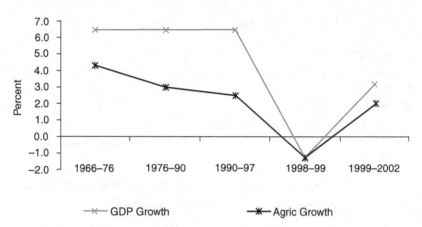

Figure 2.20. Indonesia: growth rates of GDP and agricultural GDP (percent per year, 1966–2002).

Growth, stability, and equity – Indonesia's development trilogy. Indonesia pursued three objectives through successive five-year plans (starting with REPELITA I 1969/70–1973/74). The objectives were growth, stability, and equity. C. P. Timmer calls them the development trilogy, which distinguished not only the government of Indonesia but the goals of most of the governments of East Asia along the Pacific Rim. For some three decades, from 1966 to 1996, Indonesia successfully maintained macro stability and grew. Among other things, it anchored its macro policy in the Balanced Budget Presidential Decree in 1967, which prohibited budget financing through money creation or debt creation. This helped restore and maintain financial discipline, as well as price stability. It also devalued Indonesia's currency periodically, avoiding the negative impact of the Dutch disease on agriculture – for example, in 1971 and post–oil boom, again in 1978, 1983, and 1986.

Major economic developments supportive of rural growth. Macro policy emphasizing price stability and currency convertibility provided a supportive framework for agricultural and rural growth. The Indonesian government adopted an ISI in the 1970s until the collapse of oil prices in 1983 (from USD 31 per barrel in 1981 to USD 9.75 per barrel in 1983) (Mangara, 1998: 47). Despite pursuing ISI, the government invested in rural areas, including in irrigation and market infrastructure

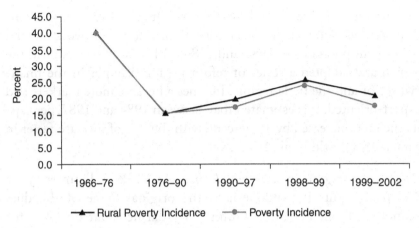

Figure 2.21. Indonesia: incidence of poverty and rural poverty (1966–2002).

Sources and Notes:

Agric/GDP: 1970, 1980, 1990, 1998, 2002: C. Peter Timmer, Senior Research Fellow, Center for Global Development. Draft June 6, 2005. "Operationalizing Pro-Poor Growth: Country Study for the World Bank – Indonesia ." Annex 2 (b) table A 2.2. Another estimate for the 1960s: 35 percent and for 2001: 17 percent. Mangara Tambunan. April 1998. "Economic Reforms and Agricultural Development in Indonesia." in *ASEAN Economic Bulletin*. Pp7–58, table 1. Also, World Bank. Little Data Book. 2003. pp 110.

Population growth: 1998–2004: World Bank. Indonesia at a glance. 09/15/05.

GDP growth: 1966–1997 – Suharto era. World Bank. Development Research Group. Rural development. March 2002. "Determinants of Agricultural Growth in Indonesia, the Philippines and Thailand". Policy Research Working Paper 2803. pp 1, table 1.1. During these three decades, population growth rate per year was 2.06 percent. An alternative estimate for the Suharto years, 1998–99 and after is in C. Peter Timmer, Senior Research Fellow, Center for Global Development, draft June 6, 2005. "Operationalizing Pro-Poor Growth: Country Study for the World Bank – Indonesia." Pp 25, 26. Post crisis, 2001–06: 4.8 percent. Source: World Bank. *Snapshot of Indonesia's economy, Pre-crisis 1993–96 to Post-crisis, 2001–06*.

Agric growth: 1960–88: real gross value added calculated from 5-year averages. Van der Eng, Pierre. 1996. *Agricultural Growth in Indonesia – Productivity Change and Policy Impact since 1880*. MacMillan Press, Inc. Table 2.3. 1985–90, 1990–97, 1999–2002: C. Peter Timmer, Senior Research Fellow, Center for Global Development, draft June 6, 2005. "Operationalizing Pro-Poor Growth: Country Study for the World Bank – Indonesia ." Annex 2 (b) Table A 2.1.

Poverty incidence and rural poverty incidence: 1976, 1990, 1996, 1998, 2002: C. Peter Timmer, Senior Research Fellow, Center for Global Development, draft June 6, 2005. "Operationalizing Pro-Poor Growth: Country Study for the World Bank – Indonesia." Annex 4 table A 4.1 Poverty incidence in 1970 was 60 percent. The estimation of poverty used a different methodology in 1990, and a different basket starting in 1996. These led to higher estimates of incidence than in the previous years. Poverty rate in 2006: 17.8 percent. Source: World Bank. *Snapshot of Indonesia's economy, Pre-crisis 1993–96 to Post-crisis, 2001–06*.

(in particular rural roads and rural electrification), research and extension services, and basic primary education. It adopted two structural
adjustment programs in 1983 and 1986, within which it devalued the
rupiah and adopted a series of reforms – for example, in the financial sector and the trade regime. Indonesia became more market- and
export-oriented. It is estimated that, between 1984 and 1987, per capita incomes increased by 16 percent, with the rate of increase faster in
rural areas (World Bank, 1990a: xv).

Substantial progress in poverty reduction. As C. Peter Timmer (June
2005b: 15) puts it, "Indonesia is the original home of the dual
economy." Remember that Gunnar Myrdal held out no hope for
Indonesia. In such a setting and with extensive poverty at independence (1945), Indonesia's achievement in poverty reduction is
remarkable. In 1967, the GNP per capita was USD 50, half the level
of India, Bangladesh, and Nigeria. By 2006, Indonesian GNI per
capita was above that of the other three countries. GNI in the four
countries was USD 1,420, 820, 480, and 640, respectively.[48] In the
1992 report of the Harvard–Stanford Poverty Team, "Interviews ...
reveal a common perception among villagers and local officials that
enormous strides have been made during the last 25 years in raising
living standards on average while also lifting many of the poorest out
of absolute poverty." (Harvard-Stanford Indonesia Poverty Report,
1992, also in Timmer, 2004: box 2) However, there is still extensive
poverty, as many people live just above the poverty line. More than
50 percent (53 percent according to the Asian Development Bank)
live on just USD 2 per day (Timmer, 2005b: 27, 31, 56). According
to World Bank data, poverty incidence declined to around 17 percent during the post-crisis years (2001–2006). However, vulnerability to poverty still afflicts around half the population, especially in
rural areas and in the eastern islands of Papua and Lampung (World
Bank, 2005c: 2).

Growth performance since the 1960s. Indonesian growth has been high
and sustained for decades. From 1960 to 1985, annual average GDP

---

[48] World Bank, World Development Indicators, 2006. More recent (World Development
Indicators, 2010) GNI/capita estimates are (USD): Indonesia, 1,880 (2008); India, 1,040
(2008); Bangladesh, 520 (2008); Nigeria, 1,170 (2008).

growth per capita was 3.5 percent (World Bank, 1993a: fig. 2). From 1961 to 1998, it was 4.33 percent (World Bank, March 2002: 1, table 1.1).[49] In late 1997–99, however, Indonesia plunged into a major crisis. After 1999–2000, there were welcome signs of recovery. However, the recovery is still considered fragile. The annual average growth rate for the 1992–2002 decade was 2.5 percent only.[50] The economic recovery strengthened and averaged 4.8 percent per year (2001–2006). Despite the severe setback of 1997–99, Indonesia's high-growth performance for decades compares favorably with that of many oil-exporting developing countries, which have, so far, squandered much of their oil wealth (Timmer, June 2005: 49).[51]

Indonesian agriculture – the importance of rice. Agriculture's aggregate growth performance since the Suharto years is given in Figure 2.20. The sector is dominated by smallholders who cultivate food crops, mainly rice, and export crops, such as rubber, palm oil, cocoa, coffee, tea, and coconut. Food crops dominate, as they account for roughly 60 percent of total agriculture value-added (Hill, 2000: 127). More than 80 percent of rice production is irrigated, of which 60 percent is located in Java (World Bank, July 3, 2003: 4). Van der Eng (1996: table 3.3, 253) argues that the Dutch colonial government (1880–1945) expanded irrigation from 2.4 to 4.9 million ha (1880–1937) and undertook early attempts at research and extension; "it did lay foundations during the 1930s and 1940s for a further acceleration of the growth of agricultural production." Growth from 1880 to 1937 was 1.9; from 1937 to 1960, 0.3; and from 1960 to 1988, 3.6 percent per year (Van der Eng, 1996: table 2.2). This estimate of long-term trends shows the much improved performance of agriculture since 1960. For more than three decades, from 1961 to 1998, agricultural growth per capita was 1.42 percent (World Bank, March 2002: 1, table 1.1). Annual growth of TFP (1971–98) averaged 0.45 percent (Timmer, 2005b: annex app. A 3.2). Apart from these aggregate measures, the story of Indonesia's agricultural performance is the story of rice. Rice is a success story, with per capita

---

[49] During these three decades, the population growth rate per year was 2.06 percent.

[50] World Bank, "Indonesia at a Glance," September 3, 2003.

[51] Timmer attributes part of Indonesia's success to its ability to use its oil wealth for rural development instead of squandering it, as many countries have done.

consumption rising by almost 60 percent between 1966 and 1992. Average rice yields nearly doubled from 2,350 kg/ha in 1970 to 4,300 kg/ha in 1990, with yields in Java being higher (Hill, 2000: table 7.1). Achieving rice self-sufficiency became a pillar of the government's strategy under Suharto in the late 1970s. The 1973–74 rice shortage on international markets and the 1976–78 outbreaks of brown plant hopper highlighted Indonesia's vulnerability. On average, Indonesia imported roughly 20 percent of world supplies. It was thus a "large" importing country.[52]

Interventions for ensuring rice self-sufficiency. To promote domestic rice production, the Indonesian government subsidized the adoption of the Green Revolution technology in HYV (e.g., irrigation, fertilizers, pesticides, improved seeds). It also guaranteed a floor price to producers, while maintaining a ceiling price for consumers. Both the producer and retail consumer prices were stable and maintained well below the trend of world prices. BULOG, the public logistics agency in charge of implementing the rice (also to a lesser extent corn, and cassava) policy, controlled imports and exports. While maintaining low and stable urban retail prices became a priority from 1966 to 1972, increasing domestic production became very important in the late 1970s. From 1978 to 1985, producer rice prices were raised sharply (Timmer, 1989: 33) (see Figure 2.22).

Was agricultural growth important in reducing poverty? The answer is yes, according to C. Peter Timmer, an expert on the Indonesian economy. Using materials from Sumarto and Suryadi's work (2003), Timmer (June 2005: 34) concludes: "Roughly two-thirds of the reduction in poverty observed during the period of fastest growth in manufactured exports was due to growth in agricultural output at the provincial level." The following tabulation was constructed by Timmer from results in Sumarto and Suryadi's presentation to the Trade, Growth and Poverty Conference in London, December 8–9, 2003. See Table 2.1.

Timmer, of course, recognizes that "[f]ull cause and effect remain to be sorted out, but the Sumarto and Suryadi results show, at a minimum,

---

[52] A country is "large" in a trade sense when its entry into or exit from a market changes market prices. The country is a price maker not a price taker.

Table 2.1. Indonesia: the Impact of Economic Growth on Poverty (Total Poverty Headcount)

Independent Variables	Total Growth Coefficient	Sectoral Growth Coefficient
Total GDP growth	−0.0254	
	(−0.90)	
Agricultural GDP growth		−1.8595
		(−3.62)**
Industrial GDP growth		−0.0664
		(−1.63)
Services GDP growth		0.0048
		(0.09)
Total population growth	0.0653	0.1193
	(2.37)*	(3.93)**
Initial poverty headcount	−0.1316	−0.1085
	(−2.96)**	(−2.55)**
Constant	0.0189	0.0524
	(0.78)	(2.16)*
Number of observations	130	130
F-Test	5.43**	7.16**
R-squared	0.1144	0.2240

Note: *t*-statistics in parentheses: * = significant at 95 percent; ** = significant at 99 percent.

that increases in agricultural output are closely associated with reductions in poverty" (Timmer, 2005b: 36). Nevertheless, he argues that agricultural growth accounts (in a causal sense) for the bulk of poverty reduction achieved. Timmer's conclusions contradict results from other researchers, however. Causal claims among these researchers assessing the quantitative importance of agricultural growth in reducing poverty contradict each other. They all wrongly infer causality from measures of statistical significance.

The marginal importance of agricultural growth in reducing poverty according to Warr and others. Warr (2002: 6, 10–11) uses regression analysis to "examine the relationship between these outcomes [decline of absolute poverty incidence in Thailand, Indonesia, and the Philippines] and the rate of economic growth in the agricultural, industrial, and services sectors." The period covered is the 1960s to 1999. To test whether the sector composition of growth matters, Warr tests and rejects the null hypothesis that it does not matter. In his analysis, "the absolute value of the estimated coefficient for agriculture was substantially smaller than

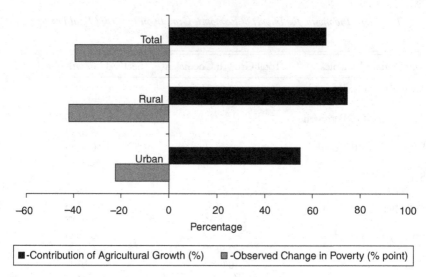

Figure 2.22. Indonesia: the contribution of agricultural growth to poverty reduction (1984–96).
Source: Timmer, C. Peter. June 6, 2005. "Operationalizing Pro-Poor Growth: Country Study for the World Bank – Indonesia." Draft. Table 4, pp 35.

the coefficients for services…. Growth in services output has been a more important contributor to reductions in rural poverty than growth of agricultural output." Fane and Warr (2003: 232) "construct a CGE model to ask how economic growth reduces poverty in Indonesia." Then, "to calculate the impact of a given increase in GDP on poverty, that is, to calculate the extent to which growth from a particular sector or factor is 'pro-poor,'" the authors subject their disaggregated model – for example, agriculture (18 sectors), manufacturing (18 sectors), services (15 sectors) – to two "shocks," namely Hicks-neutral total factor productivity increases in each sector or increases in factor supply. According to their model, the impact depends on the source of the growth. Thus the elasticity of poverty reduction in agriculture is −1.46, compared with −5.91 for services. The authors conclude that "contrary to the assumptions of many commentators, the poor do much better if a given amount of GDP growth is produced by technical progress in services or in manufacturing than if it is owing to technical progress in agriculture."

Timmer's objections to these alternative estimates. Timmer (June 2005, 53) asks: "What are we to make of these results? They fly directly in the face of the empirical results reported by Huppi and Ravallion

(1991), Timmer (1997, 2002), Warr (2003), and Sumarto and Suryadi (2003), as summarized in the discussion on sectoral contributions to poverty reduction in Indonesia." Timmer questions some of their assumptions – for example, the inability of the model to incorporate general equilibrium effects of sectoral changes; the fact that elasticities change quickly under different policy environments, a fact not captured by the CGE model; and the numerical value of 0.2 used for the Armington elasticity[53] versus the numerical value 0.1, which is more appropriate for Asian countries. Timmer finally questions the usefulness of the entire modeling exercise. He also points out that a different specification of the model can lead to vastly different results, as is shown by the results of the IFPRI model, which quantitatively explores the impact on poverty reduction of exogenous shifts in sectoral productivity. The IFPRI model concludes that agriculture has the most impact. The contradictory and confusing results of these exercises constitute clear evidence of the underlying methodological problems (see Appendix A).

Does the Indonesian case support the pro-agriculture position? So long as the results of the methodologies discussed (regression analysis, CGE modeling) are interpreted as causal explanations of agriculture's quantitative contribution, the situation will remain confused. As shown, the results contradict each other. The development performance of the Indonesian case supports the pro-agriculture (combination Pro-Ag 1) position because we do not find the combination of either (a) sustained high output and productivity growth in agriculture co-existing with persistent high rates of rural poverty and mediocre overall economic growth (combination Anti-Ag 1) or (b) stagnant low productivity agriculture co-existing with high rates of overall economic growth and low(er) rates of rural poverty (combination Anti-Ag 2).

The existence of either scenario would imply that sustained agricultural growth has no impact on either overall growth or poverty reduction. This was not the case. The Indonesian case refutes the anti-agriculture view. During the decades of sustained high growth,

[53] The Armington elasticity (Armington, 1969) is a parameter commonly used in models of consumer demand and international trade to estimate trade flows in response to price changes. It refers to the elasticity of substitution between products of different countries. The elasticity of substitution is assumed to be constant between products of different countries.

agriculture and the entire economy did well, and poverty reduction was substantial. It illustrates the combination Pro-Ag 1. Until the crisis of 1997–98, Indonesia, once considered a "basket case," was being referred to as a "miracle." Overall growth was the result not only of agricultural growth, but increasingly (as the agriculture/GDP share fell) of other major contributing factors, such as the oil boom in the late 1970s, the growth of export-oriented manufacturing as of the mid-1980s, the growth of industry more generally, whose share of GDP rose from 11 percent in the mid-1960s to 40 percent by the early 1990s, and the revolution in services (e.g., transport, communications, finance, tourism), which facilitated growth in other sectors (Hill, 2000).

II.VIII. Malaysia – GNI per capita: USD 7,230 (2009)

Introduction. Malaysia is a multi-racial country where income inequality was high in the earlier years (1950s–960s), which erupted in fierce racial riots, the most famous being on May 13, 1969. The Malaysian experience constitutes an important case to assess the contribution, if any, of agricultural development in a country where income inequality and, with it, racial tensions are major issues. Did agricultural development contribute substantially to its major growth and poverty reduction objectives?

Brief background. Malaysia is known for at least three things: its rapid economic transformation, social tensions in its multi-ethnic society, and the government's success in reducing poverty and restructuring distribution to lessen extreme inequalities of income and wealth. In 1970, the Gini coefficient of income was 0.513 for peninsular Malaysia; in 1999, it had been lowered to 0.443 for all Malaysia (Government of Malaysia, 2004: 14). Following severe race riots in 1969, Malaysia adopted the New Economic Policy (NEP) for implementation from 1970 to 1990. Its overarching objectives were to eradicate poverty among all Malaysians irrespective of race and to restructure Malaysian society so that race would not be identified with economic function and status. A distinctive focus of the NEP was improving the position of the Malays, the Bumiputeras, as a group.

Malaya as an important trading center for centuries. Malaya became independent from Britain in 1957 and formed a federation in 1963. The federation consists of peninsular Malaya, Singapore (which broke off in 1965), Sarawak, and Sabah (in North Borneo). It has long exported primary commodities and has been a major trading center. For centuries, its economic fortunes rose and fell with fluctuating international commodity prices. From the 16th century on, Malaya, Singapore, and North Borneo became important trading centers between the East and West. From the late 19th century on, exports of "indigenous and luxury"[54] products and primary commodities – for example, tin, rubber, petroleum, iron ore, and coal – became important. Trade expanded during much of the 19th and early 20th centuries until 1920, when it entered an extended period of depression. In fact, from 1930 to 1950, GDP per capita in the Malay Peninsula experienced negative growth at the rate of –0.2 percent per year (Drabble, 2000: 160). Today, Malaysia is still a very open economy.

Development strategy since independence in 1957. Since 1957, the government has adopted a highly interventionist approach to economic development. It promoted both agriculture and industry. The overarching objectives were strong growth with redistribution in favor of the Bumiputeras, who are the majority and poorer than the Chinese and Indian communities. Growth with redistribution and national harmony were overarching goals for decades. The long-term objective was to develop manufacturing as a major economic sector and source of growth, thus lessening Malaysia's dependence on agriculture and other primary activities.

Socio-economic performance over three decades. Though still not fully industrialized, the Malaysian economy has undergone rapid transformation since the 1970s (Figures 2.23 and 2.24). Its annual average real GDP growth was quite high, averaging 7.0 percent except during the 1997–98 Asian financial crisis. In the 1990s, annual growth rates averaged 9–10 percent up to 1996, declined to 7.5 percent in 1997, and plunged by –7.5 percent in 1998. Growth recovered to 5–6 percent per year in 1999 until 2001 (Weber, 2001: table 4.1). An alternative estimate puts the average annual growth rate from 1960 to 1995 at

---

[54] Indigenous and luxury products include camphor, sandalwood, hornbill beaks, birds' nests, rattans, sago, pepper, jelutong, and guta percha (the last two are used as insulators in electric cables).

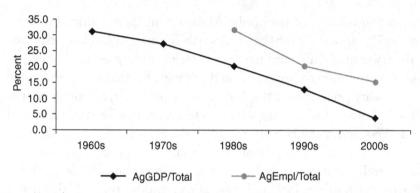

Figure 2.23. Malaysia: agricultural contribution to GDP and employment (percent per year 1960s–2000s).

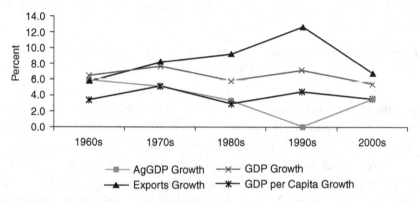

Figure 2.24. Malaysia: growth rates of selected economic indicators (percent per year 1960s–2000s).
Source: World Development Indicators, respective years.

7 percent (Abdul Aziz, 1998: 60). The incidence of poverty was also substantially reduced, from nearly 50 percent (1970) to 7.5 percent (1999) (Government of Malaysia: 2004: 15).

Substantial structural transformation since 1957. Structural changes have been profound. Primary commodities dominated merchandise exports in 1970, but by 1990 their share had shrunk to roughly a half – from 62 percent to 31 percent of total exports. Over the same period, the contribution to manufacturing exports grew from 11 percent to 59 percent (Brookfield, 1994: 95). Manufacturing has some agricultural origins, however. Processing of estate products (e.g., rubber, palm oil, timber) constituted around 22 percent of manufacturing output by 1981 (Jomo, 1993: 26).

Importance, structure, and performance of agriculture and the primary sector. Malaysia is resource-rich. Other than crop agriculture, the primary sector includes forestry (timber); tree crops such as rubber, palm oil, coconut, and cocoa; metals such as tin, copper, iron ore, bauxite, and gold; and oil and natural gas (the last two were discovered in the 1980s). Agriculture and the rest of the primary sector remain important despite their declining contribution to GDP. From 1960 and 2000, agriculture's contribution fell from around 30 percent to 5 percent of GDP. Forestry and mining in Malaysia, however, especially in Sabah and Sarawak, increased in importance by 1990. Overall agricultural output growth, which was strongest during the first plan at 6.0–8.0 percent per year (1966–70), has systematically declined: 5.0–6.0 percent in the 1970s, 4.0 percent in the 1980s (Drabble, 2000: table 11.3, 210). In much of the 1990s, the average annual agricultural growth rate was estimated to be only 0.1 percent.[55]

Socio-political importance of agriculture. Agriculture's importance, however, goes beyond its contribution to GDP, for it is home to the majority, the Bumiputeras. Poverty eradication among the Bumiputeras has been a central social goal of the government. Rural poverty, while still high, declined substantially: from 58.7 percent in 1970 to 19.3 percent in 1990. The poverty incidence at national and urban levels has also declined substantially.

Interventionist approach to promoting smallholder agriculture. The government invested heavily in smallholder agriculture and intervened directly to promote the vertical integration of agriculture with industry – the industrialization of agriculture. From 1971 to 1995, the share of total public expenditures allocated to agriculture and rural development averaged 17 percent. Only transport and social development were allocated higher shares, at 20 and 25 percent, respectively (Abdul Aziz, 1998: table 3). Important agricultural interventions were undertaken; examples are land development by the Federal Land Development Authority (FELDA, created in 1956), irrigation development schemes in the 1960s (Muda, Kemubu, and Trengganu), minimum price support

[55] World Bank, "Malaysia at a Glance," August 20, 2003.

schemes, and the provision of low-interest loans and subsidized inputs such as fertilizers, pesticides, and high-yielding seed varieties. In 1984, the New Agricultural Policy was formulated with the overarching goal of increasing incomes from agriculture, by supporting primary agriculture through research, market development, and diversification from rice and by developing agro-industry, for example, in rubber and palm oil (Brookfield, 1994: 50–55). The Industrial Master Plan (IMP) of 1986 promoted downstream activities of agriculture, particularly in rubber, palm oil, food processing, and timber, and in other resource-based industries.

Persistent dualism in agriculture despite smallholder orientation of policy. At the time of federation (1963), agriculture ranged from shifting cultivation of subsistence crops, mainly rice, by smallholders and capitalistic large-scale tree-crop estates. Smallholders also contributed to a third of total rubber planted before the depression years starting in 1920 (Brookfield, ed., 1994: 37). After the restrictions imposed on smallholders were lifted in 1929, their contribution rose further. The large estates were typically owned and managed by Westerners, mainly the British. During the 1970s, ownership and management were transferred to the Chinese and Malaysians and then increasingly in the 1980s the transfer of ownership and management to the Bumiputeras was financed by the government. By 1990, despite these changes, dualism persisted. There was some convergence in terms of productivity between smallholders on managed land (e.g., for oil palms) developed by the state and large estates, but dualism was still stark.

Agriculture's substantial but declining contribution to industrialization. In the first two decades after independence (1957), the 6–8 percent per year agricultural growth rates did contribute to investment in the non-agricultural economy through commodity export taxes. Effective rates of protection for rubber, oil palm, and cocoa were negative. To achieve the goal of rice self-sufficiency, paddy was protected. Effective protection was positive, except for some brief periods. The negative net transfer out of agriculture from 1960 to 1983 averaged 6 percent of the agricultural GDP (Jenkins and Lai, 1989: Tab.18c). Agriculture's contribution to direct taxation shrank from 9 percent of GDP in 1980 to 1 percent by 1995 (Abdul Aziz, 1998: 59–76, table 5).

Does the Malaysian case support, undermine, or modify the pro-agriculture position? The Malaysian case supports but also modifies the pro-agriculture position. It illustrates combination Pro-Ag 1 and refutes the anti-agriculture view. It showed no combination of (a) sustained high output and productivity growth in agriculture with persistent high rates of rural poverty and mediocre overall economic growth or (b) stagnant low-productivity agriculture with high rates of overall economic growth and low(er) rates of rural poverty. Instead, Malaysia sustained agricultural output and productivity growth (though declining over the years) with significant decreases in rural poverty and sustained high overall growth, resulting in rapid economic transformation in about four decades. Thus agricultural growth made a substantial though declining contribution to the transformation of the Malaysian economy and the reduction of rural poverty. It modifies the pro-agriculture view because in addition to agriculture's contribution, the leadership tapped other lucrative sources to finance its investment and development plans, such as oil, liquefied natural gas, and timber. Resource-based revenue remained a principal source of revenue for the federal government and state treasuries. Unlike many other resource-rich economies, Malaysia invested the resource rents not only in the extractive industries themselves, but also in delivering basic public goods and services (Vincent and Ali, 1997: figs. 1.5–1.7). Thus the Malaysian case does not fit the "squeeze agriculture" model, given government's substantial reinvestment in agriculture. In addition, Malaysia was successful in attracting FDI for investment, especially in manufacturing. By 1988, foreign equity as a percentage of total equity was around 58 percent (Jomo, 1993: table 3.1). From its past as a major trading center, Malaysia is still an open economy, with non-agricultural exports increasingly important earners of foreign exchange. During the earlier decades, Malaysia relied heavily on direct and indirect taxation of agriculture for public investment in the economy. In later years, agriculture's continued development benefited from being integrated into a high-growth economy. While it taxed agriculture, the government also invested in agriculture in terms of public goods and services and in terms of programs for assisting Bumiputeras.

II.IX. Tunisia – GNI per capita: USD 3,720 (2009)

Introduction. The case of Tunisia provides a contrast to Malaysia in terms of how government has promoted agricultural development to deal with high income inequality in a fairly homogeneous Arab society. Both governments were interventionist, but the specific approaches were different, and the developmental achievements, though different too, were substantial. The main question addressed here is: What was the contribution, if any, of Tunisia's sustained agricultural development to these achievements? Which of the polar views is supported, refuted, or modified?

Brief background. Today, more than 50 years after independence from France in 1956, Tunisia's development achievements are noteworthy. Until the uprisings of December 2010 (which continued into January 2011), Tunisia succeeded in maintaining, political and social stability in a region that has known significant turmoil. For decades, as a moderate Arab country in North Africa, Tunisia was viewed as an island of stability. Unfortunately this stability was not anchored in widely shared and dynamic growth. In January 2011, this seething discontent overturned a leadership which had opted for a *dirigiste* economic system, concentrating power and privilege, maintaining significant public ownership of financial institutions, manufacturing industries, and marketing companies, among other things. In the 1960s and 1970s, its economy and exports were dominated by the production of oil, natural gas, and phosphates. However, since the mid-1980s, Tunisia has become a minor net exporter of energy (Joint World Bank–Islamic Bank, 2005: table 1.1).[56] Like most developing countries, it adopted the inward-oriented ISI strategy, but since the 1990s it has been gradually opening up. The ratio of imports or exports of goods and services to GDP was around 0.4 in the late 1990s. In donor circles, the pro-Western Tunisian leadership and administration was appreciated for being stable, committed, and competent. The overthrow of Zine El Abidine Ben Ali's government (1987–2011) clearly shattered this positive image and calls for a re-assessment of what Tunisia is well known for sustained economic growth (though not spectacular like

---

[56] Oil product exports declined from 52.5 percent of total export earnings in 1980 to 9.2 percent in 2001.

South Korea's and, more recently, China's) and for major progress in socio-economic development, including a substantial reduction in poverty incidence despite significant inequality (e.g., a Gini coefficient of around 0.40 in 2000) (Joint World Bank–Islamic Bank, 2005: table 1.3)[57] (see Figures 2.25, 2.26, and 2.27).

Growth performance since the 1960s. The high growth of the 1970s was dominated by the oil boom and therefore the receipt of high oil export revenues. However, when oil prices declined in the 1980s, the government maintained high levels of investments and expenditures. As a result, financial crises ensued in the mid-1980s – high inflation (10 percent), high current deficits (11 percent of GDP), and high external debt (46 percent of GDP). These crises proved to be a turning point for Tunisia. Faced with deepening macroeconomic imbalances, Tunisia adopted a program of stabilization and adjustment, resulting in sustained annual growth rates of 3–4 percent until the mid-1990s. In 1995, Tunisia decided to increase its integration into the world economy. It signed the Association Agreement with the EU, which contains a 12-year (1996–2008) phased establishment of a free trade zone for manufactures. Despite this agreement and other bilateral trade agreements (e.g., with Morocco, Syria, Jordan, Iraq), Tunisia's most-favored-nation (MFN) tariffs are still high compared with those of other EU neighborhood countries. In particular, the liberalization of services (e.g., transport and distribution) remains very limited. The import of several important products of mass consumption – for example, cereals, sugar, tea, petroleum products, seed oils, and drugs – is still monopolized by state trading companies or public enterprises (World Bank, May 2005: 6, paras 16, 17) (see Figures 2.25 and 2.26).

Substantial socio-economic progress on several fronts. Poverty incidence fell from 40 percent in the 1960s to around 4 percent by 2000. The bulk of poverty remains rural, about 80 percent of total (World Bank, May 2005: fig. 1.1). In addition to reducing poverty, Tunisia is well known for its solid human development achievements, including its treatment

---

[57] There are other estimates of income inequality. For example, the Gini coefficient for income inequality for urban Tunisia (1985) is 0.6; that for rural Tunisia is 0.45 (Radwan, Jamal, and Ghose, 1991: 49).

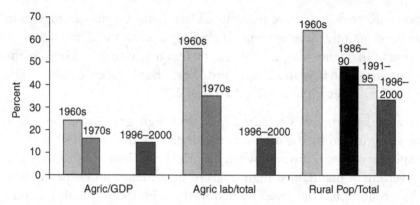

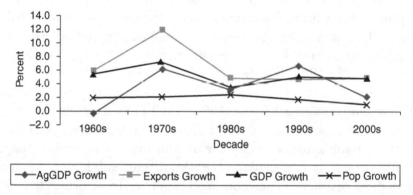

Figure 2.25. Tunisia: agricultural contribution to GDP, labor, and population (1960s–2000).

Figure 2.26. Tunisia: growth rates of selected economic indicators (percent per year, 1960s–2000s).

Sources and Notes:

Agric/GDP: 1960s, 1970s – World Bank. Kevin Cleaver. 1982. *The Agricultural Development Experience of Algeria, Morocco and Tunisia.* Staff Working Paper 552. Para 2.05. 1996–2000: World Bank Operations Evaluation Department. 2004. *Tunisia: Rural Development and Poverty Reduction 1990–2003.* Para 2.

Agric labor/total labor: 1960s, 1970s – World Bank. Kevin Cleaver. 1982. *The Agricultural Development Experience of Algeria, Morocco and Tunisia.* Staff Working Paper 552. Para 2.05.1996–2000: World Bank. *Tunisia: Agricultural Policy Review.* Decision Draft. Report # 35239-TN. Executive Summary, pp v.

Rural/urban ratio: 1960s, 1980s – World Bank. Kevin Cleaver. 1982. *The Agricultural Development Experience of Algeria, Morocco and Tunisia.* Staff Working Paper 552. Para 2.16. 1991–95: World Bank. 1995. *Tunisia – Poverty Alleviation: Preserving progress while preparing for the future.* Report no. 13993-TN. Pp 14, para 2.11. 1996–2000: World Bank. Tunisia at a Glance (2002).

GDP growth: WDI selected years.

Exports growth: WDI selected years.

Agric growth: WDI selected years.

Pop Growth: WDI selected years.

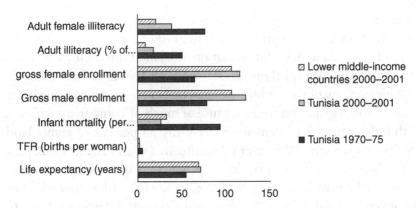

Figure 2.27. Selected human development indicators in Tunisia and in lower-middle-income countries (1970–75, 2000–01).
Source and Note: Joint World Bank-Islamic Development Bank Evaluation of Assistance. 2005. *Tunisia: Understanding Successful Socioeconomic Development.* Table 1.4.

TFR: Total fertility rate

of girls and women. For example, Tunisian women got the right to vote right after independence. The gap between girls and boys in basic education is low. More than half of university students are women. More generally, life expectancy at birth has risen and infant mortality has fallen. Adult illiteracy has decreased substantially, although there is still plenty of room for improvement. The substantial progress achieved on several fronts can be seen by recalling the situation some 30 years ago and by comparing Tunisia with the average for other lower-middle-income countries (however, progress on reducing adult illiteracy still has some way to go when compared with the average of other lower-middle-income groups) (see Figure 2.27).

Importance, structure, and performance of agriculture. In the 1950s, agriculture was a major sector, accounting for nearly a quarter of GDP. For a long time, the main objectives for the sector have been to (a) increase food self-sufficiency (hence the importance attached to cereals cultivation), (b) manage agriculture's fragile natural resources in a sustainable fashion, (c) increase employment and reduce rural–urban migration, and (d) reduce rural poverty. About 70 percent of agricultural production is in cereals, tree crops, fruits, vegetables, livestock products, and fisheries. By 2007, agriculture's contribution to GDP had fallen to an estimated 11 percent of GDP. Agriculture was no longer a major sector, but it has remained a strategic sector because it has the all-important cereals sector and is home to most of the poor. It is dualistic, with a highly skewed land distribution, the land Gini coefficient being at around 0.64 (World Bank, 2004b: para 4). The difficulties inherent in achieving any of these objectives can be appreciated when one bears in mind the arid and semi-arid nature of much of Tunisian agriculture, with only around 7 percent irrigated. Only 33 percent of arable land receives more than 400 mm of rain annually (World Bank, 1982: para 4.02). Not surprisingly, agricultural production is vulnerable to wide annual swings, as most of agriculture is rain-fed and semi-arid. Thus the growth of agricultural GDP varied from −9.9 percent (1995) to +30.3 percent (1990, 1996). The coefficient of variation on cereals, for example, is 52 percent (World Bank, June 2000: 8, paras 1–3). The yearly averages in Figure 2.26 should thus be interpreted with these wide fluctuations in mind.

A highly protected agriculture harboring low competitiveness on several fronts. Agriculture went from being a taxed sector in the early 1980s to being a protected sector, despite the recent waves of trade liberalization. Peak tariffs apply to nearly 70 percent of agricultural tariff lines, and applied rates average 67 percent. According to the World Trade Organization, Tunisia's reforms of the past two decades "have not substantially liberalised trade" (World Bank, June 2006a: viii). A major official reason is the pursuit of food self-sufficiency in the context of a highly vulnerable rain-fed agriculture competing against a highly subsidized EU agriculture. Indeed, the international competitiveness of self-sufficiency-related products on small farms is questionable – for example, durum wheat on small farms in arid areas, 44 percent of bread wheat production on small farms, and milk production (World Bank, June 2000: paras 41, 46, 66). Where it is competitive (e.g., most fruits and vegetables), it is underperforming and its EU quotas remain underused. Agricultural protection on cereals is undermining incentives to switch to these higher-value crops. There has been no trend increase in labor productivity over the past decade. Current protection policy imposes substantial costs on the rest of society: Tunisian dinar (TD) 180 million per year in compensation subsidies, 4 percent extra on the cost of living for consumers and taxpayers, and 8 percent of GDP in lost growth thanks to distorted prices. Furthermore, two-fifths of agriculture's growth represents a loss to the economy because it comes from commodities that it would cost less to import (e.g., beef and milk). Average crop yields have grown by around 2.8 percent per year (1989–2003), but what has been the contribution of TFP to total growth is unclear (World Bank, June 2006a: v, para 19). The continued protection of much of agriculture exemplifies a major short-term conflict between increasing competitiveness, on one hand (and thus raising its potential contribution to growth and poverty reduction), and assisting the more vulnerable farm households, on the other. Promoting the former would require further lowering of tariffs, which might in turn hurt, even eliminate, smallholders because they are uncompetitive. Thus there is a short-term conflict in increasing agriculture's contribution to poverty reduction.

Does the Tunisia case support the pro-agriculture position? The answer is no. The Tunisian case is one of substantial reduction in poverty within a context of steady though unspectacular overall GDP growth, with a highly vulnerable agriculture that still has many uncompetitive and low-productivity sub-sectors. Since the 1980s, agriculture has become a protected sector. We do not see scenario (a), but we see a variant of scenario (b), as discussed later. Thus, to recapitulate: (a) sustained high output and productivity growth in agriculture co-existing with persistent high rates of rural poverty and mediocre overall economic growth, and (b) stagnant low-productivity agriculture co-existing with high rates of overall economic growth and low rates of rural poverty.

The driving force behind the substantial socio-economic achievements has been the government's sustained commitment to financing social expenditures, not dynamic agricultural growth. Three distinctive features of the Tunisian experience explain the limitations of the pro-agriculture position in ways that were not emphasized in the early debates (1950s–1960s) on agriculture's role. First, the high variability of agriculture's performance and therefore the high risks involved diminish agriculture's importance. The high risks have encouraged a high rate of rural–urban migration, which is estimated to have contributed significantly to rural poverty reduction (World Bank, May 2005: 22). Second, the government's giving priority to social development and poverty reduction since independence and throughout its structural adjustment programs – for example, by cutting social

expenditures to a lesser extent than other expenditures and by promoting labor-intensive products and activities (e.g., textiles, leather
products, tourism) – was a key factor in Tunisia's achievement in poverty reduction (World Bank, August 1995: paras 6, 7). Third, agriculture, uncompetitive in some major areas, has increasingly become
a protected sector, thus benefiting from rather than generating surplus. The Tunisian case is unique in two additional respects. First, it
exemplifies the short-term conflict between promoting agriculture's
competitive growth (and hence its developmental contribution) and
protecting uncompetitive poor farm households. Second, it shows
what difference the government's giving priority to promoting broad-
based social development can make, despite a highly unequal land and
income distribution.

II.X. Brazil – GNI per capita: USD 8,040 (2009)

Introduction. The case of Brazil provides an interesting comparison
and contrast to the cases of Malaysia and Tunisia with respect to how
governments have dealt with sharp inequality in wealth and income,
in particular how they have dealt with agricultural land distribution.
Given the government's approach to inequality, what contribution, if
any, has agricultural development made to the twin objectives of sustained development of agriculture and rural poverty reduction? The
focus here is on whether the Brazilian experience supports, refutes, or
qualifies either of the polar claims regarding the role of sustained agricultural growth in overall development.

Brief background. Brazil's socio-economic, agricultural, and overall
growth experiences stand in sharp contrast to Tunisia's and Malaysia's.
Until 1980, it was one of the fastest-growing economies (World Bank,
July 1992: 43). Brazil, a country of 192 million people (2008), occupies
nearly half of all the land area of Latin America. Like Malaysia, it is well
endowed with mineral and forestry resources. It is the world's largest
producer of sugarcane and has become a major exporter of orange juice
and soybeans (Baer, 2001: 7).[58] During the food and fuel commodity price spikes of 2008, Brazil came to be known for its sugar-based

---

[58] It is the fifth-largest country after Russia, Canada, China, and the United States. Brazil is
a "large" country (in terms of affecting prices in international trade) in frozen concentrated
orange juice exports and soybeans (after the United States).

ethanol, which it subsidized in the 1970s. Brazil, however, has the dubious distinction of being highly inequitable. Income concentration has decreased somewhat, as shown by the recent income Gini coefficients. They show continued improvement in terms of greater equality from 0.574 (1981) to 0.564 (2004) (World Bank, March 2006: table 1) to 0.552 (2007) (World Bank, April 2009). There are, however, still sharp regional disparities. In the 1990s, per capita income in the northeast was still less than half of the national average, while in the more advanced regions it was more than half the national average (Baer, 2001: 4–5). In 1996, the north and the northeast accounted for 55 percent of the poor, whereas these regions had only 34 percent of the total population (World Bank, February 2006: 5). Of Brazil's 17 million or so rural poor, about 10 million live in the northeast (World Bank, May 2004: 3). The incidence of rural poverty in the northeast is around 49 percent, compared with 24 percent in the rural southeast (World Bank, April 2001: 6).[59] Brazil, an upper-middle-income country, is a land of sharp contrasts. Former president Fernando Enrique Cardoso (1995–2002) once said of his country, "Brazil is not a poor country. It is an unjust one" (Schwartzman, 2000).

Major exporter of primary commodities. Brazil has been a major exporter of many primary (mainly agricultural) commodities since its colonial days. It got its name from the export of brazilwood, which is a bark used as dyestuff in Europe. Sugar, which was introduced around 1520, remained a major export until the early part of the 17th century. In its heyday, the sugar industry was a monopoly of the Portuguese. Since the mid-1970s, Brazil has invested heavily to produce ethanol (from sugar), an alternative to petroleum.[60] In the 17th century, Brazil was valued for its gold mining in Minas Gerais (southeast Brazil) until the second half of the 18th century. Coffee was introduced in the early part of the 18th century as a specialty item and grew rapidly in the 19th century to become a major engine for growth for Brazil. Unlike sugar, which depended mainly on slave labor, coffee had free immigrant labor (mainly from southern and southeastern Europe), as

---

[59] Most of the data come from two household surveys fielded in 1996.

[60] Brazil subsidized both the car industry and sugarcane producers in the 1970s. It no longer subsidizes either. The cost of sugar-based ethanol at USD 1.40 per gallon makes it competitive even when the crude oil price declines to USD 40 per barrel (World Bank, April 2009: 79).

slavery was abolished in 1888. Minor exports were cotton and sugar. More recently, it has become a major exporter of soybeans and frozen concentrated orange juice.

Recurrent political instability until recently. Brazil has had a tumultuous past. It was a colony of Portugal from the 16th century until 1822, after which it became an independent country governed by an emperor until 1889. It was ruled by oligarchic groups until the revolution of 1930. Its first president, Getulio Vargas (elected in 1951, but in power since the revolution), killed himself in 1954. In 1964, there was a military coup. From 1964 to 1984, Brazil was under military rule. Elected presidents followed, but there was little political or financial stability. From 1985 to 1990, Brazil was led by President Jose Sarney, followed by the short-lived tenure of President Fernando Collor de Mello until his impeachment in 1992 (for corruption), then Itamar Franco until 1994, and Fernando Henrique Cardoso until 2002. In January 2003, Brazil's new president was Luiz Inacio Lula da Silva, who was re-elected for a second and last term in 2007–2010. He was succeeded by Brazil's first female president, Dilma Roussef, January 1, 2011.

Uneven but continued socio-economic development, especially since the early 2000s. Income inequality in Brazil is high even by Latin American standards. Income differences among the Brazilian population by gender and skin color account for an important part of overall income inequality, and this is due to disadvantages in wages, schooling, or both (World Bank, July 2004: xviii). One may argue that inequality per se is not a problem unless there is extensive poverty coexisting with extreme wealth. And there is extensive poverty in Brazil, although there has been a substantial decline in poverty since 2001. Poverty fell from 34.1 percent in 2003 to 29.5 percent in 2005, and extreme poverty from 14.5 percent to 11 percent over the same period (World Bank and International Finance Corporation, 2007: 56).[61] The main message with regard to poverty incidence is that it is still high, but progress in its reduction, slow between 1980 and 2000, has quickened subsequently (2003–2007). A major factor contributing to recent progress

[61] Note that the poverty incidence estimates are somewhat different between the two World Bank sources, because the poverty lines used are different. However, the message of a substantial fall in poverty incidence is the same.

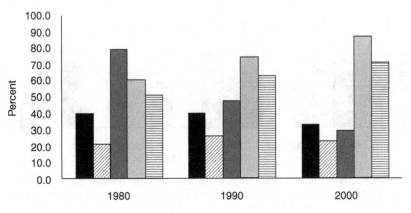

Figure 2.28. Brazil: selected socio-economic indicators (1980–2000).
Sources and Notes: World Bank. January 2004. *Brazil: Country Assistance Evaluation*. Report no. 27629-BA. Table 9.

Poverty incidence: Population below national poverty line is 22 per cent for 2001–2007. *Source*: World Bank. Brazil at a glance. 09–24–2008. Using the World Bank's definition of poverty as "less than one dollar per day", poverty headcount ratio fell from 14 to 8 percent between 1990 and 2004. *Source*: World Bank, IFC, 2007.

is the *Bolsa Familia*, a federally funded program of monthly cash payments to more than 11 million poor families who keep their children in school and under regular medical supervision. Until 2001 the socio-economic development of Brazil, an upper-middle-income country, stood in sharp contrast to Tunisia's, which was well above the average for lower-middle-income countries. However, in recent years, the Lula government's emphasis on reducing inequality and poverty through social programs resembles Tunisia's emphasis on social improvements (see Figure 2.28). These are indicative of the progress (before Lula's second term) in poverty reduction and its differential pace among groups.

Despite continued growth, little resilience to oil price shocks of the 1970s. From the end of WWII to 1979, GDP growth accelerated to 7.1 percent per year, with industrial growth at 9 percent and agricultural

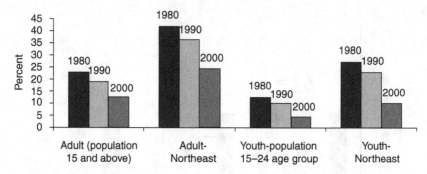

Figure 2.29. Brazil: illiteracy rate – adult, youth, and Northeast (percent, 1980, 1990, 2000).
Source: World Bank. January 14, 2004. *Brazil: Country Assistance Evaluation*. Report no. 27629-BA.
Table 9.

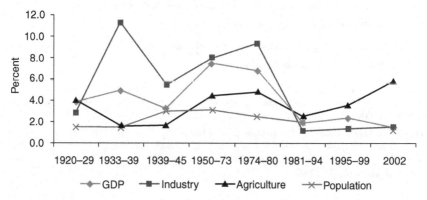

Figure 2.30. Brazil: annual growth rates of GDP, industry, agriculture, and population
(1920–2002).

growth at around 5 percent. The years from 1968 to 1973 were considered "miracle" years, as industrial growth was nearly 13 percent per
year and agricultural growth was 5.5 percent per year. The rate of GDP
growth from 1974 to 1979 dropped to 7 percent a year after the first
oil price shock of 1973. After the second oil price shock of 1979, however, growth plummeted. In 1981, for the first time GDP growth was
only 1 percent, and in 1983 it was –3.2 percent. In the 1970s after the
oil price shocks, inflation rose to 110 percent in 1980 and more than
200 percent by 1983 (World Bank, November 1991: 7–8)! Successive
governments tried to tame and control inflation, but with little success.
For an overview of Brazil's economic performance over decades until
2002, see Figures 2.29, 2.30, and 2.31.

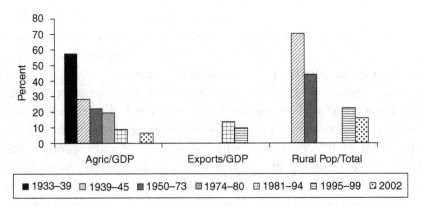

Figure 2.31. Brazil: selected socio-economic indicators (ratios) (1933–2002).
Sources and Notes:
Growth rates:
GDP: 1920–45 – Baer, Werner. 2001. *The Brazilian Economy: Growth and Development*. Praeger Publishers. 5th Edition. pp 39. 1950–2002: World Bank. January 14, 2004. *Brazil: Country Assistance Evaluation*. Report no. 27629-BA. Table 1. For the sub-period 1968–74, the annual growth averaged 11.3 percent.

Industry: 1920–45 – Baer, Werner. 2001. *The Brazilian Economy: Growth and Development*. Praeger Publishers. 5th Edition. pp 39. 1950–73: an arithmetical average of 1964 to 1973. Source: Abreu, Marcelo de P., Afonso S. Bevilaqua and Demosthenes M. Pinho. 1997. "Import substitution and growth in Brazil, 1890s – 1970s". Revised paper presented at a meeting in Paipa, Colombia, May 2–3, 1997, on Industrialization and the State in Latin America, part of the IDB Project on the Economic History of Latin America in the 20th century. http://www.econ.puc-rio.br/mpabreu/pdf/td366.pdf . 1971–94, 1995–99: Baer, Werner. 2001. *The Brazilian Economy: Growth and Development*. Praeger Publishers. 5th Edition. Appendix table A.1. 2002: World Bank. Brazil at a Glance. (09/03/2003).

Agriculture: 1920–45 – Baer, Werner. 2001. *The Brazilian Economy: Growth and Development*. Praeger Publishers. 5th Edition. pp 39. 1950–73, 1971–94: Baer, Werner. 2001. *The Brazilian Economy: Growth and Development*. Praeger Publishers. 5th Edition. pp. 66, Appendix table A.1. 1995–99, 2002: World Bank. Brazil at a Glance. (09/03/2003).

Population: 1920–45 – Schuh, G. Edward in collaboration with Alves, Eliseu Roberto. *The Agricultural Development of Brazil*. Praeger Publishers, New York, Washington, London. 1970. pp 27. 1950s to 1980s: Baer, Werner. 2001. *The Brazilian Economy: Growth and Development*. Praeger Publishers. 5th Edition. Pp 66, 8. For 1998–2004: World Bank. Brazil at a Glance 03/14/06.

Ratios:

Agric/GDP: 1933–39, 1939–45 – Baer, Werner. 2001. *The Brazilian Economy: Growth and Development*. Praeger Publishers. 5th Edition. pp 39, 47. For 1966 (in 1953 constant prices) – Baer, Werner. 2001. *The Brazilian Economy: Growth and Development*. Praeger Publishers. 5th Edition. Table 4.5. For 1974–80: Baer, Werner. *The Brazilian Economy: Growth and Development*. Praeger Publishers. 5th Edition. 2001. Appendix Table A.1. For 1982, 2002: World Bank. Brazil at a Glance. (09/03/2003)

Exports/GDP: Exports of goods and services/GDP: World Bank. Brazil at a Glance 03/14/06. The estimates are for 1984, 1994, 2003 (16.4), and 2004 (18.0).

Rural/urban population ratio: 1939–1999 – Baer, Werner. 2001. *The Brazilian Economy: Growth and Development*. Praeger Publishers. 5th Edition. Pp 3. 2001/02: World Bank. 2006. *Structural Change and Poverty Reduction in Brazil: The Impact of the Doha Round*. Staff Working Paper 3833. Pp 7.

Per capita GDP is estimated to have grown by 3.3 percent per year since 1930. World Bank. 1992. *The Political Economy of Poverty, Equity, and Growth: Brazil and Mexico*. Angus Maddison and Associates. Oxford University Press. Published for the World Bank. pp 43.

The failure of repeated attempts to control inflation until the late 1990s. Brazil's repeated struggles with controlling inflation show clearly that Brazil did not have the macro stability framework essential for uninterrupted growth and development necessary for broad-based poverty reduction. In February 1986, President Sarney proposed the Cruzado Plan I to combat inflation. Plan I allowed real wages of the poor classes to go up relative to other prices. Inflation, which abated for a while, came back with a vengeance. Brazil's economy was hit with the double problem of inflation and stagnation until 1993, despite further attempts to control inflation. After an initial lowering of inflation, the Collor Plan I in March 1990 too failed. The *Plano Real*, introduced in 1993, was an austerity plan that contained a fiscal adjustment plan and a new indexing system to gradually introduce a new currency, the URV (unidade real de valor). Inflation was reduced from 1995 to 1998. However, the fiscal adjustment was not substantial, and the government could not get through the reform of the civil service and the required accompanying reduction in personnel and salaries. Growth, which was high at 5.9 percent in 1994, declined to 0.2 percent by 1998 (Baer, 2001: 212). The Asian financial crisis of 1997–99 then exploded, leading to major outflows of foreign capital from Brazil. The major features of the *Plano Real*, in particular overvalued exchange rates and high interest rates, could not be sustained. The real was devalued by 40 percent (Baer, 2001: 216). However, this did not lead to substantial inflation, as there was high unemployment and underutilized capacity in the system. Failure to control inflation hurt the poor the most. More recently, under the Lula government, inflation fell steadily to a little more than 3 percent in 2006 (World Bank and International Finance Corporation, 2007: 45).[62]

Importance, structure, and performance of agriculture. Agriculture shrank from nearly 60 percent of GDP in the 1930s to around 10 percent in the mid-1980s and to 5 percent in 2007. The decline is no surprise, as the shrinkage of agriculture's contribution to GDP is a universal feature of industrializing economies. Its contribution to total employment also shrank, from nearly 60 percent in the 1950s to 30 percent

---

[62] The Lula government achieved a primary budget surplus even exceeding the target set by the IMF by the third year in office.

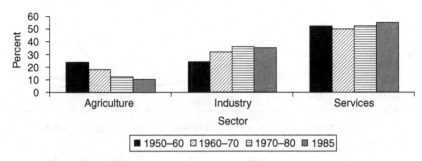

Figure 2.32. Post-WWII Brazil: sector shares in total output (1960–85).

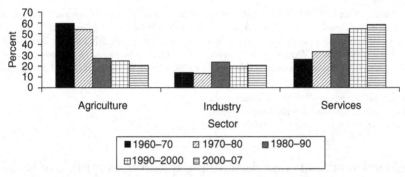

Figure 2.33. Post-WWII Brazil: sector shares in employment (1950–2007).

in the mid-1980s. This decline is also to be expected. However, when 30 percent of the labor force is producing only 10 percent of GDP (mid-1980s), this imbalance suggests that there is a problem of low labor productivity, in other words, of surplus labor. And there is this problem in Brazil, a problem exacerbated by agricultural policies that promoted capital intensity in a dualistic agriculture. See Figures 2.32, 2.33, and 2.34.

In 1987, average labor productivity in agriculture was roughly 43 percent of the national average (World Bank, July 1990: para 1.17). Yearly growth rates averaged 4 percent in the 1970s and 1980s but declined in the 1990s. Most of the growth that occurred from 1965 to 1980 came almost entirely from non-traditional export crops of soybeans (mainly in the center-west) and oranges (specifically frozen concentrated orange juice). Growth of these crops in turn came almost entirely from area expansion as opposed to increases in yields (which started only in the 1980s). In contrast to this expansion, the

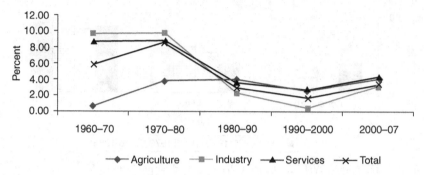

Figure 2.34. Post-WWII Brazil: sector growth rates (annual averages, 1960–2007).
Sources and Notes:
Agriculture/GDP: 1930–52 – Baer, Werner. 2001. *The Brazilian Economy: Growth and Development.*
Praeger Publishers. 5th Edition. pp 39, 47. For 1966 (in 1953 constant prices) – Baer, Werner.
The Brazilian Economy: Growth and Development. Praeger Publishers. 5th Edition. 2001. Table
4.5. For 1974–80: Baer, Werner. 2001. *The Brazilian Economy: Growth and Development.* Praeger
Publishers. 5th Edition. Appendix Table A.1. For 1982, 2002: World Bank. Brazil at a glance.
(09/03/2003).

Industry/GDP, Services/GDP: WDI respective years.
Sector shares in employment: WDI respective years.
Sector growth rates: WDI respective years.

production of food crops declined precipitously, except that of wheat,
which was heavily subsidized. Food production as a percentage of total
crop production declined from 36 percent in 1965 to 25 percent in
1980 (World Bank, July 1990: paras 2.04–2.05). By the early 2000s,
an important structural change had occurred: the agro-business sector
(primary agriculture plus agro-processing and distribution) accounted
for 25 percent of GDP and 35 percent of total employment (USDA,
2009: Brazil).

*Reducing skewed agricultural land distribution under two different
approaches to land reform.* Agricultural land distribution is an explosive
issue in many parts of the world. It is no different in Brazil, known
for having one of the most inequitable land distributions in the world.
The country's largest farms, of 1,000 ha or more, constitute only 1.6
percent of all farms but hold 53.2 of all agricultural land. The largest
75 farms, with 100,000 ha or more, control more than five times the
combined area of all small farms. Some 43 percent of land is not cultivated, and among Brazil's largest landholdings of 1,000 ha or more,
88.7 percent of arable land is permanently idle (Langevin and Rosset,

1997).[63] By 2002, the estimate was that more than 60 percent of farmland was idle (Frank, 2002). Some estimates suggest that farm returns for approximately 70 percent of family farms in Brazil are below the minimum wage per worker[64] (World Bank, April 2001: 25). Land reform in Brazil is regulated by the *Estatuto da Terra* of 1964, signed into law at the beginning of Brazil's military dictatorship. The law established that the federal government could expropriate unproductive or over-large landholdings (*latifúndia*) for the purpose of land reform and indemnify the owners with government bonds. However, the political power of Brazil's large landowners effectively precluded significant action on land reform during the military dictatorship. When the military stepped down in 1985, the civilian government announced an ambitious goal of settling 1.4 million landless families on 43 million ha over four years. However, by 1989, only a fraction of this objective was achieved – some 82,000 families were settled on 4.3 million ha (Schwartzman, 2000). Two approaches to land reform have been used.

1. *Expropriation and violence*: The pace of expropriation and settlement of poor families quickened between 1995 and 1999, under the large-scale and violent tactics of various labor organizations, in particular the Landless Rural Workers Movement (MST),[65] and the National Confederation of Agricultural Workers, which organized marginalized rural labor to occupy idle lands. This approach is confrontational. Its proponents argue that, left to its own, the federal government would give in to the interests of the landed elite, well represented in government, and would not implement its own law of 1964.

2. *Market-based land reform*: The World Bank introduced the concept of market-based land reform according to which associations of potential beneficiaries would be assisted in purchasing land. The Bank claims that its project, *Cedula da Terra* (Land Title, 1997),

---

[63] In 1996, almost 50 percent of agricultural establishments were smaller than 10 ha, occupied only 2.25 percent of total area farmed, and accounted for only 12 percent of gross farm output. By contrast, less than 11 percent of farms were larger than 100 ha but occupied 80 percent of land farmed (World Bank, April 2001: para 43). Thus, although the two sources highlight different data, the message of the sharp inequality of land distribution is the same.

[64] IPEA/World Bank/Ministerio do Desenvolvimento Agrario, Rio, August 2000.

[65] Movimento dos Trabalhadores Rurais Sem Terra.

is participatory: "The [*Cedula*] program represents the ultimate participatory process, says its manager, Luis Coirolo, because it revolves completely around its beneficiaries: They choose the land and negotiate its purchase. They decide how to use the land, what investments are required to make it productive and what technical assistance they will need." The idea that associations of the rural poor and landless negotiate directly with landowners, select the lands that best suit their needs, and purchase them at their market value is indeed at the heart of the program (Schwartzman, 2000).

Criticisms of the World Bank approach and of progress under Lula's first term (2003–2006). Non-confrontational approaches have been criticized. The World Bank's approach has been challenged on two main grounds:

1. Even if one accepts the World Bank's own evaluation,[66] that the two projects (the *Ceara Reducao da Pobreza Rural* and the *Cedula da Terra*) are successful, their scale of impact (a total of approximately 640,000 ha benefitting 23,700 households by the early 2000s) is minuscule – only 1 percent in the context of the nearly 10 million rural poor (World Bank, April 2001: 26).

2. The World Bank's approach is "subversive" (Plevin, 1999) because it relieves the government of its own legal obligation to expropriate "unproductive" land and increases the national debt, since landowners receive cash instead of government bonds. These critics argue that the Bank's approach is well liked by landowners, who receive cash instead of government bonds, can negotiate the prices with government officials rather than with potential beneficiaries who in fact have little participation, and often have little understanding of the entire process. In reality, this approach enables these large landowners to unload poor-quality land at inflated prices. The negotiated prices of land are not market prices; rather they reflect the unbalanced bargaining power of the landlords and the land poor. There is no open market for land in places where the *Cedula da Terra* operates.

---

[66] The World Bank's operations are routinely evaluated by the Independent Evaluation Group (IEG), formerly called Operations Evaluation Department (OED).

MST has not ceased to organize forced expropriations. The struggle for more land is now also against big agro-business closely allied to big landowners. The MST argues that little was achieved for the landless during Lula's first term. However, this has been disputed by the government. According to the Ministry of Agrarian Development, some 382,000 families have been given a plot of land. The goal was to distribute land to 400,000 families during Lula's first term. During that same period, the National Programme for Strengthening Family Farming (PRONAF) quadrupled the funding to agriculture, benefiting 1.9 million families; the government significantly increased the budget for the National Institute for Colonisation and Agrarian Reform (INCRA), strengthened institutions of land reform, and supported mechanisms for providing training to small farmers through extension programs (Osava, 2007). MST argues that a speedier and broader agrarian reform is required, while opponents of land reform argue that land reform has spread poverty, not wealth. So there is as yet no consensus on the progress achieved by land reform in Brazil.

Highly dualistic agriculture with two very different market orientations. Whatever the achievements of land redistribution, it has not removed dualism in Brazilian agriculture. The aggregate growth figures mask the differing performances of the two Brazilian agricultures: the large, plantation-style estates, which are high growth and are largely export-oriented, co-existing with the smallholder farm household type, either subsistence or domestic-oriented (see Figure 2.30). The first type has experienced well-known (though short-lived) commodity booms, which fueled exports for a long time – for example, sugar, coffee, and to a lesser extent cotton, cocoa, and rubber. The first type also includes large beef cattle ranches.[67] The livestock sector contributed to around 40 percent of the agricultural GDP (1980s). In the 1980s, more than 70 percent of livestock output came from extensive ranches, using traditional low-productivity technologies. In addition to logging and mining, these ranches are a major contributor to deforestation, an issue that has gained national and international attention (World Bank, May 1991: i–iv).[68] The large farms have made Brazil a major agricultural

---

[67] Cattle constitute the most important livestock activity followed by swine and poultry.

[68] Greenpeace bestowed its "Golden Chainsaw" award, for the Brazilian voted most responsible for Amazon destruction, on Blairo Maggi, the governor of Mato Grosso and owner of a farming concern that controls nearly 500,000 acres of soy, cotton, and corn plantings (Chu and Hirsch, 2005).

exporting nation, an "agricultural superpower," in, for example, orange juice, soybeans, soybean meal, soybean oil, sugar, chicken, coffee, beef, and pork (Chu and Hirsch, 2005). The technologies adopted have become increasingly capital-intensive or labor-saving over the years, with adverse consequences for the structure of employment, such as an increase in temporary, wage-earning employment. Distortions in technology adoption combined with the functioning of land markets, the structure of landownership, as well as the functioning of labor and land laws tend to sharpen the dualism between the minority class of large landowners and the majority of smallholders, semi-subsistence farms, and landless wage laborers. The employment potential of agriculture was also being undermined.

Dualism generated by structural and policy factors. The dualism characteristic of Brazilian agriculture has its roots in the colonial period of land grants. However, subsequent policy did not reduce it. There are seven major reasons. First, large landowners had incentives to invest in and expand their landholdings, as the resulting earnings would be tax-exempt. The rapid expansion of the highway network facilitated a 3.2 percent expansion rate of cropland, from 19.1 million ha in 1950 to 49.2 million ha in 1980 (World Bank, July 1992: 65). Second, continued high inflation makes land a perfect anti-inflation hedge and store of value, thus increasing incentives to amass huge holdings. Third, legislation on renting and sharecropping determines ceilings on rents and crop shares and provides permanent rights to tenants after a few years. Thus large landowners have been afraid of renting out their land for fear that the tenants would claim the land as theirs (World Bank, July 1994: paras 7.5, 7.6). Fourth, labor legislation in 1963 (*Estatuto do Trabalhador Rural*) that extended the benefits that protect urban labor to rural labor had the counterproductive effect of eliminating the traditional benefits to peasants from landlords, thus hastening the process of the proletarianization of rural labor. This in turn accelerated rural–urban migration. Fifth, the scale of resettlement under the Land Reform Law of 1964 was modest. The program lacked credibility in view of delays, cost overruns, allegations of corruption, and the like. Thus more than 40 years after the Land Reform Law, it has done little to redress the sharp inequalities in land distribution. Sixth, delivery of important agricultural services, such as research and extension and credit, were biased in favor of large farms (World Bank, July 1992: 67–69). Seventh, the inability of successive governments until the 1990s to invest in basic education for all perpetuated the highly skewed land and income distribution inherited from colonial times (World Bank, 2004c: 24). There have been significant recent improvements in coverage. The literacy rate (of the population age 15 and above) has reached 87 percent, and the gross primary enrollment rate averaged 137 percent (2001–2007).[69]

Extensive policy distortions until the reforms of 1987–92. The central objective of agricultural policy up to the 1960s and 1970s was to guarantee a stable and affordable food supply for the growing urban/industrial sector, the priority sector. Since the 1950s, agriculture has been discriminated against within an ISI strategy, the major source of discrimination being high tariffs and chronically overvalued exchange rates. There was thus a strong anti-export bias facing Brazilian agriculture (Baumann, 2002: 208–209). Outputs were implicitly and explicitly taxed; however, inputs were heavily subsidized, especially credit, not only at low nominal interest rates but at negative real rates. Researchers estimated that the resource transfer from the taxation without the credit subsidy amounted to roughly 8.9 percent of agricultural GDP for the 1975–83 period. However, if the credit subsidies are factored in, then agriculture got back some 8 percent of its GDP (1975–83) (World Bank, 2003b: 54–55). The credit subsidies were capitalized in the value of the land, which again benefited the minority of large landowners. They also encouraged capital intensity, thus undermining labor absorption and poverty reduction. In addition to these major price distortions, the government also intervened extensively in price setting, marketing, and storage.

The major reforms of 1987–92 affecting agriculture. As part of a stabilization and liberalization package agreed upon with the International Monetary Fund and the World Bank, Brazil undertook reforms that (a) removed most of the barriers to foreign trade affecting agriculture – for example, eliminating the system of foreign exchange allocation and gradually liberalizing the capital account, reducing tariffs on imported inputs (effective tariffs were reduced from around 70 percent in 1987

[69] World Bank, "Brazil at a Glance," September 24, 2008.

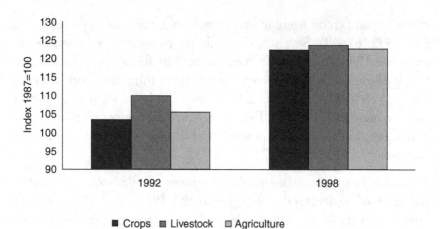

Figure 2.35. Brazil: productivity indexes for crops, livestock, and agriculture (1987 = 100, 1987–98).
Source: Bauman, Renato. 2002. *Brazil in the 1990s: An economy in transition*. Palgrave in association with St. Anthony's College, Oxford. Table 6.6.

to 15 percent in 1995) (World Bank, 2004c: fig. 22), as well as insti-tuting quantitative restrictions and eliminating taxes on exports and prior licenses; (b) removed the Brazilian government's instruments of direct market interventions and replaced them with a system of price bands – for example, eliminating the Minimum Price Program (which was unaffordable anyway by the late 1980s because of severe fiscal problems) for purchases of major grain and food crops. Subsidies for export crops, and credit for storage loans were also eliminated; and (c) dismantled state monopolies in agriculture – for example, in sugar and alcohol, coffee and wheat.

Positive impact of the reforms on agriculture. The impact of agricultural reforms on overall output and productivity growth was positive. They contributed to making large-farmer Brazilian agriculture export-ori-ented. Figure 2.30 indicates that agricultural growth since the 1990s increased relative to the earlier 1980s – around 2 percent per year. A crop and livestock productivity index with 1987 = 100 shows that growth in productivity was substantial (see Figure 2.35).

The productivity gains were mainly for major domestic food crops (e.g., rice and maize), for some major export crops such as cot-ton and soybean, but not for others, such as coffee and cocoa. Terms of trade improved for agriculture: with 1987 = 100, the index for

1998 = 129.9. The terms of trade improvement, however, benefited mainly large farms that used imported inputs. In 1995, a small fraction of the farms were responsible for the bulk of the production: An estimated 10.7 percent of farms or agricultural establishments with more than 100 ha were responsible for 53 percent of the production registered in the 1995–96 census (World Bank, 2003b: 63–63, 117–18). The impact on rural employment was, however, negative. Agricultural employment shrank by 23 percent between 1985 and 1996, while aggregate output expanded by 30 percent during the same period. The brunt of this adjustment was borne by family farm units (not large estates) and was more severe where per capita income was lowest, the northeast region (Baumann, 2002: 221–26). Thus again, the benefits of growth were skewed in favor of the better off. Therefore, whether Brazilian agriculture is under a *dirigiste* or a market-oriented and more open regime, the benefits of growth have largely bypassed the rural poor!

Does the Brazilian case support the pro-agriculture position? The answer is no; the Brazilian case refutes it. Two basic considerations are relevant. First, there are two Brazilian agricultures, not one.[70] There is the large-farmer, capital-intensive, and export-oriented one and the smallholder, traditional, domestic-market-oriented one. Second, economic performance for agriculture and the overall economy has been characterized by booms and busts; so it is hard to talk of "sustained growth performance" over decades. With respect to the large-farmer agriculture during its periods of boom, it had contributed to the overall economic development of Brazil since colonial times, but its contribution decreased after WWII under the ISI strategy that taxed and subsidized agriculture. However, several factors undermined its contribution to rural poverty reduction, in particular the high degree of inequality in land distribution exacerbated by rules that were intended to protect farm labor but in fact harmed labor's interest and the implementation of an ineffective land reform (1964). Thus (a) sustained high output and productivity growth in agriculture co-existing with persistent

---

[70] Some have argued that Brazil in the 1980s was really two Brazils, which some economists called "Bel-India" (the southern and the southeastern regions being "Belgium," and the northeastern region being "India"). "Bel-India" was coined by Edmar Lisboa, former government official and scholar (World Bank, Jan 2008: 82).

high rates of rural poverty and mediocre overall economic growth did materialize during sub-periods. The development of large-farm agriculture supports the anti-agriculture position (combination Anti-Ag 1). Furthermore, (b) stagnant low-productivity agriculture co-existing with high rates of overall economic growth and low(er) rates of rural poverty describes at times the situation of smallholder traditional agriculture. The performance of smallholder agriculture supports the anti-agriculture position too (combination Anti-Ag 2).

The low productivity of this agriculture has contributed to the high rate of rural–urban migration, thus "exporting" rural poverty to urban areas. Since the mid-1990s, agriculture's contribution to overall GDP averaged 5 percent; thus whatever impact its growth had on rural poverty reduction has also substantially diminished. In recent years, export-oriented large-farmer agriculture did well, with overall growth averaging 2.8 percent (1997–2007). However, this growth has benefited the poor more than the rich (2001–2006) (World Bank, January 2008: fig. 1). So although recent overall growth was modest – 2.8 percent (1997–2007)[71] – Brazil has made significant progress in reducing poverty and inequality through major social programs. Whatever causal link existed between agricultural growth and rural poverty reduction has been weakened by dualism and, over time, by agriculture's diminished role in the economy. In terms of poverty reduction, what mattered most in recent years was the priority given by Lula's government to social programs designed to assist the poor.

Summary. Large-farmer Brazilian agriculture did contribute to overall economic development, but its contribution to rural poverty reduction was highly constrained by structural and policy factors. The Brazilian case clearly shows that it is not just growth, but its composition and how it is achieved, that matters. Agricultural growth need not contribute to the twin objectives of overall growth and poverty reduction.

Brazil's experience in this respect provides an interesting contrast to that of Malaysia. Both share several important structural characteristics, namely dualism, land abundance and rich endowment of natural resources, and importance as a commodity exporter, with agricultural exports being major sources of growth and of foreign exchange earnings for a long time. However, a distinguishing difference is the

---

[71] World Bank, Brazil at a Glance," September 24, 2008.

importance that successive Malaysian governments have attached to equitable growth and poverty reduction. For Malaysian governments, reducing the poverty of the Bumiputeras through broad-based growth has been an overarching objective. Rural poverty declined from 58.7 percent in 1970 to 19.3 percent in 1990; overall poverty from 49 percent in 1970 and 16 percent by 2001. The governments of Malaysia invested heavily in smallholder agriculture – for example, basic rural infrastructure, research and extension, land development schemes, vertical integration of agriculture and agro-processing – and in the basic and higher education of the Bumiputeras for decades. For Brazil, equitable growth was never a priority, not even a concern, until the presidencies of Fernando Enrique Cardoso (1995, 1998) and Luiz Ignacio Lula da Silva (elected October 2002 and in 2007). Partly to counteract the stark inequality of income and asset distribution, some governments passed laws to protect labor, but these had the unintended effect of promoting capital-intensive agricultural growth. The comparison between Malaysia and Brazil shows not only that there need not be any trade-off between more equity and higher growth, but that in fact they can be mutually reinforcing. In both, whether agriculture contributed to overall development and poverty reduction was largely the result of policy. Its growth per se did not translate into broad-based increases in income and employment of the poor, as the Brazilian case shows.

The Brazilian case also provides an interesting comparison with that of Tunisia. Like the Tunisian case, that of Brazil case refutes the pro-agriculture position, but for a different reason. The reason is sustained Tunisian government commitment to assist the more disadvantaged despite the ups and downs of economic performance. Recent uprisings in no way diminish Tunisia's long standing assistance to the rural poor. Chronic high urban youth unemployment of the educated middle classes has fuelled this uprising, not the rural dirt poor (the $1 and $ 2 per day poor), the group of interest here. Tunisia's assistance to the very poor is well documented. The reason is the Tunisian government's sustained commitment to assisting the severely disadvantaged despite the ups and downs of economic performance. Thus, despite Tunisia's high income inequality[72] (much less than Brazil's) and despite an agriculture

---

[72] Admittedly, the extent of Tunisia's income inequality is far less than Brazil's. Tunisia's Gini coefficient of income inequality was around 0.4 according to the World Bank (May 2005), urban was at 0.6 and rural at 0.4 according to Radwan et al. (1991: 49).

of low competitiveness, Tunisia has succeeded in growing and reducing poverty since the end of WWII. In contrast, Brazil, including its large-farmer agriculture, has grown for decades. However, until recent years, there has been only a modest trickling down of benefits in terms of poverty reduction in Brazil.

II.XI. Chile – GNI per capita: USD 9,420 (2009)

Introduction. Since the late 1980s, both the economy and agriculture of Chile have done well. The incidence of poverty, though still high, has also been brought down substantially. However, as in Malaysia, Tunisia, and Brazil, income inequality is high in Chile. The question is, What role, if any, did agriculture play in promoting overall growth and rural poverty reduction in this context of high inequality?

Brief background. Chile has again become the envy of its Latin American neighbors. It has been one of the fastest growing economies in the world over the past two decades. Its post-WWII experience with development growth and poverty reduction is an interesting contrast to Brazil's. The structure of its economy has also changed in two important aspects: Copper exports are much less important, while agricultural exports are much more important. Chile's economy, vulnerable to international copper price fluctuations since its founding in the 1820s, was much less vulnerable only as recently as the 1990s.[73] This is a major achievement. Chile's institutional framework is also more stable than those of its neighbors and is comparable to those of OECD countries. This is reflected in high overall political stability, respect for the rule of law, and a low level of corruption. From the late 1980s through the 1990s, it grew at more than 6.6 percent per year. The East Asian crisis of 1997–98 drastically reduced its growth. However, after a downturn in 1999 (−1.1 percent growth), the economy grew at around 5 percent in 2000 and 3 percent in 2001. Its overall growth (1997–2007) averaged 3.8 percent per year (Figures 2.36 and 2.37).

Wide ideological swings from the 1930s to the mid-1970s. Before the 1930s, Chile was highly regarded, but it lost this position after the 1930s. By the 1970s, its per capita income had fallen below that of Brazil, Mexico, and Panama. During this long period, it underwent

---

[73] Chile declared independence from Spain in 1810 but gained decisive victory only in 1818.

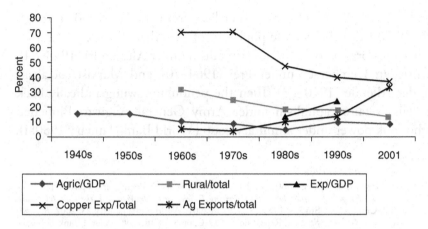

Figure 2.36. Chile: selected structure indicators (1940–2001).

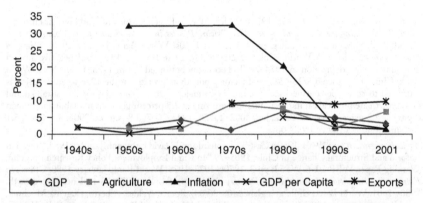

Figure 2.37. Chile: annual growth rates of selected economic indicators (1940–2001).
Sources and Notes:
Ratios:
Agric/GDP:1940s–1970s: World Bank. January 1980. *Chile: An Economy in Transition*. A World Bank Country Study. Table I-7. 1970s: Valdes, Alberto, Eugenia Muchnik, and Hernan Hurtado. 1990. *Trade, Exchange Rate, and Agricultural Pricing Policies in Chile: Volume I, the Country Study*. World Bank Comparative Studies. Table 1–2. 1980s–2001: World Bank. Chile at a glance (08/26/03). 2006: 4.1 percent. Chile at a Glance. 09 24 08.

Rural population/total population: 1960s-1980s: Valdes, Alberto, Eugenia Muchnik, and Hernan Hurtado. *Trade, Exchange Rate, and Agricultural Pricing Policies in Chile: Volume I, the Country Study*. World Bank Comparative Studies. 1990. Table 1–1.A. 2001: World Bank. Chile at a glance (08/26/03).

Exports/GDP: exports of goods & services/GDP: World Bank. Chile at a glance (08/25/05). Data in percent is for 1984, 1994, 2003 (24.2), 2004: (23.4).

Copper exports/total exports: 1960s–1970s: World Bank. January 1980. *Chile: An Economy in Transition*. A World Bank Country Study. pp 104. 1980s–1990s: World Bank. February 25, 1998. *The Kingdom of Morocco: Rural Development Strategy*. Green Cover. Report no. 16303-MOR. Volume 1. Box 4.5. The returns from bold reforms: The case of Chile.

wide ideological swings: mild socialism from the late 1930s through the 1940s; the charismatic populism of President Ibáñez (1952–58), partial restoration of orthodox capitalism under Alessandri (1958–64), Christian Democracy under Frei (1964–70), and Marxist socialism under Allende (1970–73). Then the pendulum swung radically back to laissez-faire capitalism under Army General Augusto Pinochet, who took power under a military coup (World Bank, January 1980: i).

(Figure 2.37. Source continued)

Agriculture exports/total exports: 1960s: Valdes, Alberto, Eugenia Muchnik, and Hernan Hurtado. 1990. *Trade, Exchange Rate, and Agricultural Pricing Policies in Chile: Volume I, the Country Study.* World Bank Comparative Studies. Table 1–2. 1970s, 2001: World Bank. January 23, 2002. *Republic of Chile: Country Assistance Strategy.* Report no. 23329-C. pp 3. 1980s, 1990s: World Bank. February 25, 1998. *The Kingdom of Morocco: Rural Development Strategy.* Green Cover. Report no. 16303-MOR. Volume 1. Box 4.5. The returns from bold reforms: The case of Chile. 2001: World Bank. January 23, 2002. *Republic of Chile: Country Assistance Strategy.* Report no. 23329-C. pp 3.

Growth rates:

GDP growth rate: 1940s – 1937–52, 1970s: Valdes, Alberto, Eugenia Muchnik, and Hernan Hurtado. 1990. *Trade, Exchange Rate, and Agricultural Pricing Policies in Chile: Volume I, the Country Study.* World Bank Comparative Studies. pp 4–5. 1950s–1960s: World Bank. January 1980. *Chile: An Economy in Transition.* A World Bank Country Study. Table I-5. The 1970s had negative growth rates and a major depression in 1974–75. The economy bottomed out in 1976. 1980s-2001: World Bank. Chile at a glance (08/26/03). Total factor productivity growth for the 1986 to 2000 period is estimated to be 1.9 percent per year. The other two major factors accounting for the sustained and high growth are physical capital accumulation, growing at 2.5 percent per year, and labor and human capital at 2.3 percent (World Bank, Jan. 2002: Tab.2). 1997–2007: 3.8 percent, 2006: 4.3; 2007: 5.1 percent. Chile at a glance. 09 24 08.

Agriculture growth rate: 1940s-1960s: Castillo, Leonardo and David Lehmann. January 1982. "Agrarian Reform and Structural Change in Chile: 1965–79." In Rural Employment Policy Research Program, Working Paper, WEP 10–6/WP53; pp 3. 1970s: 1973–1978. World Bank. January 1980. *Chile: An Economy in Transition. A World Bank Country Study;* pp 184. The 1970–73 had negative growth. 1980s-2001: World Bank. Chile at a glance (08/26/03). Source: Valdes, Alberto, Eugenia Muchnik, and Hernan Hurtado. 1990. *Trade, Exchange Rate, and Agricultural Pricing Policies in Chile:* Volume I, the Country Study. World Bank Comparative Studies. Table 1–1 B. 1997–2007: 5.6 percent. Chile at a glance. 09 24 08.

Inflation rate: 1950s-1970s: These are estimates of average compound annual rate for the period. World Bank. January 1980. *Chile: An Economy in Transition.* A World Bank Country Study. Table I-1, pp 12–14. 1980s: Calvo, Guillermo and Enrique G. Mendoza "Empirical Puzzles of Chilean Stabilization Policy" pp 25–54 in Perry, Guillermo and Danny, M. Leipziger, eds. 1999. *Chile: Recent Policy Lessons and Emerging Challenges,* World Bank Institute, the World Bank, Washington, D.C.; pp 28. 1990s: the decline was gradual to single digits down to low levels. Zahler, Roberto "Comment: An alternative view of Chile's macro policy" pp 55–62 in Perry, Guillermo and Danny, M. Leipziger, eds. 1999. *Chile: Recent Policy Lessons and Emerging Challenges,* World Bank Institute, the World Bank, Washington, D.C., pp 56. 2001: World Bank. Little Data Book. 2003; pp 63.

GDP per capita: 1950s-1960s: World Bank. January 1980. *Chile: An Economy in Transition.* A World Bank Country Study. Table I-5. 1980s-2001: World Bank. Chile at a glance (08/26/03).

Exports: 1970s: World Bank. 1980. *Chile: An Economy in Transition.* A World Bank Country Study. January Table III-8. The growth rate was negative for 1971–1973. 1980s-2001: World Bank. Chile at a glance (08/26/03). World Bank. Chile at a glance. (08/25/05) In annual percent, for 2003: 8.8, 2004: 8.9. For 1997–2007: 2.6 percent; 2006: 3.5; 2007: 4.1. World Bank. Chile at a glance. (09/24/08)

This long period of turmoil was characterized by high inflation, highly unstable foreign exchange rates, and almost exclusive dependence on copper exports, which contributed around 78 percent of total export revenues. The Great Depression of the 1930s hit Chile very hard (Valdes, Muchnik, and Hurtado, 1990: 8). Following the Great Depression of the 1930s, Chile adopted a highly protectionist trade policy until the 1970s. This had a major impact on agricultural performance, as the high protection implicitly taxed agriculture, despite attempts to reverse the discrimination through credit subsidies.

Major socialist reforms, 1962–73. The socialist governments undertook major reforms, including land reform (started in 1962, continued in 1967, and accelerated under Allende), support of organized labor, including major increases in wages, expropriation of large industrial firms and private banks, and price and marketing controls (rice, wheat, oilseeds, sugar, milk, etc.). Between 1965 and 1973, the land reform measures expropriated 48 percent of agricultural land. The Frei government imposed a ceiling of 80 basic irrigated hectares (BIH). Small farms, or *minifundistas,* (less than 5 ha) were largely not affected. All farms above this ceiling had their land redistributed to resident permanent workers, who were organized into collective settlements created under Frei following his Agrarian Reform Law of 1967. These were called *asentamientos.* Allende[74] formed large estate enterprises with the redistributed land that included, in addition to permanent workers, temporary labor and even sharecroppers. Pinochet reversed many of these measures.

Socio-economic crises until the mid-1970s. This was a tumultuous period first under Allende, then under Pinochet. Under Allende, real GDP per capita and real wages fell below levels achieved in 1970; agricultural output fell to levels below the 1960s; monthly inflation reached an annualized rate above 1,000 percent; and the black market exchange rate rose 10 times above the official rate. When Pinochet came to power on September 11, 1973, he set about totally restructuring the economy. The Pinochet government introduced a drastic austerity program in April 1975 and the economy plunged into a depression, the worst since the 1930s. GDP fell by more than 11 percent, and unemployment rose to 20 percent in Greater Santiago. As luck would have it, copper prices

---

[74] Salvador Allende, June 26, 1908 to September 11, 1973.

also plummeted, which entailed a resource loss of about 10 percent of GDP (1974). At the same time, the leap in oil prices wreaked havoc on an already dire situation – Chile imported three-fourths of its oil needs (World Bank, January 1980: iv–vi). The economy bottomed out in late 1976. Given these wild price swings, interpreting data for the 1970s becomes particularly tricky.

Reversing socialist reforms under Pinochet. The Pinochet administration (1973–89) was followed by democratic governments that maintained the market orientation (Alwyn, 1990–94; Frei, 1995–2002; Lagos, 2003–2005; Bachelet, 2006–2010, Pinera 2011-). The earlier years of the Pinochet administration were years of sustained reform that reversed the socialist changes and of painful adjustment to the reforms. Pinochet did not, however, entirely reverse the land redistribution under Allende. Pinochet's measures included the following: He lifted Allende's price controls, curtailed labor union political activity, devalued the peso, reinstituted the crawling peg, liberalized trade, and abolished preferential interest rates for certain sectors, including agriculture. During the debt crisis of 1982, the economy contracted severely (by −14 percent in 1982 and −0.7 percent in 1983) (Valdes et al., 1990: 5). In the early 1980s, unemployment reached some 20 percent (World Bank, 2002b: 1). It was not until 1984 that the economy began to recover, a full decade after Allende was overthrown.

Reduction of overdependence on copper exports. Pinochet opened up the economy despite the two major vulnerabilities he inherited. These were the predominance of copper in Chile's export earnings and the high debt–service ratio (World Bank, February 2002: para 1.7). Copper exports, which accounted for nearly 50 percent of total merchandize export earnings by 1989, accounted for only 31 percent of total export earnings by the early 2000s (2001). Before 1974, Chile's main traditional agricultural exports were beans, lentils, and wool. After 1974, the share of non-traditional agricultural exports, such as apples, grapes, pears, and peaches, increased dramatically (USDA, 1992). Chile has successfully diversified its export earnings from copper and restructured its agricultural trade. Agricultural exports of fruits, wine, and fish have been the star performers. Since around the mid-1980s, yearly export growth rates of agriculture have averaged 10 percent or greater (Anderson and Valdes, 2008: 125, table 4.2).

Growth performance from the mid-1980s to 2003. From 1986 to 1997, Chile's economy grew at an average rate of 7.7 percent per year, one of the highest in the world, more than twice the average in Latin America. However, during the 1990s, the growth rate suddenly declined, reaching a nadir in 1999. Productivity growth was the main factor in Chile's growth in the second half of the 1990s. The contribution of TFP to growth was 44 percent between 1990 and 1994 (World Bank, February 2004: 3).

Investment climate assessment at the beginning of the 2000s. Sustained growth rates show a resilient economy in a turbulent environment over the past several decades. A wide range of reforms covering most major areas have been put in place since the 1970s, including reforms in trade liberalization, pension and tax systems, and capital markets. The World Bank highlights a continuous commitment to fiscal discipline, which has led to a substantial decline in public debt and a policy of trade openness that has caused the value of Chilean exports to increase fourfold since 1980 (World Bank, April 2007: 13). In terms of investment climate, Chile compares extremely well with other countries (where the World Bank has made an assessment). Confidence in property rights and the rule of law is extremely high in Chile.

Substantial socio-economic progress despite high and increasing income inequality. Chile is known not only for its high growth since the late 1980s, but also for its substantial socio-economic improvements. For example, by the mid-1980s, it had achieved universal primary education. Also, despite low growth rates from the 1970s to the mid-1980s, infant mortality greatly diminished. Socio-economic improvements continued under the military government and into the 1990s. An important achievement was the decline in school dropout rates at the primary and secondary levels. Despite these improvements, however, income inequality remains high by international standards and has increased (most of the increase took place between 1994 and 1996). Only Brazil (0.61), Colombia (0.58), and Honduras (0.57) have higher Gini coefficients for income than Chile (0.56) (World Bank, 2002b: 1–2, tables 6, 12).[75]

[75] The estimate for Colombia is urban only. For comparison with the rest of the world, the Gini coefficients for income are: for the United States (2007), 0.45; Japan (2002), 0.38; France (1995), 0.33; the Russian Federation 0.42 (2009) (CIA, the World Factbook).

Falling poverty incidence and improvements in social indicators from 1987 to 2003. A combination of strong growth and well-directed social programs reduced poverty from 40 percent in 1987 to 17 percent in 1998. Some 4 percent now live in extreme poverty (World Bank, August 2001: 5). More recent (2003) data show that the incidence of poverty continued to fall (World Bank, June 2006: table 1.4). Few countries can match Chile's record of cutting poverty in half over a period of 20 years, although income inequality remains high by international standards. Adjustments for in-kind income transfers substantially reduce the Gini coefficient on income inequality. In 1998, this coefficient fell from 0.56 (unadjusted) to 0.50 (adjusted) and the ratio of the highest (richest) to the lowest (poorest) quintile fell from 20 to 11. Of the various programs considered, the subsidy to education was the main contributor to the reduction in inequality (60 percent of total transfer), followed by health (26 percent), monetary transfers (11 percent), and housing (6.5 percent). Social indicators such as enrollment in primary education, youth literacy, infant mortality, and life expectancy also improved, reaching levels close to those of advanced economies. Primary and secondary school enrollment is 106 percent.[76]

Importance, structure, and performance of agriculture. Agriculture has been a minor sector for decades. Since the 1960s, its contribution to GDP has fluctuated between 5 and 10 percent. By 2006, it had declined to around 4 percent of GDP. Its contribution to employment is more substantial, but that too declined from about 30 percent in the early 1960s to around 15 percent by the 1980s (Valdes et al., 1990: 19) and 14 percent by 1997 (United States Department of State, 2001). Its contribution to exports substantially increased from around 5 percent of total from the 1960s to nearly 34 percent by 2001. This is a major achievement, as exports themselves have grown on a sustained basis. During 1987–97, Chile's exports of goods and services grew at around 10.8 percent per year, and during 1997–2007 they grew at around 6 percent per year.[77]

Salient structural features of agricultural output. Chilean agriculture is predominantly tradable. Most of the traditional crops (e.g., cereals,

---

[76] World Bank, "Chile at a Glance," December 9, 2009.
[77] World Bank, "Chile at a Glance," September 24, 2008.

sugar beet, roots and tubers, oilseeds) and livestock are import substitutes. Some 80 percent of agricultural production is oriented toward
the domestic market (Valdes et al., 1990: 28). Wine and fruits are the
major exportables. Agriculture's highly tradable nature explains why
foreign exchange and trade policies have a major impact on its performance.[78] Almost all high-value export crops depend on irrigation,
while more generally 35 percent of all land under crops and pasture is
irrigated (World Bank, August 1994: iv).

Selected features of agricultural performance. Agricultural growth has
been low for decades until recently: from the Great Depression, during the post-WWII era, until after the removal (under the Pinochet
regime) of most of the policy discrimination (Figure 2.37). The regime
also removed the uncertainty about property rights and tenure status
(introduced by the socialist governments from 1962 to 1973). During
much of this long period, agricultural policy was determined by macro
policy to promote industrialization and import substitution. Partly to
counteract this implicit taxation, governments subsidized agricultural
credit. To satisfy urban demand for basic foods, prices of wage goods
such as wheat, rice, sugar, and oilseeds were controlled. The socialist
governments also controlled marketing. From 1970 to 1973, there was
an absolute decline in food production. This was not surprising given
the political turmoil of those years (Valdes et al., 1990: 21). For the
remainder of the 1970s, the incentives situation improved markedly.
Tariffs across all sectors were lowered, except those for commodities
such as wheat, sugar beets, and oilseeds, which had higher tariffs under
a mechanism of price bands. Most agricultural prices controlled under
Allende were freed. From 1983 to 1989, agriculture grew at a high
yearly rate of 5.8 percent, but the rate fell to 3.0 percent between 1989
and 1992 (excluding forestry and fishing sub-sectors, the rate fell to
1.5 percent), while overall GDP grew at 6.1 percent per year during
that period (World Bank, August 1994: i). The average annual growth
rate of an export-oriented agriculture was 5.6 percent (1997–2007).[79]
Estimates of effective protection for major commodities (estimated
for the 1960–84 period), including those of livestock, were negative
from 1960 to 1969 and then turned positive for selected years until

[78] Beef became non-tradable after 1975 regulations on foot and mouth disease.
[79] World Bank, "Chile at a Glance," September 24, 2008.

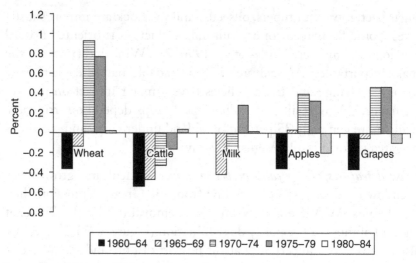

Figure 2.38. Chile: rates of protection (1960–84).
Sources and Notes:
Effective Protection Coefficients (EPC) for Wheat, Cattle, Milk, Apples, Grapes: 1960–
1979: Valdes, Alberto, Eugenia Muchnik, and Hernan Hurtado 1990. *Trade, Exchange Rate, and
Agricultural Pricing Policies in Chile: Volume I, the Country Study.* World Bank Comparative Studies.
Table 3–8. These commodities account for around 43 percent of total value of crop production in
1969 (pp 71). In the later years, there was an increase in the share of fruit production. The above
are the most important commodities and representative of the policy regime. These coefficients
measure the average direct and indirect price interventions on agricultural producers, 1960–84.

1984. See Figure 2.38. By the mid-1980s, total crop and livestock productivity was considered low by international standards (Valdes et al.,
1990: 28).

More equitable agricultural land distribution under Pinochet. In addition
to a change in the price and trade framework under Pinochet, there was
a major change in land distribution and tenure security. Agricultural
land was more equitably distributed even after Pinochet returned some
28 percent of expropriated area to the former owners (Valdes et al.,
1990: 30). He did not completely reverse Allende's land reform, since
he did not return to the feudal *latifundia* landownership structure.
Comparing 1965 and 1979 data on land distribution shows that the
major difference was decreased concentration of land in large farms
(defined as greater than 80 BIH). Land greater than 80 BIH occupied
55.3 percent of total land in 1969; by 1979, it occupied only 21 percent
of total. The two middle-sized farm categories were the 5.1–25.6 BIH
and the 25.6–64 BIH groups. Their respective shares changed from

12.7 and 22.5 percent in 1969 to 38.7 and 22.2 percent in 1979. The share of the *minifundistas* (5.1 BIH) also changed from 9.7 percent to 14.0 percent. Four percent of formerly privately owned land was held by government agencies (Valdes et al., 1990: table 1–8).

Land distribution and operating farm sizes by the late 1990s. Small farmers remain important. Small farmers consist of subsistence farmers and small farmers with 12 ha or fewer of crops and pasture.[80] According to the 1997 census (the latest available),[81] the total estimated number of farmers was 330,000, of which 103,000 were small subsistence farmers and 175, 000 small farmers. This group of small farmers – 84 percent of farmers – controlled 25 percent of total farmland and contributed to 25–30 percent of agricultural GDP. Medium-size farms numbered 17,000, and there were around 9, 500 large farms (Anderson and Valdes, 2008: 128).[82] These larger farmers – 16 percent of total farmers – controlled 75 percent of farmland and contributed to 70–75 percent of agricultural GDP. Chilean agriculture is dualistic, with a highly unequal land distribution, but not a *latifundia* system. Farm sizes changed in different regions depending on the crop mix. Thus, in the central regions, the heart of the fruit and wine export sub-sector, farm size increased as the number of farms decreased. The reverse happened in the southern regions, where wheat and traditional crops – grains, milk, beef – are produced. There, the number of farms increased and farm sizes decreased. In the dairy, pork, and poultry sub-sectors, average operating size increased, while the number of units decreased. According to preliminary results of the 2007 Agricultural Census, there was a substantial increase in the number of corporate farms: in 1997, corporate farms occupied less than 50 percent of total land under individual farms; by 2007, the percentage rose to 82. Average operating size increased from 84 to 109 ha (OECD, 2008a: box 1.2).

---

[80] Small farmers are divided into three groups: subsistence, transition, and consolidated. In terms of irrigated land, subsistence farmers have 1.8 ha, transition 4.0 ha, and consolidated 7.6 ha (Foster and Valdes, 2008: 5).

[81] The information from the 2007 census was still being processed as of the beginning of 2009.

[82] These numbers total 26,500, constituting only 8 percent of total. Together with the number for small farmers, they add up to only 304,500 total farms, not 330,000. So some numbers are missing.

The benefit to agricultural labor and small farmers from a dynamic, export-oriented agriculture. The dynamic growth of fruits, vegetables, and wine exports in the central regions of Chile has significantly contributed to increased rural employment and thus lower poverty. With lower rural poverty, there have also been lower rates of rural–urban migration. Valdes and Jara argue that these developments – less rural poverty and rural–urban migration – have been due primarily to the fact that exports are much more labor intensive than the production of import substitutes, such as wheat and sugar. They point out that it is not the export orientation per se that mattered but rather the labor intensity of the activities, which in Chile's case coincides with exports (Anderson and Valdes, 2008: 152). Much of this expanded employment is in terms of salaried labor of a seasonal nature, reflecting the seasonality of agricultural production and the increased flexibility of labor markets, which became a hallmark of doing business under the Pinochet regime. Most small farmers, however, live in the southern regions, where traditional import competing agriculture (e.g., wheat, dairy, and beef) predominates. According to OECD (2008a: 14), the high growth of the competitive agricultural (mainly horticulture and wine) sub-sectors has done little over the past 15 years to "improve the farm-derived incomes of the majority of agricultural households. Rather the gains in total incomes have come from the farm household either diversifying its sources of income or leaving the sector for more remunerative work."

Access to rural non-farm jobs critical in rural poverty reduction. As in many other countries, access to RNF jobs and incomes has become an increasingly important way to reduce rural poverty and increase rural incomes. Indeed, salaried agricultural workers who rely primarily on agricultural work have a high poverty incidence of around 24 percent. For single-person farms relying entirely on agricultural income, poverty incidence is similar, at around 23 percent; however, for those with less than 50 percent of household income from agriculture, the poverty incidence drops to around 7 percent (2003) (Foster and Valdes, 2008: tables 7, 8). Opportunities in RNF tend not to be alternatives to primary agriculture, but rather complementary.

Does the Chile case support the pro-agriculture position? The answer is no. Agriculture did make some contribution, as it was taxed for years, but it has been a minor sector for decades. Poverty reduction was achieved primarily through non-agriculture measures. For decades since the mid-1980s, we see scenario (b): stagnant low productivity agriculture co-existing with high rates of overall economic growth and low(er) rates of rural poverty. Chilean agriculture is, however, dualistic in that the export-oriented, irrigated sub-sector (e.g., fresh fruits and vegetables), and fisheries are competitive and have been doing very well. The growth of that large-farmer agriculture has contributed to the reduction of rural poverty by generating seasonal employment. But it is access to RNF jobs, government investments in rural infrastructure and services, and benefits from government's social programs that have made the critical difference in poverty reduction.

The Chilen case shows that even though agriculture is not a major sector and not a major contributor to overall growth and poverty reduction performance, its growth performance can be significant for overall development, for it has contributed to the diversification of the overall economy. This diversification in turn is a key factor strengthening Chile's resilience to external shocks, hence increasing its ability to sustained high growth. Up to the 1990s or so, Chile's vulnerability was due largely to its overwhelming dependence on copper prices. This dependence was a major reason Chile was so badly hit by the Great Depression. It is no accident that Chile's downturn following the East Asian crisis of 1997–98 was much milder than that following the earlier external shocks.

SECTION C
Review of Selected Quantitative Assessments of the Contribution
of Agriculture to Overall Growth and Poverty Reduction

Introduction. The case studies presented in the preceding sections assess the contribution of agriculture to overall economic development and poverty reduction in a wide variety of contexts by seeking to refute the two polar views on agriculture's contribution instead of seeking to confirm either view. As already shown, confirmations prove nothing, as contrary positions have been confirmed. The central methodological message of a Popperian approach is that outcomes inconsistent with a hypothesis constitute more powerful evidence against the hypothesis than positive statistical correlations can generate in favor of the hypothesis. The following discussion highlights the contrast between the methodological approach of this book and the method of statistical correlations that is prevalent in the literature.

It is methodologically and theoretically wrong to infer causation from statistical relationships. In recent years, the debate about the relative contribution of agriculture to overall growth and poverty reduction has been couched in terms of econometric estimates. We illustrate this by drawing on work by Timmer, Valdes, and Foster, as their reviews of the literature address this question precisely (Timmer, May 2005; Valdes and Foster, 2005). Our fundamental point bears repeating, namely that it is well accepted that the leap from statistical association to structural causality is wrong on methodological grounds.[83] Measures of statistical significance are precisely that, no more, no less. "McCloskey and Ziliak (1996: 97–114) look carefully at a large number of empirical studies in economics and conclude that researchers seem not to appreciate that statistical significance does not imply economic significance" (Kennedy, 1998: 64). It is also misleading on theoretical grounds, including the

---

[83] "It is usually assumed that movements in the dependent variable are caused by movements in the independent variable(s), but the existence of a relationship between the variables proves neither the existence of causality nor its direction. Using the dictionary meaning of causality, it is impossible to test for causality. Granger developed a special definition of causality which econometricians use in place of the dictionary definition; strictly speaking, econometricians should say 'Granger-cause' in place of 'cause' but usually they do not. A variable x is said to Granger-cause y if the prediction of the current value of y is enhanced by using past values of x" (Kennedy, 1998: 66).

policy implication that typically follows. One important policy implication of asserting that the primary sector contributes less to poverty reduction than the other two sectors is that a lower priority is recommended for investment in the sector. This is misleading because it ignores two important features of the dynamic process of successful agricultural transformation, as shown in the cases of England, Japan, and the United States, among other industrialized countries. These features are the following:

1. The interlinked and dynamic nature of sector and overall growth;
2. The fact that the size of agriculture (in terms of its contribution to GDP) shrinks the farther along it is on its transformation path.

The first feature means that one cannot infer the relative importance of a sector in promoting overall growth and poverty reduction just by measuring the relative contribution of that sector to GDP. Why? It is because that measure ignores benefits from agricultural and rural diversification, including demand-induced spillover and multiplier effects. The second feature is the well-known paradox whereby a thriving agriculture contributing to a growing economy shrinks in relative size over time. Thus its smaller relative size over the course of development is a sign of its sustained productivity and output growth, not a sign of its weakness. Given other considerations, it may still be correct to advocate lowering the priority of investing in agriculture, but it would be wrong to infer it from these estimates. Furthermore, this approach ignores all that has been learned about the critical importance of the overall framework of macro-economy, trade, and institutions in driving growth and poverty reduction. This overall framework may be the major causal factor, and not growth in this or that sector.

Defending or undermining agriculture's importance using econometric estimates is invalid. Timmer, and Valdes and Foster, counter the anti-agriculture intelligentsia by arguing that agricultural development generates quantitatively significant externalities and reduces poverty. Are their arguments methodologically valid? Simply put, they argue that agriculture contributes significantly to overall growth and that its contribution to increasing the incomes of the poor is greater the more equitable the income distribution. This is an important argument. The issue is the way they establish it. Specifically, they have recourse to econometric estimates that do the following:

1. They quantify linkages with other sectors through multipliers that are between 2 and 3 – for example, agriculture multipliers through consumption and production linkages.
2. They show that through these multipliers, agriculture contributes to overall growth and, via such growth, to poverty reduction as evidenced by positive growth–poverty elasticities; these elasticities are higher the lower the degree of income inequality.
3. They measure the "true" size of agriculture (the concept of an expanded agriculture) by estimating "the extent of agriculture's inter-industry links to other sectors [as it] would determine its real size and importance to the overall economy." (Valdes and Foster, 2005: 5) Their message is that agriculture's contribution should be judged by the larger contribution to GDP, not only by the contribution of primary agriculture alone to GDP. For example, for Chile, Mexico, and Colombia, the percent increase in share due to forward and backward linkages is significant (between 28 to 89 percent increase above the official estimates of primary agriculture alone). Furthermore, "the Inter-American Institute for Cooperation in Agriculture (IICA, 2004) also produces generous estimates of an 'expanded agriculture.' For Latin America and the Caribbean, IICA's expanded agricultural GDP represents about 30% of national output." Valdes and Foster, (2005: 6) rightly argue that these are overestimates of agriculture's contribution "because any industry's GDP could be attributable to contributions from various sectors."
4. They quantify the magnitude of spillover effects for Latin America. Valdes and Foster (2005: 9) use Bravo-Ortega and Lederman's (2005) estimates of cross-sector growth elasticities, which they (wrongly in our view) interpret as the "impact of a 1 percent increase in one sector's GDP on another sector's GDP." They find that "[i]n all [Latin American] countries except for Uruguay, agricultural is positively related to subsequent non-agricultural growth, and this relationship for 10 of the 20 other [Latin American] countries is considerably above the regional average cross-sector growth elasticity of 0.12, with some countries

having very high elasticities of cross-sector growth impacts (e.g., Chile, Jamaica, Guatemala, Argentina and Brazil)" (9). In other words, on average, for the region, a 1 percent growth in agriculture is associated (they interpret this as causal, however) with a 0.12 percent growth in non-agriculture (excluding food processing) and 0.18 percent growth (including food processing). They do say that the Granger causality test "suggests but does not really prove causality in a mechanical sense" (Valdes and Foster, 2005: 11). Yet they argue that the results quantify the contribution of agriculture. "For non-LAC [Latin American] countries, one finds that agriculture 'contributes' about 1.5 times the size of the sector ... For LAC [Latin American] countries, agriculture contributes about 1.8 times its size..." (2005: 10). So it is not clear whether they argue that the results are only suggestive or whether they claim that the estimates quantify the contribution in a valid way.

5. They measure the "elasticity of connection": the percent responsiveness of the average incomes of the lowest quintile to a percent increase in agricultural growth. Timmer (2002: 1527–1534) estimates elasticities ranging from 0.8 for the lowest quintile to greater than 1.0 for the highest quintile. He finds that in economies where the income gap is "large" (i.e., when the income gap between the lowest and the highest quintile is twice as large as the average income; this income gap is also considered bad), the poor are weakly connected to the growth process; in other words a highly skewed distribution is associated with a weak trickle-down effect. Using the same measure of income gap, Timmer finds that in countries with "good" income distribution, "labor productivity in agriculture is slightly but consistently more important in generating incomes in each of the five quintiles. Furthermore, agriculture has a noticeable 'anti-Kuznets' effect" However, "[a] similar anti-Kuznets effect is seen from the non-agricultural sector." Furthermore, Timmer finds that "[t]he contrast with countries where the relative income gap is large – more than twice the average per capita income – is striking. In [such an economy, for] the poorest quintile, workers are virtually disconnected from the national economy.... And growth in agricultural productivity is no more successful in alleviating poverty than growth in the non-agricultural productivity.... Indeed the rich benefit considerably

more from agricultural growth in countries with large income gaps, no doubt because of highly skewed distribution of land." (Timmer, 2005: 1531, 1534)

Timmer's estimation of the elasticity of connection, though highlighting an interesting feature of an economy, cannot be used to strengthen the case in favor of the greater (than non-agriculture) effectiveness of agricultural growth on poverty reduction. His estimates are consistent with the commonsense view that the less equitable the income distribution, the less the poor benefit from growth. His estimates do not give us more insight than that and say nothing about the role of agriculture in poverty reduction. Moreover, using cross-country estimates, Bravo-Ortega and Lederman (2005) come to the opposite conclusions. They find that "the elasticities of connection (the direct effects on poverty) are higher for non-agricultural than for agricultural growth across quintile groups.... The elasticities of connection for agriculture compared to non-agriculture are even less in the case of Latin America, where the agriculture elasticities fall relative to non-LAC developing countries and the non-agriculture elasticities increase."(Valdes and Foster, 2005: 13, table 3)

6. They show, according to Valdes and Foster (2005:13–14) that "[r]elative to its GDP share agriculture has a greater impact on poverty reduction than non-agriculture. Agriculture's GDP share averages 0.12 for LAC [Latin American countries] and 0.22 for non-LAC developing countries. Relative to their shares in GDP, on average, agriculture's contribution to raising the incomes of the poorest is at least 2.5 times that of non-agriculture (2.5 for LAC, 2.9 for non-LAC developing countries)."

In sum, various types of econometric estimates are used to argue for the quantitative importance of agriculture in promoting overall economic growth and poverty reduction. A problem is that econometric estimates of statistical significance are also used to prove the contrary, as we saw earlier; for example, the India study by Beesly et al. (2004) contradicts results obtained by Ravallion and Datt (1996). The fact that these studies contradict each other is good evidence that the method of inference is wrong. And there is no independently replicable way to resolve contradictions. The inference leap from statistical to causal significance is at best a hypothesis that requires further testing: "Economists will simply have to face the fact that econometric studies of country data will not be able to establish causality" (Tsakok and Gardner, 2007: 1146).

What is the empirical content of these estimates? Confirming instances, econometric or not, do not prove anything. To quote Popper (1961: 134): "This is the reason why the discovery of instances that confirm a theory means very little, if we have not tried, and failed, to discover refutations. For if we are uncritical we shall always find what we want: we shall look for, and find, confirmations, and we shall look away from, and not see, whatever might be dangerous to our pet theories. In this way it is only too easy to obtain what appears to be overwhelming evidence in favour of a theory which, if approached critically, would have been refuted. In order to make the selection by elimination work, and to ensure that the only the fittest theories survive, their struggle for life must be made severe for them."

At best, empirical estimates provide valuable insights to deepen our inquiry, not to end it. How should we then use these econometric estimates? There are several useful ways. (a) They can provide valuable insights to deepen our understanding of the functioning of the economy; (b) they can be promising entry points to deepen our inquiry, not to end it[84]; and (c) better still, their insights can be complemented by further analysis of the broader historical and socio-political context in which they occur. On the basis of these correlations and our understanding of the broader structural context, we should then develop refutable hypotheses that we test following Popper's methodology (Berkson, 1989: 166–70).[85] Why should we do so? There are two main reasons. One is to reduce or, better still, avoid repeating the "painful lessons"[86] that the rush to policy implications of some widely accepted empirical

---

[84] It has long been known that causal inference from regression estimates is problematic. "Indeed causal arguments based on significance tests and regression are almost necessarily circular.... Correlation is not the same as causation: statistical technique alone does not make the connection" (Freedman, 1991: 292, 301).

[85] To test within the Popperian approach, one can use various analytical tools, including regression analysis and simulation exercises (Johnston 1970: 397) or complement existing historical information with sample survey data designed especially to test predictions of the maintained hypothesis (or hypotheses).

[86] This phrase is from Binswanger (1994).

"truths" have caused. We need to test the applicability of our causal claims before deriving general policy implications and acting upon them. Today's acceptance of regression coefficients as causal factors of universal applicability resembles the acceptance of the Prebisch–Singer thesis (1950) – of deteriorating secular terms of trade for primary commodities – as an empirical truth without any attempt to test it. Such acceptance proved to be costly to millions.[87] This thesis, popular not only among academic economists, but also among many politicians of the developing world, largely provided the intellectual justification for import-substituting industrialization (ISI), a strategy that, with the hindsight of more than 50 years, has clearly undermined rather than promoted development for so many.[88] Moreover, the flimsy basis for policy conclusions based on these regression coefficients also makes development economics prone to fads.[89] Faddism is problematic for any discipline. For the economics of agricultural growth in developing countries, it has been costly, as it has undermined investment in agriculture. As pointed out by Timmer (2005a: 23, 28), support for agriculture has dwindled because of "donors who have been distracted from their core mission by development faddism and pressures from single-issue groups ... and partly because there is no accepted core of development theory, and only hotly contested empirical 'truths', faddism has long dominated donor thinking about

[87] Developing a test of this thesis within the Popperian framework is a challenging task, especially as such empirical testing of refutable hypotheses is unchartered territory in development economics. The objective of testing this thesis would be at a minimum to understand under what conditions this secular decline (if it actually exists) would hurt primary commodities exporters and under what conditions it would not. More generally, within the framework of Popper's methodology, how to develop refutable tests is discussed in Berkson (1989) (see also Appendix A).

[88] As Eicher and Staatz (1998: 10) put it, "The 'secular-decline hypothesis' became an article of faith for some development economists and planners, reinforcing the tendency to downplay agriculture's potential for development."

[89] It would be interesting to ask development practitioners what they would agree on as having constituted fads – defined as development approaches that would "solve" the development puzzle. Would they agree with Timmer (2005a: 28) that these include community development of the 1950s; ISI of the 1960s; reaching the poorest of the poor of the 1970s; structural adjustment programs of the 1980s; sustainable development of the 1990s; and back to community-driven development (CDD) of today. I would add the training and visit extension system à la Daniel Benor of the 1970s and 1980s; integrated rural development and basic needs of the 1970s; privatization of the 1980s; and micro-credit dispensed by NGOs.

appropriate development strategy."[90] Faddism inevitably trivializes development economics. This is most unfortunate as development economics tries to come to grips with one of the most stubborn and vexing social problems of our time, widespread and persistent poverty amid plenty.

[90] Timmer (May 2005a: 28) also rightly points out that "[p]artly because of so many new topics on the development agenda," donor attention has been diluted and diverted from core developmental mission. I would argue that this proliferation itself shows the methodological disarray of the field of development economics. Researchers and practitioners cannot but realize that complex causal structures are at work, and their use of regression coefficients to justify policy recommendations cannot adequately do justice to the complexity of the situation; hence more and more items are added to the development agenda to make up for the deficit of understanding.

SECTION D
Is Success in Agricultural Transformation Important for Overall Development? What We Learn from This Selective Review

Conclusive refutation of the "squeeze agriculture" position. The development experience of the People's Republic of China from 1949 to 1979 is conclusive evidence that for economies with dominant agricultures, you cannot "squeeze agriculture," transfer the surplus for investing in industry, and achieve industrial status; that is, you cannot "leap forward," as the Chinese put it, or, as is often said, you cannot "catch up with the West." During this 30-year period, the central government fully implemented the "squeeze agriculture" strategy. In particular, it tried different collectivization experiments, monopolized marketing and trade of major staples, and fixed input, output, and factor prices. In fact, it is hard to imagine what more the government could have done to implement that strategy and still keep a semblance of social consensus and stability. Armed with distorted prices and a powerful state machinery to implement its strategy, the government was able to maintain a high (around 25–30 percent of GDP) savings and investment rate to promote heavy industrial development. Despite substantial heavy industrial growth, the Chinese leadership under Deng Xiaoping chose to fundamentally reorient the "squeeze agriculture" strategy, costly in terms of forgone growth, consumer welfare, and efficient resource use. During this 30-year period, China did industrialize, but such industrialization proved to be a hollow victory. Low incomes remained prevalent, poverty was still extensive, and China was still not the industrial power it wanted to be. For the Communist Party of China, its leadership was at stake.

Substantial but not universal evidence in favor of the pro-agriculture position. If "squeezing agriculture" does not work, does promoting it work? At a general level, our answer is a qualified yes. To repeat, the main operational issue between the two polar views is whether one needs to invest in agriculture for the sector to play its full developmental role, or whether neglect and exploitation of the sector is a better developmental strategy. That the sector plays an important role in the economic life of a country at the early stages of development is not at issue, for it cannot be otherwise. Agriculture is typically the dominant sector in terms of its contribution to GDP and employment-cum-income. To assess the accuracy of the claims made by both polar views, in this review we have chosen country cases differing in almost all aspects (resource endowments, historical and institutional legacies, etc.) but with only three common features, either an important agricultural sector or a substantial reduction in poverty or both. We have chosen countries that refute and support either polar view. Based on the development experiences of selected major industrial countries and post-WWII developing countries, the following assessment of agriculture's role in long-term overall development and poverty emerges:

1. Where agriculture has done well for at least several decades in a country's economic development and transformation, the overall economy has also done well. Doing well simply means having sustained high growth rates of agricultural output and productivity and of the entire economy, with broad-based increases in income and substantial decreases in poverty. Such were the experiences of England, the first country in the world to industrialize, and of Japan, the first non-Western country to industrialize. Important post-WWII examples include Taiwan, China, from the 1950s to the 1970s and the People's Republic of China after 1979. The state of Punjab, India, the home of the Green Revolution in India has had high agricultural growth rates and low poverty incidence rates, whereas Bihar and Orissa have experienced the reverse: stagnant agricultures with a high incidence of poverty. At the national level, in India's closed economy (until the reforms of the 1990s), persistent low agricultural growth rates (punctuated by some years of higher growth rates in the early to middle 1990s) and GDP growth rates averaging 4 percent per year (1950–89) saw a steady but slow reduction in poverty, with only moderate increases in average incomes.

2. While the aforementioned experiences are supportive of the pro-agriculture position, they also show that the benefits in terms of widespread income increases and poverty reduction, rural and urban, can materialize only after a substantial lag. Much depends on the distribution of income, wealth, and economic opportunities. For example, in 18th- and 19th-century England, with a skewed income and wealth distribution and laissez-faire

capitalism, the poor, rural and urban, did not benefit for decades after the onset of both revolutions. In Japan, the Republic of Korea, and Taiwan, China, where governments valued equitable growth and implemented land reform and other reforms to level the playing field, the benefits of growth were broad-based.[91] In the People's Republic of China, rural households did benefit during the earlier years following the 1979 reforms, but income disparities have grown wider between coastal and inland regions, and between rural and urban households.

3. Where the income benefits to the rural poor did materialize during the course of agricultural transformation, access to RNF income and job opportunities was an important contributing factor, as in, for example, Taiwan and the People's Republic of China. Increases in agriculture income were not enough. This is true even for American agriculture, which has shown sustained productivity growth for decades. Although there has been increasing land concentration and inequality in sales value in American agriculture, the distribution of farm household incomes in 1990 was more equitable than in 1950. In addition, the incidence of poverty among farm families was less than among urban households in the 1990s than in the 1960s. Access to non-farm sources of income has made the difference – it reduces rural income inequality and widespread poverty. A productive agriculture is necessary but not sufficient for broad-based rural poverty reduction.

4. In dualistic agricultures, with high inequality in the distribution of income and land, agricultural growth by itself was far from sufficient to substantially reduce poverty on a broad base. Governments had to resort to special measures to reduce widespread poverty in the course of development. Land reform has leveled the playing field in only a minority of East Asian countries, removing the root cause of dualism. However, increasing income inequality in the People's Republic of China in recent decades shows that land reform is not sufficient to ensure equity in the distribution of growth benefits over time. The substantial poverty reduction in Malaysia, Tunisia, Chile in the 1990s, and Brazil in recent years shows that land reform is not necessary

---

[91] It is interesting that, in all three cases, the United States played a key role in the land reform.

either. What is necessary is sustained government commitment to building a more equitable society.

5. The relative contribution of agriculture is diminished for small, open, export-oriented economies, which benefit from substantial inflows of foreign exchange, through aid, remittances, trade in non-agricultural commodities, FDI, and so on. In these countries, their developmental growth and poverty reduction were financed by non-agricultural surplus. Witness the cases of Portugal, Ireland, and the Republic of Korea, three high-performing economies. However, even in these countries, the development of agriculture was not neglected. Its development was such that the sector did not act as a constraint on overall growth. The agricultures of Portugal and of Ireland benefited from substantial EU aid. There was considerable investment in South Korean agriculture, making it one of the most productive and, since the 1970s, one of the most protected.

6. Though still not successfully transformed, agriculture made a substantial contribution to overall growth and poverty reduction where governments gave priority to its development, as in the case of Malaysia and Indonesia. The Malaysian experience stands in stark contrast to Brazil's. They are both resource-rich, with dualistic agricultural economies. In Brazil, large-farmer agriculture did well but left the poor behind. In Malaysia, the government priority on reducing the poverty of the Bumiputeras was translated into substantial investments to assist this group. Agriculture was taxed in the earlier years, but part of that surplus was plowed back into the sector. This priority made a major difference to the income growth and poverty reduction of the Bumiputeras. Indonesia stands out as a major oil exporter that consistently gave priority to promoting smallholder agriculture and to achieving rice self-sufficiency. During the decades of high growth, agriculture and the entire economy did well, registering substantial reductions in poverty, until the East Asian financial crisis of 1997–99.

7. The cases of Tunisia and Chile show that both the pro- and anti-agriculture positions can be too simplistic in countries where agriculture is not the major sector but cannot be ignored for socio-economic reasons. Tunisia was oil-exporting until the mid-1980s.

Its agriculture is drought-vulnerable, but it is home to the majority of the poor. Copper dominated Chile's economy, constituting both the strength and the vulnerability of the economy. In both countries, the governments succeeded (although to different degrees) in achieving steady overall growth, increasing incomes, and reducing poverty, despite inequitable land distributions and despite poor performance in large parts of their agricultures. Thus their experiences undermine the pro-agriculture positions. However, they do not support the anti-agriculture position either, because the development of agriculture rather than its naked exploitation still makes better economic sense. Chile's high-growth competitive agricultural export sub-sector constitutes a welcome diversification of the economy, contributing to both overall growth and the economy's resilience in the face of the ups and downs of the copper market. Tunisia's government still faces the challenge of developing a competitive agriculture, without hurting the rural poor in the short run. Subsidizing an uncompetitive sector while it is working out this longer-term sustainable growth strategy makes more socio-economic sense than discriminating against a vulnerable sector where most of the poor still reside.

How to develop agriculture, not whether to develop agriculture – that is the question. In our review of the wide range of country experiences, the weight of the evidence is that agricultural development does indeed matter. The "squeeze agriculture" approach has been refuted. China is the most dramatic case of such refutation. Our main operational conclusion from assessing the relative accuracy of the two polar positions is that the focus of policy and research attention should be on how best to promote a successful process of agricultural transformation, not whether to promote it or not. It is striking that although farming is one of the oldest activities of humankind, the fact that only a minority of countries have succeeded in transforming their agricultures is strong evidence that this developmental task is far from trivial. Part Two focuses on the "how."

SUCCESS IN AGRICULTURAL TRANSFORMATION: WHAT MAKES IT HAPPEN?

Introduction to Part Two

Part One argued that success in agricultural transformation does matter. Whether agriculture is the primary engine of growth or not, Part One showed that agriculture has and therefore can make an important contribution to overall growth and poverty reduction. Part One took a long and broad view of the process by analyzing a wide range of country cases drawing upon economic history and post-WWII experiences worldwide. Thus the focus of policy and research attention should not be on whether to promote a successful process of agricultural transformation, but on how to do so. Part Two focuses on the how.

The basics needed are not in question: Traditional modes of production have to be replaced by technology and economic organization of farming that will generate sustained increases in agricultural productivity. This transformation requires investment. The main question then is: What are the conditions for such investment on a sustainable basis? Part Two addresses this question. What do we know about this? To address the latter question, Part Two hypothesizes that five conditions must be in place for a sustained period to achieve success in agricultural transformation:

1. A stable framework of macroeconomic and political stability. Central and local governments are able to enforce peace and order.
2. An effective technology-transfer system. Research and extension messages reach the majority of farmers.
3. Access to lucrative markets. The majority of farmers face expanding markets of paying customers. To them, investing in agricultural and rural production is good business.

4. An ownership system, including a system of usufruct rights that rewards individual initiative and toil. It is feasible for farm/rural families to gain monetarily from risk taking and hard work.
5. Employment-creating non-agricultural sectors. As agriculture becomes more productive, it must shed labor, which, unless absorbed into non-farm jobs that pay as well as agriculture, would simply constitute exporting farm poverty to other sectors.

The strong version of the proposed hypothesis is that a lack of even one of these conditions will undermine sustained agricultural growth and its transformation. If one or more of these conditions fails to hold, yet agricultural development occurs, the strong version of the hypothesis is refuted. However, if these five conditions exist but agriculture is still moribund, this would mean that these five conditions are not sufficient. Specifically, Part Two addresses four main questions:

1. Can we find one agriculture that is of sustained high productivity and growth that does not meet all of these five conditions? If so, our hypothesis is refuted. We consider three major high income agricultural exporting countries.[1]
2. If these five conditions exist but agriculture is still not of sustained high productivity, then they are not sufficient. Can we find any such country where agriculture has been important for a long time?
3. If one or more of these conditions do not exist, and yet agriculture is successfully transformed, then the strong version of this hypothesis is refuted. Can we find any country for which this is the case?
4. To maintain these five conditions over decades requires commitment from competent successive governments to investing in and delivering public goods and services in agriculture and rural areas. The benefit to the sector and economy expected from such sustained public investment is an incentive and market environment that promotes short- and long-term private investment among

---

[1] Unless otherwise indicated, GNI data for all countries cases presented are from World Bank: World Development Indicators, September 2010

the majority of farm/rural households in agriculture. Smallholders in much of the developing world have not benefited from such a commitment. Why? What can or should be done about it to promote success in agricultural transformation?

Chapters III and IV address questions 1 and 2; Chapters V and VI deal with questions 3 and 4. Chapter VI argues that a thriving private agriculture is built on public foundations. As Wolfensohn, ninth president of the World Bank Group, is reported to have said, "Government is in the driver's seat." Recognizing that only governments can create the environment needed for success in agricultural transformation, the focus is on how governments establish and sustain the five conditions. The age-old challenge of agriculture, namely that of "feeding the world" (Federico, 2005), must be achieved for all, while we respect the demands of our fragile environment and adjust to climate change. It is clear that achieving successful agricultural transformation in future decades will be even more demanding than what it has been so far. This point has been forcefully made by McCalla (2000: 10), who pointed out, "In fact, we may have to raise output with less and less water and do it in a resource-friendly way." How to shape the changing role of agriculture in order to generate economic surplus on a broad basis will continue to challenge policy makers, practitioners, and researchers alike. Synthesizing two hundred years of the economic history of agricultural development throughout the world, Federico (2005: 1) rightly says that "agriculture is an outstanding success story." Agricultural development has been successful in averting the Malthusian catastrophe in large parts of the world. The challenge will be to build on this success and extend it to all in our increasingly interdependent world.

Finally, it should be apparent to all that although this book discusses some 30 country cases, it has left out most of the agricultural countries of our world.[2] Countries chosen in this book are those whose

---

[2] The 30 or so countries are (in order of the discussion): pre- and post-WWII: England, Japan, and the United States; post-WWII: Ireland, Portugal, the Republic of Korea, Taiwan, China, India, the People's Republic of China, Indonesia, Malaysia, Tunisia, Brazil, Chile, Canada, Australia, New Zealand, Argentina, Ghana, Egypt – lower and upper – the Philippines, Mexico, Morocco, Pakistan, Venezuela, Botswana, Haiti, Myanmar, Turkey, Singapore, and Hong Kong.

experiences constitute tests of the hypotheses being evaluated. If time and space had permitted, many other countries would have been considered, using the same methodology. These tests would be most welcome, as they have the potential for strengthening the hypotheses put forward in this book.

III

Necessary Conditions

Introduction

Summary. Although "newly" established, Canada, Australia, and New Zealand are high-income industrialized economies. Primarily urban, their agriculture and agro-food sectors nevertheless remain important earners of foreign exchange. Since their founding and over the 20th century, their governments have been able to achieve success in the transformation of their agricultures. Their agricultures have benefited from meeting the five conditions. As in most OECD countries, their agriculture and agro-food sectors received substantial market-distorting price supports and subsidies after WWII. Economists rightly argue that these subsidies reduce the efficiency of global resource allocation, hence global growth. However, the success of their agricultural transformation raises the difficult question of whether these subsidies have played an essential role in such transformation. The sustained high productivity performance of agriculture in Australia and New Zealand without these price-distorting subsidies make a strong case that they are not.

Country cases chosen and question addressed. We first consider the cases of Canada, Australia, and New Zealand, three "New World" countries with land-abundant agricultures.[3] They are major agricultural exporting countries that are also industrialized high-income countries – hence our rationale for choosing them. The main question is: Do they meet the five conditions hypothesized earlier? To repeat, successful agricultural transformation has two main components: (a) productivity

---

[3] Canada: On July 1, 1867, the British North America Act united Canada as a single country of four provinces. Australia: The Constitution of Australia came into force on January 1, 1901, when the colonies collectively became states of the Commonwealth of Australia. New Zealand: Self-government was granted in 1852. The process of independence was gradual from then on. New Zealand adopted the Statute of Westminster of 1931 in 1947. New Zealand does not celebrate any independence day. This statute declared Britain's dominions "equal in status."

increases sustained over a period of at least two to three decades and (b) sustained income increases of the majority of farm/rural households. We rule out agricultures as being "successfully transformed" in cases where only a minority of rural households participate in and benefit from economic growth. In the three case studies chosen, we consider the manner in which the five conditions are being fulfilled. For all three countries, there is still relative rural poverty, as average rural incomes are generally lower than average urban incomes. But they do not have the absolute poverty that the one dollar or two dollar per day poverty line of the World Bank entails. Their socio-economic development over decades has a broad base.

Effect of government intervention on agricultural protection in the country cases selected. As in other OECD countries, these three countries intervene (or did until the late 1970s) quite extensively in the operation of their agricultural markets. The situation in Canada is different from those in Australia and New Zealand.

- Canada reduced its financial support to farmers in the 1980s and 1990s, but in the 2000s it raised its support again, while Australia and New Zealand virtually ended their decades-long subsidy assistance.[4] The Producer Subsidy Equivalent (PSE)was estimated to be 21 percent of adjusted value of production in Canada in 2004, compared with 18 percent in the United States and 34 percent in the EU (15) (Krakar and Longtin, 2005).[5]
- During the earlier period, in Australia and New Zealand, the high protection accorded to manufacturing was an implicit tax on agriculture. From the 1900s to the early 1970s, these countries adopted an inward-oriented, import-substituting strategy. Tariff revenue accounted for around one-fifth of all government revenue. The tariffs were at very high levels given their per capita income levels, the highest in the world at that time (1870). The high tariffs were supplemented in the 1930s by quantitative

---

[4] In 2006, Canadian farmers received CAD 16,600 on average per farm, a total budgetary outlay of CAD 3.8 billion (OECD, 2008a).

[5] Producer Subsidy Equivalent (PSE) is an indicator of the annual monetary value of gross transfers from consumers and taxpayers to support agricultural producers, measured at farm gate level, arising from policy measures, regardless of their nature, objectives, or effects on farm production or income.

restrictions and were raised even more in the 1960s. Thus by the 1970s, the tariffs on manufacturing were the highest among OECD countries (Anderson et al., 2008: 9). To counteract the tax, the governments implemented policies of direct assistance to agricultural producers such as input and output subsidies, regulatory interventions, and price stabilization schemes. As a result of both the implicit taxation of the sector (through protection on manufacturing) and direct assistance to agricultural producers, the latter were taxed around 10 percent (1955–59), and later around 6 percent (1975–79), while in New Zealand the implicit taxation rates were 16 and 6 percent, respectively (Anderson et al., 2008: table 4).[6]

- During the later period, from the 1970s to 2000s, Australia dismantled the protection on both industry and agriculture; in New Zealand, the process started in the 1970s, gathered momentum in the mid-1980s, and was virtually completed by 2000. Thus the Nominal Rate of Assistance (NRA) for Australia was 0.5 percent and that for New Zealand 2.4 percent for 2000–2004 (Anderson et al., 2008: table 4).[7] Anderson et al. (2008) argue that the removal of these distortions in agricultural (and manufacturing) incentives maintained for more than a century generated a substantial reform dividend. In both countries, overall growth and the rate of multifactor productivity growth (MFP) in agriculture accelerated.

III.I. Canada – GNI per capita: USD 42,170 (2009)

Brief background. Canada has been transformed from a largely agricultural and rural economy to a high-income industrialized and urban economy since the end of WWI, a period that has seen the

[6] These are measured by the Relative Rate of Assistance (RRA), which is made up of the average percentage of the Nominal Rate of Assistance (NRA) of the tradable components of agriculture relative to the average percentage of the NRA to the tradable components of the non-agriculture sector (Anderson et al., 2008). The NRA is the increase in revenue, including payments not tied to production due to government policy intervention.
[7] This is a measure of the financial support from government policy. It is defined as an increase in gross revenue from sales of product relative to the no-policy situation. A positive number means positive support. See http://www.fao.org/DOCREP/006/J1866E/j1866e11.htm, which explains these different measures.

impressive growth of manufacturing, mining, and service sectors. In 1900, agriculture contributed to 25 percent of GDP, falling to around 5 percent in the 1970s (TD Bank Financial Group, 2007). Today, primary agriculture contributes to around 2 percent of GDP (2002) (Canadian Federation of Agriculture, 2008). The broader agriculture and agro-food sector contributes to 8 percent of GDP (early 2000s) and accounts for one in seven Canadian jobs, three-quarters of which are beyond the farm gate (Skogstad, 2007: 26). By the end of the 20th century, the agriculture and agro-food sector was exhibiting high productivity growth, far above that of the business sector. Between 1997 and 2003, the annual multi-factor productivity growth rate of primary agricultural production (which includes forestry, fishing, and hunting) was around 3 percent (exceeding that of industry, which was 1.5 percent). Canada was the fourth-largest exporter of agriculture and agro-food products after the EU (15), the United States, and Brazil (Krakar and Longtin, 2005).[8] Canadian scholars distinguish four stages in the transformation of Canada's agriculture: from a staples sector in the late 19th century to a mature staples economy in the early 21st century (Skogstad, 2007).

The manner in which the five conditions are fulfilled. Over more than a century, successive Canadian governments have put in place and maintained the five conditions:

1. *Condition on stability*: Over the span of the 20th century, Canada experienced political and price stability, and the government enforced law and order. During the 1970s and 1980s, however, Canada did experience inflation of 5–10 percent per year following the oil price crises and commodity price hikes. Canada also had large and rising fiscal deficits from the mid-1970s to the mid-1990s. In fact, all three countries analyzed here, Canada, Australia, and New Zealand, suffered from high inflation from the mid-1970s through the 1980s. This inflation is referred to as the Great Inflation (Nelson, 2005: 135–36, figs. 1–3). So for Canada up to 1972, the annual rate of inflation averaged 2 per-

---

[8] By 2007, it was the fifth-largest exporter, after Australia (TD Bank Financial Group, 2007).

cent. After 1992, the inflation rate again averaged 2 percent per year (Thiessen, 1999: 2).

2. *Condition on an effective technology-transfer system*: The need for agricultural research was recognized more than a hundred years ago. The first step took place in 1859 when Reverend Abbé Pilote founded the first Canadian School of Agriculture at Sainte Anne-de-la-Pocatière, Quebec. In 1886, Parliament passed a bill establishing five experimental farms. The research station and experimental farm system expanded to more than 40 research establishments from coast to coast. Today, the overall responsibility for the adequacy of research rests with the federal authorities, while provinces have jurisdiction over agricultural teaching and extension. Many farmers operate on a relatively small scale, under differing climate, soil, and other conditions. They cannot afford to finance, organize, and conduct research; thus, because such work is in the public interest, most farming and food research is financed directly or indirectly by governments.[9] The research function is shared by Agriculture Canada and other federal agencies, provincial departments of agriculture, provincial research councils, faculties of agriculture in universities, veterinary medicine, and private industry. Food research complements conventional agricultural production research to provide an abundant variety of high-quality foods. During a century of research, plant varieties and animal strains have been improved; good soil conservation practices have been implemented; losses by insect pests and plant diseases, animal disease, drought, and frost have been reduced or overcome; economical methods of storage and food preservation have been discovered; and better means of using food crops and animal products have been developed (*Canadian Encyclopedia*, 2011).

3. *Condition on access to lucrative markets*: Access to markets was progressive and took various forms. In 1930, one-third of all

---

[9] This situation is, however, changing rapidly as farm sizes have increased significantly over the past decade or so. Farm sizes at and below $250,000 per year dropped by nearly 22 percent from 1996 to 2006, while those at and above $2.5 million per year increased by more than 143 percent over the same period. Smaller farms still dominate in numbers, but farms with an annual revenue of $500,000 and higher, while accounting for only 11 percent of all Canadian farms in 2005, contributed to 55 percent of total farm sales (Sparling and Laughland, 2008: fig. 1).

Canadians lived on farms; by 1941, one-quarter did. During this period, when a high proportion of Canadians were members of farm households, the Canadian Wheat Board (created temporarily during 1919–21 and restored in 1935 under farm pressure) was given monopoly powers to sell prairie grain. The federal government stabilized the prices of 11 commodities, including grain, dairy, and meat products. The federal government also provided income support programs starting in the late 1930s; one of these was the Canadian Agricultural Income Stabilization Program to protect farmers from sudden drops in their incomes due to circumstances beyond their control (Office of the Auditor General of Canada, 2007). From around 1945 to 1975, there was substantial federal government assistance to agriculture in the form of subsidized credit (which promoted mechanization), further expansion of the price stabilization measures initiated in the 1940s, and entering into international trade agreements. An important initiative of this period was the development of national marketing boards for dairy, poultry, and egg producers, with the mandate to control domestic supply and to protect domestic markets from imports. More recently, there was increasing regional market integration – for example, via the Canada–U.S. Free Trade Agreement in 1989 and the North American Free Trade Agreement in 1994 (NAFTA).

4. *Condition on an ownership system, including a system of usufruct rights that rewards individual initiative and toil. It is feasible for farm/rural families to gain monetarily from risk taking and hard work*: Canada has always recognized and enforced the system of private property rights for white settlers. However, on the Canadian prairies the Indians were confined to specific reserves, with all other land passing to the Crown. Property was held by the aboriginal population on a collective basis, in accordance with their traditions. Therefore, from the very beginning, the status of property rights for white settlers on the prairies was different from those of Indians. A white settler could obtain the standard 160-acre homestead for a nominal $10 fee, which after a three-year proving-up period became fully privately owned. The settler could then use his or her land as collateral when buying

equipment, animals, and building materials. There were also preemption and railway lands available as and when the farm needed to expand. Indians were not, however, permitted to apply for homestead or preemption land, and so were confined to their reserves, where there was also no spare land onto which they could subsequently expand their farms, should they have been successful (Ward, 2006).

5. *Condition on employment-creating non-agricultural sectors*: Non-agricultural employment and income have become increasingly important for smaller farms. In rural Canada, 1956 was the first year non-farm rural population exceeded farm rural population; by 2001, only 11 percent of the rural population was farm (Olfert, 2006). Between 1980–81 and 2000–2001, employment in agriculture declined by 6.8 percent, while in agriculture and agro-food combined, it increased by 31.2 percent. Thus about 78–93 percent of rural employment was not in agriculture. In 2000, farm families with incomes above $10,000 had 75 percent of their income off-farm. Growth in the rural economy, farm and non-farm, was closely tied to urban growth. By the 1990s, the share of non-farm income in total farm household income averaged 80 percent, being made up of wages and salaries, non-farm self-employment, pension, investment, among other things (Canadian Government, 2006). Large farms, earning more than $250,000 in gross revenues per year, earn most of their income through farming. Also, on a per farm basis, they receive the highest in program payments. Farm households, earning between $10,000 and $249,999, are highly dependent on off-farm income.[10] In 2004, off-farm employment income was the main contributor to the increase in total off-farm income and represented close to 70 percent of total off-farm income of farm families (Agriculture and Agri-Food, Canada, 2007). Essentially, the rural economy is no longer to be equated with the agricultural economy, and the engine of the rural economic growth has increasingly become the urban economy.

---

[10] Average family income of farm and non-farm households in Canada was $50,000 (2000–2002). In 2004, the average farm household net worth was $900,000 (Canadian Government, 2006: fig. 2).

III.II. Australia – GNI per capita: USD 43,770 (2009)

Brief background. The performance of Australian agriculture is a major achievement, particularly as it is in one of the "driest parts of the world, with by far the oldest, most infertile, most nutrient-leached soils of any continent" (Henzell, 2007). Australia is subject to extreme climatic variations, which have an inevitable impact on farm incomes and the entire economy.[11] An old saying was that the Australian economy rode on the sheep's back. As in other high-income industrialized economies, the relative importance of agriculture has shrunk dramatically over the past century. During the early part of the 20th century, agriculture contributed to 25 percent of GDP and 70–80 percent of export earnings. Agriculture's contribution (of raw and unprocessed commodities) to exports remained substantial at around a quarter of total export earnings per year (e.g., 22 percent in 2003–2004). As the overall economy industrialized and was transformed, agriculture's relative share kept declining: to 14 percent in the 1960s, 6 percent in the 1980s, 4–6 percent during the last two decades of the 20th century, and 3 percent in 2003–2004. By 2003–2004, it employed 4 percent of Australia's workforce, down from 9 percent in the late 1960s. On the basis of an assessment of the direct and indirect role of agriculture in the Australian economy, however, the size of the farm-dependent industries is estimated to be 12 percent of GDP (1998–2004) (Econtech, 2005).[12] Food and beverage processing is the largest Australian manufacturing industry. Moreover, in absolute terms, output since the 1960s has grown at 2.4 percent per year, with the growth due primarily to high productivity growth. Over the past 25 years, annual multifactor productivity growth has averaged 2.3 percent, higher than in the market sector, at 1.1 percent (Australian Government Productivity Commission, 2005).[13] According to ABRARE (Australian Bureau of

---

[11] For example, in the drought of 2002–2003, a drop of 19 percent of gross agricultural production led to a decline of 1 percent of GDP (Hedley and Lu, 2004).

[12] Similar studies have been undertaken for the United States, United Kingdom, and Canada. They all show that despite primary agriculture's small size, there are strong links between agriculture and the rest of the economy, so that the farm-dependent sector is much larger.

[13] The market sector excludes the following: property and business sectors, government administration and defense, education, health and community services, and personal and other services.

Agriculture and Resource Economics), productivity grew from 100 in 1953 to 343 in 2002, declining to 261 in 2003 due to the drought and increasing again to 332 in 2004 (Mullen, 2007). The index is highly variable, reflecting mainly seasonal conditions. Productivity growth in agriculture has been around three times that in the economy as a whole and has markedly outpaced the decline in terms of trade facing farmers over the past 15 to 20 years (1990s on).

The manner in which the five conditions are fulfilled. Over the 20th century, since Australia became a federation on January 1, 1901, successive Australian governments have put in place and maintained the five conditions.[14] It is interesting to note the differences from and similarities to the Canadian situation. The fulfillment of the five conditions is as follows:

1. *Condition on stability*: The 20th century was generally a period of relatively low inflation, and the government enforced law and order. There were standout decades of high inflation, however: the second decade of the century and the 1970s and 1980s. Very much like the situation in Canada and much of the world, the oil price shocks and domestic inflationary pressures in the 1970s resulted in a long period of high inflation – an annual average of 10.4 percent in the 1970s and 8.1 percent in the 1980s. The 1990s saw a return to very low inflation rates, with inflation averaging around 2 percent per year. While the low inflation in the 1990s is impressive in itself, the comparison with previous periods is even more striking given the strong economic growth experienced during the second half of the 1990s (Australian Government, Department of the Treasury, 2002).

2. *Condition on an effective technology-transfer system*: Institutionalized agricultural research and development as well as farmers' own experimentation have been important factors in the creation of new knowledge and technical advances in Australian agriculture. Industry and government contributions fund research and development, which is undertaken mainly by public sector researchers and departments of agriculture. It is estimated that agricultural

---

[14] The Commonwealth of Australia Constitution Act (UK) passed on July 5, 1900, and was given royal assent by Queen Victoria on July 9, 1900.

research and development has driven 85 percent of the 2–4 percent per year productivity growth evident in many agricultural sub-sectors over a sustained period (Australian Government, Ministry of Agriculture, 2005). Australia's agriculture has a history of innovation; this includes the introduction of the stump jump plough and combine harvester at the turn of the 20th century, improvements in ground preparation, and disease and weed control through the use of advanced chemicals and fertilizers, large-scale irrigation via artesian water and dams, and the use of satellite technology to aid in land use decisions and to guide and control spraying and preparation equipment. The adoption of new and improved technologies, together with increased mechanization of many aspects of agricultural production, has increased labor productivity. Australian farmers are also better educated than they were two decades ago. Access to effective technology transfer has contributed to impressive results. According to a study by Coelli and Prasada Rao (2003) comparing total factor productivity growth across 93 agricultural producers in the world, Australia's performance compares well with other countries in the OECD over the past two decades and is similar to the level in the United States. TFP growth in the broadacre[15] and dairy sectors is highly variable from year to year but has increased over the past several decades. Between 1977–78 and 2000–2006, productivity growth in the broadacre sector has averaged 1.5 percent per year. In the dairy sector, it has averaged 1.2 percent per year. Between 1953 and 1968, productivity in broadacre grew by 2 percent per year and after that period by 2.5 percent.

3. *Condition on access to lucrative markets*: Australia found markets for its agriculture from the early days, as exports have always been important for Australia's agriculture and accounted for up to 80 percent of its export earnings until the late 1950s. The export of beef and mutton to the United Kingdom started with the advent of refrigeration. Export markets drove the expansion of meat production, and the 1932 Ottawa agreements granted preferential access for Australia to British markets. When this agreement

---

[15] Broadacre crops are the following: winter crops – wheat, barley, oats, canola, and lupins; summer crop – grain sorghum.

expired in the 1960s, the market focus shifted to the United States, Japan, the USSR, and the Middle East. In recent decades, the government has assisted agro-business and other businesses through the Australian Trade Commission (Austrade), a business-focused statutory authority within the Foreign Affairs and Trade portfolio. Austrade is dedicated to helping Australian businesses – particularly small and medium enterprises – find export and investment opportunities overseas, through the resources of its offices in Australia and in more than 90 cities around the world. Since the 1990s, the focus has shifted to the ASEAN countries, a region with some of the fastest-growing economies in the world. The institutions for facilitating marketing have evolved over the years. Thus:

- At the onset of WWII, the Australian Wheat Board (AWB) was established to stabilize prices and meet wartime demand, and the AWB was allowed monopoly control of the domestic market for 40 years. The security of a fixed price, soil improvement, disease-resistant varieties, and improved cultivation techniques led to further expansion of the wheat belt. Domestic wheat marketing was deregulated in 1989 (Economicexpert. com, 2003).
- In the late 1970s and early 1980s, Australia operated supply management types of schemes in the dairy industry, and buffer stock and reserve price schemes in the wool industry.
- From the mid-1980s on, as part of a wider program of microeconomic reform, government began to dismantle statutory marketing arrangements and price support schemes, which provided the bulk of the support. Effective rates of assistance (ERA), which averaged 13 percent in the 1970s, declined to 5 percent by 2003–2004.[16]
- Australia has, however, several producer-based organizations in major commodity groups that support market promotion programs. These programs are funded by a grower levy and also receive government funds. For example, the objective of the

---

[16] ERA is the dollar value of measured assistance divided by unassisted value added. For agriculture, this assistance includes tariff assistance, assistance provided by domestic regulatory, and pricing arrangements.

Supermarket to Asia Council (1996) is to increase Australia's food exports to Asia. The Council brings together government and industry leaders, who work to maximize Australia's food export potential to Asia. Another example is the Australian Meat and Livestock Corporation (AMLC), which exists to improve the production of Australian meat and livestock, to protect market access, to ensure the best possible delivery of the product, and to encourage the consumption of meat. The AMLC focuses its efforts in Japan, the United States, South Asia, Europe, and the Middle East. The Australian Dairy Corporation (ADC) focuses on maximizing overseas trade and market access opportunities and reinforcing trade access gains by promoting Australia's image as a reliable supplier of quality products. The ADC is funded by the Australian dairy industry and by its own trading activities. No funds are provided by the government. Other corporations exist for fresh produce, wine and brandy, and wool.

Today, a major market access issue for Australia is the reform of international agricultural markets. As a relatively small economy (in a trade sense, a price taker), Australia has a strong interest in the maintenance of an effective rules-based trading system as well as in the liberalization of trade in agriculture, goods, and services. Reflecting this interest, Australia has taken a lead role in the agriculture negotiations and is chair of the Cairns Group coalition of WTO members that advocates outcomes for agriculture that would substantially improve market access, reduce trade-distorting domestic supports, and eliminate export subsidies (Cairns Group, 2005).

4. *Condition on an ownership system, including a system of usufruct rights that rewards individual initiative and toil. It is feasible for farm/rural families to gain monetarily from risk taking and hard work*: As in Canada, the original inhabitants and the white settlers were treated differently with respect to landownership, among other things. The right to own land was a key component of the Anglo-Saxon culture that colonized Australia. The white settlers, many of them known as squatters in 19th-century Australia, were granted land even as Britain declared Australia

terra nullius (empty land), thus dispossessing the Aborigines, who had inhabited the vast continent for thousands of years.[17] The issue of land rights is particularly problematic in the case of mining rights (Yunkaporta, 2008). Britain was fully aware of an indigenous population when it sent the first fleet of convicts to Botany Bay in 1787. However, according to the government, "The people could not be considered owners of their land. They were simply primitive and happy occupants" (Moore, 2001). Terra nullius certainly provided the rationalization for the initial British invasion of Australia. The concept also helped to bring the land fully under the settlers' control by legitimizing Britain's "claim of effective proprietorship that is made by the physical occupation of that land" (House, 2001).[18] Many squatters were given leasehold rights, which could be converted into ownership with security of tenure for a fee after a certain number of years. During the 19th century, several pieces of land legislation formalized squatting (Wikipedia, 2009). The interested reader can consult an eventful history of confrontations and corruption as squatters and free settlers battle over land (Spooner, 2005).

5. *Condition on employment-creating non-agricultural sectors*: The increased share of off-farm employment and income in rural household income is a common feature of most OECD countries.[19] The share of agricultural employment has shrunk significantly since the start of the 20th century, when agriculture itself was nearly 25 percent of total GDP. By the 1960s, agriculture was 16 percent of GDP, and agricultural employment was 10 percent of total employment. In the 2000s, the share of both has shrunk to 3 percent of their respective totals (2005–2006) (Anderson et al., 2008: table 1). However, the contribution of off-farm income – that is, off-farm wages and salaries, investment dividends, rents and other business income, and government social support payments – has averaged 65 percent of total income of broadacre

---

[17] As of 2010, no settlement satisfactory to them had been reached with the government of Australia.
[18] The 1992 Mabo judgment finally freed the continent of *terra nullius* as a legal doctrine.
[19] Mexico, an OECD country, still has a major problem with off-farm employment. See the later discussion of Mexico.

families between 1989–90 and 2002–2003.[20] Agriculture and closely related sectors generated 12 percent of GDP (2005), although primary agriculture's contribution to the GDP was around 3 percent in 2002–2005 (ABRARE, MAF, 2006). The difference between what primary agriculture employed – about 3 percent, and around 17 percent when farming and related industries are concerned – is significant (in absolute terms employing 1.6 million Australians). Half of these jobs are in six capital cities (ABRARE, 2007). The significance is that the non-farm sector, a substantial portion of which is in agro-processing, is generating the bulk of jobs.

III.III. New Zealand – GNI per capita USD 26,830 (2009)

Brief background. New Zealand has been considered an agricultural country since the 19th century, when the introduction of refrigerated transport (1890s) allowed its sheep and dairy industries to expand so as to provide the United Kingdom with meat, wool, butter, and other agricultural products.[21] New Zealand says of itself that "[i]n the global context, New Zealand can be described as being in the business of pampering the palates and passions of the world's more prosperous citizens" (Government of New Zealand, 2004). New Zealand does not export staples, but products with higher income elasticities. With increasing mechanization and the rapid growth of other sectors, the proportion of the population working in agriculture (including fishing and forestry) declined steadily from about 37 percent in 1901 to 9.4 percent in 1999 (New Zealand Agriculture). Unlike the case in most other OECD countries, agriculture is still a very important part of the economy of New Zealand. Agriculture is mainly pastoral farming, but it also includes horticulture. In 1984, on the eve of New Zealand's economy-wide market liberalization, primary agriculture accounted for around 7 percent of GDP. The share of primary agriculture had declined from 15 percent in 1960 to 5 percent in 1999 (Johnson, 2000). In 2008,

---

[20] Broadacre industries surveyed were wheat and other crops, mixed livestock crops, sheep, beef, and sheep-beef.

[21] New Zealand today is primarily urban – around 72 percent of the population now lives in cities – but agriculture is still the main export industry (Wikipedia, 2009).

it stood at 4–5 percent. When agro-business is included, the contribution rises to around 14 percent (1986–87) and 17 percent (1999–2000) (Lamble, 2005). Agriculture is also a significant contributor to employment and exports. For employment, the contribution ranges from about 9 percent of total employment under the narrow definition to around 30 percent under the wider definition. Growth in TFP since 1970 is considered one of the highest among OECD countries. Since the 1984 reforms, productivity has increased by 4 percent per year (Johnson, 2000). There are other estimates: 7.7 per annum since 1984, mainly in horticulture, according to Philpott, and an increase of more than 30 percent in average productivity as a result of drastic cuts in inputs, according to Kalaitzandonakes, Spinelli, and Bredahl (1993). These productivity increases enabled New Zealand to regain competitiveness (1990–92), which it had lost from 1986 to 1989, according to the index of competitiveness published by the New Zealand Institute of Economic Research (Sandrey and Scobie, 1994). New Zealand today is famous for having a thriving agriculture without subsidies, in the form of market-distorting price supports for its farmers.

The manner in which the five conditions are fulfilled. Throughout the 20th century, New Zealand's governments have succeeded in establishing the five conditions, despite severe difficulties at times, as when New Zealand lost its major export market, Britain; in 1955, Britain bought nearly 66 percent of New Zealand's exports (Wikipedia, 2009), but on January 1, 1973, Britain formally joined the Common Market of the European Union.[22] The fulfillment of the five conditions has been thus:

1. *Condition on stability*: Like Canada and Australia, New Zealand was able to maintain macro and political stability throughout most of the 20th century, despite short periods of inflation and political tension. There were inflationary periods, as during the international oil and food commodity price crises of the late 1970s and 1980s. From around 1974 to 1988, New Zealand

[22] New Zealand's economy was turned toward Great Britain for historical reasons. New Zealand was declared a dominion by a royal proclamation in 1907. It achieved full internal and external autonomy by the Statute of Westminster Adoption Act in 1947, although this merely formalized a situation that had existed for many years. Great Britain applied to join the Common Market of Europe in 1967.

experienced more than 10 percent annual inflation (*New York Times*, 1988). There was tension over land between settlers and the original inhabitants, the Maoris, which quickly led to further conflict. In the 19th century, the New Zealand governor had begun buying up land from the Maoris to appease those colonists who wanted more land available to them. However, in the 1970s, a Maori political movement demanding compensation gathered steam, and a number of young Maoris staged protests to gain attention for the cause. In the 1980s and 1990s, academics and government officials finally began to take real notice of Maori grievances. In 1995 and 1998, the government gave the Ngai Tahu and the Waikato-Tainui tribes NZ$170 million each worth of land and monetary compensation (Faucette, 2008).

2. *Condition on an effective technology-transfer system*: Effective technology transfer existed way back. Livestock is of primary importance in New Zealand's agriculture.[23] Vaccines for farm animal diseases were introduced in New Zealand early in the 20th century and were initially produced by government laboratories. The development of the privately owned Tasman Vaccine Laboratories in the 1950s, together with the importation of drugs by companies such as Burroughs Welcome and Coopers, made a wide range of vaccines available. More recently, both the Ministry of Agriculture and Forestry and commercial vaccine companies have developed a range of vaccines for sheep against infectious conditions that cause abortion (Veterinary Services, 2008). The effectiveness of the technology-transfer system, among other things, has contributed to a sustained average rate of multi-factor productivity growth of 1.8 percent per year from 1926–27 to 2000–2001. Disaggregated in three sub-periods, it was 1 percent between 1926–27 and 1955–56, rising to 2.2 percent from 1956–57 to 1982–83 and to 2.6 percent from 1983–84 to 2000–2001 (Hall and Scobie, 2006). Hall and Scobie estimate that investment in domestic research and development has generated an annual rate of return of 17 percent. They also emphasize the importance of access to foreign knowledge in a small, open economy.

---

[23] Horticulture is next, but it is of growing importance.

3. *Condition on access to lucrative markets*: New Zealand has always
   been a trade-oriented economy. As a member of the British
   Commonwealth, it enjoyed special treatment for its agricultural
   products. As late as 1964, New Zealand's main trading partner
   was the United Kingdom. In 1966, the UK purchased two-thirds
   of New Zealand's total exports (World Bank, 1968: 110). To the
   UK, it exported 61 percent of its meat production (lamb, mutton,
   beef, veal), 94 percent of its butter, and 87 percent of its cheese. This
   ceased when the UK joined the EU in 1973 and Commonwealth
   preference was abolished. New Zealand had to find new markets and it did. By 1998–99, exports to Britain were only 6 percent of total. New Zealand's most important trading partners in
   the late 1980s when it undertook the reforms were the United
   Kingdom, Germany (West, before 1989), and Italy in the EC,
   Australia and Japan, the United States, and Canada. After the
   reforms, the major new markets became Australia, Japan, Korea,
   China, and Southeast Asia. From 1970 to 1989, New Zealand's
   exports increased by 95 percent, while global trade grew by more
   than 150 percent. This relatively slower growth was due to its concentration in markets that were themselves contracting and were
   highly protectionist (Sandrey and Scobie, 1994). Since 1990, New
   Zealand has been actively developing free trade relationships with
   its neighbors. The "Closer Economic Relations" (signed in 1983)
   with Australia has created a single market of some 22 million
   people. New Zealand has a free trade agreement with Singapore
   (2001); with Singapore, Brunei, and Chile, New Zealand formed
   the Trans Pacific Strategic Economic Partnership (2005), initiated
   a free trade deal with Thailand (2005) and with China (2008), and
   has been discussing (2007) a deal with the Gulf states.

4. *Condition on an ownership system, including a system of usu-*
   fruct rights that rewards individual initiative and toil. It is feasi-
   ble for farm/rural families to gain monetarily from risk taking and
   hard work: New Zealand recognized and enforced private property rights for white settlers but not for the original inhabitants
   (until June 25, 2008). It also put in the foundations of a more
   equitable land distribution for the white settlers. The history of
   white settlement was not always peaceful. The increasing number of early-19th-century settlers led to violent conflict over land

between the Maoris and the white settlers, called Pahekas.[24] In the 1880s, New Zealand's economic activity centered in the South Island and on the export of wool, principally from the great pastoral estates. With the advent of refrigeration, the economic frontier shifted northward, stimulated by the export of dairy products and frozen meat. Thus refrigeration and technology developments in dairying underpinned the drift north. The shift was also accompanied by a broadening of the base of landownership.[25] By the 1920s, small and medium farms dominated, and the landownership in New Zealand became broad-based. The opportunities for dairying and mixed farming on newly opened lands in the North Island diffused the issue of land monopoly that had loomed large in New Zealand political economy in the 1890s. The moves toward wider landownership in New Zealand enabled small and medium farmers to gain from the trade-related rise in land prices. Crown land, following the extinguishing of Maori rights, was alienated in a variety of ways, including sale of the freehold and various types of lease. There were two main stages:

1. Up to 1890, the great majority of Crown land transfers were of the freehold category, especially for the better-quality land.

2. After 1890, public policy, stimulated partly by the opportunities for dairy farming arising from refrigeration, was directed toward unlocking the alleged "land monopoly" and promoting denser settlement and smaller farms. The leasing of smaller acreages of Crown land was facilitated by new legislation in 1892. Before 1892, "perpetual" leases were subject to renewal and revaluation after 21 years and included a right to purchase the freehold. The system was then extended, by creating

---

[24] War broke out between the settlers and the Maoris, and the New Zealand Land Settlement Act of 1863 led to land confiscation without due process or compensation. It was not until June 25, 2008, that the New Zealand government signed a treaty with a group of Maori tribes to compensate them for land confiscated by the Pahekas. This treaty transferred 170,000 ha of forestland worth NZ$319 million into Maori ownership. There was also an official apology by the Crown and an agreement of a corrected historical account of past events (Faucette, 2008).

[25] However, bringing more of the richer, wetter lands of the North Island into productive use also depended upon the construction of a transport infrastructure, on the pacification with the Maoris, and on the land policies of government.

"leases in perpetuity" (actually for 999 years), charged at 4 percent each year of the initial valuation and not subject to revaluation. The secretary for Crown lands, Percy Smith, argued that such leases were practically the same as freehold and carried rights of sale, sub-lease, mortgage, or disposition by will, although they had conditions, such as a requirement to occupy and improve the land.

The system was intended to encourage closer settlement by keeping the capital cost of new farm formation low and to encourage the improvement and utilization of land. Subsequent legislation gave leaseholders a right to purchase the freehold. Average farm size fell after 1890, and activity in the rural land market accelerated. Selling land had become cheap and simple in New Zealand after the Torrens system of land registration was adopted in 1870.[26] The New Zealand state was able to clearly establish property rights in the rural sector at the initial stages of colonization. It allowed for the extension of property rights for the new waves of white settlers, while at the same time kept a tight control over the destination and uses of public land. By doing so, it facilitated the access to land to a large part of the population, effectively preventing the control of land by oligarchic groups. By 1914, only around 25 percent of farmland remained genuinely leasehold (Greasley and Oxley, 2005: 7). New Zealand's history of land distribution and settlement is often contrasted with that of Uruguay, where a very different pattern characterized the institutions of the rural sector. This early history has had major consequences for later development (Scaniello and Porcille, 2006: 9–10).[27]

5. *Condition on employment-creating non-agricultural sectors*: As in other industrialized high-income OECD countries, the bulk

[26] Titles to land were not held in the form of deeds, but by registration at a land office. The advantage was in providing secure titles at low cost, and without survey, the system diminished barriers to the frequent transfer of rural land. The data arising from land transfers under the registration system are an important source of price information, given the frequency with which rural land changed hands.

[27] In Uruguay, the access of the population to land was a highly conflictive process that the state could not organize properly, being unable to resist the pressure of large landowners, the financial demands produced by frequent fiscal crises, and the military and political power of the *caudillos*, of paramount influence among those of the rural population who had neither formal property titles nor leasing contracts protecting their interests (Scaniello and Porcille, 2006: 9–10).

of job creation has been outside agriculture for decades. Non-agricultural rural employment and incomes became particularly important during the reform period, when many farms were losing money because they had to readjust to the new relative price structures. The economic adjustments entailed a substantial decline in land values; a restructuring of output away from the formerly subsidized sheep production toward more beef, dairy, and deer; decreased employment; and the exit of high-debt farms. Many had to find alternative and additional forms of employment and incomes. After the painful adjustment period (the worst period was during 1984–90), restructured farms regained profitability.[28] An estimated 1 percent (800 farms) of farms had to leave the land (Sayre, 2003). The need to earn off-farm income also became widespread. According to a survey undertaken in 1992–93 by the Ministry of Agriculture and Forestry (MAF), earnings from off-farm work averaged $15,000 to $22,000 depending on farm type.[29] Some 73 percent of all farms sampled reported some source of off-farm incomes. Off-farm income, which is received by the majority of farmers in New Zealand, is likely to be increasingly important in the future. Off-farm employment in particular is likely to increase in more densely populated rural areas and in districts within commuting distance of urban areas. In this, rural areas reflect the trend toward pluri-activity in New Zealand as a whole (MAF, 2008). Rural incomes are now more diversified, with rural tourism a vibrant sector.

[28] The painful adjustments were bearable (i.e., not socially destabilizing) thanks to an increase in private and public assistance schemes. The Adverse Events Family Income Support Scheme, initiated in 1988–89 because of the drought, is now in place to support family income.

[29] For comparison, median market income fell from $39,000 to $32,000, by 17 percent, from 1986 to 1991.

IV

Necessary but Not Sufficient Conditions?

Introduction

Summary. Only during the last decades of the 20th century were Ireland and Portugal finally able to put together the five conditions. An important condition is related to the landownership structure. Although both Ireland and Portugal ended the 20th century with predominantly private ownership, there were other structural features that tended to undermine incentives for long-term tenancies and investments in agricultural productivity. The cases of Ireland and Portugal do not refute the hypothesis that the five conditions are necessary. However, their experiences do emphasize the importance of two other factors for successful transformation: (a) the age structure and educational makeup of the farming population and (b) the long time – more than two to three decades – necessary for achieving broad-based high productivity and improved incomes for the majority of farm/rural families. Indeed, a review of selected worldwide experiences shows that the time dimension varies substantially across countries.

Country cases chosen and question addressed. Part One considered the cases of Ireland and Portugal, two industrialized economies that have been star performers. Ireland, long considered a backward agricultural region of Great Britain, became known as the "Celtic Tiger" in the span of a generation (1960–2000). Portugal, long considered a Third World economy in Europe, transformed its economy in the space of 15 years or so (1986–2000). One striking fact about the performance of these two countries is the marginal contribution of their agricultures to their overall economic performance. To repeat, Part One argued that the case of Ireland does not support the pro-agriculture view and, similarly, the case of Portugal does not support the polar pro-agriculture view. This chapter reconsiders the process of their agricultural transformation to assess whether in fact their agricultures did or did not meet the five conditions. If they did but still have not been successfully transformed, this would mean that the five conditions are not sufficient. If they did not meet the five conditions, the experience of these countries would corroborate (but not confirm) the proposed hypothesis.

IV.I. Ireland – GNI per capita: USD 44,310 (2009)

Brief background. At independence (for 26 of its 32 counties) from Great Britain in 1921, Ireland's GDP per capita was a little more than half of Britain's. In 2006, it surpassed Britain's, albeit slightly: USD 45,580 versus USD 44,970.[1] The star performance of the Irish economy occurred during the 1990s following the 1987 reforms that opened the economy, reduced government spending, lowered tax rates, and attracted FDI. Agriculture, the contribution of which was around a third of GDP in the 1920s, now contributes some 3–4 percent (2000s). Throughout these intervening decades, did Irish agriculture meet the five conditions?

Were the five conditions fulfilled and if so, how? It is well known that Irish agriculture received substantial EU funds after Ireland joined the European Economic Community (EEC) in 1973. The contribution of EU payments to farm family income (FFI) has been substantial; for example, for 2007, it was 84 percent of FFI (Connolly, Kinsella, and Moran, 2008: 1). In what incentive and market environment were these received? The incentive and market environment was shaped not only by the receipt of these substantial subsidies, but also by the 1992 EU MacSharry reforms and the Agenda 2000. Over the broad sweep of the 20th century, the environment for agriculture was characterized thus:

1. *Condition on stability*: During most of the post-WWII period, Ireland enjoyed stability. However, it experienced prolonged periods of political instability during the earlier part of the 20th century. Gillmor (1987:175) identified 1960 as the "date of demarcation" in the economic and political history of Ireland's

---

[1] World Bank. World Development Indicators, 2006. GNI per capita for the United Kingdom is USD 47,930 (2008).

agriculture.[2] Prior to that date, Ireland experienced tumultuous times, which had a negative impact on its agricultural production (which is mainly livestock). Shortly after independence in 1921,[3] it waged a bloody civil war (June 28, 1922, to May 24, 1923), which is alleged to have claimed more lives than the war of independence. In the 1930s, under the nationalist and isolationist policies of the Fianna Fáil party, Ireland waged a costly economic war with Britain (its biggest agricultural market before accession to the EEC in 1973), which imposed retaliatory special duties and quotas on Irish agricultural imports.[4] From 1958 to 1972, there was stability and prosperity. Indeed, this first period of sustained growth is labeled Ireland's "first golden age" (MacSharry and Padraic, 2000: 54). From the early to middle 1980s, the economy was characterized by extensive government spending: It was 54 percent of GDP in 1986, with high inflation; 20 percent per year in the early 1980s, with high unemployment; and 17 percent during 1985–87. Price stability returned following the 1987 reforms as annual inflation rates averaged 3–4 percent (Gwartney et al., 2009). Ireland's phenomenal economic growth took off during the 1990s, a period of domestic political and price stability. More recently, since the global financial crisis of 2007–2010, Ireland is again fighting for its economic survival. It is clear that economic success has constantly to be fought for, as the case of Argentina shows (see Chapter V).

2. *Condition on an effective technology-transfer system:* Throughout most of the 20th century, although Ireland had a technology-transfer system, its effectiveness varied over the years. Its primary focus also changed from productivity increases to more generalized assistance to farmers. Since 1900, when the Irish

---

[2] According to Gillmor (1987: 169), 1960 represents a watershed year that marked a major transformation in the modern agricultural and economic development of the Irish Republic.

[3] The Irish war of independence took place from January 21, 1919, to July 11, 1921. Violence, however, continued through 1922.

[4] The measures were undertaken in retaliation against the government of the Republic of Ireland's refusal to pay to Britain land annuities "arising from a programme of tenant purchase prior to independence." During 1931–35, Irish agricultural exports to Britain were halved (Gillmor, 1987:167).

Department of Agriculture and Technical Instruction was established, Ireland has had an agency for delivering extension services. The effectiveness of the system during the tumultuous years of the early 20th century is questionable, as evidenced by the fact that the Free State of Ireland's commercial livestock sector fared poorly in comparison with that of Northern Ireland (Gillmor, 1987: fig. 4, 175).[5] In 1958, a national agricultural institute for agricultural research and extension was created.[6] This institute played a large role in applied agricultural research and in disseminating its results (Kennedy et al., 1988: 64). In the 1980s, budgetary pressures obliged development agencies to charge for their advisory services (Curtin, Haase, and Tovey, 1996: 108–109). Then again (since 1988), the extension advisory services arm of the Agriculture and Food Authority of Ireland – Teagasc – became responsible for assisting farmers on agricultural production issues. Its client base is estimated to have been more than 40,000 farmers out of a potential farming population of 130,000 throughout Ireland (Farrell, McDonagh, and Mahon, 2008).[7] The effectiveness of this agency may be inferred from the fact that the period of the 1950s to the mid-1980s is labeled the "productivist era." One estimate of multi-factor productivity growth from 1954 to 1986 is 2 percent per year (Glass and McKillop, 1990). During this period, the emphasis was on intensive production and increased productivity. Annual labor productivity growth in agriculture between 1990 and 2003 averaged 3.5 percent, lower than the EU-15 at 4.8 percent, and the United States at 4.5 percent (National Competitiveness Council, 2006: fig. 5). Teagasc considers the very success of this "productivist era" in terms of food surpluses to have contributed to a change in the policy environment and a concerted effort to reduce productivity. In 2005, Teagasc launched the "Options for Farm Families Programme," which was based on a radically different approach. Instead of focusing on productivity,

[5] Now referred to as the Republic of Ireland.
[6] The Irish name for the Agricultural Institute is An Foras Taluntais.
[7] Ireland's Central Statistical Office's Household Budget Survey defines a farm household as one in which the head of the household is a farmer or a retired farmer and there is at least one other farmer in the household (O Brien and Hennessy, 2008: 31).

it took a holistic approach to assisting farmers in their new environment. This approach stresses the multi-functionality of agriculture – multi-functionality in terms of providing environmental services, wildlife and habitat preservation, and recreation. The program also requires the active participation of the client farmer to jointly (with the extension agent) find solutions (Farrell et al., 2008).[8]

3. *Condition on access to lucrative markets*: Access to lucrative markets was difficult for Irish farmers for much of the 20th century, when Britain was its main export market. Access improved toward the end of the century. Over this long period, there were distinct ups and downs. The issue was not just access, but how lucrative the markets were. Ireland's markets, domestic and foreign (mainly Britain until 1973), experienced slow growth for a long time. Moreover, Britain subsidized its own farmers through deficiency payments and other improvement grants and allowed market prices to find their own level. The relatively open British market was intensely competitive, and prices received by Irish farmers were often unattractive (Kennedy et al., 1988: 214). Specifically, the market environment for agriculture went through four major phases:

   (a) During the first phase – the decade after independence (1921) and before the protectionist party of Fianna Fáil came into power (March 9, 1932) – agricultural prices collapsed after the WWI boom. Although agriculture was considered the most important sector for the newly independent country, the new government provided no price support for agriculture, and agricultural budgetary expenditures were less than 2 percent of total (1922–23) (Kennedy et al., 1988: 37).

   (b) The second phase was protectionist. It lasted from the 1930s until WWII. An important measure adopted was wheat support: wheat was subsidized, with its price being double the world price by 1936. During WWII, wheat was being promoted for self-sufficiency reasons as well. Sugar beet and horticulture were also protected. The all-important

---

[8] The program has, however, been criticized for being poorly implemented, and client response to this new approach so far is muted.

dairy sector received huge financial incentives from the Irish government. The export-oriented cattle industry, however, suffered from the protectionist policy and the economic war with Britain during the 1930s (Gillmor, 1987: 170–71). The protectionist phase ran out of steam because of the small size of the domestic market. Market access and buoyancy did not improve during most of the 1940s and 1950s. The war years of the 1940s were characterized by extensive rationing. The 1950s were traumatic, as terms of trade deteriorated for Ireland and the government adopted a deflationary budget.

(c) During the third phase, roughly 1958–72, agriculture experienced sustained growth as terms of trade improved, the government adopted expansionary fiscal policies, and the AIFTA was signed (December 1965). Policy had become much more outward-oriented. The market environment improved significantly and so did agriculture's growth rate. Under AIFTA, the British fatstock guarantee was extended to a higher tonnage of Irish exports, subsidies were available at an earlier stage to store cattle, the butter quota was almost doubled and concessions were made to exports of cheddar cheese. Also, the government of Ireland's expenditure on price supports to farmers grew from 3.6 to 19.5 percent of aggregate farm income (1960–70), accounting for 2.6 percent of GDP at factor cost (Sheehy, 1980: 297).

(d) The fourth phase was initiated by Ireland's accession to the EEC. With accession (1973), agriculture benefited from substantial price increases, market expansion, and EEC funds for restructuring. Farmers received a 45 percent increase in real prices during 1971–78 (Sheehy, 1980: 297). Irish agricultural output had access to an expanded market and an inflow of substantial subsidies. Times were good, but they did not last. The late 1970s were marred by the oil price spikes of 1979 and world recession. During 1978–80, real prices received by Irish farmers fell by nearly 21 percent; during 1980–85, they fell by a further 16.5 percent (Sheehy, 1988: 22–23). The 1980s were a period of gloom and doom that fortunately also came to an end with the fundamental reforms of 1987, which succeeded in attracting massive inflows of FDI. The Celtic Tiger was unleashed. During the period of the MacSharry reforms (1992), market access for agricultural produce was ensured but production was also curtailed.

4. *Condition on an ownership system, including a system of usufruct rights that rewards individual initiative and toil. It is feasible for farm/rural families to gain monetarily from risk taking and hard work.* By the mid-1980s, Ireland had a system of private ownership that rewards individual initiative and toil; however, incentives for long-term tenancies were weak until the late 20th century. Widespread landownership is a proud achievement of the Irish people, after centuries of dominance by England and after the successful struggle of the Land League to win back the "Land of Ireland for the People of Ireland." Landownership had become synonymous with national independence. By 1999, Ireland's farm structure was characterized by the dominance of owner-operated smallholdings – 50.2 percent of total (1–5 to 10–19 ha) – followed by medium holdings – 34.6 percent (20–29 to 30–49 ha) – and a small minority of large farms – 15.2 percent (50–100 ha and above) (Bielenberg, 2002: 3–4).[9] Ireland's tumultuous history of land tenure explains the strong attachment Irish farmers have for their smallholdings and the disincentives to developing long-term tenancies. Some key events during this long history of struggle date centuries back, from the time when Henry II (1154–89) laid claim to the land of Ireland and redistributed the conquered lands among those loyal to him, to the 20th century, when England repurchased the land from the landlords to resell to Irish tenants. The key events are the following:

(a) Henry VIII (1491–1547), known as the lord of Ireland, later the king of Ireland, took away the lands surrendered by Irish kings and re-granted their land to them as "earls."

[9] These percentages are computed from Bielenberg (2002: table B). The respective percentages for 1975 are 62.2 (small); 28.7 (medium), and 8.6 (large). Thus it is clear that a quarter of a century ago, the number of smallholdings was much higher and the number of large holdings much lower (Bielenberg, 2002: 4).

(b) The British Penal Laws (1695) restricted Irish Catholics in many areas including the fact that they were forbidden to own land, to school their children, to vote, to be lawyers, or to hold public office.[10]

(c) Over subsequent centuries, most of Ireland was seized by the monarchs of England as the lands of various leaders of rebellion were declared forfeit and re-granted to others.

(d) Thus, in 1641, nearly 40 percent of the land was owned by Catholics; by 1688 (Cromwell's era), it was only 20 percent; and by 1714, it was as little as 7 percent (Bielenberg, 2002: 1).

(e) By the beginning of the 17th century, the only legal forms of land tenure were those recognized under English law – for example, estates held by sole owners, tenancy in common, joint tenants, and coparceners. Thus Irish forms of land tenure were no longer recognized as legal.

(f) The Great Famine (1845–49) was a watershed event. The heavy toll – 1 million deaths, 2 million emigrants, mainly to the United States, and massive evictions (as thousands could not pay the rent) – catalyzed opposition to the English occupation in the form of the Land League.

(g) The Land Purchase Acts of 1903 and 1909 (the precursors of which were the Land Acts of 1870 and 1881) set the framework for government purchase of land from the landlords to be resold to Irish tenants. The Irish Land Commission (1881) paid the former landlords in land bonds, while the new owners spread out their payment to the British government over 40–60 years in the form of annuities. The imputed rent was much lower than what they formerly had to pay as tenants. These Land Purchase Acts have largely shaped the land tenure system that prevails in modern Ireland. They enabled Irish tenants to own the land they were farming.

(h) The legislative framework as implemented by the Land Commission (up to 1985) was to buy up large farms (especially in congested districts) and sub-divide them.

---

[10] William III and Mary II were the monarchs of England, Scotland, and Ireland who instituted the penal laws. The Glorious Revolution of 1688–89 had deposed James II and installed William and Mary as joint sovereigns.

(i) The Commission also bought up for resale the land from landowners who did not cultivate the land themselves.

(j) As a result, there were virtually no long-term tenancies between 1909 and 1965, for landlords who wanted to rent out their land feared compulsory purchase by the Commission. So their only options were to use conacre for tillage lands and agistment for the grazing of livestock, for a maximum period of 11 months.[11] These arrangements were under licenses, not leases, and it was the landlord's duty, not the licensee's, to maintain the property (e.g., fencing, manuring, maintenance of drainage).

(k) In the Land Act of 1984, the government completely changed its policy, which was undermining long-term rentals. Concerned that its policy did not give security of tenure for long-term capital investments in the land, it abolished the compulsory purchase powers of the Land Commission and made long-term leasing legal again.

(l) While the number of long-term tenancies increased, conacre and agist still prevail in Irish agriculture.

Knowledgeable analysts of Irish agriculture however point out that the decades-long (from 1909 until 1984) policy bias in favor of small owner-operated farms and against long-term tenancies is an important reason Irish agriculture today is characterized by many non-viable small farms (Bielenberg, 2002: 4). There is more than 20th-century government policy, however. As Kennedy et al. (1988:216) put it well, "Historical and cultural factors had combined in Ireland to create an intense sense of attachment to the family holding which militated against any system of tenure other than outright ownership."

5. *Condition on employment-creating non-agricultural sectors*: When Ireland's macroeconomy took off during the 1990s, the condition on employment-creating non-agricultural sectors was fulfilled, as indicated by successive National Farm Surveys (NFS). Indeed, the period of high economic growth turned Ireland from a labor-surplus to a labor-scarce economy, with increased

---

[11] Conacre is the letting of a portion of one's land for a single crop. Agistment is the taking in and feeding of somebody else's cattle for a fee.

labor participation rates for females. According to the NFS 1995, in 36.5 percent of farms, the farmer or his spouse had an off-farm job. By the NFS 2006, the figure had jumped to 58 percent. Indeed, some 40 percent of farm households had off-farm income; and almost 30 percent of the farming population was sustainable only because they had off-farm income (O'Brien and Hennessy, 2007: 18, 4). It is clear that the viability of many farms depends on the continued availability of off-farm sources of income. The pull of greater remuneration off-farm and the push of declining real farm incomes (average farm incomes declined by 17 percent in real terms) combined to increase farm household dependence on off-farm employment and income during the Celtic Tiger period (O'Brien and Hennessy, 2007: 192). The shift of labor from agriculture toward industry and services had started around 1960. By 1973 – the year of the accession to the EEC – agriculture provided only 24 percent of total employment, which further declined to only 5 percent of total by 2006. Unemployment fell from a high of 16 percent (1988) to 4 percent (2007) (O'Brien and Hennessy, 2007: 10–11) Most of the employment growth occurred in the newer sectors, such as electronics, pharmaceuticals, medical instrumentation, and international financial services, as well as older sectors, such as construction and tourism. For farmers, off-farm employment was mainly in construction and traditional manufacturing. For farmers' spouses, off-farm jobs were typically in teaching, nursing, or clerical occupations.

Has Irish agriculture been successfully transformed? Irish agriculture has not yet been successfully transformed. Over the course of the 20th century, it traveled a long and bumpy road. The five conditions came together late in the 20th century. Agriculture's competitiveness is still a concern, especially if a freer agricultural trade environment is allowed to materialize. Specifically, there are concerns about low and declining productivity, the substantial number of small unviable holdings, and the relatively low income-cum-poverty of farm households.

- *Slowdown in productivity*: Until well after WWII, Irish agriculture was still characterized by the traditional low-input, low-output system, with land productivity much lower than the "generality of European countries" (Kennedy et al., 1988: 215).[12] In addition, analysts point out that the massive monetary injection into Irish agriculture following EEC accession in 1973 did not give a major boost to production and productivity. The impact was primarily monetary (Sheehy, 1980: 297). Estimates of TFP growth vary, but estimates pertaining to more recent decades suggest a slowing down of productivity growth. For example, Glass and McKillop (1990) estimate that TFP grew at roughly 2 percent per year over the period 1954–86. Still another estimate suggests a decline from 1.5 for the 1980s to 0.7 percent annual growth for the 1990s. Yet another estimate shows a decline from 2.3 (1984–89) to 1.5 percent annual growth (1990–98) (Matthews, Newman, and Thorne 2006: 15–16). The suggested recent slowdown is consistent with the comment by Miller, who spent a year (1999) working in the Irish dairy sector.[13] Comparing Ireland with New Zealand, he noted that "research findings have been slower to get out and be adopted by the farming community." Matthews et al. (2006) attribute the slowdown in productivity in large part to the CAP policies of the MacSharry era (1993–2004) – for example, production quotas and various other restraints, including payments conditional on productivity restraints.[14] Milk quotas, however, started much earlier, in 1984.

- *Unviable smallholdings*: Bielenberg (2002) argues that there are too many small unviable holdings and too few long-term tenancies. This agrarian structure undermines incentives to undertake long-term capital investments required for sustained productivity increases. On the basis of estimates of positive correlation between levels of efficiency, on one hand, and farm size, soil quality, and

[12] Data for 1955 indicate that output per acre of agricultural land in Ireland was lower than in any other Western European country, and was a little more than one-fifth that of the Netherlands and one-third that of Denmark (Kennedy et al., 1988: n. 4, 225).

[13] Miller spent a full year (1998) working in Ireland as part of an exchange between the Consulting Officer Service, and Teagasc, the Irish agency responsible for all agricultural research, consultancy, education, and extension.

[14] During the McSharry era, direct payments increasingly replaced output price supports as a way to maintain farm incomes. Under the 2003 Luxemburg Agreement, the majority of direct payments were decoupled from production.

extension use, on the other, some researchers argue that the predominance of smallholdings is likely to undermine Irish competitiveness in a free trade (less protected and subsidized) environment (O'Brien and Hennessy, 2007: 61).[15] In addition to this structure, the age and education profile of many small farmers is feared to undermine good farm management and adaptation to technical change. In 1981, 44 percent of farmers were aged 55 and over. Only 4 percent of farmers had attended third-level colleges or received any training in agriculture (Kennedy et al., 1988: 218). By the mid-2000s, 25 percent of farmers were older than 65. Almost 50 percent were older than 55. This age imbalance itself is viewed as a result rather than the prime cause of economic and social decline. This age imbalance then exacerbates the original decline, thus setting in motion a vicious circle (Curtin et al., 1996: fig. 2.4, 79–80).[16] Few of these farmers have availed themselves of a government scheme that enables farmers to retire at the age of 55 due to their strong attachment to their farms and lifestyles. This strong attachment is evidenced by the very few farms – 0.1 percent – that went on sale in 1999, when farm prices were very high (O'Gorman, 2006).

• *Relative low–income–cum–poverty concerns*: Despite the substantial financial help given to farmers for decades, there is still a sizable relative poverty problem among farmers.[17] "If poverty is measured by household incomes 50 percent less than the average, some 25 percent of all farmers would qualify" (Sheehy, 1992: 6). By the mid-2000s, "one in five Irish farmers lives in poverty, defined as an annual income less than £7,000" (O'Gorman, 2006). The CAP commodity price support programs, while assisting all farmers, were regressive and actually contributed to widening the disparities between large and small farms, and therefore increased the relative poverty of small farms (Curtin et al., 1996: 115).

---

[15] Note that farm size and efficiency vary inversely in South African agriculture, according to Van Zyl, Binswanger, and Thirtle (1995).

[16] This vicious circle is referred to as the "principle of circular and cumulative causation."

[17] Almost $11 billion was allocated for the period 1993–99 from the EU's Structural and Cohesion Funds. During the 1990s, living standards rose from 56 percent to 87 percent of the EU average. (Ireland Economy)

IV.II. Portugal – GNI per capita: USD 20,940 (2009)

Brief background. Portugal, considered a Third World economy in the 1960s, has now joined the ranks of high-income, industrialized countries. Consistent with the universal pattern of structural economic change, the contribution of agriculture to GDP declined from 30 percent in 1950 (Avillez, Finan, and Josling, 1988: 7) to around 3 percent by 1998 (Bandarra, 2002: 44). When Portugal joined the EC (then EC-12, now EU-27) in 1986, its GDP per capita was about 53 percent of the EU average; by 2008, it reached 75 percent.[18] However, while Ireland's GDP per capita is well above the EU average, Portugal's is one of the lowest in Western Europe (2005–2007). In this process of fundamental transformation of its economy, has its agriculture been successfully transformed? Did it meet the five conditions?

Were the five conditions fulfilled and, if so, how? In assessing the framework for Portugal's agriculture over the 20th century, the differences and similarities between Portugal and Ireland are of particular interest. One striking historical difference is that Portugal was a major colonial power for almost seven centuries, whereas Ireland never had any colony. In fact, Ireland was itself under Great Britain's domination for centuries. Another important structural difference is the dualism in Portuguese agriculture – *minifundia* in the north and *latifundia* in the center and south (Moreira, 1989: 72) – whereas Irish agriculture is dominated by small and medium holdings. One striking recent similarity is the policy environment for Portugal's agriculture after accession to the EC in 1986. Also, Portugal, like Ireland, went through watershed events throughout the 20th century. Late in the century, the watershed events were the 1974 revolution and the 1986 accession to the EEC, which marked a fundamental reorientation of Portugal, from a colonial power under authoritarian rule to a democratic nation-state becoming integrated into Western Europe (Syrett, 2002: 2). This reorientation is evident with respect to the exis-

---

[18] In purchasing power parity terms.

tence/non-existence of the five conditions, which characterized the environment for agriculture. Thus:

1. *Condition on stability*: Portugal has known long periods of stability and instability in the past century. It entered the 20th century as a monarchy and ended it as a Western democracy. For the decades in between, it was under a dictatorship. There was stability during the Salazar dictatorship, albeit through repressive means, and after 1985. The transitions were messy. Over the first quarter of the 20th century, Portugal experienced a tumultuous last decade of the monarchy and a chaotic first Republican era (1910–26). These difficult times were punctuated by strikes, demonstrations, assassinations, financial crises, and high inflation. Some oft-cited events are as follows:

   (a) student demonstrations at the University of Coimbra in 1907;
   (b) assassination of King Carlos I and the heir, Prince Luis Filipe, on February 1, 1908;
   (c) massive anti-monarchy demonstrations in 1909;
   (d) the Republican Revolution of October 4, 1910;
   (e) the exile of the last king, King Manuel II;
   (f) the murder of the republican leader Sidonio Pais (1918);
   (g) a brief civil war;
   (h) a monarchist restoration and insurrection (1919);
   (i) the assassinations of several prominent conservative figures (1921); and
   (j) another election, in 1922.

The ballot box, however, did not lead to any stable government. Between 1910 and 1926, Portugal had 45 governments. (Baioa Fernandes, and de Meneses, 2003: 4)! This unstable period was followed by a military coup and dictatorship (1926–33), which promised stability, order, and discipline. However, there continued to be constant power struggles within the army and between the army and its opponents. Salazar as finance minister solidified his power by his ability to restore financial order and stability. Under his long dictatorship (1933–74), he concentrated political and economic power for himself and his clique. Under the *Estada Novo* (New State), Salazar controlled inflation and imposed political stability through repressive means, including exiles and censorship. The regime fell in a coup on April 25, 1974, over whether to keep the colonies.[19] A broad majority in the army and in the population was against the regime's policy of keeping the colonies. The Carnation Revolution of April 1974 was a major turning point for Portugal. It marked the end of authoritarian rule at home and of imperial rule abroad. Turbulence continued, however, for a whole decade after the revolution (1975–85). This period has been referred to as the "lost decade," as (a) political instability was inevitable with socialist and pro–free market forces battling for control; (b) inflation surged with the two oil price shocks[20]; (c) remittances fell as Europe went into a recession; while (d) the government had to devote considerable resources to assist some 600,000 refugees from war-torn former colonies (Corkill, 1999: 67–69). It was indeed a difficult time.

2. *Condition on an effective technology-transfer system*: Evidence indicates that this condition was largely not fulfilled before Portugal's accession to the EC on January 1, 1986.[21] After accession, there was an injection of substantial EU funds for structural improvements and for technology transfer. On the eve of Portugal's accession, agriculture was considered backward – "thirty years out of date" (Monke et al.). According to Monke et al. (1986), Portuguese policy makers took little interest in the development of the agricultural sector before the 1974 revolution. As a result, the agricultural sector was incapable of generating endogenous technical change because of the "dearth of agricultural sector research capacity and the ineffectiveness of an extension service in identifying producer needs or disseminating research results" (Monke et al., 1986: 325). The World Bank (1978: 3.19) found the system of agricultural research and extension services to be "seriously understaffed, short of funds, and isolated from actual farm problems in every way." Whatever government intervention existed was essentially limited to market regulation and the administration of subsidies for

---

[19] The last 20th-century Portuguese colonies were as follows: in Africa – Angola, Cape Verde, Guinea-Bissau, Sao Tome and Principe, and Mozambique; in India – Goa, Daman, and Diu; in China – Macao; in Indonesia: Timor Este. The independence wars in Portuguese Africa started in the early 1960s.

[20] Inflation fluctuated between 16 and 29 percent per year during 1975–85 (Corkill, 1993: 121).

[21] The period 1986–96 is considered a transition period to full membership. The transition period for agriculture, initially 1986–96, was extended to 2001.

privileged groups such as wheat and olive producers and dairy processors. Regions like the small and fragmented farm sector of northern Portugal (e.g., in Tras os Montes) were largely neglected (except for milk and dairy product subsidies). A regional development project in Tras os Montes (1989) found that the region's system of research and extension was weak and uncoordinated (World Bank, 1989: 3.22–3.25). This neglect contributed to the low average levels of technology, productivity, and income of this region, considered some of the lowest in Europe (Monke et al., 1986: 318). Lains (2003: table 4), however, argues that there were significant productivity increases during three sub-periods from 1850 to 1950, and new production techniques including improved technical assistance to farmers played some role. For example, labor and land productivity grew at 1.45 and 2.29 percent per year, respectively, during 1927–51 compared with 2.29 and 1.53 percent per year, respectively, in Denmark during 1930–60. Lains (2003: 18–20) argues that these increases materialized despite the absence of major institutional changes. By that, he means that there was no change in landownership, in the organization of production, or in the introduction of new production techniques. Instead, there were increases in demand, which was itself generated by higher overall economic growth, improved transport and market infrastructures, and improved technical assistance to farmers. These favorable factors, however, were not sufficient to change the "extreme backwardness of Portugal's agricultural sector." Agriculture was virtually stagnant during the subsequent two decades: its growth averaged 0.9 per year during the 1953–55 to 1973–75 period (World Bank, 1978: 1.01).

3. *Condition on access to lucrative markets*: Before accession, this condition was fulfilled mainly for large farmers who sold to Salazar's corporate marketing agencies. After accession, all farmers had to compete with EU-set price levels, which, in many cases, were lower than under Portugal's price policy in the early 1980s. Thus the condition regarding access changed under different political and policy regimes, and given that Portuguese agriculture is dualistic, the condition varied for different farm sizes and regions. During the Salazar period (1933–74), large commercial farmers (farms 100 ha and larger) of the central region of Ribatejo o Oeste, and the southern region of Alentejo and Algarve faced

different market access conditions from the traditional small (farms 1.0–1.5 ha) farmers of the northern region of Tras os Montes, Entre Douro e Minho, the Beira Litoral, and Interior. Under the *Estado Novo* of the Salazar regime, large landowners[22] received generous price policy support, while small subsistence farmers of the north were left to fend for themselves (although milk was subsidized at different levels).[23] The small farmers were further hampered in their market access by poor rural infrastructure. Not only smallholder agriculture was thus hampered; all agriculture was, as there was chronic underinvestment in rural infrastructure (Corkill, 1993: 63). Given its corporatist approach, the Salazar government had total marketing control (including control over imports and exports), over cereals, livestock products, oilseeds, fruits, and wine. State marketing boards were monopsony buyers of domestic cereals and oilseeds and offered producers guaranteed prices. Domestic meat and poultry producers received prices above world levels, while their feed costs were subsidized. Successive governments negotiated favorable trade deals for Portugal – in 1972 with EFTA; in 1972 and 1976 with the EEC. After the 1974 revolution, during the socialist period under Soares, government continued to set prices on a wide range of commodities, including many production input subsidies favorable to farmers. In the 1980s, the budgetary costs of government's price policy had become untenable. Subsidies on milk were reduced; grain import monopoly was liberalized, thus allowing foreign competition; and many input subsidies were reduced or removed. After 1986, transition arrangements negotiated with the EEC took effect. Because Portugal was a member of the EEC, commodity prices had to conform to EEC-set levels, which in Portugal's case, meant that they fell. The tendency for most commodity prices to fall continued under the reforms of 1992 and Agenda 2000.[24] As already indicated, however, agriculture did benefit from substantial EU funds – 700 million

---

[22] Large landowners of the center and the south were important political supporters of the Salazar regime.

[23] Cheese was also subsidized by means of restrictions on imports implemented through the government monopoly that controlled all trade in dairy products, the Junta National de Productos Pecuarios (JNPP).

[24] The main exceptions are potatoes, white *vinho verde*, rice, and sunflowers (Pearson et al., 1987: 26–27).

ECU[25] was allocated to the Programa Especifico de Desenvolvimento da Agricultura Portuguesa (PEDAP) (Corkill, 1993: 100).
4. *Condition on an ownership system, including a system of usufruct
   rights that rewards individual initiative and toil – It is feasible for farm/rural families to gain monetarily from risk taking and
   hard work*: This condition was fulfilled to the extent that land
   was largely privately owned, whether on small or large farms.
   However, there were features of the agrarian structure in the
   south and the north that undermined rewards for risk taking and
   hard work. Portugal had a dual agrarian structure at the time of
   the de facto land reform of 1974. The south was feudal, while the
   north was (and still is) dominated by small, fragmented farms.
   According to the 1968 Census of Agriculture, more than three-
   fourths (77.3 percent) of landholdings were less than 4 ha, while
   0.5 percent of holdings occupying 45 percent of land were in
   units of 100 ha or more (World Bank, 1978: annex 4, table 1).
   The *latifundia* structure of the south was characterized by absentee landlords and landless workers. The *minifundia* of the north –
   small and fragmented farms – were owner-operated, but poverty
   and heavy emigration made farming a residual or secondary
   activity of low productivity for many who were forced to seek
   higher incomes elsewhere. Land was left under management by
   relatives or women left behind, and sharecropping arrangements
   were widespread. Moreover, the legislation on rentals (following
   the 1974 revolution) favored tenants to the detriment of owners. That too undermined rentals and the long-term investments
   they could entail (Moreira, 1989: 78). In the late 1970s, following
   the de facto land reform, the south had another problem: uncertainty. The uncertainty showed up in numerous amendments to
   agrarian reform legislation, while communists and socialists bat-
   tled over the future form of the agrarian structure. As a result,
   the south had many types of ownership structures – collective
   farms (communists), producer cooperatives (socialists), private
   large landowners, small private farms, and state-owned lands.
   The September 1977 Law (No. 77/77) clarified in which districts

---

[25] ECU, the European currency unit, is a composite monetary unit consisting of a basket of
European Community currencies that served as the predecessor of the euro.

expropriation and nationalization could occur, set limits on maximum acreage,[26] pledged to restore illegally occupied land (restoration started in 1978), and guaranteed written and duly registered tenancy agreements for a minimum of six years, with the option of one three-year renewal and with rent to be paid in cash and not to exceed a maximum to be set by government (World Bank, 1978: annex 4, VI, VII).[27] With the de facto land reform and the subsequent legal pronouncements and clarifications, Portugal did away with the feudal agrarian structure of the south and, over time, the uncertainty that the reform had generated.

5. *Condition on employment-creating non-agricultural sectors*: This condition was fulfilled only late in the 20th century. Surplus agricultural and rural Portuguese laborers have been able to benefit from this condition to the extent that they have emigrated, received substantial EU funds,[28] and joined the labor force of the growing urban economies of Portugal. These employment avenues were largely not available until the 1960s. Under the Salazar regime (1933–74), an estimated 1.98 million Portuguese emigrated (32 percent of them clandestinely); however, nearly three-fourths of the emigration occurred during 1961–74. Before 1960, the typical emigrant was a single male, age 15–35, predominantly from a rural area. Up to 1960, a large percentage of the emigrants went to Brazil; after 1960, they went primarily to Western Europe, mainly France and Germany (Baganha, 1998: 10).[29] Despite such substantial emigration and a rapid decline in agricultural employment – from nearly 50 percent of total employment in 1950 to around 27 percent in 1975 – considerable disguised unemployment remained (Corkill, 1993: 25). In

---

[26] The basic farm size exempt from expropriation was 30 ha or less, but no more than 300 ha, subject to a maximum of 70,000 points. The scale employed to assess the points is based on Portugal's cadastral classification (World Bank, 1978: annex 4, sec. 17)

[27] Analysts point out that the restrictions placed on rental rates have had little impact on such rates. Most producers bypass official regulations in favor of informal agreements (Pearson et al., 1987: 76–77). With respect to the small and fragmented farms of the north, policy has sought to promote land consolidation and to impose legal limits on fragmentation.

[28] In the 1990s, the EU transfer funds amounted to more than 3 percent of GDP (Baer and Leite, 2003: 746).

[29] Most of the emigrants to Western Europe were from the industrial sector, not the primary sector. The remittances from all the emigrants made a significant contribution to the GDP. As a share of GDP, the contribution rose from 2 percent in the 1950s, to 4 percent in the 1960s and 8 percent in the 1970s (Baganha, 1998: 11).

some areas, like Alto Tras os Montes and Douro, the rural population continued to decline, as there was not sufficient growth in non-agricultural rural employment, especially for youth. In fact, the outflow has left an aging population. To retain educated rural youth, efforts to promote rural tourism and agro-processing have been launched in recent years (Syrett, 2002: 68–71). The option of joining the urban labor force has improved since 1985, as Portugal's transforming economy has been rapidly converging toward EU income levels (Syrett, 2002: table 1.3).

Has Portuguese agriculture been successfully transformed? Portugal's agriculture has not yet been successfully transformed. Decades of further adjustment are likely to be required. Productivity levels are still low and rural poverty levels still substantial by EU standards (Freire and Parkhurst, 2002: 14, 19–21). During the last decades of the 20th century, Portugal was putting together the five conditions. By the first decade of the 21st century, the long process of the transformation of Portuguese agriculture had begun. During much of the 20th century, agricultural policy sought to keep food prices low for urban consumers while also benefiting feudal landlords, supporters of the Salazar regime. Specifically, it protected and subsidized the feudal landlords of the south and center but neglected the small farmers of the north (except for the subsidy on milk and dairy products) by using a host of price and marketing controls. Following EEC accession, the different agro-ecological regions and farmer groups began to adjust to a very different incentive and market environment. For example, in the northwest, wine monoculture has expanded, while milk and dairy products (highly subsidized and a major source of income for small farmers before accession) have faced declines in real prices. In the northern interior, many small farms have disappeared and thus made way for large areas of reforestation generating industrial wood, for which there is a high demand in the EU. In the center and south, where large farms (200 ha and larger) predominate, grain, cattle, olives, and wine have grown in importance, as EU support for these products has been substantial. In the river valleys and irrigated areas, intensive cultivation of fruits, vegetables, and rice has increased. This has been an ongoing process of transformation in response to evolving CAP policy and incentives.

V
Missing Conditions

Introduction

Summary. Among the many agricultures that have so far failed to transform themselves successfully, we find that at least one of the five conditions is not fulfilled. This finding strongly suggests that these five conditions are jointly necessary. However, it is still possible that the hypothesis is not universally applicable. If future research identifies an agriculture that has been successfully transformed but has not met one or more of the five conditions, then the sphere of applicability of this hypothesis must be redefined. A striking feature of this hypothesis is how unsurprising any of these conditions is. Indeed, many development practitioners have even called them "obvious." What is not so obvious is why so many governments have not been able to create and maintain these "obvious" conditions for decades.

The country cases chosen and question addressed. This chapter tests the proposed hypothesis by considering cases where one or more of the five conditions do not exist. Under these circumstances, if agriculture is successfully transformed nevertheless, that would constitute a refutation of the strong version of the proposed hypothesis. Can we find any case? No. Instead, we find that where one, but usually more than one, condition is missing, the productivity and growth performance of that agriculture is problematic. Its ability to successfully transform is severely constrained. We consider each condition in turn.

V.I. Condition 1: A Stable Framework of Macroeconomic and Political Stability – The Central and Local Governments Are Able to Enforce Peace and Order

There is a substantial literature quantifying the high correlation between political instability, poor economic performance, and widespread poverty.[1] The case of sub-Saharan Africa (SSA) is often cited (Fosu, 2002). It is no accident that the two countries in SSA that have so far fared the best economically, Botswana and Mauritius, have succeeded in maintaining political stability in the post-WWII period analyzed by Fosu (2002: table 1 [1958–86]).[2] Fortunately, over the 1994–2004 decade, political and macro stability has improved significantly in SSA. According to the IMF, the index of political instability has declined from 21 percent (1994) to 10 percent (2004) (International Finance Corporation, 2007: fig 3.1). Since 2002, the number of armed conflicts has been significantly reduced, fiscal deficits and inflation have been lowered, and growth has accelerated (Binswanger-Mkhize and McCalla, 2010: 3577). Macroeconomic and political instability is certainly not unique to SSA. Several Latin American countries have also known tumultuous periods in the 20th century. Argentina is a case in point.

Recurrent macroeconomic and political instability in Argentina undermines the successful transformation of its well-endowed agriculture[3]. We take the case of Argentina to illustrate the importance of this condition because Argentina's agriculture is favorably endowed, and yet did poorly for decades. Argentina's comparative advantage in agriculture is considered to be greater even than that of the United States.[4] Deep soils, temperate climate, adequate rainfall, and good access to sea freight endow Argentina with exceptional potential for agricultural production. Nevertheless, its agriculture and economy did poorly from approximately 1950 to 2000. Its per capita income was higher than that of the United States in 1900; yet today it is still a developing country.[5] The stability condition was not fulfilled time and again – Argentina had to endure recurrent political and macroeconomic instability during most

---

[1]   High correlation by itself does not mean causation or, even less, the direction of the causation, but it can signal an important empirical regularity indicative of deeper causes that should be analyzed.

[2]   GNI per capita in Botswana was USD 6,240 (2009), and in Mauritius, it was USD 7,240 (2009). World Bank, World Development Indicators, September 2010.

[3]   World Development Indicators, September 2010: GNI per capita, USD 7,570 (2009).

[4]   Compared with the United States, Argentina has a longer growing season with milder winters and equal if not superior soil fertility in a larger proportion of its total land area (Schnepf, Dohlman, and Bolling, 2001).

[5]   Argentina declared independence from Spain on July 9, 1816.

of the post-WWII period. We choose Argentina also because it is the home of Raul Prebisch (1959), who advocated import-substitution industrialization to be financed by taxing instead of investing in agricultural development and promoting its exports.[6] The following are some of the main events marking this long period of instability:

- Juan Peron – elected twice in 1946 and 1951 – became increasingly authoritarian, and Argentina underwent a military coup that exiled him in 1955.
- Argentina then entered a long period of military dictatorships with brief intervals of constitutional government.
- The former dictator, Peron, returned to power in 1973, and his third wife, Isabel Martinez de Peron, was elected vice president.
- After Peron's death in 1974, she became chief of state, assuming control of a nation teetering on economic and political collapse.
- In 1975, terrorist attacks by right- and left-wing groups killed some 700 people.
- The cost of living rose some 355 percent, while strikes and demonstrations were constant. On March 24, 1976, a military junta led by Lt. General Jorge Rafael Videla seized power and imposed martial law.
- The junta has been accused of thousands of murders, political arrests, and the disappearance of thousands more. While violence declined, the economy remained in chaos.
- During the 1960s, annual inflation hovered around 30 percent. However, by the mid-1980s and early 1990s, it had skyrocketed to annual rates in excess of 1,000 percent.
- Argentina's currency overvaluation when measured against its purchasing power parity vis-à-vis foreign exchange rates exceeded 100 percent throughout most of 1980s and into the 1990s.[7]

---

[6] An examination of Argentina's PSE – a measure of net government domestic support to the agricultural sector of the economy – during 1985–93 reveals that the overall policy regime was a net drag on the agricultural sector (Schnepf et al., 2001).

[7] Purchasing power parity is a theory of the long-run equilibrium exchange rates between two currencies, based on the relative price levels of the two countries. It states that the exchange rate between one currency and another is in equilibrium when their domestic purchasing powers at that rate of exchange are equivalent. This equilibrium exchange need not be the official exchange rate. In the case of Argentina, it means that with the overvalued Argentine peso, one can buy x percent more of imported items at the official rate than at a lower

- By the end of the late 1980s, Argentina's economy was plagued by huge external debts and hyperinflation.
- As the 1983 elections approached, inflation hit 900 percent, and Argentina's foreign debt reached crippling levels.
- In October 1983, Alfonsin handed the Peronist Party its first defeat since its founding. However, Alfonsin himself had to resign a month later amid riots over high food prices, in favor of a new Peronist president, Carlos Menem.
- In 1991, Menem promoted austerity measures. But beginning in 1998, Argentina suffered its worst recession in a decade. GDP per capita declined by 22 percent between 1998 and 2002 (World Bank, October 2005: executive summary).
- In 2003, following drastic liberalization and privatization reforms, the economy rebounded under Kirchner.

Thus, despite Argentina's exceptional agricultural potential, recurrent instability combined with other unfavorable policies undermined Argentina's long-term agricultural performance (Sturzenegger and Mosquera, 1990). During 1961–2005 the value of agricultural output increased 158 percent in Argentina compared with 241 percent in Chile and 439 percent in Brazil (World Bank, July 2006: viii). Rural poverty is still also high for a middle-income country – GNI per capita of USD 7,570 (2009).[8]

V.II. Condition 2: An Effective Technology-Transfer System – Research and Extension Messages Reach the Majority of Farmers

Without this condition, agricultural output can grow, but it can grow extensively only so long as the land/labor ratio remains favorable. Increased population pressure on resources requires sustained growth in productivity or intensive growth, which in turn requires

rate that would have reflected actual purchasing power (See Appendix B). When an official exchange rate is overvalued, it means that the country's imports valued in domestic currency are too cheap, and its exports valued in foreign currency are too expensive, relative to the equilibrium exchange rate.

[8] Disaggregated data from the 2001 census show that in rural areas (narrowly defined as locations with fewer than 2,000 inhabitants), 30 percent of that population (or 1.3 million) was classified as people with unsatisfied basic needs. Indigenous peoples face a poverty rate that is in excess of two times the rate of the non-indigenous population (World Bank, April 2007).

effective technology transfer. With primarily extensive growth, the process of transformation of agriculture and possibly of the entire economy remains limited. The case of Ghana clearly shows this. We choose Ghana also because it resembles Argentina in some important respects – agricultural endowment with substantial economic achievements. Ghana is well endowed agriculturally but lost considerable economic grounds after independence (March 6, 1957). At independence, Ghana was the most prosperous SSA country other than South Africa. As the first African country to gain independence from Great Britain, Ghana had a per capita income comparable to that of the Republic of South Korea in those years. However, after more than 50 years of development, Ghana is still a low-income country – GNI at USD 700 (2009) – while South Korea is an upper-income country – GNI at USD 19,830 (2009).[9] Also, like Argentina, Ghana went through a long period of political and price instability – the period encompassing the military coup against Nkrumah in 1966 until the installment of the Provisional National Defence Council by Jerry Rawlings in 1981. Fortunately, since 2000, productivity seems to be growing. During 2001–2004, agricultural growth was driven by land expansion, increasing yields, or both. Over the long term, however, agriculture grew, due mainly to area expansion rather than productivity growth. Thus a majority of the labor force remains in low-productivity agricultural activities that inevitably yield low earnings (low even when compared with levels achieved in other African countries).

The weakness of the technology-transfer system limits the structural transformation of Ghanaian agriculture. Agriculture has always been important for Ghana – in 1970, the agriculture/GDP ratio was 51 percent; by 2005, it was 36 percent. Yet agricultural research does not get the attention it deserves. Ghana had an established agricultural research system well before independence, but since the late 1970s, this system has suffered from severe underfunding. Ministry of Agriculture extension staff pointed out that contact with research staff is inadequate and that the results of research are not relevant to farmers' needs (World Bank, May 1991: 13). These problems contribute to

---

[9] World Bank, World Development Indicators, September 2010. Ghana is considered an African success story by the World Bank.

the substantial yield gaps in all crops across Ghana, although poor-quality land is scarce. Cocoa yields average 350 kg/ha in Ghana compared with 740 kg/ha in Côte d'Ivoire.[10] National average cassava yields are 12 mt/ha compared with 30 mt/ha in Brong Ahafo (a region located in midwestern Ghana between the Ashanti region and the Côte d'Ivoire border). The technology exists to raise productivity, but farmers have yet to fully exploit the opportunities. Adoption is low because of disconnects between research and extension, and because of poor access to critical complementary inputs.[11] The staple foods of maize and cassava dominate food crop production in Ghana. Average farmer yields for sorghum are 1,000 kg/ha compared with 3,000 kg/ha by farmers using technical advice (World Bank, May 1991: annex 1). Whatever expansion has occurred has been mainly through area, not yields. Yields have remained largely stagnant (World Bank, November 2007: table 2.4). The use of modern agricultural techniques remains limited. However, since 2001, there has been some evidence of productivity gains. The limited extent of agricultural transformation has also meant that over the entire 1980–2005 period, Ghana's economic structure has remained fairly stable (World Bank, November 2007: 32). Ghana is a small open economy with exports accounting for 40 percent of GDP in recent years. The limited extent of structural transformation is evident in that Ghana has not diversified its exports since the 1970s. Cocoa, gold, and timber still account for 70 percent of its total commodity exports (World Bank, November 2007: 38). As a result, Ghana's economy is still very vulnerable to commodity price shocks.

V.III. Condition 3: Access to Lucrative Markets – The Majority of Farmers Face Expanding Markets of Paying Customers; To Them, Investing in Agricultural and Rural Production Is Good Business

Throughout much of the developing world, agriculture was severely discriminated against under the strong urban bias that characterized countries espousing the ISI. Lipton (1977) pointed out that the

[10] Yields of Indonesian cocoa beans range from 400 to 800 kg/ha. Indonesia is the world's third-largest producer, after Côte d'Ivoire and Ghana.
[11] There are other problems. In some instances, incentives do not exist to make productive investments as uncertainties on the marketing side deter farmers from taking the risks.

underdevelopment of rural areas was due largely to being bypassed in development spending. The 18 country studies that Krueger, Schiff, and Valdes (1991) edited estimated the extent of taxation of agriculture (1960–84) and analyzed the policy instruments used.[12] The estimates of Nominal Protection Rate (NPR) clearly show that the extent of the discrimination was substantial.[13] In all countries analyzed, the NPRs were –0.25 percent and above. For example, the NPR estimates (percent, 1960–84) are as follows: Asia: –25.2; Latin America: –27.8; Mediterranean: –25.2; and sub-Saharan Africa: –51.6 (Krueger et al., eds., 1991: vol. 1, tables 1–2). The overall incentive and marketing environment generated by agricultural price policy and the extent of rural infrastructural development largely determine market access. Taxation to finance the ISI undermined the access of myriad smallholders to lucrative markets, and thus to higher incomes. The case of Egypt during the post-WWII period illustrates the key importance of access to lucrative markets for both the shorter-term performance of agriculture and its longer-term successful transformation.

Extensive government of Egypt intervention in marketing undermined smallholders' access to lucrative markets[14]. The case of smallholders in Egypt exemplifies the debilitating impact of limited access to lucrative markets on achieving successful transformation of agriculture. For the majority of small farmers and landless peasants, the market environment for agriculture was not good under the ISI strategy of Nasser and even under the more liberalized policy well into the 1980s. To promote industry and to achieve food self-sufficiency, the government intervened directly through price and marketing controls, and indirectly through trade and foreign exchange policies. Agriculture is well endowed in Egypt, in that it has year-round irrigation, fertile riparian silts, and long sunlight hours, which have made possible a

[12] The countries are: Asia: Republic of Korea, Malaysia, Pakistan, the Philippines, Sri Lanka, and Thailand; Latin America: Argentina, Brazil, Chile, Colombia, and Dominican Republic; the Mediterranean: Egypt, Morocco, Portugal, and Turkey; and Sub-Saharan Africa: Côte d'Ivoire, Ghana, and Zambia.

[13] A Nominal Protection Rate is the ratio of domestic to border price of a commodity. A numerical value of zero indicates neutral protection; negative means discrimination or taxation; positive means positive support. For a fuller discussion of the method of assessing agricultural price policy within the partial equilibrium framework, see Tsakok (1990).

[14] World Development Indicators, September 2010: GNI per capita for Egypt, USD 1,800 (2009).

high cropping intensity estimated at 190 (1980) (Cuddihy, 1980: ii).[15] However, agriculture was substantially taxed and controlled through price fixing, marketing monopolies, and quotas. Estimates of the long-run tax rate on the sector averaged 30 percent (1970s), contributing to reducing average agricultural incomes by 25 percent less than the rest of the economy. Taxation of export crops was also implicit through the overvalued exchange rate (mainly from 1960 to 1972). In some years (1973–76), some crops were more highly taxed, as in the case of cotton (60 percent) and rice (80 percent), and some were highly protected, as in the case of wheat and livestock/meat (Cuddihy, 1980: iii–viii; table VII-4). The overall taxation rate was reduced to around 12 percent between 1973 and 1980 (Dethier, 1989: abstract.) Thus, from about 1950 to 1975, Egypt adopted the classic tax-farmers-cum-subsidize-urban-consumers strategy. Farmers' incomes were reduced by LE 1.2 billion (despite the rhetoric of helping smallholders), while consumers gained LE 1.02 billion and the government gained LE 179 million (1974–75) (Cuddihy, 1980: 116).[16]

Large farmers in Egypt were not so constrained. As to be expected, the labyrinth of controls did not promote incentives for sustained efficiency and productivity; nor was its impact equitable. The larger farmers were better able to circumvent or benefit from the system through various means, such as bribery, getting scarce credit and other subsidized inputs, violating quotas, and shifting their production toward non-controlled crops. In the heyday of Arab socialism, the production plans were complemented with mandatory membership in state-run cooperatives. Cooperatives were meant to transform rural Egypt under Nasser because it was alleged that "peasants have a natural interest in socialism" (Dethier, 1989: 30). This did not happen. What did happen, and not surprisingly, was that large farmers dominated the cooperatives. They knew how to manipulate the controlled system to their advantage. Violation of cotton and rice quotas was pervasive, with the probability of violation increasing with the size of the holding. Farmers

[15] However, agriculture is land- and water-scarce and labor-abundant. The average density ratio of agricultural cultivated land to population has declined from 0.48 *feddan* per person (1950) to 0.19 *feddan* (1999) (El-Ghomeny, 2003: 93–94). A *feddan* is equal to 0.42 ha, or 1.04 acres.

[16] LE denotes Egyptian pounds. However, LE denotes Lower Egypt when compared with Upper Egypt, UE.

would divert the use of subsidized fertilizers from, say, cotton to non-controlled and therefore more lucrative crops, as in horticulture. Every year, thousands of farmers preferred to pay fines rather than conform to the production plans government had for them. By the mid-1970s, the horticultural sub-sector was getting a definite boost as farmers (typically large farmers who could invest and take the risk) tried to evade the taxation of controlled crops (e.g., cotton).

In Egypt, two agricultures emerged with differential market access. Distorted incentives and differential degrees of market access for different commodities and farmer groups, maintained over decades, gave rise to a dualistic agriculture. By the early 2000s, Egypt had two distinct agricultures. By the early 1980s, the growth performance of horticulture and livestock was distinctly better than that of the other crops. These two sub-sectors benefited from the absence of price and quantitative controls and good access to subsidized inputs, the best of all possible worlds! The expansion of commercial poultry production exemplifies what favorable market access can do. During the 1960s, 80 percent of poultry production was from the village. By 1985, commercial poultry production was more than half of total supply (Dethier, 1989: 24). With Sadat's *Infitah* policy – the Open Door policy (April 1974) – there was a surge of private-sector investment in agro-processing, the bulk of which was for poultry and egg production. Maize and soybean meal, main components of poultry feed, were mainly imported by government and sold at subsidized prices. In contrast to these high-growth sub-sectors, the market environment for traditional crops (cotton, rice, wheat, maize, and sugar) was not good, although it did improve. In 1974, their prices were substantially increased, although they were still taxed; for example, for cotton and rice, prices increased by 14 percent (1974–80) (Dethier, 1989: 50, table 2.3). In fact, from 1960 to 1985, estimated effective protection rates for these crops, from both direct and indirect intervention, were substantially negative, ranging from −12 to −74 percent (Dethier, 1989: 95, table 3.7).[17] By the 1980s, the local rural elite had

---

[17] An Effective Protection Rate (EPR) is the ratio of value added at domestic to border prices. The NPR compares only the output prices; the EPR takes into account the prices and quantities used of tradable inputs. Both measures show what producers gain (lose) as a result of government intervention affecting the prices of their outputs and inputs.

figured out how to circumvent the distorted system to their advantage. The elite used its *shilla* network (clientelist network) to get access to the best markets and to tap public resources.[18] Unlike the rural elite, the majority continued to face two main types of obstacles to market access: the negative incentive framework generated by regulated markets (until the reforms undertaken within the Economic Reform and Structural Adjustment Program, March 1990) and the underdeveloped state of physical transport, communications, market intelligence, and marketing infrastructure (World Bank, 1993b: xvi). The latter reflects the much reduced share of public investments in total public investments: from around 14 percent (excluding the share that went to the Aswan High Dam, 1962–66) to 7 percent (1988–92) (World Bank, 1993b: 6). Market access improved with market liberalization measures of the 1990s, especially for farmers in Lower Egypt (LE) who had good access to expanding domestic and foreign markets and for large farmers who could afford to evade the remaining controls (e.g., on cotton). Improved market access contributed to the higher growth rate estimated at around 3.4 percent for the 1990s, a distinct improvement from the growth rate of earlier decades, which averaged 2.2 percent per year during the years when population growth averaged 2.5 percent per year (1939–87) (Hansen, 1991: table 1.1).

Farmers in Upper Egypt have poor access to lucrative markets for higher-value crops. The performance of the agricultural and rural economy of Upper Egypt (UE) illustrates the importance that differential market access in UE and LE makes. Smallholders in UE have poor access to lucrative markets for higher-value crops. This poor access is a major reason for the low share of non-traditional (or high-value) crops in UE's total cultivation. In UE, higher-value crops occupy only 7 percent of cultivated land (1996–2005), whereas in LE the share is 57 percent of total. Traditional (or low-value) crops thus dominate in UE; they occupy 93 percent of total cultivated land. Two major factors accounting for the limited share of non-traditional crops in UE are: (a) poor transport, communications, and marketing infrastructure (in particular,

---

[18] The downfall of Hosni Mubarak, president for nearly 30 years brought about by the massive uprisings of January 25 to February 11, 2011 throughout Egypt, but most notably in Tahrir Square, Cairo and in Alexandria, is eloquent testimony of the rage of the people being locked out of economic opportunities and political freedom for decades.

inadequacy of the cold chain) that would guarantee product quality in transport and handling; it is estimated than 20 percent of fruit products and 40 percent of vegetable products in UE are lost in transport and handling; and (b) the much smaller size of landholdings in UE than in LE, which means that the smaller UE farmers are more dependent than larger farmers on local traders. The smaller farmers get lower prices than the larger farmers. Livestock products are important in both UE and LE. However, in LE, better access to centers of growing demand means more income from livestock products too. Thus LE, which is better located and better served by marketing infrastructure, has better access to the thriving urban centers of the north delta and to overseas demand. The only centers of growing demand in UE are in Aswan and Luxor, two important tourist centers (World Bank, June 2006: ix–xii).

V.IV. Condition 4: An Ownership System, Including a System of Usufruct Rights That Rewards Individual Initiative and Toil – It Is Feasible for Farm/Rural Families to Gain Monetarily from Risk Taking and Hard Work

This condition is not fulfilled in the case of the Philippines, where recurrent land conflicts between landless peasants and smallholders, on one hand, and the landed oligarchy, on the other, has undermined agricultural performance and limited poverty reduction. The ownership system refers not only to land, but especially to farmers' relationship to the land they till. In the Philippines, the implementation of successive land reforms over decades has not yet resulted in an equitable land distribution and ownership system, such that the majority of farm/ rural families have received ownership and title to the land they expect to receive. Land conflicts are still rife (Asian Legal Resource Centre, 2009). A brief background including relevant history is in order.

Brief background on the Philippines' post-WWII agricultural and economic performance[19]. The experience of the Philippines with land reform stands in stark contrast to that of its East Asian neighbors: the Republic of Korea, Japan, Taiwan, China, and the People's Republic of

---

[19] World Development Indicators, September 2010: GNI per capita for the Philippines, USD 1,790 (2009).

China, where land reform has had a transformative impact not only on agriculture but on the entire economy. The land reform process was swift and equitable. Moreover, land redistribution was viewed as only one component, albeit a key one, in an overall package to make agriculture productive and profitable for the majority of smallholders. The socio-economic performance of the Philippines is particularly disappointing because right after the end of WWII, and despite extensive wartime destruction, the Philippines had one of the highest per capita incomes in East Asia, above that of the Republic of Korea, Taiwan, and Thailand. However, by the beginning of the 21st century, its per capita income had long been overtaken by Korea and Taiwan (in the 1950s) and by Thailand (in the 1970s) (Balisacan and Hill, 2003: 4).[20] Per capita agricultural output barely grew in the Philippines – 0.04 percent per year during 1961–98 (Akiyama and Larson, eds., 2004: 455–522, table 11.1). From 1980 to 2000, the average yearly agricultural growth rate was 1.65 percent well below the annual rates achieved by several East Asian neighbors – for example (in percent), Indonesia at 3.04, Thailand at 2.80, Vietnam at 3.74, and China at 4.71. At a GNI per capita of USD 1,790 (2009),[21] the poverty incidence was estimated at 28.1 percent nationwide, urban at 14.4 percent, and rural at 41.5 percent (2006).[22] Poverty is mainly rural poverty, at around 75 percent of total. While yearly agricultural growth has risen since 2000, it has not been primarily through productivity growth. Between 1980 and 2000, TFP growth stagnated at around 0.2 percent per year (World Bank, 2009b: tables 1.4, 2.1, 45). Failure to fulfill condition 4 on a landownership system that rewards individual initiative and toil for the majority has contributed to the disappointing performance of the Philippines' agriculture. This problematic agrarian structure has deep roots that go back to at least the Spanish conquest.

High inequality in the agrarian structure in post-WWII Philippines is rooted deep in history. Skewed landownership dates back to Spanish

---

[20] The GNI per capita for the Republic of Korea and that for Thailand are (current USD) 19,690 (2007) and 2,750 (2005), respectively (World Bank, "Country at a Glance," September 28, 2007; August 13, 2006). That for Taiwan is USD 16,471 (2006), http://www.dgbas.gov.tw/.

[21] World Bank, World Development Indicators, 2009.

[22] World Bank, World Development Indicators, 2009, has 22.6 percent (poverty head count ratio) at USD 1.25 per day (purchasing power parity, PPP) and 45 percent at USD 2.00 per day, PPP.

colonial days (1596–1896). In pre-Hispanic times, communal owner-ship of land prevailed, with individual families given usufruct rights over particular parcels of land. In return, families had to perform particular obligations to the local elite, the *datu*. The Spanish intro-duced private ownership, the concept of legal title to a parcel of land. There were few extensive Spanish-owned *latifundios* typical of Latin America. The more typical landholding pattern was one of more mod-est holdings owned by native elites and part-Chinese *mestizos*. Many of the native cultivators lost their land through a money-lending sys-tem known as the *pacto de retroventa*, under which loans were secured by land. The Spanish land registration acts of 1880 and 1894, the introduction of cadastral surveys under the United States, and the Torrens land registration system of 1913 each afforded opportuni-ties for large-scale land grabbing. The enmity engendered by the land grabbing and other land-related injustices is undimmed by time, fuel-ing recurrent peasant unrest. The history of the Philippines is replete with peasant uprisings, with tenure-related grievances providing the impetus for many of these revolts. The first recorded peasant uprising in which agrarian issues figured prominently was in 1745. There has been no significant improvement in the distribution of income and assets since independence in 1946 (U.S. colonial administration lasted from 1898 to 1946).[23]

Skewed land distribution breeds abuse of power and rural discontent in the Philippines. The Gini coefficient for land actually increased after WWII. It rose from 0.53 in 1960 to 0.57 in 2006, indicating high and increased inequality, especially in comparison with the East Asian median Gini coefficient of 0.41 (World Bank, 2009b: 51–52). Since WWII, farming in the Philippines has been characterized by a pre-ponderance of small farms (1971 and 1980 censuses), except for large plantations in the export sector (e.g., pineapple plantations, which are dominated by two multi-nationals). About 85 percent of all farms had fewer than 5 ha. This small farm size accounted for 50 percent of

---

[23] Under the U.S. colonial administration, there was the Hukbalahap (People's Army Against Japan) rebellion of the mid-1940s, when the Philippines was occupied by the Japanese. During the Japanese occupation, many landlords fled to the major cities. Many of them collaborated with the Japanese. Landlord–tenant relations were exacerbated during the occupation.

total farm area. About 65 percent of all rice and corn farms had fewer than 3 ha (Intal and Power, 1990: 23–24, table 7.11). By 2002, the average farm size was 2.2 ha (World Bank, 2009b: table 2.6). There is nothing wrong with small farms per se, as the productivity performance of small farms in Taiwan amply demonstrates. What is wrong is that the inequity in land distribution provides fertile ground for abuse of power by the landed oligarchy and outbreaks of violent rural discontent. What is also wrong is that landlessness is acute and growing (Hayami, Quisumbing, and Adrioano, 1990). In 1952, Robert S. Hardie wrote: "Chronic economic instability and political unrest among tenants has culminated in open and violent rebellion. The rebellion derives directly from the pernicious land tenure system; it is but the latest in a long and bitter series" (Monk, 1990: 9). Hardie's analysis of rural poverty and unrest included the following problems: (a) farm rentals were oppressive, as most tenants paid 50 percent of the gross product; (b) net family income from farm operations was woefully inadequate for a decent standard of living, and income from outside sources was also woefully inadequate; (c) interest rates on borrowed money were onerous; annual rates of 100 percent were common, and rates of 200 percent and higher were not unusual; (d) lack of adequate economic storage, marketing, and buying facilities forced farmers to sell at low prices and buy at high prices; (e) guarantees against ruinous prices were non-existent; and (f) institutions conducive to growth and strengthening of democratic principles were neglected. Hardie's report, written at the request of the U.S. government, was completed in the fall of 1952, more than 50 years ago. The report was buried. Ever since then, successive Filipino governments have been grappling with the problems Hardie identified.

After more than five decades of land reform, there is still an unfinished agenda in 2009. Unlike the land reforms in East Asia, progress on land reform in the Philippines has been slow. Under successive administrations, the reform momentum was unable to break through the grip of repeated resistance from the landowning elite. The first attempt at land redistribution was the Friar Land Act (1903) under the U.S. colonial administration. It was followed by many more attempts – in 1933 (tenancy, U.S.); 1954, 1955 (tenancy and redistribution, Magsaysay);

1963, 1971, 1972–85 (Operation Land Transfer, Marcos); and 1988 (Comprehensive Reform Agrarian Program, Aquino and Ramos). Implementation under all the administrations stretched over years. Over time, various measures to dilute or undermine implementation were continuously brought forward – for example, reduction in the initial scope of the program through extended deliberations in the cabinet; insistence by private landowners that public lands be first disposed of before expropriating private lands; conversion of agricultural land to non-agricultural uses; transfers of land to one's relatives, friends, and straw people; 10-year exemption for commercial farms; and debates regarding the fixing of levels for retention limits in an effort to raise the limits. Just prior to the Aquino government, only 4 percent of Philippines' 7.8 million ha had been acquired. The new law under Aquino would involve the incremental distribution of less than 100,000 ha, barely 1 percent of cultivated farmland, to fewer than 100,000 families, or 3 percent of the present landless. Between them, the Aquino and Ramos governments completed 57.9 percent of the planned reform of rice and corn lands by the end of 1993. This element of reform accounts for 20.3 percent of the land area for which ownership has been distributed (public lands) or redistributed (private lands). Compulsory acquisition, however, accounted for a little more than 2 percent of the reform program as implemented through the end of 1993. So neither the authoritarian regime of Marcos nor the more democratic regimes of Aquino, Ramos, and, so far, Macapagal-Aroyo have been successful in significantly reducing the sharp inequality of land distribution or the insecurity of land tenure. For example, some 71 percent of distributed titles are collective instead of individual titles, as initially prescribed by Law RA 6657 (World Bank, 2009b: 9). By not resolving the deep-seated problem of agrarian unrest, the long-drawn-out and faulty process of implementation of land reform has undermined investment and productivity increases. It has prolonged uncertainty and prevented producers from using land as collateral. Moreover, the current system of conflict resolution is "cumbersome and inefficient and works to the advantage of landowners" (World Bank, 2009b: 3). Thus, for more than five decades, the power of the landowning elite has been reaffirmed time and again.

V.V. Condition 5: Employment-Creating Non-agricultural Sectors – As Agriculture Becomes More Productive, It Must Shed Labor, Which Unless Absorbed in Non-farm Jobs That Pay as Well as Agriculture Would Simply Constitute Exporting Farm Poverty to Other Sectors

This condition is fulfilled when there is sustained high growth in the overall economy. Under these favorable circumstances, higher agricultural productivity sheds farm labor, which is at the same time "pulled" into growing non-farm labor markets. This condition is not fulfilled when farm labor is being pushed out of agriculture instead of being pulled up into an expanding non-agriculture sector, a problem typical of low-productivity–low-growth or dualistic agricultures. Under these circumstances, in this increasingly globalized economy, rural migrants venture farther afield in search of living wages. Mexico and Morocco are cases in point, although the specifics of their situations necessarily differ. In both countries, agriculture is dualistic and of low productivity for most smallholders. The employment-generating growth of the overall economy has not been sufficient to "pull" farm/rural labor into expanding job markets. Instead, the disguised unemployment problem of rural areas with their extensive poverty has spilled over into urban areas already burdened with high unemployment. Both countries are known for high and sustained rates of rural–urban migration, domestic and in particular foreign.

The case of Mexico – high rural migration in search of jobs farther and farther afield[24]. Rural migration has been an ongoing process in Mexico, but in recent decades it has increased by leaps and bounds: by 182 percent between 1980 and 1994 (the year NAFTA was signed) and by 452 percent from 1980 to 2002 (Mere, 2007: 3). There has been a steady and massive emigration since the 1940s, to major centers such as Mexico City, Monterrey, and Guadalajara (Grindle, 1988: 30). Surplus labor from the central regions of Mexico was attracted to the large irrigated farms of the north, especially during the decades of high agricultural growth (1940–70). The 1970 census showed 1.2 million migratory farmworkers representing more than 20 percent of the rural population, following the harvests from one part of Mexico to

---

[24] World Development Indicators, September 2010: GNI per capita, USD 8,920 (2009).

another (Cockcroft, 1998). The United States has been an important destination for a majority of rural migrants from Mexico (Garcia and Gonzalez Martinez, 1999: 1).[25] The rural migrants who cannot afford to be unemployed join the informal urban labor market and so are not officially listed as unemployed (Fleck, 1994). Thus the official open urban rate of unemployment is low in Mexico, but this does not mean that overall unemployment is low (as Mexico has a dual labor market). Urban underemployment is high, and returns to self-employed labor are low (2000) (World Bank, June 2007: 4).

The case of Morocco – high rural migration in search of jobs farther and farther afield[26]. Morocco also has become a major source of migrants in Western Europe since the 1960s (Focus Migration, 2009). As in Mexico, migrants have been primarily rural. In the 1970s, the mountainous Rif area in the province of Nador in the north was a major source of emigrants filling unskilled jobs in manufacturing, trading, or the mines of northern France. The Souss in the south was also a major center of emigration. A 1981 study by the Insitut National de Statistique et d'Economie Appliqué (INSEA) emphasized the changing character of emigration: the emigration of necessity, of the poor rather than of those who primarily want to supplement other activities and to become rich (Collyer, 2004: 16, 18–19). In the 1990s, the urban unemployed also emigrated. The latter phenomenon is to be expected given that open urban unemployment averaged 22 percent in 2000, much higher than the 16 percent in 1990. Unemployment among youth (age 15 to 24 years) has been even higher – well over 30 percent since the early 1990s. Not only is urban unemployment high, but its duration is long – the average duration of unemployment was 41 months (2000) (Agenor and El Aynaoui, 2003: 9–10).

Brief background on Mexico and Morocco. Both Mexico and Morocco have known periods of high growth, but these have not been sustained or shared and were not rooted in TFP growth.

---

[25] In fact, by the end of the 20th century, the majority of Latinos residing in the United States were of Mexican origin and their Mexican American descendants (Chicanos). They account for the vast majority of migrants working in agriculture and related industries (U.S. Bureau of Census, 1997). The vast majority of Mexican immigrants to the United States are *campesinos* and rural proletariats from Guanajuato and other states of Mexico's central plateau region (Garcia and Gonzalez Martinez, 1999: 1–2).

[26] World Development Indicators, September 2010: GNI per capita, USD 2,790 (2009).

- *Mexico*, an upper-middle-income OECD country (1994), has a GNI per capita of USD 8,920 (2009) and a relatively small agriculture – agriculture/GDP ratio averaging 9–10 percent in 1987 and 4–5 percent in 1997–2007. Given the relatively small size of agriculture and the per capita income level, one may expect this condition of adequate employment-creating non-agricultural sectors to be fulfilled, but it is not. Mexico still has a substantial rural population plagued by poverty and a lack of sufficient high-productivity jobs – some 23 percent of the total population is rural, and poverty, averaging 18 percent, is mostly rural (2001–07).[27] Agriculture participated in the historic expansion of the Mexican economy as it rose at an annual rate of 6 percent through the mid-1960s. Economists were hailing Mexico as an "economic miracle" (prematurely as it turns out), as Mexico enjoyed three decades (1940–70) of 6 percent per year growth rate. However, TFP growth, which averaged 4.5 percent per year in the 1940s, declined to a little more than 1 percent in the 1950s and 1960s, fell to zero in the 1970s, and turned negative in the 1980s to mid-1990s. Annual TFP growth in Mexican agriculture was 1.5 percent per year (1980–2001), smaller than the 2.3 percent per year of the period 1961–80 and smaller than that of all major Latin American competitors (World Bank, June 2007: 254). More recently, agriculture grew by only 0.4 percent per year in the 1980s, and the economy grew at 1 percent per year during the same period.
- *Morocco*, a lower-middle-income country – GNI per capita USD 2,790 (2009) – experienced average annual growth of 2.6 percent in 1988–98 and 4.5 percent in 1997–2007. On a per capita basis, annual growth was 0.8 and 3.2 percent, respectively.[28] Agriculture is still an important component of the economy: the agriculture/GDP ratio averages 15 percent (2000–2006). Agriculture still accounts for 44 percent of jobs, 50 percent of which are unpaid farm-family aid (World Bank, June 2007: 76). Like Mexico, Morocco is a case where overall growth has exhibited periods of dynamism (in the 1960s), but it has not been sustained since

---

[27] World Bank, "Mexico Country at a Glance," September 24, 2008.
[28] World Bank, "Morocco Country at a Glance," September 24, 2008.

the 1980s. Moreover, TFP growth has not contributed to overall growth over the past 35 years! (World Bank, March 2006: 9). Furthermore, given the growth of the labor force relative to the growth of the economy, the non-farm economy has not been able to absorb, at remunerative wages, surplus agricultural labor. Most jobs continue to be informal, low-skill, and low-productivity. The informal sector generates 39 percent of non-agriculture jobs and 90 percent of commerce jobs. A sustained annual growth of at least 6 percent is estimated to be necessary if the Moroccan economy is to employ the expected new entrants to the labor market (World Bank, June 2007: 75–76). Morocco faces an additional problem: high volatility in its growth, as its agriculture is drought-vulnerable, resulting in wide swings in its growth (e. g., +23 percent in 2006, – 20 percent in 2007). The wide swings wreak havoc (World Bank, March 2010: fig 1.1, table 1.1).

Adequate access to employment-creating non-agricultural sectors in Mexico. This condition did not materialize for much of smallholder agriculture in Mexico, particularly in the rain-fed regions of the center and south, and even during the decades of high growth during 1940–70. Indeed, employment for rural labor and at above poverty levels has been a long-standing problem, rooted in unequal development since Spanish colonial times.[29] The Mexican Revolution (1910– to around 1920) was preceded by rapid economic growth, but with concentrations of wealth and income under Porfirio Díaz (1876–1910). During this period, peasant communities lost much of their land to the expanding estate sector. After Porfirio Díaz, large-scale units of production soon put small-scale producers, individual artisans, traders, the peasantry, and the proletariat in a precarious position, being better able to monopolize markets, control job and wage conditions, and ensure rapid economic expansion. Thus, despite impressive economic growth during the Porfiriato, real wages dropped from 40 to 36 centavos a day, a pittance. Malnutrition continued, and average life expectancy remained about 30 years (Cockcroft, 1998: 86). Following the "miracle" period (1940–70) was the "lost decade" of the 1980s, during which there again was insufficient employment-creating non-agricultural growth

[29] From 1810 to 1822 Mexicans won national independence.

to absorb the surplus rural labor force. More recently, overall growth has been mediocre – it averaged 2–3 percent per year and agricultural growth 1–2 percent during 1987–2007.[30] The high income inequality – Gini coefficient estimated to be 0.51 (1992–2002) – also limited the employment-creating capacity of any growth (Verner, 2005: fig. 3.5). An important factor contributing to this problem – of surplus rural labor and inadequate non-agricultural employment – was government policy favoring the capital-intensive farming of the wealthy. Its ISI policies also gave subsidies (including on credit) to rich industrialists. In contrast to the limited support given to *ejido*-type holdings,[31] liberal credit was made available to private freeholders. Many of the latter turned out to be politicians, highly placed bureaucrats, and their cronies, the so-called nylon or artificial farmers. The overvaluation of the peso (until 1948, when it was devalued by 40 percent) also made agricultural machinery relatively inexpensive, thus undermining employment generation.

Adequate access to employment-creating non-agricultural sectors in Morocco. Some 50 years after its independence from France (1956), slowing down "excessive" rural–urban migration continues to be a major sociopolitical preoccupation of the government of Morocco. Surplus farm labor has remained a major problem, and its employment prospects have been constrained by lack of sustained, high productivity growth (agricultural and non-agricultural). Most farm laborers toil in a low-productivity rain-fed sector, vulnerable to increasingly frequent and devastating droughts. Agricultural value added has stagnated in the sector: from DH 670 in the early 1960s to DH 710 during 2000–2004 (World Bank, June 2007: 1, 279).[32] The continuing high urban unemployment partly explains why rural migrants are going farther afield.[33] Adequate access for farm/rural labor to employment-creating sectors

---

[30] World Bank, "Mexico Country at a Glance," September 24, 2008.
[31] *Ejidos* are communally owned lands. They are "rural communities modeled after a mixture of soviet-style collectives and pre-colonial indigenous social structure" (World Bank, June 2001: executive summary). *Ejidos* have had a complex history since the Mexican Revolution of 1917. In Mexico, land reform lasted from 1917 to 1992. In 1991, President Carlos Salinas de Gortari put an end to the constitutional right to *ejidos*, citing the low productivity of these lands.
[32] DH: dirham, the currency of Morocco. 1 USD = 7.7309 DH (September 29, 2009).
[33] The recent uprisings (February 21, 2011) have multiple roots, including high urban youth unemployment, extensive underemployment urban and rural, and pervasive corruption.

thus remains a major goal of government policy. In its latest agricultural strategy – the *Plan Maroc Vert* (2008), the government of Kingdom of Morocco estimates that some 8–10 million farm laborers suffer from chronic underemployment.[34] One promising measure that the government has been promoting is the development of rural tourism. The great beauty of Morocco's countryside and villages, and its distinctive art, culture and cuisine, attract thousands – around 150,000–200,000 tourists every year (Magharebia, 2008).[35] Whether it will be from rural tourism or from the implementation of the *Plan Maroc Vert*, or both, the vast majority – nearly 70 percent of all farmers – micro-holders and smallholders who occupy only 26 percent of total land (1996 Census of Agriculture)[36] – will benefit from greater demand for their labor as well as the goods and services they sell.

[34] Population estimates for Morocco (2001–2007, in millions) are: total, 30.9; rural/urban ratio, 44:56; rural, 13.6; agricultural, 10.9; urban: 17.3 (World Bank, "Morocco Country at a Glance," September 24, 2008).

[35] The goal of the tourism industry was to attract 10 million visitors to Morocco by 2010. The focus was to be not only on the beaches but on the interior as well, including isolated villages, oases and deserts, and majestic mountain regions.

[36] This is from the latest agricultural census (*Recensement General Agricole*, RGA 1996).

VI

The Public Foundations
of Private Agriculture

Introduction

Summary. The successful transformation of agriculture depends on generations of farmers investing in agriculture because it is profitable for them to do so, despite the inevitable ups and downs of farming. In order for such risky production to be profitable, it requires, at a minimum, sustained government investment in the delivery and proper functioning of public goods and services accessible to all farmers. Government delivery of public goods and services over decades creates an environment within which the majority of farmers, not just the privileged few, can perceive and seize market opportunities, take risks, diversify their income and employment portfolio, and achieve financial success, however defined by the farmers themselves. Sustained public investment in and delivery of public goods and services accessible to the majority of farmers lays the foundation for a thriving private agriculture because they jointly provide an environment of stability and opportunity for all farmers, enabling them to achieve what they want most, financial strength and security in good times and bad.

Focus of the chapter. The systematic testing of the proposed hypothesis shows that despite the great variety of country conditions, there is a common pattern in the conditions necessary "to get agriculture moving" (Mosher, 1966). The insights derived all point to the central role of government in the process. Government cannot actually grow the food or successfully order farmers at gunpoint to do so. But only government can create the environment that encourages farmers to produce for the market and profit from it. For better or for worse, government support makes the critical difference. Where it has made a positive difference, this support essentially consisted of government's ability to deliver public goods and services accessible to the majority of farmers and over decades. This was not sufficient but absolutely necessary. This chapter argues for focusing on this critical role of government in help-ing to make successful agricultural transformation happen.

Organization of the chapter. Why is this the focus, and what are the practical implications of such focus? Specifically, the chapter first com-pares this focus with the prevailing insights on what gets agriculture "moving" and why these insights have been largely disregarded by gov-ernments in many developing countries. It is clear that the hypothesis proposed and tested in the preceding chapters is fully consistent with prevailing insights. So what is different? What is different is the focus on the role of government over long periods of time, several decades at least. The central thesis is that this role is essential for development. No amount of foreign aid can substitute for a committed and devel-opment-minded government taking charge.[1] Governments in much of the developing world have been unable to adequately fill this basic supportive role. Why? Several political economy explanations have been advanced and are therefore considered here. In assessing the role of government in agriculture, this chapter is guided by the thesis put forward by Root (2006: 4): "Transforming uncertainty into risk is how countries grow rich. Lack of institutions that make managing risk pos-sible is the root cause of disparity in economic performance between developed and developing countries." Agriculture is the sector *par excel-lence* on which to test this thesis, since the sector is highly vulnerable to natural calamities (e.g., sharp weather fluctuations, outbreaks of pest attacks) and zigzag market fluctuations. In addition to these, farmers are also subject to uncertainties created by government – for example, with respect to land distribution, landownership, and market access. Root rejects the conventional wisdom that it is the absence of capital (the "financing gap") that undermines development. Root (2006: 221) adopts Frank H. Knight's distinction between measurable risks and immeasurable uncertainties.[2] Root's thesis implies that countries that have successfully transformed their agricultures have given farmers

---

[1] Indeed, some argue that foreign aid has made matters worse, as in *The Aid Trap* (Hubbard and Duggan, 2009).

[2] "The practical difference between the two categories, risk and uncertainty is that in the former the distribution of the outcome in a group of instances is known (either through calculation a priori or from statistics of past experience), while in the case of uncertainty it is not true" (Knight, 1921: 233).

tools to transform the pervasive uncertainties of agriculture into calculable risks. Does the evidence support his thesis? This book argues that these tools include the five necessary conditions. This chapter assesses the extent to which Root's thesis helps explain what kind of political economy motivates governments to establish and maintain the five conditions, and why sustained delivery of public goods and services is essential. At the outset, what constitutes public goods and services, with special reference to agriculture and the rural sector, is defined.

Concept of public goods and services. Goods and services are public when their consumption is such that "all enjoy in common in the sense that each individual's consumption of such a good leads to no subtractions from any other individual's consumption of that good" (Samuelson, 1954: 387–89). The benefits of the consumption go beyond the enjoyment of private individuals (in economic jargon, benefits external to the individual are called "externalities") but are internal to the society at large. In lay people's terms, the entire society, not just individuals, enjoys the consumption. A textbook definition is: goods and services that can be used by any one person without affecting the supply to all other people and for which it is impractical to charge individually. Examples frequently cited of non-rivalrous and non-excludable consumption are national defense and the enforcement of law and order. A major financial implication is that the consumption of these public goods and services cannot be limited to those who pay for them. So private markets cannot be relied upon to be the sole suppliers. Private markets fail under these circumstances. The existence of these public goods and services gives rise to the free-rider problem, namely the problem of users who cannot be excluded from such consumption even if they do not pay. They can ride freely. Therefore, the government must step in because there would be an under-supply if the supply of such goods and services were left totally to private markets.[3] Society would be worse off.

Some real-world examples of public goods and services, with particular reference to agriculture. Examples abound, although there are sometimes controversies over what constitutes public and private. An example of a pure public service would be the dissemination of information of public

---

[3]   The contrary case is that of public bads – negative externalities like pollution and waste disposal, where individuals inflict costs on society through their private behavior. In such cases, the behavior must be taxed; otherwise, there would be an oversupply.

interest, such as that on weather and other natural events, and regulation regarding food safety. However, to complicate matters in the "real world," many goods and services have both public and private goods elements – called quasi-public goods/services. For example, at sector and micro levels, some goods and services must be provided in bulk to be economically feasible because of economies of scale; examples are major thoroughfares such as roads and waterways; piped water and electricity; dams, potable water supply, and irrigation networks; and telecommunication services. Another important example for the future of agriculture is the financing of agricultural research and the dissemination of its findings as extension messages. This can be a private or public good/service depending on the content of the research, the nature of the benefits generated, and the average income level of the farmers relative to the cost of providing the service. McCalla (2000: 10) argued that the global agriculture of the future will have to "come from knowledge-based agricultural intensification, using modern science and biological technology." Schultz (1964: 175–206) argued strongly in favor of public investment in the human capital of farmers – providing basic literacy, agricultural training, and research and extension services, public health facilities that improve life expectancy and the vigor and vitality of farm people – because such investments are essential to the transformation of traditional agriculture into modern agriculture.[4] The individuals who are trained benefit, but because society as a whole also benefits from these investments, they are quasi-public. There is a wide consensus that at an economy-wide level, some important public goods and services are the achievement of peace, social cohesion, and public security; the maintenance of political and price stability; the proper functioning of institutions for competitive market functioning; the enforcement of law and order; the proper functioning of law courts; and the dispensation of justice. In our globalized world, global public goods and services are becoming increasingly important for agriculture; among these are the safety of internationally traded foods; bio-security and the containment and eradication of communicable diseases; reduction in greenhouse gas emissions of agricultural

---

[4] "The key to growth is in acquiring and using effectively some modern ... factors of production" (Schultz, 1964: 178). Schultz correctly points out that his thesis has "radical social and economic implications" (1964: 175). He identifies the transformation of agriculture in Denmark (1870–1900), Japan (1880–1938), and Israel (1950s) in support of his thesis.

technologies, carbon sequestration, as well as mitigation of and adaptation to climate change; and knowledge of development (Stiglitz, Spar, and Habib, 1999). It should be clear from this list that the demarcation between a public good and a public bad is not hard and fast. It changes over time depending in part on changing social values regarding what constitutes a public good versus a public bad, and in part on the state of technology and the efficient scale of production, considered economical and therefore financially sensible. Thus, if law and order were not valued, these would be public bads, and war and violent conflict would be considered public goods. Similarly, the demarcation between private and public can also be a matter of judgment and ethics, for many important goods and services contain both elements. To development practitioners who see the ugly face of poverty the world over and dream of unlocking the great potential of everyone, in particular the poor, reducing poverty is a public good.

VI.I. Prevailing Insights into What Gets Smallholder Agriculture Moving and Why They Have Been Largely Disregarded

What gets agriculture moving? There is a broad consensus among mainstream agricultural economists and development practitioners as to what agriculture needs to "get moving." Schultz (1964: 5, 17, 205–206) argued that the transformation of agriculture is an investment problem. But it is not primarily a problem of the supply of capital. "It is rather a problem of determining the forms this investment must take.... Once there are investment opportunities and efficient incentives, farmers will turn sand into gold." Again, "The key variable in explaining the differences in agricultural production is the human agent, i.e., the differences in the acquired capabilities of farm people." Schultz emphasized the critical importance to farmers of having "the skill and knowledge to use what science knows about soils, plants, animals and machines.... The knowledge that makes the transformation possible is a form of capital, which entails investment – investment not only in material inputs in which part of this knowledge is embedded but importantly also investment in people." Schultz thus identified as critical government investment in developing scientific technology and extending the knowledge to farmers; investment in the education of farmers so they understand and use the technology;

and creating an incentive framework enabling them to want to invest in the new technology. Tomich et al. (1995: 166) emphasized the need for governments to pursue broad-based development and to provide the "six I's." These are innovations, inputs, incentives, infrastructure, institutions, and initiative. This recommendation is fully consistent with Schultz's, except that Tomich et al. emphasized the importance of these six factors operating at the same time. According to Timmer (2005a: 19), who synthesized past insights "There is no great secret to agricultural development. Mosher (1966) and Schultz (1964) had identified the key constraints and strategic elements by the mid-1960s. New agricultural technology and incentive prices in local markets combine to generate profitable farm investments and income streams that simultaneously increase commodity output and lift the rural economy out of poverty (Hayami and Ruttan, 1985). The process can be speeded up by investing in the human capital of rural inhabitants, especially through education, and by assisting in the development of new agricultural technology, especially where modern science is needed to play a key role in providing the genetic foundation for higher yields." The glaring fact is that although "there is no great secret to agricultural development," agriculture in large parts of the developing world is still of low productivity with widespread poverty. Why?

Why have most governments neglected their agricultures, in particular their smallholders? There is an extensive literature discussing the main reasons for the neglect and discrimination – for example, Krueger et al. (eds., 1991), Eicher and Staatz, (1998), and the World Development Report 2008 (World Bank, 2007b). In view of this extensive literature, only the key notions with implications for the role of government are presented here. Notion after notion provided little reason to invest in agriculture and the productive capacity and well-being of smallholders.

- For decades (since the 1950s), it was thought that smallholder farmers were backward and unresponsive to price incentives, and hence could be taxed without fear of undermining agricultural growth, because national development was synonymous with industrialization and urbanization (Binswanger, 1994). The investment needs of agriculture were disregarded, and governments taxed agriculture to invest in industry. Cheap food for cities had to be ensured. Urban bias (well into the 1980s) was pervasive, in both mixed-market and communist systems. Fighting against this bias was Lipton (1977), among others. Lipton argued that urban bias in overvalued exchange rates, state procurement, and public spending decisions made it impossible for hardworking and innovative smallholders to get a fair return on their efforts (Cortbridge and Jones, 2006: 9–11).

- Academics such as Albert Hirschman (1958: 109–110) also condemned agriculture. Using the concept of linkages, Hirschman argued that "agriculture certainly stands convicted on the count of its direct stimulus to the setting of new activities through linkage effects – the superiority of manufacturing is crushing."

- Prebisch and Singer (1950) asserted that secular terms of trade would turn against primary exports, including agricultural exports. Thus whether low-income countries invest in primary sectors such as agriculture does not help their development. The dependency theorists argued that underdevelopment was the result of the dependence of low-income countries (the "periphery") on the expansion of rich industrialized countries (the "center"). For them, low-income countries were exploited in the process, as trade was a zero-sum game. Investment in agriculture does not make sense within this worldview.[5]

- There was also the communist/socialist camp (e.g., China, the Soviet Union, and Cuba), which advocated public ownership and collectivization. For this camp, advanced agriculture required large state farms using big machinery capable of exploiting economies of scale. It disregarded the necessity and power of private material incentives, as well as the key importance of local knowledge and responsiveness of farm households in decision making. For example, in China's production teams, the work-point standard (wage rate) was identical for all workers irrespective of individual contribution, depending on differential skills and hours put in. The inevitable free-rider problem was prevalent (Lin

---

[5] It appears that what has come to be known as the Prebisch–Singer thesis of the secular decline in agriculture's terms of trade was arrived at independently according to Toye and Toye (2003).

et al., 1996: 80–81). To make matters worse for agriculture, Mao's China believed in leaping into industrialization and taxed agriculture through prices and procurement to do so (see Chapter II). Small-scale agriculture was considered incapable of improvement by Marxist economists like Baran (1952), who argued that broad-based capitalist development among poor farmers was impossible without violent social revolutions.

- The "basic needs" period of integrated rural development (IRD, 1970s and 1980s) recognized the need of smallholders for basic public goods and services. However, neglect of the substantial economic, financial, and administrative requirements of such integrated delivery made the approach unsustainable. IRD projects were mainly donor-financed, and governments did not continue to finance them.

- Political support for land reform in most developing countries (except for Japan, the Republic of Korea, the People's Republic of China, and Taiwan, China all in the early 1950s) did not succeed in bringing about the redistribution of agricultural land and other assets to the majority of small and landless farmers to the point of shifting the balance of socio-political and economic power in favor of this majority.

- In the 1980s and 1990s, preoccupied with structural adjustment programs and regaining fiscal balance, many developing country governments privatized parastatals and drastically reduced the little budgetary support they were allocating to smallholder agriculture and rural households. By and large, the private sector did not step into rural areas where government withdrew. Thus smallholders were again left with even lesser access to basic public goods and services in rural areas.

Important as these factors were, critics can rightly point out that they explicitly omit the single most important factor explaining why smallholder agriculture has chronically been deprived of the public support it needs to thrive in most of the developing world: the political economy that shapes government decisions and budgets. Political economy considerations are intended to explain why governments do what they do, not just what they do. There are several variants within the political economy approach to understanding the determinants of government policy decisions. Which variant best explains the chronic neglect of smallholder agriculture in much of the developing world?

VI.II. Political Economy Explanations: Alternative Theories of Governments' Neglect of Smallholder Agriculture

Is the persistent underdevelopment of agriculture in large parts of the developing world a puzzle? If one assumes that governments are "agencies whose job is to maximize social welfare and public policy is viewed as a set of choices made by governments to secure society's best interests," then government behavior in much of the developing world is incomprehensible (Bates, 1998: 235). It is therefore essential to reject this view of government if one accepts the reality of widespread poor governance and to entertain political economy explanations. Distributional issues – allocation of resources and the costs and benefits of policies – are at the heart of political economy considerations. Three major variants are of interest here:

1. Bates argues that one should not view government as a unitary actor, but rather as a pluralist entity, and public policy as an "outcome of political competition among organized groups." Thus, according to Bates, governments are "agencies which seek to stay in power" (Bates, 1998: 235–38). Governments should be viewed as primarily self-serving entities, willing and able to sacrifice the welfare of the majority for their own political survival. The predatory policies of many governments severely taxing smallholder agriculture certainly support this explanation. Bates also gives many examples, such as the government of Ghana subsidizing farm input programs to ration scarce inputs to politically loyal farm organizations, while taxing the majority of cocoa farmers through its low cocoa price policy. This view of government cannot, however, explain why the Taiwanese government adopted agricultural policies (in the 1950s–1970s), including a thorough land reform, that benefited the majority of agricultural and rural households (Fei et al., 1979). The Taiwanese government succeeded in promoting equitable growth.
2. In Olson's (1971) framework, governments are manipulated by lobby groups. Small groups organize in powerful lobbies, whereas

large groups do not. "The multitude of workers, consumers, white collar workers, farmers, and so on are organized only in special circumstances, but business interests are organized as a general rule" (Olson, 1971: 143). Olson would explain the heavy taxation of agriculture in developing countries through the lack of vigorous lobby action by smallholders. Speaking of the United States, "The most striking fact about the political organization of farmers in the United States is that there has been so little. Farmers on the whole have not been well organized, except perhaps in recent years" (Olson, 1971: 148).[6] Binswanger and Deininger (1997) also emphasize smallholders' "low potential for collective action" as a major reason "why inefficient policy regimes persist." Small farmers in developing countries, unlike farmers in industrialized countries, today constitute a major proportion of the total population. Typically, their costs of communication are high, as they are geographically widely dispersed and have inadequate access to rural transportation and communications networks. As a result, they rarely if ever organize. Like Bates, Olson is not able to explain the agricultural policies of the Taiwanese government. The Kuomingtang government strengthened existing local organizations –farmers' associations formed under Japanese rule (1895–1945) – and drew upon their participation to implement its policies from the very beginning. There is no evidence that these associations lobbied to shape government's agricultural policy (Shen, 1970).

3. De Mesquita and Root (2000: 1) point out, "How to govern for prosperity is likely to be the most important policy puzzle of the twenty-first century." According to them, the answer to the puzzle lies in the nature of political incentives wherein leaders need only satisfy a small group to stay in power. When it is not in the survival interest of leaders to promote the welfare of the majority, bad economics becomes good politics. Root (2006: 17) argues that social inequality – sharp inequality in the distribution of wealth and power – is a fundamental cause of divided governments, polarized societies, and inability to reach consensus about

---

[6] De Gorter and Swinnen (2002: 1905) point out that Olson's framework does not explain why the U.S. government heaped subsidies on farmers in the 1930s when farmers represented about 25 percent of total U.S. population.

collective goals, in particular policy reforms to promote pub-
licly beneficial agendas. Thus, in societies with high inequality of
wealth and power, leaders can stay in power by distributing private goods to these select few. These governments resort to "cli-
entelistic channels of private influence." Consumed with the need
for their own survival, such governments plunder their countries'
resources instead of building for the welfare of current and future
generations. Within this type of political economy dynamics, the
short- and long-term interests of the majority – smallholders,
numerous and poor – get ignored. This argument seems promising, as it explains why smallholders have been chronically ignored
in large parts of the developing world and why the only exceptions have been some East Asian countries whose governments
have drastically reduced socio-economic inequality through land
reform and other measures. De Mesquita and Root's thesis can
explain why so many governments in highly unequal societies
have not been able to transform uncertainty into risk, thus leaving their countries (in our case, their agriculture, which often is
the dominant sector) mired in stagnation and extensive poverty.
Essentially, they argue that "bad economics is good politics" when
leaders' prime interest in their own survival does not coincide
with serving the people's interest in a better life.

The discussion that follows presents and tests De Mesquita and Root's
thesis applied to the case of the underdevelopment of smallholder
agriculture.

The logic of patronage politics demands bad economics. Cronyism is the life
blood of patronage systems but has no place in competitive systems
based on merit. Patronage politics thrives when patrons dispense private goods to reward their supporters. Root (2006: 26) calls this small
group of supporters the "winning coalition." With the loyal support of
this coalition, many autocrats have enjoyed greater political longevity
than their counterparts, elected officials in democracies. The very logic
of this modus operandi requires that the size of the winning coalition be small (consisting of, e.g., party elites, heads of the military,
big landlords and corporations, and warlords) to keep patrons' largesse
plentiful, thus enabling them to sustain their grip on power. The larger
the size of this coalition, the thinner must be the spread of private

goods. The logic also requires policies that maintain the status quo of skewed distribution of income and wealth. Largesse to this narrow clique comes at the nation's expense. Not only are the nation's resources plundered, but such sharp disparities breed social polarization inimical to broad-based growth, as Pakistan, Venezuela, and many other developing countries with sharp disparities exemplify. When patronage politics prevail, the nation is doubly robbed. This first occurs when the elites privatize public resources. It occurs a second time when the opportunity cost of the resources is diverted away from investment in the delivery of basic public goods and services. There is more. Private investment is undermined when rules of competitive market functioning are violated for the benefit of the few; instability, uncertainty, and distrust reign; competitive markets cannot flourish; and social polarization paralyzes a nation's ability to develop the consensus required to undertake long-term investments in order to promote the productivity and resilience of its people. Patronage politics distorts incentives, thus undermining the productivity potential of the entire economy, of both the rich and the poor.

Sharp disparities in wealth and power breed instability and uncertainty. In dualistic economies, whether the government is pro-rich or pro-poor, where country leaders exploit sharp disparities in income and wealth to strengthen their grip on power, the poor will suffer, irrespective of how much aid is poured in or how resource-rich the nation is. In both cases, the governments are unable to provide a stable political framework or invest in and deliver basic public goods and services. Pakistan and Venezuela illustrate both cases.

- *Autocratic rule in Pakistan breeds corruption and instability:*[7] Sharp disparities in income and wealth coupled with extensive poverty provide fertile ground for coups and armed conflict along religious, tribal, or ethnic lines. Since its founding (1947), Pakistan has already had three military coups, first under Field Marshall Ayub Khan (1958–69), then General Zia Ul-Haq (1977–88), and most recently General Pervez Musharraf (1999–2008). In March 1971, grievances by East Pakistan (now Bangladesh) of economic exploitation by current-day Pakistan led to a civil war.

---

[7] World Development Indicators, September 2010: GNI per capita, USD 1,020 (2009).

Due primarily to geopolitical alliances, Pakistan has been the third-largest recipient of aid since 1960. After 1982, Pakistan received around USD 5 billion of U.S. aid (Root, 2006: 167, 182). This abundant aid has, however, largely bypassed the common people, for Pakistan exemplifies the growth-inhibiting nature of the politics of high inequality.[8] The powerful elite consists of 22 families owning 66 percent of industry, 97 percent of the insurance sector, and 80 percent of banking. In agriculture, only 0.1 percent of landlords owned 500 acres or more, occupying 15 percent of Pakistan's land (Root, 2006: 163). The Gini coefficient for landholding was 0.62 (2001–2002) (Anwar, Kureshi, and Ali, 2003: 8). Successive autocratic regimes – for example, those of Ali Jinnah, the founder (1947–58), Ayub Khan (1958–69), Zulficar Bhutto (1972–77), Zia Ul-Haq (1977–88), elected governments of Benazir Bhutto (1988–90 and 1994–97), and Nawaz Sharif (1990–93 and 1997–99) – all used corruption to solidify their grip on power, operated state funds in non-accountable ways, and filled public civil service posts with their supporters while bypassing standard civil service criteria. This patronage system has been characterized thus: "The faces did change from time to time ... but the stranglehold of this elite group accounting for less than 1 percent of the population on the affairs of the state has remained unscathed. The capture of institutions of the state and the market by the elite is complete" (Root, 2006: 168–69).[9]

- *Personalized rule in Pakistan breeds not only political instability, but also uncertainty for the millions outside the clique*: Personality-driven politics is inherently unstable, and instability and uncertainty go hand in hand. Whether pro-rich or pro-poor, successive Pakistani governments undermined the rule of law to maintain their winning coalitions. As a result, the millions outside this inner circle are unable to trust the state to provide even the most

[8]   The United States, like all donors, faces a dilemma. The dilemma is whether the assistance goals of the donor would be better served if the donor worked with the existing regime despite corruption and other negative governance traits or whether it would be better to wait until a better regime came along (Heckelman and Coates, eds., 2003: 206).

[9]   Assessment by Ishrat Hussain, former World Bank official with long years of experience in the Pakistan government.

basic public services, such as law and order, enforcement of contracts, justice, and security.[10] Extensive government intervention in the functioning of private business without any checks and balances on its power to issue or extract favors has been fertile ground for corruption. For example, Ayub Khan issued licenses and permits to his favorites. Under the banner of populist policies, Zulficar Bhutto raided public coffers to enlarge the public sector but left the privileges of the rich untouched, nationalized industries, and extracted kickbacks from import licenses issued under its import-substitution policies. Democratically elected Benazir Bhutto was known for taking shares of companies that benefited from import licenses. The parliament of the democratically elected Nawaz Sharif was composed primarily of feudal lords and industrialists, many of whom bought their seats in office. As a result of this spoils-based governance, business success, instead of being admired, is suspect because such success is built on political access rather than competitive merit. Given the predatory state, private business has every incentive to keep correct information regarding its business statistics secret. In such an environment, official information is also suspect. The thinness and unreliability of market information inevitably undermines efficient and competitive market development. Unable to trust the state or private business, many of the poor have turned to Islamic fundamentalism as a final refuge for law and order.

- *A high degree of inequality, social polarization, and political instability is not unique to Pakistan – the case of Venezuela*[11]: Like de Mesquita and Root, Easterly (2001: 263–83) argues that countries with a high degree of inequality tend to suffer social polarization, economic gridlock, and persistent low growth and underdevelopment. Venezuela, a middle-income country with a GDP per capita of USD 10,150 (2009), is a good case in

---

[10] The extensive flooding in Pakistan, which started on July 22, 2010, the worst in 80 years, has destroyed what little public infrastructure, such as roads and bridges, existed. Some 20 million people, an eighth of the population, were said to have been severely affected (*New York Times*, September 24, 2010). This major devastation is inevitably testing the ability of the government to deliver basic assistance to millions.

[11] World Development Indicators, September 2010: GNI per capita, USD 10,150 (2009).

point.[12] The beautiful capital city of Caracas, "the poster child for inequality," is ringed with shantytowns (Easterly, 2001: 264). The Gini coefficient for Venezuela was (for the 1980s–1990s) 0.5 for income and 0.9 for land (World Bank, July 2002: fig. 2.2a, b). Its billions of oil profits fuel distributional wars rather than investments in broad-based development.[13] Despite its oil wealth and populist policies, including nationalization under the highly controversial figure of President Hugo Chavez, the average Venezuelan has 22 percent lower income in the 2000s than in the 1970s (Easterly, 2001: 264). Poverty incidence measured by the National Institute of Statistics was nearly 47 percent in 2000, with extreme poverty[14] at 18 percent. The poverty incidence rose to nearly 53 and 23 percent, respectively, in 2004 (UNICEF, ILO, World Bank Group, 2006: fig. 3). For more than a century since it first declared its independence from Spain (July 5, 1811), it has experienced frequent periods of political and policy instability, dictatorship, and revolt. More recently, since the late 1980s, with worsening macroeconomic imbalances, the government embarked on a major stabilization-cum-adjustment program, including extensive trade liberalization, called El Gran Viraje (1989–92). Fiscal discipline and market orientation gave way to violent protests (called the "Cherokees March") from lobbies of powerful farmers and feed grain processors. The pendulum then swung back to protectionism. But again, the costs soon became unsustainable as the fiscal deficit rose to nearly 7 percent of GDP by the end of 1995, in part due to the costs of these subsidies. Venezuela thus continued to swing back and forth between unsustainably high protection and the rigors of market discipline. In the 1990s, Venezuela experienced two military coup attempts in 1992, the ouster of President Perez on corruption charges in 1993, and a banking crisis in 1994,

---

[12] Venezuela's ranking with respect to the environment for doing business is low. Out of a sample of 183 countries, its ranking is 177, compared with 1 for Singapore (World Bank and International Finance Corporation, 2009: 1).

[13] Venezuela's petroleum era started in the 1920s. Before then, Venezuela's economy consisted primarily of subsistence agriculture, raising cattle, and exporting coffee, cocoa, and gold. There was also great disparity of incomes and extensive poverty (World Bank, 1961: 28–29).

[14] The extreme poverty line measures only the consumption cost of a food bundle, with no services included.

when President Caldera took office.[15] In the 2000s, Venezuela continued to suffer from political and macro instability, a deep recession, and high inflation – above 30 percent in 2003 (World Bank, 2007b: box 1). Under the banner of Bolivarian socialism, Chavez (1999–present) is using welfare programs as a way of redistributing funds from the oligarchy to his supporters, the poor. It remains to be seen whether Chavez, who sees himself as a champion of the poor, will be able to find the socialist path to macro and political stability, and to building the national consensus essential to achieving broad-based development and prosperity.

High developmental cost of a skewed distribution of income and wealth a common but not an inevitable problem. Are the cases of Pakistan and Venezuela the exceptions or the rule? Empirical evidence strongly suggests that a highly skewed distribution of income and wealth often engenders a power structure inimical to political stability and broad-based growth in large parts of the developing world. However, a high degree of inequality is not an insurmountable obstacle to achieving poverty-reducing growth. Chile after Pinochet is a well-known counterexample, as Chile has a high degree of inequality, with a Gini coefficient of income of 0.56 (World Bank, 2002b: 1–2, tables 6, 12), but has substantially reduced poverty since 1990 and achieved high growth.[16] Moreover, its government apparatus is known to be relatively efficient, with little corruption (Lopez and Miller, 2008: 2680). Botswana is another counterexample. Inequality of both assets and income is high – Gini coefficient of around 0.56 during the 1980s and 1990s (Acemoglu, Johnson, and Robinson, eds., 2003: 85). It is clear that much depends on country leadership and the economic philosophy and strategy it adopts. Examples of political instability and low growth

---

[15] Venezuela has had democratic elections since 1958. It decisively gained its independence from Spain in 1821 (the wars of independence lasted for 10 years, from 1811 from 1821) under the leadership of Simón Bolívar, a national hero greatly admired by Chavez. Since then, it has experienced frequent periods of political instability, dictatorship, and revolt.

[16] Poverty incidence was reduced from 40 percent in 1987 to 17 percent in 1998. Barely 4 percent now live in extreme poverty (World Bank, August 2001: 5). The rural headcount poverty measure fell from more than 50 percent (1980) to 23 percent (2000) (Anderson and Valdes, eds., 2008: 130). While the lessons to be drawn from Chile's experience remain controversial, what is not controversial is the fact that poverty reduction has been substantial and growth has been high.

in Latin America are often quoted – for example, the macroeconomic instability in most of Latin America over the past three decades, in particular in Argentina, and the high frequency of coups d'état and political assassinations (Root, 2006: 99–103; Edwards, Esquivel, and Marquez, 2007: 1–5; Blanco and Grier, 2007).[17] For sub-Saharan Africa, low economic growth is attributed largely to political instability as measured by the frequency of coups d'état on the continent (Fosu, 2002; Nel, 2003: 626). Nel (2003: 626), however, rightly points to the conflicting results that would obtain if one were to infer causality from measures of statistical significance between income inequality and political instability.[18] We still do not know, as Kanbur (2005: 225) reminds us, that "identifying policy variables that lead to equitable growth is the first level of hard questions that analysts and policy makers face on growth, inequality and poverty." Not only do we not know what these are, empirical evidence from the East Asian "tigers"[19] shows that there is no necessary trade-off between inequality and growth during the earlier stages of growth. These East Asian countries grew, and resource allocation became more equitable. Trade-off between growth and equity was once believed to be the case based on Kuznets's empirical work showing an inverted U relationship between inequality and growth. The fundamental question is not only under what conditions the curve does or does not exist, but also what kinds of inequality are socially destabilizing and growth inhibiting.

VI.III. Is Patronage Politics a Key Factor Undermining Smallholder Agriculture?

How has patronage politics undermined smallholder agriculture? De Mesquita and Root (2000) argue that bad economics is good patronage politics. The autocratic leaders are concerned mainly with satisfying their winning coalition by distributing private goods extracted at the nation's expense. These leaders thrive in a highly unequal system.

---

[17] Blanco and Grier (2007) examined a panel of 18 Latin American countries from 1971 to 2000. In their sample, there were 20 coups d'état, 451 political assassinations, 217 riots, and 113 crises that threatened to bring down the sitting government.

[18] "Large-n cross country regression studies to date have produced conflicting results" (Nel, 2003: 626).

[19] The four "tigers" are Hong Kong, the Republic of Korea, Taiwan, China and Singapore. The newly industrializing economies of Southeast Asia are Indonesia, Malaysia, and Thailand (World Bank, 1993a: xvi).

Although a high degree of inequality does not necessarily lead to bad economics, as the cases of Botswana and Chile show, it often does.[20] Where great inequality distorts not only power sharing, the system of patronage politics is prone to political instability, which inevitably breeds uncertainty and undermines risk taking. Such a system cannot promote broad-based development. The underdevelopment of smallholder agriculture is one of its major casualties. More generally, Collier (2007) argues that three-quarters of the world's "bottom billion" have suffered from prolonged periods of poor governance and poor policies (Binswanger-Mkhize and McCalla, 2010: 3638).[21] The hallmark of the environment in which patronage politics flourishes is threefold: pervasive uncertainty, rampant corruption, and a large component of government public expenditure allocated to private goods and services. What is the evidence? The discussion that follows explores the evidence. Specifically, it considers whether these three structural features are found in countries where smallholder agriculture is underdeveloped. Before considering these cases, however, it is important to appreciate the characteristic features of agriculture (in particular that of smallholders) that make the sector highly risky. This appreciation enables us to better understand the nature of public support required.

The many faces of uncertainty in agriculture, in particular for smallholders. It may be difficult for the urban world to fully appreciate the decentralized decision- and knowledge-intensive nature of agricultural production and marketing within an environment subject to major shocks (Timmer, 1988: 291–300). For subsistence agriculture, farmers are concerned primarily with uncertainties due to weather fluctuations, pest attacks, and the onslaught of other natural calamities. Millions of

[20] A high degree of inequality in Chile is still very problematic, as Lopez and Miller (2008: 2692) point out. Although Chile is not corrupt in the usual sense of the word (e.g., kickbacks, bribery), domination of elite ideology has been through "control of mass media as well as of certain key think tanks and universities.... This ideology emphasizes that enforcing existing income or profit taxes and removing their loopholes is a bad idea because it would promote less investment and the exiting of capital outside the country in search of lower taxes. Hence, in lieu of taxing income, profit and resource rents, policy makers are advised to maintain one of the highest VAT which effectively shifts the burden of taxation from the elites to the rest of society."

[21] "[For] the one billion who are stuck at the bottom ... their reality is the fourteenth century: civil war, plague and ignorance. They are concentrated in Africa and Central Asia, with a scattering elsewhere" (Collier, 2007: 3).

small farmers must decide what, when, and how to plant, harvest, and store without any guarantee that natural conditions will be favorable enough for a good harvest. For commercial agriculture, the range of uncertainties increases by leaps and bounds: (a) fluctuations in domestic prices (including interest rates) of inputs, outputs, and factors of production (land, labor, and capital); (b) changes in foreign exchange rates and trade regimes; and (c) changes in government policy in terms of taxes, subsidies, and other interventions affecting agricultural terms of trade and on-farm technology uptake. This is not all. For smallholders, there is more to worry about. Do they have tenure security on their small plots of land? If they are sharecroppers, will the formula for sharing the harvest be maintained or worsened as the competition for land intensifies? Since agricultural income is typically inadequate for household use, most smallholders must also sell their labor in the non-farm sector, rural or otherwise. What kinds of employment opportunities and wages can they expect? For farmers who have borrowed against the value of their land and the expected harvest, the vagaries of nature and of markets can wreak havoc on their capacity to service their loans. Farmers can lose, whether the harvest is good or bad: When there is an abundant harvest, prices plummet and farmers can lose. This is usually referred to as the "farm problem." When natural calamities strike, farmers can also lose their entire harvest and livelihood. Is it any wonder that farmers, from generation to generation and the world over, want to leave the farm!

VI.III.I. *Pervasive Uncertainty*
Main channels under government control generating uncertainty in agriculture. At a fundamental level, farmers' relationships with the land they till and the markets in which they operate inevitably have an impact on the risks they can take. Farmers everywhere operate within the legacy of government policy on land and property rights, as well as on infrastructure development and market access. What kinds of risks farmers can take within this framework largely determines what kinds of farmers they can be. They must thrive as risk takers. Does the legacy of government policy in these two areas help farmers take risks throughout the long chain from farm production to final sale? Too often, it seems not. Country evidence clearly shows that social conflict in the case of agriculture is typically generated by: (1) highly unequal distribution of land (and increasingly

water);[22] (2) tenure insecurity; and (3) inadequate infrastructure and poor access to markets hurt farmers' ability to take risks. In so doing, they undermine smallholder development. The case of the People's Republic of China, however, shows that equality of land distribution alone does not necessarily entail tenure security. Thus:

(1) *Agricultural land – inequitable distribution*: Land policy and administration have been of determining importance in agricultural performance. Land distribution, if considered equitable and speedily implemented, and land administration, if considered competent and just, are major sources of stability and risk reduction, essential for increasing productivity, as the case of Zimbabwe dramatically exemplifies.[23] The uncertainties that surround the process of land redistribution and use have been due mainly to unresolved social conflicts in different parts of the world.

(a) *Social conflict in Sub-Saharan Africa*: Inequities in land distribution in many parts of the world, whether arising from colonialism or feudalism, have been socially destabilizing. For example, in Zimbabwe, the redistribution of land from the minority of white farmers to the majority of poor black farmers has been an explosive issue for decades. During nearly a century of colonial rule (late 1880s–1980), the British and Dutch settlers expropriated the best agricultural lands of the Shona and Ndele peoples by crushing their uprisings (1885–96) and legitimizing the ownership of the whites by giving them titles, while the blacks, confined to the 23 percent of the worst land in designated native reserves, were governed only by customary law. Thus, by 1919, Southern Rhodesia (at independence on April 18, 1980, became Zimbabwe) had a dualistic agriculture. The war of liberation was fought over land (Pazvakavambwa and Hungwe, 2009: 138–40).[24] In South Africa, at the end of apartheid (1994), 86 percent of

---

[22] With increasing water scarcity, especially under certain climate change scenarios, conflicts in water use and resolution of water rights are looming as a major problem of asset distribution, for land without water is of little value.

[23] World Development Indicators, 2010: GNI per capita, USD 350 (2005, latest estimate available).

[24] Thus the issue of land transfer and distribution from the minority of white farmers has poisoned politics for decades, even before the Lancaster House Agreement (1980) was signed between Great Britain and Zimbabwe, in which Great Britain said it would fund a willing seller/willing buyer land reform to the tune of 44 million British pounds.

all farmland was in the hands of a minority of whites – 10.9 percent of the population, with approximately 60,000 owners. At the same time, 13 million black people, most of them poverty-stricken, remained crowded in the former homelands[25] (Lahiff, 2009: 170). This highly inequitable land distribution rooted in the history of colonization and exploitation generates high unemployment, poverty, and social tensions. Land distribution issues are also problematic in many other parts of SSA; for example, they are politically explosive in Sudan and increase poverty in many countries of East Africa where land scarcity and concentration in the smallholder sector is increasing (Jayne et al., 2003: 261–65).[26]

(b) *Social conflict in Asia*: In the People's Republic of China, it was the ability of the Communist Party to rally the countryside around the promise of land reform that eventually gave the Communists victory over the Kuomingtang (Zhou and Bourguignon, in Binswanger-Mhize et al., eds., 2009: 121). In much of land-scarce and labor-abundant developing Asia, the success or failure of post-WWII land reforms to create a unimodal land distribution has had a determining impact on the subsequent distribution of economic opportunities, political power, and social peace – for example, in the Philippines, where land conflicts are still raw despite more than five decades of land reform (see the earlier discussion of the Philippines), and in the state of Bihar, India, where large inequalities of landownership persist despite land reform, which started in 1950 (World Bank, 2005b: 7).

(c) *Social conflict in Latin America*: Except for Cuba, "incomplete land reforms" characterize Latin America, where the demand for land by the dispossessed has been a source of major revolutions and political upheavals (Mexico, Bolivia, Cuba, and Nicaragua, Chile under Allende, Guatemala under Ardenz, and El Salvador), but the issues of inequity and poverty remain

---

[25] Homelands are what were referred to as native reserves, into which the blacks were pushed as the white British and Dutch settlers took the best agricultural land. These reserves constituted only 13 percent of South Africa (Lahiff, in Binswanger-Mhize et al., eds., 2009: 170).

[26] The countries are Ethiopia, Kenya, Uganda, Mozambique, and Zambia (1990–2000, data from representative household surveys).

(de Janvry and Sadoulet, 2002). Land reform (1958–63) in Cuba has been a major platform of the Communist government under Castro since 1958. The expropriation of land under large landholdings, including 480,000 acres of land owned by American corporations, collectivization under cooperatives, and state farms have contributed to thousands fleeing to the United States and to the imposition of the U.S. trade embargo against Cuba since 1960. In Latin America, the dualistic structure of *latifundia* co-existing with *minifundia* grew in the 19th century as a minority of rural oligarchs obtained control of huge tracts of land and kept the native populations as subsistence farmers (e.g., in Bolivia, Ecuador, Guatemala, Honduras, and Peru) on small plots of land (Furtado, 1976: 68–80).[27] In Nicaragua, a major platform of the Sandinista revolution was land reform (1981–85), during which land was confiscated at gunpoint and redistributed as cooperatives. In Brazil, where the poorest 40 percent own barely 1 percent of the land, while 3.5 percent of the landowners hold 56 percent of arable land, the Landless Workers Movement (MST) was still calling for faster and broader land reform during President Lula's second term (2007–2010). For decades, the MST has been organizing confrontations for land expropriations (Osava, 2007).[28] In 19th-century Argentina, the government chose to dispose of public lands by making grants of huge blocks of land to individuals and then later to private development companies (Sokoloff and Zolt, in Edwards, Esquivel, and Marquez, eds., 2007: 95–96). Contrast this to the approach taken in the largely Anglo-Saxon "New World."[29]

(d) *Contrast with the largely Anglo-Saxon countries of the "New World"*: Historians often contrast the Homestead Act of 1862 in the United States and the Dominion Lands Act of 1872 in Canada with the land policy adopted in Argentina.

---

[27] The Gini coefficient of inequality of land distribution in Latin America ranges from 0.62 in Mexico to 0.85 in Brazil and Argentina and 0.9 in Venezuela (World Bank, July 2002: table 1.3, figs. A2.8, A2.9).

[28] The MST and the Brazilian government disagree on how much progress the Lula government made on land reform after Lula's first term (2003–2006).

[29] The "New World" refers to the sparsely populated lands discovered and colonized by the European colonial powers: North and South America, Australia, and New Zealand.

In North America, the land policy created a system of family farms of fairly equal size, thus removing a potential source of social conflict as in Latin America. Historians also contrast the more egalitarian land policy adopted in New Zealand in the 19th and early 20th centuries with that of Uruguay, where large landowners and *caudillos* (political bosses, over-lords, military chiefs, certain strongmen) got their way (see the earlier discussion in Chapter III on New Zealand).

(2) *Agricultural land – tenure insecurity*: Tenure insecurity has multi-ple causes and comes in several forms. While there are no survey data that show its extent in rural areas in the developing world (Deininger, 2003: xxv), anecdotal evidence suggests it is wide-spread. In some countries, the weakening of customary tenure systems and the co-existence of different property rights regimes gives rise to confusion, resulting in tenure insecurity and the inadequate functioning of land markets. The problem is often compounded by weak land administration. For example,

(a) In some sub-Saharan African countries where there have been long years of conflict (e.g., Mozambique, Rwanda, Angola, Southern Sudan, Northern Uganda), there may be a breakdown of traditional rules that used to make customary land tenure sys-tems secure. In areas ravaged by the AIDS/HIV pandemic, the customary rights of widows and orphans are not protected. In some cases, customary land tenure systems do not provide protec-tion against incursions by outsiders, including government offi-cials at the national level (Van den Brink et al., 2006: 13–15).

(b) Although Ghana is land-abundant, access to agricultural land is a problem, according to Nyanteng and Seini (2000). Their research shows that although individuals may not have diffi-culty in accessing small parcels of land for farming, their ten-ure security is often threatened by the lack of clarity in their right to transfer use rights to others (ISSER survey, 2007).[30] This difficulty may be due to a lack of clear titles. Land in the northern region of Ghana is communally owned, and con-trol over it is in the hands of the land priest, variously known

---

[30] Institute of Statistical, Social and Economic Research (2007), State of Ghanaian Economy Report (2006), University of Ghana.

as *tendana*, *tigatu*, or *totem*. However, Migot-Adhola et al. (1991), using data from some regions of Rwanda and Kenya, question the widespread view that indigenous tenure systems that assign land rights to the community discourage long-term investments in land improvements.

(c) Tenure insecurity is also problematic in other parts of the developing world. For example, in Nicaragua, tenure insecurity is pervasive in the agrarian reform sector.[31] This typically hurts the rural poor who received confiscated land under the Sandinista regime (FSLN, 1979–90). In Nicaragua, tenure insecurity has two causes. One is land that was given by the state but which the state did not own or did legally own but gave to ineligible beneficiaries. The other is land that was given to cooperatives but that disintegrated subsequently in the 1990s and did not have proper procedures for privatization or for debt restructuring (World Bank, October 2003: 2–3).

(d) In Morocco, there are complex land tenure systems (private on 75 percent of land and on the remaining 25 percent, various forms of collective, use-only, tribal, agrarian reform, and state-owned). This complexity is problematic. On the private land, only 30 percent of the land has formal registration titles (of which only 40 percent have been updated), while the remaining land is under *Moulkya*, a traditional Muslim system of land registration. The *Moulkya* system does not eliminate conflicting claims of ownership. The Moroccan Land Administration Agency (ANCFCC) has not been able to keep up with the system of titling such that, as of 2006, it would take it some 12 years to deal with the then-existing backlog (World Bank, June 2007: ch. 15)![32]

(e) The more equitable allocation of land use rights in the People's Republic of China to rural households under the Household

---

[31] During 1981–85, thousands of acres of land were expropriated and converted into cooperatives. These lands, organized under cooperatives, constituted the Agrarian Reform Sector. In the 1981 Agrarian Reform Law, the Sandinistas expropriated unused farms, properties of absentee landlords, and unproductive land. Prior to the July 17, 1979, power takeover by the Sandinistas (Frente Sandinista de Liberación Nacional, FSLN), 4 percent of landowners occupied 52 percent of arable land.

[32] The Moroccan Land Administration Agency is called the Agence Nationale de la Conservation Foncière, du Cadastre et de la Cartographie (ANCFCC); World Development Indicators, September 2010: GNI per capita, USD 1,000 (2009).

Responsibility System (1979) does not ensure tenure security, as the thousands of land seizures of valuable farmland (typically peri-urban along the east coast) for economic projects demonstrate. Thousands of cases of corrupt local government officials and private business colluding to seize farmland without adequate compensation have been reported by the *Economist* (2005). Farmers have virtually no effective legal recourse for obtaining justice, as the law courts are controlled by local Communist Party officials, according to Human Rights Watch. Not surprisingly, violent protests have erupted. The central government has become increasingly concerned about the rural instability generated by these incidents. To protect farmers, it passed the Rural Land Contracting Law (2002), according to which "any organization or individual is not allowed to expropriate or illegally limit the land contracting rights of farmers." Document No. 1 of 2008 encouraged the establishment of rural land registries, which would give farmers legal certificates to their contracted land (Zhou and Bourguignon, in Binswanger-Mhize et al., eds., 2009: 131). It remains to be seen whether these will in fact ensure tenure security.[33]

With respect to infrastructure development and access to markets:

(3) *Infrastructure*: To market successfully, farm households need, at a minimum, access to infrastructure and market systems linking their immediate neighborhoods to their customers. Inadequate linkages make the process of and returns from marketing highly uncertain. While there has been a significant increase (World Bank, June 1994: fig. 3) in access to infrastructure (e.g., paved roads, power, telecom, potable water) in low- and middle-income developing countries, millions of smallholders remain isolated by poor transport and communications infrastructure. What is required to link farmers with their markets is a complex set of both hardware and software, from paved rural roads to fully enforced and competitively structured contracts between farmers

[33] Improper seizures continued into 2010, as the case of businessman Gu Kui of Chengdu (capital of Sichuan) shows. Gu Kui is suing the Chengdu city government (Wagner, in *Der Spiegel*, August 13, 2010).

and their business partners upstream and downstream.[34] This section focuses only on the basics, for if these do not exist, the more sophisticated links will not either. Rural Sub-Saharan Africa is singled out as being particularly poorly equipped. An estimate of only 40 percent of rural Africans live within 2 kilometers of an all-season road, compared with some 65 percent in other developing countries (World Bank, Africa's Infrastructure, 2009c). The low population densities of SSA make matters worse because these make the cost per capita of investment high. There are fewer and less developed roads in SSA than there were in Asia at the time of the Green Revolution (1960s) (World Bank, 2007b: box 2.1).

(a) Large areas of rural Asia, where most of the world's poor live, however, also lack market access. For example, in rural Pakistan, where about 100 million people live (two-thirds of the total population), one in every five villages is still not accessible by all-weather motorable roads (Essakali, 2005: 1).[35] Even in rural India, where the Green Revolution took off in the state of Punjab in the 1960s, inadequate rural infrastructure and market access is problematic for millions, especially the rural poor. The government of India is well aware of this and thus created the Rural Infrastructure Development Fund (RIDF), first launched in 1995–96 to assist states in rural infrastructure development. Irrigation projects, and rural roads and bridges, have been the two main expenditure categories from the RIDF. After more than 10 years of the RIDF, the states that made the least use of the funds to improve their rural connectivity are also some of the poorest states: Bihar and Orissa, with poverty rates of around 50 and 44 percent, respectively (1999–2000). In 1996–97, after the RIDF had just started, more than 50 percent of villages in Bihar and Orissa had yet to be connected (Meenakshi, 2008: 15–16, tables A1, A2).

---

[34] The public goods component of agricultural marketing includes the availability and accessibility of (a) transport and communications infrastructure; (b) support services, such as the establishment of grades and standards; (c) dissemination of market information; (d) public security; and (e) contract enforcement. (The World Bank has several publications on the functioning of markets. For more discussion, see for example, World Bank 2001c, 2002d, and more recently background paper to World Bank, 2007b by Dorward, Kydd, and Poulton).

[35] In Pakistan, an estimated 42 million people live below the poverty line (Essakali, 2005:1).

In an already risky sector, that of smallholders whose margin of error is already slim, uncertainties due to recurrent land-related conflicts, tenure insecurity, inadequate transport and communications infrastructure, and poor access to markets condemn millions of them to a low-level equilibrium trap.

To what extent has patronage politics been responsible for these uncertainties? Where smallholder agriculture is underdeveloped, we find that governments have not been able to remove or significantly reduce uncertainties with respect to land use and market access. Often highly inequitable distribution of wealth (e.g., land) and power prevailed, providing a good context for patronage politics to thrive. However, would it be correct to say that power distortions under patronage politics are always responsible? The answer is not obvious. It depends largely on how one analyzes and interprets the contrasting cases of India and China. India is a representative democracy, and patronage politics should not be the determinant of public action. Root (2006: 116–50), however, argues that the corruption of patronage politics is rife in the allocation of government resources – for example, "a jungle of tax breaks, dodges and exemptions," the granting of licenses and permits, and the control of state-owned sectors. In addition, Root (2006: 121) points out that the "Congress Party created a patronage network that empowered or co-opted local power brokers or 'big men,' offering access controlled by the party in exchange for their local influence to gain electoral support." The People's Republic of China is under a one-party system. The Communist Party waged a bloody land reform to eliminate the landlord class and imposed egalitarian land distribution. Yet with the success of the post-1979 economic reforms, income inequality again increased, and the land use rights of rural households were again threatened by corrupt and powerful local government officials. Are these the workings of patronage politics as well? If so, then the causal linkages among these variables – equality or inequality in the distribution of land, wealth, income, and economic power generating an environment of uncertainty inimical to broad-based and high-productivity growth – need to be further investigated and tested.

VI.III.II. *Rampant Corruption*
Does rampant corruption of patronage politics undermine smallholder agriculture? The second feature of patronage politics is rampant corruption.

Corruption, like a cancer to the body politic, robs millions of opportunities for a productive and dignified life. The 2011 riots in many parts of the Arab world is a powerful reminder that the rage of the people against corrupt, incompetent and elitist governments cannot forever be suppressed.[36] The destructiveness of corruption cries out to be understood. On the basis of corruption perception indices and anecdotal evidence, there seems however to be no simple causality between degree of corruption and the extent of the damage that such corruption inflicts on broad-based economic growth, including the well-being of smallholders where relevant. Corruption seems to be both a cause of mismanagement and a consequence of a larger institutional collapse. Specifically, there are four main reasons:

1. Rampant corruption exists both in countries where smallholders have done poorly – the Philippines – and where they are doing better (since the mid-1990s) without any decrease in corruption – Bangladesh (World Bank, July 2007: 127).[37]
2. Smallholder incomes and livelihoods have substantially improved under regimes criticized for being very corrupt – for example, Indonesia, with a CPI at 2.6, and the People's Republic of China, at 3.6.
3. The least corrupt countries are also some of the best-performing economies. Thus, in those few countries praised by Transparency International (2008) for low levels of corruption, economic management, including the use of public funds, has benefited the majority. These few countries in the developing world are: in sub-Saharan Africa, Botswana,[38] with a CPI at 5.9 (36th)[39]; in Latin America, Chile at 6.9 (23rd); in East Asia, Singapore[40] at 9.2 and Hong Kong[41] at 8.7 (4th and 12th, respectively). Thus, since no

---

36 The 2011 riots in the Arab world started in Algeria (January 8), Tunisia (January 14), Egypt (January 25), Yemen (January 27), Jordan (January 29), Bahrain (February15), Iran (February 15). Libya (February 16), and Morocco (February 20)
37 World Development Indicators, September 2010: GNI per capita, USD 590 (2009). The Philippines received a Corruption Perceptions Index (CPI) of 2.3; Bangladesh, 2.1. The respective country rankings were 141 and 147 out of 180 countries surveyed. The least corrupt country according to this index was Denmark, at 9.3 (Transparency International, 2008).
38 World Development Indicators, September 2010: GNI per capita, USD 6.240 (2009).
39 Surprisingly, hunger increased in Botswana between 1990 and 2005 (Binswanger-Mkhize and McCalla, 2010: 3591).
40 World Development Indicators, September 2010: GNI per capita, 37, 220 (2009).
41 World Development Indicators, September 2010: GNI per capita, 31,420 (2009).

country with good governance has suffered from sustained low growth, one can hypothesize a strong positive causal relationship between quality of governance, on one hand, and growth performance, on the other (however, we still do not know what the direction of the causation is).

4. Countries with the highest levels of corruption as measured by the CPI – Haiti at 1.4 (177th), Myanmar at 1.3 (178th), and Somalia at 1.0 (180th) – are also the most severely mismanaged, with dire consequences for economic performance and citizen well-being. Recent natural disasters have cast global attention on the havoc that years of corruption and mismanagement have inflicted on Haiti and Myanmar. The 7.0 earthquake that hit Haiti on January 12, 2010, has laid bare the ineffectiveness of USD 2.6 billion of foreign aid since 1984 (Roc, 2009: 2). The earthquake dealt a devastating blow to a Haiti already brought to its knees by centuries of political instability and political violence.[42] The category 3.0 typhoon that hit Myanmar on May 5, 2008, exposed the extensive poverty and vulnerability of the population after years of isolation, economic mismanagement, and rampant corruption (the military coup occurred in 1962). Somalia, infamous for being a failed state and a pirate kingdom, has been torn by conflict since its independence in 1960 and especially since President Mohammed Siad Barre was overthrown (1991). Since then, warlords, pirates, and clans have fought over resources (Blair, 2008). These extreme cases of institutional collapse emphasize the strong empirical basis for the

---

[42] The Haitian Revolution (1791–1803) was the first successful revolt of slaves against their white French masters. It was very violent and claimed thousands of lives: slaves, about 100,000; whites, about 24,000 (Wikipedia, "Haitian Revolution"), http://en.wikipedia.org/wiki/Haitian_Revolution. Dictatorships and instability have dogged Haiti since then. The 19th century had its dictator in Faustin I, from 1847 until he was deposed in 1859 by General Fabre Geffard. A succession of provisional governments followed. During the 20th century, Haiti again had a string of dictators, the more recent ones being "Papa Doc" and "Baby Doc." Respectively they were François Duvalier (1957–71) and his son Jean-Claude Duvalier (1971–88), who fled into exile to the French Riviera. They were followed by Manigat (1988, for only 4 months) and General Namphy (also short-term, 1988), who was toppled by General Avril, followed by the elected leftist radical Jean-Bertrand Aristide (1991, then 1994–96). He was also toppled by the Duvalier loyalists, who installed General Cedras. Aristide went into exile for three years in the United States (1997–2001), was back again from 2001 to 2004, and then went to South Africa in 2004. René Preval was president from 1996 to 2001 and again in May 2006 to the present. He was prime minister in 1991 under Aristide.

increasing attention given to the quality of governance as a caus-
ative factor in socio-economic performance.

However, because the phenomenon of corruption itself is complex, and
information on its extent partly subjective, there is no basis for simple-
minded inferences from the corruption indices to negative impact on economic performance (Thompson and Shah, 2005: 6–9).[43] Finally, there is
no evidence that corruption necessarily undermines economic growth and
social development. Quite the contrary seems to be the case. The experience of the United States is a case in point. Bribery was routine in the
United States during much of the 19th century, but corruption declined
between 1870s and 1920. Today, a super power, the United States is known
for having one of the less corrupt governments (Glaeser and Goldin, eds.,
2006: 20–21).[44] Thus, while it is reasonable to argue that in general rampant corruption hurts smallholders, we do not have a universal theory on
its causal link with economic performance. A case-by-case investigation is
necessary in order to hypothesize and test the causal links.

VI.III.III. *An Expenditure System Biased toward*
Private Goods and Services

Tax systems in many developing countries are highly constrained to deliver
public goods and services to the poor. According to Chu, Davoodi, and
Gupta (2000: 34–36), the tax system of many developing (and transition) countries is a weak tool to reduce the inequality of income and
wealth. This is a major difference between tax systems in developing
countries and those in industrial countries. Moreover, the tax structures in developing countries are regressive,[45] as they are dominated by
indirect taxes[46] and have a limited menu of capital and wealth taxes.
Furthermore, they have a low tax-to-GDP ratio, are plagued by weak

---

[43] The subjective nature of corruption perception rankings is recognized to be problematic. The
ideal would be to assemble outcome data in addition to subjective data. "The art of measuring governance requires a theory for the selection and aggregation of both outcome and
subjective data capable of influencing long and short-term policy" (Besancon, 2003: 6).

[44] The CPI for the United States was estimated to be 7.3, with a ranking of 18 out of 180 countries (Transparency International, 2008).

[45] Regressive means that the tax burden on the poor is higher relative to their income or expenditure than on the rich. In terms of benefits of government spending, regressive means that
the benefits to the poor are smaller than those to the rich, relative to their respective incomes
or expenditures.

[46] Indirect taxes are taxes on sales and value added and are ultimately paid by consumers
through higher prices.

tax administration, including widespread tax evasion, and corruption. Of the 36 overall tax systems studied, only 13 were found to be progressive; the rest were either regressive or neutral. The expenditures on public services such as education, health, and transfer programs were progressive, but many of them were poorly targeted.[47] In the 1980s, under the pressure of structural adjustment programs and given the high debt burden, expenditures on debt repayment and the military remained high,[48] while social expenditures such as those on education and health and on public goods such as roads, schools, infrastructure, and agricultural research were substantially curtailed (Ebel, 1991: table 11, 29, 46–47). How meaningful is the level or composition of public expenditure as an indicator of the effectiveness of impact? For example, increased health outcome and educational status depend on the level of governance, among other things. According to Rajkumar and Swaroop (2002: 23, 4), a survey of 250 primary schools in Uganda[49] revealed that they received only 13 percent of the budgetary allocation for non-wage expenditure; the rest just disappeared! The use of budgetary data has these and other limitations.[50] Given such limitations, public expenditure data are at best indicators of broad tendencies.

Public expenditure support in selected smallholder agricultural economies – the public–private split where patronage politics rule. One important way that governments show their allegiance is how they raise public

[47] Government spending is said to be poorly (well) targeted if the poorest quintile's share of the benefits from such spending is smaller (larger) than that of the richest quintile.

[48] As a percentage of central government expenditure, these two expenditures (in 1990) were around 61 for Pakistan, 48 for Chile, and 49 for Indonesia. The lowest was 31 for Egypt, and the highest was 85 for Jordan (Ebel, 1991: table 11).

[49] World Development Indicators, September 2010: GNI per capita, USD 460 (2009).

[50] The main strength of the public expenditure data is that they can capture important priorities of governments, as public expenditures are scarce resources, especially if the data series stretch over decades. The hypothesis is that the actual priorities of government manifest themselves in the struggle that determines budget allocations. Data on public expenditures, however, are a limited source of information for testing this hypothesis. The main reasons are that (a) expenditure data are typically short-term; (b) expenditure on a good or service is often not translated into actual delivery of the good or service because of the low efficiency and effectiveness of public expenditures; (c) the split between public and private is not always clear-cut because some goods/services have both public and private goods elements; (d) expenditure items are misclassified (e.g., in Nicaragua; see World Bank, December 2001 : 4); (e) expenditure allocations are often not actual sums spent (usually they are much less); and (f) in many highly indebted countries (e.g., in Sub-Saharan Africa), foreign aid is a major component of public expenditures, and therefore donors' priorities – not necessarily the recipient country's – prevail (Lele, ed., 1991: 8). For more discussion, see Shah (ed., 2005).

money and on what they spend it. Focusing on this split can be particularly revealing, provided that the reader appreciates at the outset the strengths and limitations of public expenditure data for the questions addressed here. Despite a substantial literature on public expenditure reviews and their developmental impact, a breakdown of public expenditure data into public and private goods and services is rare (Allcott, Lederman, and Lopez, 2006: 5).[51] The following cases highlight the importance of the public–private split:

- *Latin America*: Lopez (May 2005) investigated precisely this public–private split (he calls private goods "non-social subsidies") in 10 countries of rural Latin America (1985–2000).[52] On average, the split was 45 percent public and 54 percent non-social, or private. What Lopez includes in public goods are the following: technology generation and transfers, rural roads, and communication and information services. The bulk allocation in spending, namely on non-social subsidies, went entirely to benefit well-to-do farmers, and these included credit subsidies and irrigation. Lopez also argues that such a significant share of government expenditures on non-social expenditures reduces the income of the rural poor. Lopez (May 2005) argues that underinvestment in public goods in rural Latin America is a major reason agricultural growth has been mediocre even after the countries removed the heavy anti-agriculture bias generated by macro and trade policies. In a related paper, using 1985–2004 Latin American data, Lopez and Galinato (2007) argue that a higher ratio of private to public goods expenditure tends to worsen poverty and increase income inequality. This is an important hypothesis that should be tested in other contexts. Lopez and Miller (2008: 2681), however, remind us that it is not only the public–private split that is relevant for assessing the pro-public impact of the tax system,

---

[51] An example of a review where the composition was by origin of funding and by sector, and not by public–private split, is the public expenditure review of Nicaragua, a highly indebted country (World Bank, December 2001, 2008). The two expenditure reviews show that most of the expenditure was foreign-funded and the effectiveness of such aid needed improvement. The composition of the expenditures did not necessarily reflect governments' priorities. In agriculture, aid for projects was poorly targeted, including programs for which the public service component was unclear (World Bank, December 2001 annex I).

[52] The 10 Latin American countries are Costa Rica, Dominican Republic, Ecuador, Honduras, Jamaica, Panama, Paraguay, Peru, Uruguay, and Venezuela (Lopez: 2005, 14).

but also the way taxes are raised. Thus, although the expenditure content of Chile's system is "clearly tilted in favor of the low income classes," the tax system has not reduced the high degree of inequality in Chile because the system as a whole is pro-elite. Specifically, the tax base is narrow, the rents accruing to natural resources are not taxed, and the tax system is highly dependent on indirect taxes, and is full of loopholes and exemptions.

- *India*: Another important case is that of Indian public expenditures on agriculture and rural areas. India is a major agricultural nation of smallholders, and it spends a relatively large amount of its GDP on agriculture. In recent years, the central and state governments of India spent about 23 percent of agricultural GDP on agriculture and rural development. In agriculture alone, they spent 12.3 percent (1990–93 data), compared with 6.4 percent in China (World Bank, June 1999: table 3.1).[53] World Bank analysts argue that despite these substantial sums, their effectiveness is undermined by "inadequate composition and low efficiency" (World Bank, June 1999: 13). Why? They point to the large and increasing share being allocated to input subsidies, which benefit mainly the better-off farmers. Data on public expenditures (1981–82 to 2002–2003) show that over this period the share allocated to subsidies on food, fertilizers, power, and irrigation[54] increased, while investment (this category was not disaggregated) decreased. The mix of public and private goods elements in these subsidies is controversial. Public investments were only 13.6 percent (1999–2000) of the total subsidies spent on food and fertilizer (central government expenditures)[55] and on power and irrigation (state government expenditures) (World Bank, 2005b : table 2.9). This crowding out of growth-enhancing public expenditures (e.g., the public expenditures on research and development, livestock, dairy, and fisheries) started in 1986 (World Bank, June 1999: A2.5).

---

[53] This level of spending exceeded that of many Asian economies, except the Republic of Korea and Thailand. Despite this, the average annual growth rate of agriculture of 2.46 percent (1990–96) was below that of selected comparator countries; e.g. (in percent), China, 6.50; Pakistan, 3.7; and Thailand, 2.82. However, the Republic of Korea had a lower growth rate of 1.73 percent (World Bank, June 1999: 13).

[54] Credit is also subsidized, but since it has a small budgetary outlay, it is often not included.

[55] Food and fertilizer subsidies from the central government benefit urban consumers of food and urban producers of fertilizers (fertilizer companies).

The Tenth Plan (2001–2002 to 2006–2007) of the government of India recognized that this declining trend is problematic (Ministry of Agriculture, 2002, and Planning Commission, 2002). These subsidies are also a major cause of the underlying fiscal crisis confronting the central and state governments (Vaidyanathan, in Morris and Morris, eds., 2003: 236). Whether these subsidies primarily promote or do not promote the public interest (and which group in the public) is, however, controversial since these subsidized goods have public and private elements. Those in favor of and those against these subsidies point out the following:

(a) *In favor*: Although the use of agricultural inputs and the consumption of food grains are strictly private (they are rival in consumption, that is one person's consumption of A precludes another person from consuming the same A) given their importance in production and consumption, these subsidies "helped in achieving self-sufficiency in food grains, fair sharing of gains and technology and public investment between the farmers and the consumers, improved economic access to food, and the development of backward and dry-land regions...."Thus, the benefits of input and food subsidies have been shared by "all sections of society, i.e., surplus producing farmers, other farmers who are net producers of food grains, landless laborers, urban consumers and the industry" (Acharya, 1997a, b; Purohit and Reddy, 1999: 63).

(b) *Against*: Subsidies for canal irrigation and power are highly inequitable. To begin with, few of the subsidies actually reach farmers. Most accrue to state irrigation departments. A significant share of the power subsidy is lost through pilferage and improper metering. The farmers who actually benefit from these subsidies are farmers who irrigate their land, not the landless rural poor. It is estimated that irrigated crops capture twice the level of subsidies that rain-fed crops receive, even though rain-fed agriculture accounts for two-thirds of India's cropped area and two-thirds of the rural poor (World Bank, June 1999: 3.13). The wealthier states get more. When measured by subsidy per unit of gross cropped area or subsidies as a percentage of agricultural GDP, the wealthier states (e.g., Gujarat, Maharashtra, Tamil Nadu) have the highest shares (Gulati and Narayanan, 2003: 194, fig. 6.5a). By concentrating the benefits among a few farmers and states, it has strengthened the vested interest and political resistance to keep these subsidies in place.

(c) *Against*: A case can be made that during the earlier years of the Green Revolution (late 1960s and early 1970s), the input subsidies were considered important for promoting risk taking, especially among small farmers to facilitate their adoption of a more productive technology. It was thus in the public interest. The adoption of the Green Revolution did take off. In the 21st century, more than 25 years since the introduction of the Green Revolution techniques, it is debatable whether these subsidies are necessary to induce risk taking for higher productivity.

• *Indonesia*: A third important case is that of Indonesia under three decades of President Suharto's New Economic Order (1967–98). Indonesia is well known for achieving sustained growth, thus substantially reducing poverty and improving mass literacy, including that among girls, while maintaining a fairly equal distribution of income, estimated at a Gini coefficient (for household expenditures) of 0.33, compared with Malaysia at 0.50 and Thailand and the Philippines at 0. 45. The share of national income going to the poor increased (Timmer, 2004: 3, table 1). Indonesia started from an extremely low base – nearly 70 percent of the population was "absolutely poor."[56] Even Myrdal, a Nobel laureate (with Friedrich Hayek), pronounced in his *Asian Drama: An Inquiry into the Poverty of Nations* (1968) that "no economist holds out any hope for Indonesia"! These remarkable achievements materialized despite crony capitalism.[57] There was definitely patronage politics. Despite this, the government invested heavily in public goods and services – for example, rural infrastructure such as roads (including farm-to-market roads), communications networks, market infrastructure and ports, irrigation and water systems, and education and

[56] Hunger was widespread, as average food intake was 1,600 kg per day (Timmer, 2004: 12).
[57] According to Timmer (2004: 5, 55), "Most of the coalition supporting Suharto was, in fact, held together by the corrupt distribution of economic resources, often in the form of lucrative access to easily marketable commodities, such as oil or timber (i.e., the rents from natural resources)." "Large-scale ethnic (Chinese) businesses bought protection from Suharto and his military allies and received lucrative import and operating licenses in return."

health – which benefited the majority of smallholders. Interestingly, the social expenditures are not considered to have been well targeted, especially in the earlier years, but over time, the poor also benefited significantly (Timmer, 2004: 43). In the earlier years (1960s-1970s), the government funded these expenditures mainly from donor aid; in the later years (1980s on), from oil revenues.

The Latin America case illustrates the importance of the public–private split for the income growth of the rural poor. The India case illustrates the controversies inherent in assessing the public impact (negative or positive) of public expenditure data. The Indonesia case shows that patronage politics does not necessarily mean neglect of smallholder development. The Indonesia case also shows the determining impact of country leadership.[58] For the autocrat Suharto, economic growth to benefit the rural poor was a key national objective. Thus, while patronage politics seems to undermine development spending in many parts of the developing world, it is not a universal phenomenon. Each case must be analyzed separately.

VI.III.IV. *Summary*

Has patronage politics been the main factor undermining smallholder agriculture? The patronage politics thesis of de Mesquita and Root does go a long way in explaining why and how governments have neglected smallholder development, but puzzles remain. While it is true that many governments concerned primarily with strengthening their winning coalition have failed to build systems for the greater good (e.g., reducing uncertainties and improving market access for smallholders), corruption and cronyism alone have not determined the effectiveness of economic management. Other factors can also

---

[58] In addition to leadership, another variable whose importance has been difficult to integrate into causal explanations has been the cultural factor as embodied in the actual mix of personalities and their value systems. How a development outcome is rooted in the complex interaction among structural characteristics of an economy – the cultural environment with its values for savings, investing, and concepts of equity and social responsibility; and government intervention, among other things – comes to life in a simulation game called "Exaction" (Chapman and Tsakok, 1989). This game was developed to be used as a training tool at the World Bank for development practitioners seeking to understand the dynamics of agricultural development so as to better promote it. One of the main messages of this simulation game is the culture-cum-personality dependency of any development outcome, not just the personality of the government, but also the personalities of the people who make up the economy. Much has been written about its different "runs" and possible lessons learned for development practitioners.

make a difference. Leadership is one such factor.[59] The causal links among the four variables – patronage politics, public expenditures biased against the public good, the public–private split, and the public impact of public expenditures – are complex. Controversies that arise in understanding this nexus cannot be settled mechanistically, that is, by solely appealing to certain ratios. The India and Indonesia cases show that more understanding is necessary with respect to the strengths and weaknesses of the economy, the distribution of wealth and poverty, the goals of government, and the quality of leadership, among other things. In addition, it is also necessary to consider (a) the vision of a good society that government and people embrace; (b) their economic philosophy, especially with respect to social equity or justice; and therefore (c) what the government considers its role should be in realizing that vision. Policy controversies are rooted in these fundamental differences.

VI.IV. Success in Agricultural Transformation: Governments Are in the Driver's Seat

Only governments can create the environment for promoting or undermining sustained development. Success in agricultural transformation requires the five conditions to be in place, all conditions resulting from sustained government action. This hypothesis was systematically tested earlier. So far, it has not been refuted, which means we can be guided by it. Simply put, jointly these conditions give farmers the stability, the opportunity, and the incentives needed to invest in agriculture and profit from it. No matter how hard farmers work, they cannot jointly produce such an environment. For better or for worse, only governments can do it. Governments are in the driver's seat,[60] whether they are "big" or "small." To date, government intervention in the developing world has largely not provided the environment of support and opportunity that smallholders need to thrive. As pointed out, there is a substantial literature analyzing what went wrong.[61] Therefore, the

---

[59] Timmer (ed., 1991: 290), makes the same point: "Personalities also matter. Leadership qualities and personal values of individual leaders can wreck a rural economy, as in Tanzania or rescue it from decades of urban bias, as in Indonesia."

[60] Applied to development, this phrase is attributed to James D. Wolfensohn, ninth president of the World Bank Group (1995–2005).

[61] For example, Krueger et al. (eds., 1991), who argue that government intervention generated by general economic policies (indirect) at macro, foreign exchange, and trade levels (in the

focus here is not on what went wrong per se, but on selected interventions, which are recurrent and controversial. In developing countries, these are subsidies on inputs and, in rich countries, price supports, a variety of quantitative interventions, and substantial border protection. Understanding the controversies that these interventions have generated can help us better assess what types of support agriculture needs and therefore what kinds of drivers development-minded governments should be.

The controversy over the predominance of subsidies on inputs and other private goods. One recurrent controversy concerns subsidies on private goods that supporters allege are for the public good. Available evidence cited by the World Bank (2007b: 114–15) indicates that public expenditure in agriculture has often been "diverted from agricultural investments to subsidies ... defined as payments from public budgets to essentially private goods such as agricultural inputs." Thus, the percentage of public budgets allocated to input subsidies was 37 for Argentina (2003), 43 for Indonesia (2006), 75 for India (2002), and 75 for Ukraine (2005); for input subsidies and parastatals, 26 for Kenya (2002–2003); and for fertilizer subsidies and maize prices, 80 for Zambia (2003–2004). Those against (e.g., the World Bank)[62] and in favor of these subsidies argue thus:

- *Against*: The argument is threefold: (a) they crowd out needed expenditures on public goods and services, like market infrastructure, research and extension, natural resource management, and other high-return investments in public goods and services; (b) they benefit primarily richer farmers, who because of their political clout successfully defeat chances of their reduction (in short, such public expenditures are growth-reducing and inequitable); and (c) at a global level, the substantial producer support in OECD countries hurts developing countries, mainly by artificially lowering the prices they can receive for their agricultural

18 selected countries) has a greater impact on agriculture than do agriculture-specific (direct) policies. By and large, they find that indirect policies have had a greater impact than direct policies and that severe discrimination has been the rule.
[62] The opinions are those not only of the World Bank but of other researchers as well. See Lopez (2005: 218–220) on the underinvestment in public goods of many developing countries and the high opportunity cost of such underinvestment – forgone agricultural growth that is environmentally sustainable and poverty-reducing.

exports.[63] If the producer support were removed, such removal would raise the export prices developing countries could obtain and thus lead to a major increase in the welfare gains of these countries, a gain valued at five times the current annual flow of aid they receive (World Bank, 2007b: 10–11).[64]

- *In favor.* The supporters argue that they are important for promoting technology transfer and national food security (e.g., Indonesia, India, and Zambia) and for national food security (again), environmental stewardship, and improving income distribution as the income of rural households is on average lower than their urban counterparts (OECD).

This controversy reminds us that subsidies are easy to start and virtually impossible to stop. The case of the Common Agricultural Policy (CAP, since 1962), and the U.S. Farm Bill of 2008 (a continuation of agricultural subsidies since the New Deal of the 1930s) are two good cases in point.

"The rich industrialized countries all protect their agriculture; why should we not?" This sentiment is often expressed by developing countries, which, in frustration, have to deal with the substantial protection of OECD countries (except New Zealand and Australia since the 1980s). Yes, indeed, why not, if such price support is seen as necessary to successfully transform one's agriculture. But is it? This is the question. The weight of the evidence suggests it is not necessary. True, in all cases of successful transformation, there has been sustained government support. There has been no case of success within a laissez-faire approach. For example, the case of Taiwan shows that in the formative years (1950s–1970s) the government undertook basic structural reforms, institutional strengthening, and infrastructure investments. There was no price support and protection. In fact, agriculture was taxed and contributed to industrial investment (see the earlier discussion of Chapter II on Taiwan, China). Yet agriculture became a major

---

[63] It is true that this substantial financial support has declined from 36 percent (1986–88) to 30 percent (2003–2005) of the gross value of farm receipts. For 2007, agricultural support amounted to 23 percent of gross receipts, down from 26 percent in 2006 and 28 percent in 2005 (OECD, 2008b).

[64] The distribution of welfare gains and losses, however, varies among the countries, depending on the actual commodity in question and the status of each country as importer or exporter of the commodity.

engine of growth and development. Thus are price support and high protection necessary? There are three main considerations:

First, there are cases where price support and protection have not resulted in an agriculture and rural sector of high productivity generating broad-based income increases for the majority of rural households. For example:

- *Among middle-income countries*: The case of Turkey[65] shows that the substantial agricultural protection for decades – in terms of price support and protection through complementary forms of quantitative interventions – was fiscally destabilizing and did not result in agriculture with high output and high productivity growth. By the late 1990s, agricultural subsidies had contributed to severe fiscal deficits threatening the very stability of the entire economy (World Bank, March 2004: i, 1). The fiscal problem was brought under control in part through the Direct Income Support program (DIS, 2000)[66] and drastic reductions in price support. Thus, despite decades of price support and other protection measures and despite the great potential of Turkey's agriculture, agricultural productivity is low,[67] land and income inequality is high,[68] and rural poverty is substantial at 34 percent (urban at 22 percent).[69] Even though agriculture's share of GDP was around 10 percent by the early 2000s, subsistence and semi-subsistence farming is still important (European Commission, July 2009). Thus Turkey's price support and large degree of protection of agriculture for decades has not succeeded in transforming the sector. After Turkey drastically reduced its fiscal deficit, including the level of agricultural protection, and regained macroeconomic

---

[65] World Development Indicators, September 2010: GNI per capita, USD 8, 730 (2009).

[66] Producers received an income transfer not related to what they produced and sold. The support was decoupled.

[67] For example, yields (1998) of wheat and milk are a third to a quarter of yields in high-productivity agriculture (FAO, 2000).

[68] Inequality of income as measured by the Gini coefficient was 0.45 (1994) and 0.46 (2001) (World Bank, 2003a: vol. 1, 25). The Gini coefficient for land ownership is 0.6 (1980) (Hansen, 1991: table 6–8). More recent writings discuss the sharp inequality but do not give a Gini estimate.

[69] This is not the extreme poverty line of USD 1 per day, but the national poverty line (IFAD, 2006, also World Bank, August 2005). Extreme poverty is virtually non-existent. Absolute poverty is highest in eastern and southeastern Anatolia.

stability, the annual growth of its economy rose to average 7.5 percent (2002–2006) (World Bank, April 2008: 5).

- *Among low-income countries*: The case of India clearly shows that continued and substantial expenditures on private goods have not transformed agriculture. The effectiveness of the support given to Punjab agriculture since the mid-1960s to promote the technologies of the Green Revolution illustrates the pros and cons. Punjab agriculture has benefited from subsidies on a wide range of production inputs and from guaranteed minimum support prices. "The 1970s and 1980s were the heydays for the state's agriculture as productivity of both [wheat and rice] crops increased rapidly, farm incomes rose, poverty declined, and the state led the Indian agriculture scene" (World Bank, September 2003: 1). However, by the 1990s, growth of output and productivity had slowed down dramatically and environmental problems had surfaced – overexploitation of groundwater and deterioration of water quality. The point is not that these support measures did not benefit farmers and rural livelihoods. They did. But their continuation (over 40 years),[70] even expansion over the later years, has become problematic.

Second, as the cases of Australia and New Zealand show, the structure of OECD[71] price supports and protection is not necessary to achieve a thriving agriculture. The Australian and New Zealand post-reform experiences do make a strong case for a thriving agriculture without such protection and price supports. By 2005–2007, the nominal rates of assistance[72] for Australia were zero for both exportables and importables; for New Zealand, they were 0.6 and 8.9, respectively (Anderson et al., 2008: tables 2, 3). However, there are critics.

---

[70] In 1966, high-yielding varieties of wheat from Mexico were first planted in the Punjab.

[71] The OECD member countries are (2008) Australia, Austria, Belgium, Canada, Chile, the Czech Republic, Denmark, Finland, France, Germany, Greece, Hungary, Iceland, Ireland, Italy, Japan, Korea, Luxembourg, Mexico, the Netherlands, New Zealand, Norway, Poland, Portugal, the Slovak Republic, Spain, Sweden, Switzerland, Turkey, the United Kingdom, and the United States. The OECD was established in 1961. Its basic objectives are as follows: to achieve the highest sustainable economic growth and employment in member countries, while maintaining financial stability; to contribute to sound economic expansion in member and non-member countries; and to contribute to the expansion of world trade on a multi-lateral, non-discriminatory basis in accordance with international obligations.

[72] NRA measures protection afforded by policy. For Australia, in terms of measures of domestic market support and border market support they were both zero; for New Zealand, they were zero and 1.3, respectively (Anderson et al., 2008: tables 2, 3).

- *Australia*: Australia dismantled its protective structure more gradually than did New Zealand. It started in the 1970s and was completed by 2000, by which time all anti-agricultural bias had been removed. Such reform was part of a wide-ranging reform. Despite lower protection, agricultural productivity, like the rest of the economy, experienced a growth surge in the 1990s. For example, TFP growth of broadacre crops between 1989–90 and 1998–99 averaged 3.6 percent, compared with an average of 1.5 percent between 1977–78 and 2006–2007. The lower recent rate is due partly to drought (ABRARE, 2009). This TFP growth is a major achievement, especially as Australia is drought-prone.[73] The critics, however, point out that despite the higher growth of agriculture and the entire economy, the poverty rate, variously defined, did not decrease despite the higher growth (Brotherhood of St. Laurence, 2002). There is also concern with the privatization of extension services as fee-based extension advisory services were introduced in Tasmania in 1982. This model has encountered two major drawbacks. First, face-to-face contacts with farmers have decreased substantially and with them the free flow of information among farmers. Second, the extension services have been constrained in promoting information and techniques in the public interest, for example, techniques promoting sustainability. To promote the public interest component of farming, government has had to resort to more regulation of agriculture and forestry, a feature of concern with farm organization leaders (Bloome, 1993).
- *New Zealand*: The fiscal and financial crises of 1984 provided the urgency for reform. It was the Federated Farmers of New Zealand that proposed to the Muldoon government the removal of the agricultural subsidies (1982).[74] They argued that the control of inflation (to which the subsidies contributed) was more important to them as farmers than the receipt of subsidies, much of which was to compensate for the inflation (in turn caused by all the subsidies!). Furthermore, as in Australia, agriculture reform was part of

---

[73] There were periods of drought in 1994–95, 2002–2003, and 2006–2007.
[74] Although Muldoon of the National Party did not accept the proposal, the proposal started a national debate. The Labour government, which was swept into power in 1984, started to implement the proposal.

an economy-wide reform program. The dismantling of the system of price supports and other forms of protection (1984) was painful to many farmers. An estimated 1 percent of total commercial farmers were forced to leave the farm. The transition period lasted around six years. It was not until 1990 that land values, commodity prices, and farm profitability indices started to stabilize and rise. Among rich countries, New Zealand stands out as still being an important agricultural country, with agriculture contributing to around 12 percent of total employment, 17 percent of GDP (late 1990s), and 5 percent of GDP by 2009 (Sayre, 2003; United States Department of State, August 2009). Since the reform, agriculture has become more export-oriented.[75] Together with horticulture and forestry, it contributes to 65 percent of export receipts (Ministry of Agriculture and Forestry, 2003). One therefore cannot say that the removal of price supports and other subsidies has destroyed its agriculture. The rate of TFP growth in the farm sector since 1970 has been one of the highest in the OECD (Johnson, 2000: 15). However, there are critics of the reform. The price of the liberalization reforms was paid by those least able to pay it, the poorer households. In fact, the Save the Children organization ranked New Zealand 4th worst on an OECD child poverty league table. One in every six children was living in poverty (Save the Children, 2005). Income inequality has increased. The Gini coefficient of income rose from 0.353 (1984) to 0.404 (1996) (Dalziel, 1999: table 2). However, the degree of inequality stabilized in the early 2000s, although it is still higher than the OECD average of 0.300 (Ministry of Economic Development, 2007: table 1.10). With respect to commercialization of extension services, the same concern (as in Australia) has been voiced as to whether a private model can adequately serve the public interest elements in farming and forestry.

Finally, today there is no doubt that the system of price support and high protection has rightly come under severe criticism for being costly and inequitable. Developing countries as a bloc are expected to gain substantially from agricultural trade and subsidy reform (McCalla

---

[75] The contribution of agriculture and food to exports was 44 percent during 2000–2004, the largest sectoral contribution (Anderson et al., 2008: table 1).

and Nash, 2007). Even the OECD has long accepted the necessity
of reform. The transfer efficiency of the support (the percentage of
the support that ends up as additional income to farm households) is
low: only 25 cents out of every dollar of price support becomes farmers'
income (OECD in Washington, 2003). Input suppliers end up cap-
turing a large part of the price support intended for farmers. Larger
farmers, not the smaller farmers, are major beneficiaries. Furthermore,
the support has had the perverse effect of taxing relatively poorer consumers to benefit the incomes of well-off producers. Moreover, at a
global level, better-off farmers gain at the expense of the worse off.[76]
The farm subsidies have become a very divisive issue in World Trade
Organization trade negotiations.[77] In our increasingly interdependent
globalized world economy, where sharp disparity in incomes and livelihoods between rich and poor is socially destabilizing, should this costly
and inequitable OECD approach to agriculture transformation be a
model?

Since governments are in the driver's seat, how they drive is critical. If governing for prosperity is one of the greatest challenges of our times, then
the challenge should include how government can support the majority
of households and small entrepreneurs while minimizing adverse efficiency and distributional consequences of such support. As the controversial cases of public support discussed earlier show, subsidies are hard to
remove and their unintended adverse consequences spill way beyond one's
borders. They also show, however, that in all cases of progress, government
was part of the solution. The necessity of government intervention was
accepted by Adam Smith, for whom the proper functioning of government was limited to "three duties of great importance: (i) the provision
of military security; (ii) the administration of justice; and (iii) the duty
of erecting and maintaining public works and certain public institutions
which it can never be for the interest of any individual, or small number of
individuals to erect and to maintain because the profit could neither repay
the expense to any individual or small number of individuals, though it
may frequently do much more than repay it to a great society" (Blaug,

[76] For example, the U.S. cotton subsidies hurt the poorest countries (World Bank, 2007b: 11).
[77] Witness the difficult trade talks following the Doha Round in Qatar in 2001. There have
been subsequent talks almost every other year, during which participants have wrestled with
such issues as rich countries' farm subsidies, poor countries' mechanisms to protect poor
farmers in the event of sudden price falls, and market access for special products.

1997: 57).[78] Thus, to build a "great society," Smith advocated government intervention and its support for social arrangements that would harness the powerful motive of self-interest. He did not advocate a pure laissez-faire system.[79] This is why Smith talked of "systems of political economy," not only of the "the invisible hand," to build the wealth of nations. To harness private self-interest to build the wealth of nations, a well-functioning government is necessary. The many cases of successful and unsuccessful agricultural transformation show that this is still a central challenge.

VI.V. What Makes It Happen: The Public Foundations of Private Agriculture

The five conditions revisited – their public good/service nature: The five conditions jointly generate an environment of stability and opportunity within which farmers, large and small, have the incentives to invest in agriculture's productivity and growth in such a way as to achieve personal financial success, however defined. By promoting their own interests, they develop and transform agriculture. In so doing, they enable governments to achieve national goals of food security at all times, good and bad – income, employment, and export growth; environmental sustainability; and widespread poverty reduction. All these goals have private and public goods elements. The task for government is to harness farmers' private incentives and local knowledge and complement them with public goods and services. Each of the five conditions is a public good or service (or an important element thereof). Thus:

1. *The stability condition* is generated not only by responsible macroeconomic management, but also (and more fundamentally) by a system in which law and order are enforced within a socio-political context where social conflicts can be resolved fairly and peacefully. The divisiveness of agricultural land issues, as in, for example, the Philippines, Zimbabwe, and Nicaragua, clearly

---

[78] Blaug, quoted from Adam Smith's *An Inquiry into the Nature and Causes of the Wealth of Nations*, Book IV: "Of Systems of Political Economy," ch. 9. The first edition was published in 1776, the fifth and last in 1789.

[79] Smith's concept of the "invisible hand" is often compared to that of Bernard de Mandeville's (1670–1733) *Fable of the Bees* (1714), in which he states, "Private Vices by the Dextrous Management of a Skilful Politician may be turned into Publick Benefits." Mandeville thus advocated some sort of social/political mechanism to transform private vices into public benefits.

shows that perceived equity in the distribution of assets is a public good. People's concept of what constitutes social justice, no matter how nebulous or subjective it may be, is a powerful determinant of social cohesion. The achievement and maintenance of socio-political stability thus have deep roots in people's aspirations for a good life and governments' ability to meet them.

2. *The effective technology-transfer condition* requires a system of agricultural research, extension, and training that private individuals or groups of individuals will or will not build, depending on whether these individuals can appropriate the benefits by profitably charging for the use of the results. In developing countries, conditions for such profitable appropriation typically do not exist. These include inadequate private property rights enforcement, the high costs of providing the service due to high transport costs and more generally inadequate infrastructure of all types, the length of the gestation period involved, and the low educational level and purchasing capacity of farmers (Pardey et al., 2007: 17–18). In short, the very factors that make countries underdeveloped make the supply of effective technology transfer a public service with a very high social return. In addition, the types of research of most relevance to developing countries have been those related to self-pollinating crop varieties (e.g., wheat, rice, soybeans, common bean, chickpea) and disembodied (not embodied in any particular product) farm management practices. These features make these technologies the least appropriable of all. Finally, given economies of scale of operation of technology-transfer systems, many developing countries are too small to achieve an efficient scale. Thus possibly the best thing the government can do is develop a capacity to tap into a worldwide system like the Consultative Group on International Agricultural Research (GCIAR).[80] In the current context of climate change and the need for adaptation, access to agricultural research results can make the difference between conflict-free or conflict-ridden adaptation.

---

[80] The mission of the CGIAR is "to achieve sustainable food security and reduce poverty in developing countries through scientific research and research-related activities in the field of agriculture, forestry, fisheries, policy and environment." http://www.cgiar.org/who/index.html.

3. *The access to markets condition* is entirely a public service given the economies of scale involved in the network of infrastructure hardware required. The software component of the access – consisting, for example, of rules of market functioning, contract and property rights enforcement, dissemination of public information, and security of persons and property – depends entirely on public delivery (either finance or regulation).[81] Except for some minor roads, even if farmers organized they could not supply the scale and quality typically required. Access to markets also has a policy component in that it depends on public policy agreements on trade, foreign exchange, and food safety. In this globalizing world economy, there are tremendous opportunities for smallholders to benefit from the supermarket revolution and increased urban demands for organic, high-value, and ready-to-eat foods. According to Reardon (2006: 81), the most important markets for small and medium farmers in developing countries are domestic urban markets, not exports, for the latter constitute a small part of the overall agro-food market facing smallholders.[82] Government investment in a well-functioning market infrastructure is essential to enable smallholders to tap into this new engine of demand growth for their products.

4. *The ownership system, including usufruct rights, condition* is entirely a public service that rests on past policy on land distribution and ownership status, and on current land administration capability. Land distribution has been one of the most divisive issues the world over, and enforcement of private property and usufruct rights has been undependable in many developing countries due to weak land administration capabilities, among other things. It is the government's sole responsibility to set the rules and enforce them. The private sector can provide the legal and technical skills needed to implement these rules.

5. *The employment creation in non-agricultural sectors condition* exists as an important option for farm households to diversify their

---

[81] The actual delivery of these public goods and services can be contracted out to the private sector, but the government is responsible for infrastructure development. Government can develop public–private partnerships, introduce competition among potential suppliers, develop a regulatory framework for the proper functioning of existing infrastructure, etc. (World Bank, June 1994: box 1; World Bank, World Development Report, 2004).

[82] The estimate of exports from small and medium producers in developing countries is 3 percent of their total production and 5 percent of their marketing amount.

sources of income and employment in countries where governments have succeeded in promoting sufficient non-farm growth to generate demand for migrating or excess farm labor.[83] How well rural–urban migrants are integrated into non-agricultural sectors is dependent not only on options generated by non-farm growth, but also on the availability of public goods and services like employment centers, schools, and basic health centers, and accessibility of transport and information networks. Delivering basic services – for example, in health, education, and transport – for all, especially the poor, is government's responsibility.[84] Even the ability of rural–urban migrants to integrate successfully into urban life is dependent on their level of education and skills, results of previous human capital formation, largely at public expense.

It is important to note that establishing these five conditions is a task that goes well beyond the usual set of policy tools typically considered "agricultural." What is usually considered agricultural is only a small subset of these conditions. Maintaining these conditions for decades requires that governments have a long-term vision of peace and prosperity for all and anchor the realization of this vision in competent and clean administrative structures.[85] The building of such structures to deliver public goods and services makes the critical difference in governance. Singapore rightly sees good governance and therefore an effective government as a strategic issue of national development (Ali, 2000).

The five conditions revisited – transforming uncertainty into measurable risks? Farming is not only highly uncertain, but subject to very specific risks (OECD, 2009: 11–16). Farmers must plant, but whether they

---

[83] Given the precariousness of agricultural life for many poor, their ability to diversify their income base through access to non-agricultural jobs can mean survival in downturns. There is increasing evidence that non-agricultural incomes are very important for them. For the rural non-poor, the latter sources of income are also very important (Fan, ed., 2008: 63).

[84] The benefits of education and health go well beyond the individuals involved. Society as a whole also benefits. Equally important is the equity consideration when the poor receive basic education and health services (World Bank, 2003d: 32–35).

[85] The experience of Hong Kong is instructive. Corruption was rampant in the 1950s and 1960s. Starting in the mid-1970s, Hong Kong's leadership put in place a five-pronged approach to eradicating corruption and building a clean and competent civil service. Hong Kong is consistently rated as one of the least corrupt places in Asia (Au Yeung, 2000). Singapore also shares this honor.

will reap and sell profitably is up to nature and markets. In addition to such uncertainties, many risks are non-insurable because of information asymmetries[86] and high transaction costs associated with collecting information about the probabilities or with pooling systemic risks.[87] Add to this already complicated situation the adverse impact of climate risk.[88] The five conditions are not focused on coping with any specific types of risks, but together they create an environment that helps farmers manage risks better. They do so by strengthening farmers' resilience in several ways. First, by removing one major source of shock and uncertainty, the macro and political stability condition enables farmers to allocate their energies more productively. Second, by giving them access to a richer set of productive and profitable technologies, the technology-transfer condition improves their understanding of how best they can deal with biological production risks. Adaptation to climate change is particularly important in the years ahead. Third, by expanding the number of markets farmers can reach and the information base to access them, the market access condition gives farmers improved understanding of more market options. Fourth, by guaranteeing farmers' ownership or usufruct rights to the land they till, farmers have the tenure security they need to invest. Fifth, by enabling farmers to diversify their employment and income portfolio, the employment creation condition strengthens farmers' resilience to negative income shocks arising from farming. Together, the five conditions generate an environment of stability and opportunity, for the whole is greater than the sum of its parts. This is necessary but not sufficient for facilitating risk management. Farmers in the highly performing agriculture of rich countries do enjoy such an environment, and yet their governments

---

[86] There is asymmetric information when one party can hide important information from the other party in a transaction; thus a farmer who knows best the risks his crops or livestock rearing are prone to can hide that information from the potential insurer. This situation in turn gives rise to two other problems: (a) adverse selection, as when a farmer with diseased animals buys insurance but the insurer cannot have the correct information on the probabilities; and (b) moral hazard, as when a farmer who buys the insurance has the incentive to incur the damage against which he took the insurance. In both cases, private insurance business is not viable.

[87] Systemic risks occur when the probability of an entire region suffering from the same calamity (e.g., droughts, floods) is the same. In such cases, risks within that region are not diversified. Viable insurance requires the pooling of different risk profiles.

[88] For example, Australia has been experiencing increasing climate volatility dramatized by the disastrous 2002 drought (Chance, 2003).

resort to additional measures to assist them deal with risk.[89] The environment created by the five conditions would facilitate development of the next step to effective risk management, namely access to futures and options markets, among other things (Debatisse et al., 1993).

Success in agricultural transformation transforms lives. Success in agricultural transformation constitutes more than sustained output and productivity increases and broad-based income increases for farm/rural households. It transforms the everyday lives of millions of those in farm/rural households. Sustained productivity increases that raise the income levels of the majority of farm/rural households also serve as a catalyst for virtuous circles of human development.

What makes it happen? Decades of government commitment are required to implement a holistic approach to agricultural transformation. Governments must govern for the prosperity of all – sustained increases in agricultural productivity and incomes for the majority of farm/rural houses. Experience to date of both success and failure clearly shows that there is no single path, but there is a pattern to success and failure. There are two important characteristics of success.

1. A holistic approach is a key characteristic of success. Conceptually, holistic means understanding the interdependence of the different parts that together make the whole. Practically, holistic means that piecemeal measures that are not integral components of an overall strategy are of limited effectiveness at best. More often than not, these piecemeal measures do not work. Operationally, governments must view agriculture as an integral component of an entire open economy. Holistic, however, does not mean everything has to be done at the same time. This is impossible. The effectiveness of piecemeal social engineering is determined by the role assigned to it within a larger strategy.

2. Long term is another key characteristic of success. In the frenetic pace of our modern world, where instant results are required for

---

[89] Not only do they have access to price support mechanisms (with the adverse unintended consequences already discussed), but they can also use market-based risk management instruments traded in commodity futures and options markets. One such instrument is a standardized futures contract, which is an agreement to buy or sell a commodity for delivery in the future at an agreed-upon price that may be satisfied by delivery (rarely used) or offset (a compensating option). For more discussion, see Debatisse et al. (1993).

political economy reasons, building the foundations of highly performing agriculture may not be popular.[90] The challenge for policy makers and development practitioners alike is to develop strategies and identify measures that deliver short-term success with long-term achievements. This is an art, a great art, but not a science. Constant experimentation and monitoring of small-scale attempts are essential to learn, to scale up, and to move forward, as development contains many puzzles and mistakes will be made. This approach is skill- and time-intensive. To value and support such an approach, government commitment, in developing and industrialized countries, must be anchored in a vision of a just society, where the well-being of the poor and less fortunate matters to those in power.[91] Writing about the bottom billion, Collier (2007: 3–4) expresses the same concern.[92] In our global world, social disintegration caused by poverty knows no borders. We all live in a global village.

To date, experience shows that the poor lose the fight over resources unless they have an ally in government. The political economy literature reminds us time and again that it is the imperative of pleasing the rich to gain their support rather than promoting the interests of the majority for a better life that drives policy. Politics is in command, for better or for worse. The transformation of agriculture will succeed when those who control the purse strings understand that it is in their enduring interests to promote it. What are the main reasons it has not happened so far? Agriculture is one of humanity's oldest occupations.

---

[90] Timmer (ed., 1991: 293), raises the same concern. He discusses the "short-time horizon of so many governments" as being a threat to creating and maintaining a favorable economic and institutional environment for positive growth results to continue.

[91] A nation's wealth also depends on the social conscience of the rich and powerful. It is noteworthy that there has been a strong tradition of philanthropy in one of the richest industrialized economies, the United States, ever since its founding. Philanthropists and philanthropic institutions include, e.g., John Harvard (1607–38), Benjamin Franklin (1706–90), the Peabody Fund (1867), Andrew Carnegie (1835–1919), the Ford Foundation (1936), and the Rockefeller Foundation (1913). Recent examples are Mayor Bloomberg (New York City) Warren Buffett and Bill and Melinda Gates. Mark Zuckerberg, founder of Facebook, also signed up to the "Giving Pledge," an initiative of Buffet and Gates. (National Philanthropic Trust, http://www.nptrust.org/philanthropy/history_philanthropy_1700s.asp).

[92] "The twenty-first century world of material comfort, global travel and economic interdependence will become increasingly vulnerable to these large islands of chaos. And it matters now" (Collier, 2007: 3–4).

The technologies have been developed – all along the chain from production to marketing, processing, storage, and final sale.[93] Demand exists, and its potential is likely to increase with urbanization, globalization, and overall income growth. Cities must have food security or else the entire superstructure of our exchange economy will collapse. Urban dwellers cannot be food self-sufficient. The will of the farmers to produce and profit exists. For smallholders barely eking out a decent livelihood, nothing can be more motivating than having market opportunities and being able to exploit them.

Will governments govern for the prosperity of all? However, will the opportunities and support be available to all? This is the question. Will governments invest in and deliver the public goods and services essential for successful agricultural transformation? Will they focus on doing what only governments can do: deliver public goods and services accessible to all in order to generate an environment of stability and opportunity for growth and prosperity for all? In developing countries, no amount of foreign aid can substitute for this essential government role. Foreign aid can be effective only when it is allowed to focus on the constraint it can best relieve: funding. The technical component of aid is effective to the extent that it is a technical partnership. It cannot be a substitute for development-minded governments taking charge. Foreign aid can be effective only when governments cease to be the problem and become instead a decisive part of the solution.

---

[93] Binswanger-Mkhize and McCalla (2010: 3581) point out that the science and technology divide between SSA agriculture and that of the rest of the world is growing wider because of underfunding of science and technology institutions in SSA and because of rapid changes in international biotechnology and private agricultural research. Moreover, the uniqueness and the heterogeneity of African agricultural environments make opportunities for borrowing technology from other regions more difficult.

APPENDIX A
A Note on the Research Methodology of This Book

Introduction

This appendix sets out the methodology of research undertaken in this book and how it compares with three widely used approaches to assessing and learning about causality from non-experimental data. These approaches use the following:

1. Case studies as anecdotes to support or illustrate selected hypotheses about some aspect of growth, development, and poverty reduction and to glean lessons;
2. Cross-country regression analysis to estimate statistically significant or significant Granger causality coefficients, from which inductive inferences are derived to form the basis of universal statements about impact and causality; and
3. General equilibrium or sector-wide modeling to assess the magnitude and direction of impact of given exogenous shocks to the economic system as structured in the model.

The approach here differs from these three. The book develops testable hypotheses to explain well-known events in economic development. Then it tests these hypotheses against rival theories, using both cross-country data and case studies drawn from economic history and post-WWII development.

A.I. Proposed Approach using Cross-Country Data and Case Studies

The approach proposed here rests on three propositions. The first two are widely accepted, but the third, still largely unknown among practitioners in economic development and academic economists, is controversial in some quarters. The three propositions are as follows:

1. Inductive generalizations from particular instances are invalid. David Hume (1711–76) argued in his book *Enquiry into Human Understanding* (1748) that such inferences from repeated particular instances to universal claims may be psychologically motivated but do not constitute proof of objective, actual causation.

2. Correlation is not causation. This is routinely pointed out in econometrics textbooks (Gujarati, 2003: 22–23). Correlation may or may not be the result of causation. Therefore, one can validly infer neither the existence of causation nor its direction from correlation coefficients. However, correlations can be informative and can serve as tests of hypotheses and as a fruitful start of research.

3. Confirmations are highly informative only when they discriminate between rival, testable explanations of the same phenomena (Popper, 1965). Superior hypotheses are those that survive refutations in crucial tests, not simply those hypotheses for which confirmations are found. Using the current methodology of inductive inferences, theories of economic development are regularly confirmed, only to be contradicted shortly thereafter by new evidence or a new analysis of the evidence. As a result, the field is full of theories that are both confirmed and contradicted by evidence.

The focus on potential and actual refutations is the hallmark of Popper's methodology and stands in sharp contrast to the current inductive approach. In his methodology, Popper makes use of a well-known logical principle, namely the asymmetry between confirmation and refutation: Countless clear confirmations cannot establish the truth of a universal claim, but one clear refutation can refute a universal claim. Thus finding another white swan cannot prove that all swans are white, but finding one black swan can demolish the universal claim that all swans are white. Stating the same principle in terms of logical relations, in logically valid arguments truth flows from premises to conclusions, and falsity flows from conclusions to premises. True premises cannot have a false conclusion, but false premises can have a true conclusion. Thus a true universal hypothesis cannot be refuted, but a false hypothesis can be confirmed.

So to assess the relative accuracy of competing universal hypotheses on growth and development, the book tests them by seeking to refute them. This is counterintuitive to the prevailing practice, which is to find confirmations, based on an inductive use of econometric measures of statistical significance. The prevailing approach to getting theory to emerge is to do regression studies on the data. Regressions are run on a number of variables in the data, usually in the hope or expectation that some of the variables are a cause of the others.[1] Although most regression studies correctly refer to their results as correlations and associations, yet they almost invariably proceed to incorrectly make policy recommendations that interpret these correlations as causation. When it is found that a correlation exists, the "null hypothesis" is refuted, and a theory of a causal relationship is confirmed and considered established. It is logically invalid to infer causality from statistical significance. Although logically speaking a "null hypothesis" is an alternative theory, it provides no guidance on where to test to further our understanding, as it contains no theory of causation. Applied and policy-oriented economics rests on making claims on the nature of causation. However, a "null" hypothesis is null in the sense of having no such understanding. It is no wonder that this latter approach has led to contradictory claims, as evidenced by several recent studies, including those on agriculture's role in promoting pro-poor growth (Timmer, May 2005a).The dubious value of refuting the null hypothesis to seek corroboration was already pointed out by Freedman (1991: 310) quoting Meehl (1978: 817): "The almost universal reliance on merely refuting the null hypothesis as the standard method for corroborating substantive theories in the soft areas is … basically unsound."[2]

This book proposes an alternative approach that does not lead to these contradictions. Instead of making universal claims based on specific instances, we posit universal claims that explain specific instances and then use further research to test these universal claims against testable rival theories.

A.II. Popper's Methodology of Science: Refutations of Bold Conjectures

The research approach here is based on Popper's methodology of science. Popper argued that confirmations by themselves are relatively easy to find and are not very informative. As already stated, Popper's

---

[1] Regression models have been used in the social sciences at least since 1899 (Freedman, 1991: 291).

[2] Freedman (1991: 310) points out that Meehl's article entitled "Theoretical Risks and Tabular Asterisks: Sir Karl, Sir Ronald, and the Slow Progress of Soft Psychology" argues that the good knight is Karl Popper, whose "motto calls for subjecting scientific theories to the grave danger of refutation. The bad knight is Ronald Fisher whose significance tests are trampled in the dust."

methodology makes use of the logical strength of refuting instances. A key feature of Popper's methodology is that rival testable theories give us much more guidance. If two theories predict a lot of existing data and conflict over what should happen in some cases, then we can look at those data as a "crucial experiment." Popper's methodology is designed to promote the development and testing of such rival theories.

Popper's main recommendations are as follows:

1. Formulate your theory in a way whereby you can clearly specify in advance what would constitute a refutation.

   Popper observed people "immunizing" Marxism and Freudianism from refutation – for example, by dismissing those who disagreed as having "false consciousness," surreptitious changes in the meaning of terms, and so on. Popper's point is that such immunizations also drain a theory of its predictive power. "Bold hypotheses," those daring to go beyond the data they are intended to explain, are the most likely to inform us about reality when they are tested.

2. Try to identify situations most likely to refute your theory. Develop or take advantage of competing theories that give conflicting predictions.

   Here the ideal is to have robust rival theories, not just a null hypothesis. Then we can look at many areas and have an idea of how to fruitfully modify the theory when it is refuted.

3. Discover cases that refute your theory or its alternatives.

   Many strong economic theories have been refuted in their original form. The question is what happens next. But for there to be a "next," we have to discover the refutations. Then we have clues for the next step.

4. Respond to refutations by developing a new testable theory of the economic system that can explain deductively the previous refutations and confirmations.

   This fourth step may be the most crucial; it is the process of inventing a new theory that can explain the past refutations and confirmations. Two points are central. First, this process is a creative one. A study of the data is critical, but the theory will not simply "emerge" from the data; it has to be imaginatively created.

Second, it is vital not to weaken the explanatory power of theories by ad hoc modifications – modifications for which there are no further tests.

How proponents and opponents of a theory respond to its refutation is the key to whether research in a field will grow or stagnate. If the advocates "save" theories by ad hoc lists of exceptions or by surreptitious changes in the meaning of terms, then the field will be stagnant. If advocates and rivals alike creatively produce new testable explanations of confirmations and refutations, then the field will learn and grow.

A way of summarizing Popper's view of productive methodology is that a theory is an instrument for probing the nature of society, just as it is an instrument for probing the physical world. Observation and experiment are only as informative as the theories that are being tested. Thus bold theorizing and severe testing are keys to progress.

A.III. Seeking Refutations, Not Merely Confirmations, as Empirical Tests of Hypotheses: Practical Considerations

Popper's recommended methodology is difficult and risky. Being able to refute a hypothesis and learn from the refutation is demanding. There are several practical considerations.

First, it is important to formulate a hypothesis in a refutable way even before collecting relevant data; otherwise, either it is impossible to refute, or the refutation is not informative. For the refutation of a given proposition to be informative and serve as a useful guide to further research, the proposition itself must exclude at least one observable event. Only then does it have empirical content. If a statement or claim can be stated in a way that makes it consistent with all conceivable events (i.e., it can always be confirmed), then it is irrefutable; that is, it is devoid of empirical content. When claims concerning the functioning of some aspect of the economic system of interest are irrefutable, then we need to first reformulate the claims so that they have empirical content. Unfortunately, as Johnston (1970: 369) stated, "the literature relating to agriculture's role in economic development deals with a subject that is vast and not clearly defined." In reformulating the hypotheses to make them refutable, there is always the danger that they will become trivialized.

Second, refutations are conclusive only relative to data. That is, if there is full agreement on the data, then an unambiguous conclusive refutation is possible. However, refutations are likely to be non-conclusive when there are ambiguities and disagreements regarding the observational data, a situation typical in economics. In the latter case, the research focus should be on coming to an agreement on the formulation of the claim and the accuracy of the relevant data. The soundness of both exercises can be objectively checked by third parties. A resolution can then be obtained through a process of open debate. Even if disagreement persists, the process of resolving the disagreement itself will be informative.

Third, while confirmations do not prove the truth of a universal statement, some confirmations are more informative than others: the case when data confirm one hypothesis but refute its rival. Such a case then constitutes a "crucial" experiment because it helps discriminate between two rival hypotheses.

Fourth, even though correlations cannot establish causality, they contain useful information about patterns and regularities. Identifying a pattern can be the first step to understanding a phenomenon. The next step is to develop a testable theory to explain the correlation. The third step is to independently test the theory with new data, which may include further correlations. Here again, the guide to what is an "independent" test is essentially that a rival theory will predict different results in that new test.

APPENDIX B
Glossary of Selected Economic Terms

B.I. Computable General Equilibrium (CGE) Modeling

General equilibrium obtains when demand and supply are equal in all markets that make up an economy or an entire system. They are in equilibrium. A model is a theoretical construct that captures the essential elements of the structure of and the interrelationships between these demand and supply functions. The model is expressed in terms of mathematical equations. The empirical magnitudes for the different variables in the equations are obtained from data. Using computing power, CGE modeling refers to the use of algorithms to solve the equations and quantify the impact of selected changes on variables of interest. CGE is often contrasted to partial equilibrium analysis, in which selected markets are analyzed (hence partial) assuming other markets within the overall system are unchanged. A recent example of the first exercise is the analysis of the impacts of changes in public spending on growth and poverty reduction of a "typical" Sub-Saharan African country (Lofgren and Robinson: 184–224). Examples of the second are in Tsakok (1990: 158–82).

B.II. Efficiency

There are four main variants of the concept of efficiency: allocative (or economic) and productive, and for each of these, static and dynamic. Economic efficiency is achieved when the least-cost combination of inputs is used to get a given output. Economic efficiency thus depends on both relative input and output prices and on technology. Productive efficiency is achieved when the least number of inputs are used to produce a given output. What is included in the set of productively efficient combinations depends only on technology. To find the economically efficient option, information on relative prices is required. The achievement of static efficiency refers to the continual search for improvements within a fixed set of initial conditions on prices and technology, whereas dynamic efficiency refers to increasing productivity as the initial conditions themselves change.

B.III. Elasticity

This is the degree of responsiveness of one variable to another. So the price elasticity of demand (supply) is the responsiveness of quantity demanded (supplied) to a unit change in price. Elasticity has numerical values along a demand or supply curve, varying from infinity to zero. When the value is greater than zero but less than 1, it is considered inelastic – the case of necessities. Consumers have limited flexibility to cut back in the case of a price increase. So a unit increase (decrease) in the price will generate less than a unit decrease (increase) in the quantity demanded. When the value is greater than 1 but less than infinity, it is considered elastic – the case of most consumption goods (economists label these "luxuries"). With these goods, consumers have much more flexibility in responding to price changes. A value of infinity means that consumers will buy infinite amounts at a given price but nothing at all at even the slightest change in price. A unitary value means that quantity demanded changes by exactly the same amount as the unit change in price. In models of consumer behavior and international trade, an Armington elasticity is assumed to estimate the response of trade flows to price changes. The parameter used usually assumes constant elasticity of substitution among products of different countries (see use of Armington elasticity in Indonesia case study, Chapter II, Section B).

B.IV. Gini Coefficient

This coefficient was developed by the Italian statistician Corrado Gini in 1912. In economics, the Gini coefficient is used to measure the degree of concentration or dispersion or inequality of income and land. It can range between zero – the case of perfect equality, in which everyone has the same thing – and 1 – the case of perfect inequality, in which one person has everything. The higher (lower) the number, the more unequal (equal) is the distribution. It is also used in other fields; for example, in ecology, it is used as a measure of biodiversity.

B.V. Gross Domestic Product (GDP)

This is a measure of the total flow of goods and services produced in an economy over a given period of time, usually a year, valued at market prices, and then aggregated.

There are several variants of the measure of this flow, depending on whether distinctions are made between (a) domestic and foreign ownership; (b) depreciation in the value of assets used to generate the flow of goods and services; and (c) taxes and subsidies. Which distinction is made depends on which aspect of aggregate economic performance is of interest.

B.VI. Gross National Product (GNP) and Gross National Income (GNI)

Gross national product is the GDP including the income arising from investments and possessions owned abroad. Gross national income is the GDP plus income accruing to domestic residents abroad from investments abroad less income earned in the domestic markets accruing to foreigners abroad.

B.VII. Hicks Neutral Technical Change

This is a change in technology that affects the use of labor and capital in the same way. In changing the scale of production, the change is not biased in favor of using more or less of labor or capital. The change in scale equally affects both inputs.

B.VIII. Median, Mean, and Mode

The median is the number that divides the bottom 50 percent of a data set from the top 50 percent. It is different from the *mean*, which is the average number obtained by summing all the observations of the data set and then dividing this sum by the number of observations. The difference is that the median has a frequency distribution attached to each number in the data set. The *mode* is the value that occurs most frequently in a data set. A distribution function tells how frequently a certain value occurs. Distribution functions have different shapes. If the distribution is unimodal, it has one highest point or peak on the middle value; this shape is also referred to as a bell shape. "Bimodal" means two peaks; "multimodal" means several peaks. A fairly equal distribution of landholdings is unimodal, and an unequal one can be bimodal (cases of Taiwan and Colombia, respectively, in Tomich et al., 1995: box I.2). If the distribution is skewed to the right, this means the peak occurs at lower values – for example, there are more poor people with small plots than there are high-income people with large plots.

B.IX. Multiplier

This is the number by which an initial injection of expenditure into the economy is amplified above the value of the initial injection. Thus, if USD 100 is initially injected into an economy and it generates USD 400 of income in the economy, then the value of the multiplier is 4.

B.X. Net National Product (NNP) and Net National
Income (NNI)

Net national product is GNP minus depreciation. Depreciation is the reduction in value of an asset through wear and tear in the process of production. Net national income is NNP minus indirect taxes.

B.XI. Protection Coefficients

These are measures of agricultural support or taxation on producers and consumers, resulting from a variety of measures such as price supports, import tariffs, and subsidies on inputs. They show the extent to which agricultural policy has transferred income in favor of (or reduced income against) a particular commodity or group. Transfers to producers come largely from consumers paying higher prices (higher relative to the non-intervention situation) and from taxpayers (Josling, 1975). The major ones used by the OECD and the WTO are, respectively:

- *Producer (Consumer) Subsidy Equivalent (PSE)*: A measure of the value of the monetary transfers to (from) agricultural producers (consumers) resulting from agricultural protection. This measure is also referred to as Producer Support Estimate. When expressed as a percentage, it shows how much of the income of the producer (consumer) received (lost) from that given activity was due to the policy of protection. It can be used for inter-country, inter-commodity, and inter-year comparisons. For example, the PSE as a percentage of value of gross farm receipts was the highest for Switzerland, at around 75 percent (2000–2002), and lowest for Australia, at around 5 percent (2000–2002) (OECD, 2003).

- *Aggregate Measure of Support (AMS):* This is determined by calculating a market price support estimate for each commodity receiving such support, plus non-exempt direct payments or any other subsidy not exempted from reduction commitments (made during the Uruguay Round Agreement on Agriculture in 1998), less specific agricultural levies or fees paid by producers. It differs from the Producer Support Estimate (PSE) in many respects. The most important difference is that price gaps in the AMS calculation are estimated by reference to domestic administered prices and not to actual producer prices and that external reference prices are fixed at the average levels of the 1986–88 base period. In addition, many budgetary transfers included in PSEs are excluded from the AMS.

There are many other categories of price comparisons that show the extent to which a given commodity or group has received more or less income compared with the situation in which the policy affecting the price ratios did not exist (e.g., nominal protection rate). Which ones are used depends largely on the questions being asked and the data available (Tsakok, 1990: ch. 3).

B.XII. Purchasing Power Parity (PPP)

This is a theory that, in the long run, the equilibrium exchange rates between two currencies will reflect the relative price levels (hence, the purchasing power of currencies) in these two countries. According to the theory, when the official or market exchange rate in country A is overvalued (undervalued in country B) relative to the PPP, then holders in A of the overvalued currency (undervalued in B) will buy too (relative to PPP) much (little) of imports (exports from B), and sell (relative to PPP) too little (much) of its exports (imports into B). If market forces of arbitrage were allowed between the two countries and exchange rates were allowed to float in order to reflect relative demand and supply, then PPP predicts that the overvaluation in A's currency would be eliminated by the rise in prices of B's exports to A. As inflation rises in B, A's currency would then buy less of B's exports to A. As an example, suppose at USD 1 = 8 renminbi (RMB, Chinese currency), the USD is overvalued (the RMB is undervalued). Then over time, arbitrage forces can drive the exchange rate to the USD 1 = 4 RMB, approximating the PPP level. In the real world, many factors would prevent the PPP from obtaining –for example, import and export restrictions of various kinds and exchange rates not allowed to float. While the concept of PPP is simple – exchange rates adjust to reflect relative purchasing powers and inflation rates – the actual measurement of PPP can be very complex and controversial.

B.XIII. Quintile

This is a fifth, or 20 percent, of the population.

B.XIV. Regression Analysis and Coefficients

Regression analysis is a statistical tool to estimate the quantitative relationships between variables, based on a given set of data. If there is a theory explaining how these variables are causally related, regression analysis estimates these values or coefficients between a dependent and independent variable(s) and, on the basis of these coefficients, predicts values of the dependent variable, conditional on the numerical values of the independent variable(s). The inference of causation is based on theory, not on the numerical values of the estimates. One can never infer causation on the basis of regression coefficients alone (Gujarati, 2003: 22–23). Causality cannot be logically inferred from statistical relationships, no matter how statistically significant the coefficients are.

B.XV. Small and Large Countries

In international trade, a "small" country is one that is a price taker, because its share of the international market in a given commodity is small; a "large" country is a price maker, because its share is big. In other words, when a "small" country enters or leaves the international market in a given commodity, such entry or exit does not affect the level of international prices of that commodity. "Small" and "large" in a trade sense have nothing to do with physical size as such. Thus the tiny island of Zanzibar used to be a "large" country in clove trade, until the collapse of clove plantations following the revolution of 1964.[1] Zanzibar was overtaken by Indonesia in the international clove trade.

---

[1]   The 1964 revolution by local Africans ended some 200 years of Arab rule on the island.

B.XVI. Social Equity

This is the concept of social justice: fair access to opportunity and resources, equal treatment, and equal opportunity. There is no disagreement with the concept per se, but with what concretely constitutes equitable distribution and treatment in the real world of resource and opportunity allocation. It is a value judgment. In the world of development, many consider differences in income and wealth positions of different groups to be extreme and the distribution inequitable when lower-income groups suffer from severe malnutrition and food insecurity, and have very limited access to basic education and health care services, while upper-income groups have luxurious lifestyles. It is not just the differences in wealth and income per se that are considered inequitable, but the co-existence of such differences with extensive poverty on one side and lavish lifestyles on the other. The core concerns of social inequity are twofold: increasing concentration of income and wealth in the hands of the top quintile, on one hand, and declining share of income and wealth by the bottom quintile, on the other.

B.XVII. Spillover Effects

These are the effects of an activity or process that go beyond – hence spill over – the intended target of the activity or process. The idea of *spillover* and *externalities* is similar: impact that goes beyond intended boundaries. The impact can be positive – for example, an increase in literacy positively affects the quality of citizenship, thus benefiting social functioning beyond the individuals becoming literate – or negative – for example, chemical pollution from a given plant undermines the health of people totally unrelated to that plant.

B.XVIII. Total Factor Productivity (TFP) Growth

Productivity is the quantitative and qualitative relationship of output to inputs. Higher productivity growth means greater output growth for a given input growth. Growth in TFP is a measure of growth in output not accounted for by growth in inputs. Thus, if inputs are multiplied by 2 but output grows by more than 2, that extra growth is a measure of TFP growth. When inputs are used more efficiently, productivity grows. TFP growth can be due to technological, organizational, or social improvements, among other things. TFP growth is the fundamental reason for growth in wages and consumption, hence in standard of living. TFP growth is the bedrock of higher consumption. The estimation of TFP can be controversial.

B.XIX. Value Added

This is the additional price over the cost of producing an output that can be charged to customers. It is the value that is added to the inputs by the production process.

APPENDIX C
Supporting Tables

England

Table C.1. *Indices of Sustained Agricultural Production Growth 1700 = 100 (1700–1850)*

	1700	1750	1800	1850
Output[a]	100	121	159	272
Output[b]	100	127	191	285
Sown arable area	100		135	199
Total area	100		138	132
Land productivity[a]	100		115	207
Land productivity[b]	100		138	216
Crop productivity[c]	3.05 (1300)			6.73
Livestock productivity[c]	1.04 (1300)			6.56
Labor productivity[a]	100	126	141	197
Labor productivity[b]	100	134	170	206
Wheat yields	100	123	136	180
Cereal yields	100	135	158	250

Note: Wheat yields are from Hampshire, Lincolnshire, Norfolk, and Suffolk. Cereal yields are from Norfolk and Suffolk.
[a] Population method.
[b] Volume method
[c] In wheat bushel equivalents. The base comparison year is 1300 rather than 1700.
Source: Overton (1998: table 3.11).

Table C.2. *Contribution of Agriculture and the Spatial Distribution of Population, 1700–1880*

	1770s	1800s	1880s
Agric./GDP	43		10
Agric. pop/total	55	36	6
Rural/urban			33/67

Sources and Notes:
Agric./GDP: Chambers and Mingay (1966: 208, n. 1).
Agric. pop.: Mingay (1996). For this period, the ratio between rural and urban population is not given. According to Arnold Toynbee, by 1831 the agricultural population constituted only 28% of the total population (Toynbee, 1884: Sec. VIII),
Rural and urban population: Toynbee (1884: Sec. II).

Table C.3. *Indexes of Key Prices – Wheat, Agricultural*
Money, and Real Wages: 10-Year Averages
(1700–49 = 100), 1700s–1840s

Period	Wheat	Money Wage	Real Wage
1700s	100	97	97
1730s	93	102	108
1770s	147	110	74
1800s	267	207	78
1820s	189	183	96
1840s	176	162	91

Note: The Corn Laws were repealed in 1846.
Source: Overton (1998: table 3.1).

Table C.4. *England and Wales: Key Features of the Agrarian Structure 1851*

	Small Farms, 100 Acres or Less	Medium Farms, 101 to 300 Acres	Large Farms, More Than 300 Acres
Farmers ('000)	134	64.2	16.8
Farmers (% of total)	62	30	8.0
Acreage (% of total)	22	45	33

Source: Chambers and Mingay (1966: 93, 132).

Japan

Table C.5. *Agricultural Growth Performance (Percent per Year, 1880–1969)*

Period	Total Output	Productivity	Gross Value Added	Productivity
1880–1935	1.6	1.2	1.6	1.3
1876–1938	1.6	1.2	1.6	1.4
1945–65	3.4	1.1	3.1	2.9
1947–69	3.6	1.6	3.3	3.4
1950–60[a]	4.4		4.2 (4.0)	

[a] Data from Tomich et al. (1995). Total output refers to farm output and the figure in parentheses refers to net value added.
Source: Yamada and Hayami (1979: tables 2–1, 2–4a, 2–4b).

Table C.6. *Indices of Agricultural Performance*

	1880	1920	1960
Output (net of seed and feed)	100	205	334
Total inputs	100	119	174
Total factor productivity	100	172	192

Source: Tomich et al. (1995: table 3.2).

Ireland

Table C.7. *Growth Performance of Economy and Agriculture (Percent, Annual Average, 1980s–2000s)*

	1980s	1990s	2000s
GDP growth	3.1	7.0	6.1
Agric./GDP	11.0	6.8	2.5
Agric. labor/total labor	16.3	11.7	6.8
Agric. growth	2.3	1.7	–3.1

Source: World Development Indicators.

Portugal

Table C.8. *Growth Performance of Economy and Agriculture (Percent, Annual Average, 1960s–1990s)*

	1960s	1986–91	1990s
GDP growth	7.0	3.8	3.0–3.5
Agric./GDP	27.0	6.0	2.9
Agric. growth	2.0	–3.5	–2.1
Agric. Labor / total labor	42.0	13.0	5.0

Note: The 1975–85 period was a decade of crises.

Sources and Notes:

GDP growth: 1960s, 1986–91: Corkill (1993: 17, 28, 117, 126). 1990s: "Economic Survey of Portugal: Policy Brief," *OECD Observer*, April 2001.

Agric. growth: Corkill (1993: 17–28). 1986–95, 1995–2001: decline in agricultural output. Communication from the Commission to the Council and the European Parliament, "Report on the Situation in Portuguese Agriculture, Brussels, June 19, 2003, paras 3.1, 3.3, Secs. 4–6.

Agric./GDP, Agric. labor / total labor: 1960s: Pintado (1964: table II). Mid-1980s: Corkill (1993: table 3.2). 1990s: Bandarra (2002:44, 46 tables 1, 2). Agro-industry contributed another 5.4% of GDP (1998).

Republic of Korea

Table C.9. *Growth Performance of Economy and Agriculture (Percent, Annual Average, and Ratios, 1960s–2000s)*

	1960s	1970s	1980s	1990s	2000s
Agic. GDP/total	38.0	26.2	13.4	6.6	3.8
Agric. GDP growth	5.4	3.4	2.0	1.1	0.4
Export growth	30.1	22.8	11.5	14.2	12.2
GDP growth	8.3	8.3	7.7	6.3	5.2
GDP per capita growth	5.6	6.3	6.4	5.2	4.7
Agric. empl. / total			26.8	13.8	9.1

Source: World Development Indicators.

Table C.10. *Agricultural Growth Performance (Percent per Year, 1920–69)*

Period	Years	Total outpour	Input[a]	Total Productivity	Partial Productivity, Labor and Land[b]	Gross Value Added	Input[a]	Total Productivity
Pre-war	1920–39	1.62	1.62	−0.01	1.14 (0.90)	1.38	0.44	0.94
					1.52 (1.28)			
War	1939–53	−0.32	0.04	0.32	0.53 (0.51)	−0.36	−0.57	0.22
					0.36 (0.33)			
Post-war	1953–69	4.36	2.38	1.95	2.49 (2.40)	4.27	1.46	2.76
					3.29 (3.20)			
Whole period	1920–69	1.94	1.41	0.52	1.40 (1.28)	1.81	0.48	1.32
					1.76 (1.63)			

[a] The first input column includes non-farm current input; the second input column excludes non-farm current input.
[b] The estimates of partial productivity for labor and land are on a total output basis and, in parentheses, on a value-added basis.
Source: Ban (1979: tables 4.1, 4.5a, 4.5b).

Table C.11. *Selected Growth Rates (Percent per Year, 1946–73)*

Period	Production	Input[a]	Productivity	Output	Input[a]	Productivity
1946–52	0.83	2.15	−1.29	0.88	2.15	−1.24
1952–54	10.87	3.42	7.20	10.54	3.42	6.88
1954–65	3.99	2.51	1.44	3.89	2.51	1.35
1965–73	2.79	0.65	2.13	2.23	0.65	1.57
1946–73	3.41	1.94	1.44	3.21	1.94	1.23

[a] The input columns include non-farm current input.
Source: Ban et al. (1980: tables 20, 21).

Table C.12. *Korea, Taiwan, China, and Japan: Growth Rates*
(Percent per Year, 1920–73)

Period	Korea		Period	Taiwan	Period	Japan	
	Rice	Total		Total		Rice	Total
1920–25	2.35	1.25	1910–19	2.72	1889–1914	1.37	1.54
1925–31	3.16	2.77	1920–29	5.19	1914–39	0.73	0.72
1931–36	2.84	3.50	1930–39	3.32			
1920–40	1.62	1.47	1906–40	3.19	1889–1939	1.01	1.13
1910–38	4.0						
1910–38	15.5[a]						
1956–73		3.5					

[a] Refers to rice exports to Japan.
Sources: 1920–40, 1956–73: Kang and Ramachandran (1999: table 1). 1910–38: Ramachandran (1995: table 1).

Taiwan, China

Table C.13. *Growth Performance of Economy, Agriculture, and Exports*
(Percent per Year, 1960s–2000s)

	1960s	1970s	1980s	1990s	2000s
GDP growth	9.5	10.3	8.2	6.5	4.1
Agric. GDP growth	2.7	2.8	1.2	−0.2	−0.6
Export growth	22.4	19.8	11.6	7.7	9.2

Source: World Development Indicators.

Table C.14. *Growth Performance of Agriculture (Percent per Year, 1913–70)*

Phase of Development	Period	Total Production	Total Output	Gross Value Added
Initial phase, Japanese rule	1913–23	2.7	2.8	1.9
Agricultural transformation	1923–37	4.0	4.1	3.8
Retrogression under war	1937–46	−4.9	−4.9	−3.9
Recovery	1946–51	10.3	10.2	9.2
Continued rehabilitation	1951–60	4.6	4.7	4.1
Sustained development	1960–70	4.1	4.2	3.3
Pre-war period	1913–37	3.5	3.6	3.0
Post-war period	1946–70	5.5	5.6	4.8

Note: Output is total production minus agricultural intermediate inputs; gross value added is output minus non-farm current inputs.
Source: Lee and Chen (1979: table 3.1).

India

Table C.15. *Annual Growth Performance and Key Ratios (1960s–2000s)*

	1960s	1970s	1980s	1990s	2000s
Agric. GDP/total	42.5	38.9	32.0	27.6	20.4
Agric. GDP growth	2.0	1.3	4.4	3.2	2.9
Export growth	5.4	10.6	4.8	12.0	15.1
GDP growth	4.0	2.9	5.7	5.6	7.2
GDP per capita growth	1.6	0.6	3.4	3.7	5.6
Agric. empl/total				67.4	
Pop. growth	2.3	2.3	2.1	1.8	1.5

Source: World Development Indicators.

Table C.16. *Growth Performance of Economy and Agriculture (Percent 1980–2002)*

	1980/81–1990/91	1991/92–1992/93	1993/94–1994/95	1995/96–1996/97	1997/98–2001/2002
GDP	5.8	5.4	7.9	7.3	5.5
Agric. GDP	3.1	6.0	5.4	9.4	1.7

Sources: World Bank (2002a: table 1.1). The source for the period 1997/98–2001/2002 is World Bank, July 2003, *Sustaining Reform, Reducing Poverty*, table 5.1.

Table C.17. *Growth Performance of Economy and Agriculture (Percent per Year, 1980–1998)*

	1980/81–1990/91	1988/89–1989/90	1989/90–1990/91	1990/91–1991/92	1991/92–1992/93	1992/93–1993/94	1993/94–1994/95	1994/95–1995/96	1995/96–1996/97	1996/97–1997/98	1989/90–1997/98
GDP	5.8	6.5	5.7	0.4	5.4	5.0	7.9	8.0	7.3	5.0	5.6
Ag GDP	3.1	1.8	3.8	-2.3	6.0	3.7	5.4	0.2	9.4	-1.0	3.4

Source: World Bank "India: Evaluating Bank Assistance for the Agricultural and Rural Development – A Country Assistance Evaluation. Operations Evaluations Department," Working Paper Series, 2002, table 1.1. An alternative set of estimates of annual agricultural growth are: 1982–92, 3.0%; 1992–2002: 3.0%. World Bank, "India at a Glance," August 25, 2003.

Table C.18. *Agricultural Growth in the States of Bihar, Orissa, Punjab and at National Level (Percent per Year, 1967–2001)*

State	1967–88	1980/81–1990/91	1990/91–2000/2001	1994/95–2001/2002[a]
Bihar		2.8	−0.1	3.8
Orissa		2.8	1.1	
Punjab	4.5	5.0	2.6	
All India	2.8	2.9	3.0	3.0

Note: The growth rates are gross state domestic product (GSDP).

[a] Refers to Divided Bihar. Bihar split into two states in 1993–94, Jharkand and Bihar; 1994–95 is the first year for which data for divided Bihar are available.

Sources: Bihar and Orissa: 1980/81–2000/2001, 1994/95–2001/2002: World Bank, *India: Bihar: Towards a Development Strategy*, October 21, 2003, draft, table 1.4; Ahluwalia (2003: table 1).
 Punjab: 1967–88: Bhalla (1995: table 3.1). 1980–2001: Ahluwalia (2003: table 1). 1990/91–2000/2001: World Bank (July 2003 a: para. 3) (September 2003). 1967–88: Bhalla (1995: table 3.1). 1980–2000/2001: Ahluwalia (2003: table 1). 1994/95–2001/02: World Bank, *India: Bihar: Towards a Development Strategy*, October 21, 2003, draft, table 1.4.

Table C.19. *Poverty Incidence Using Two Methodologies: Rural Headcount Ratios (Percent)*

State	Official Methodology			Adjusted Estimates		
	1987–88	1993–94	1999–2000	1987–88	1993–94	1999–2000
Bihar	53.9	58.0	44.0	54.6	48.6	41.1
Orissa	58.7	49.8	47.8	50.4	43.5	43.0
Uttar Pradesh	41.9	42.3	31.1	34.9	28.6	21.5
Madhya Pradesh	42.0	40.7	37.2	43.7	36.6	31.3
Haryana	15.4	28.3	7.4	13.6	17.0	5.7
Punjab	12.8	11.7	6.0	6.6	6.2	2.4
All India	39.4	37.1	26.8	39.0	33.0	26.3

Note: Deaton and Dreze (2002: Table 2a) adjusted the official estimates to make the estimates derived from data of the 55th round of Central Statistical Office (CSO) comparable to those of the 50th round. The rationale for the adjustments is that the methodology used after the 50th round (1993–94) is different from that of previous rounds; therefore, the estimates of headcount ratios derived are not comparable. The subsequent rounds used "thin" samples, meaning smaller samples were in the field for only six months instead of the customary year and with a different sampling design. The results of such samples yield results that are inconsistent with other data showing rapid economic growth. In addition to the adjustments for the questionnaire, adjustments were made in price indexes which affect the poverty line itself.

Overall, their reassessment showed that poverty had declined more or less evenly during the entire period even before the liberalization measures of the 1990s. Specifically "six years prior to 1993–94 and not only in the six years subsequent to 1993–94" (Deaton and Dreze, 2002: 6). In addition, income disparities increased in the 1990s, within states and especially within urban areas, with the southern and western states doing much better than the northern and eastern states, as well as between urban and rural areas.

Note also that the estimate of poverty incidence by the World Bank is 29% (2000) (World Bank, December 2003; 2003a: 109).

People's Republic of China

Table C.20. *Growth Performance of Economy and Agriculture and Key Structural Ratios (Percent per Year, 1952–2002)*

	1952–57	1965–75	1978–84	1982–92	1992–2002
GDP	6.0–7.0	6.0–7.0	9.4	9.7	9.0
GDP per capita	3.0	3.0	8.0	8.1	8.0
Agric. GDP	4.9	3.8	7.3	4.6	3.7
Population	2.2	2.2	1.4	1.4	0.8
Exports		3.4		14.0	
Exports/GDP			11.3		25.3
Agric./GDP	57.7		30.0		15.0
Agric labor/total	83.5		68.7		50.0
Rural/urban	89/11				62/38

Note: These growth rate figures are country-wide averages. The growth rates in coastal provinces were higher. For example, the coastal provinces grew at 9.7% per year between 1978 and 1995. There are two alternative estimates of China's GDP growth rate from 1978 to 1995 in Chai (ed., 2000a: box 1.1. These are 8.0 and 6.8%.

Sources and Notes:

GDP. China experienced sharp ups and downs during the earlier period of 1952–78. The Great leap Forward (1958–60) experienced negative growth of up to –30% and during the Cultural Revolution (1967–77) negative growth of up to –10% in World Bank, 1997b. (ed. fig. 1.3). For the pre-reform period, Rawski (1979: 767) states that "specialists now agree that China's economy has experienced substantial growth over the last three decades. Estimates of annual GDP growth cluster around 6–7." These rates are much higher than the rates from Perkins (1994: 42, n. 1), who put it at around 4.8% for 1952–78. For 1978–95, the annual rate is 9.4 % in World Bank, 1997 b. : table 1.1. 1982–2002: World Bank, "China at a Glance," August, 29, 2003. 1997–2007, average annual growth 9.5% (World Bank, "China at a Glance," September 24, 2008).

GDP per capita: 1950–78, 3.0%, and 1978–95, 8.0 % in World Bank, 1997 b. 1982–2002: World Bank, "China at a Glance," August 29, 2003. 1997–2007: 8.7% per year (World Bank, "China at a Glance," September 24, 2008).

Agric. GDP: 1952–57, 1965–75: Perkins and Yusuf (1984: table 3–3); an alternative estimate for 1952–78 is 2.9%, for 1978–1984, 7.7%, and for 1984–87, 4.1% (Lin in Chai, ed., 2000: table 1); for 1978–84, Perkins (1994) (in Chai, ed., 2000). Still another estimate for 1952–78 is 1.9%, for 1978–87, 6%, and for 1984–87, 3.4% (Lardy, 1990: table 1). 1982–2002, World Bank, "China at a Glance," August 29, 2003. 1997–2007, 3.7% (World Bank, "China at a Glance," September 24, 2008).

Population growth rates: yearly average at 2.2% between 1957 and 1975 (Rawski, 1979). The one-child policy was instituted in the late 1970s. By the late 1970s, the rate declined to less than 1.4% (Perkins and Yusuf, 1984). The annual growth rate during the 1996–2002 period averaged 0.8% (World Bank, "China at a Glance," August 29, 2003). 2000–2007: 0.6% per year (World Bank, "China at a Glance," September 24, 2008).

Exports: Perkins (1994) (in Chai, ed. 2000). 1997–2007, annual growth of exports of goods and services averaged 22.7% (World Bank, "China at a Glance," September 24, 2008). *Exports/GDP*: *Exports of goods and services/GDP*: World Bank, "China at a Glance," September 8, 2005; a more recent estimate for 2003 is 34.2% and that for 2004 is 39.7%.

Agric. labor/total labor: 1952: China National Bureau of Statistics, 2002, table 3.2; 1980 and 2000: Tang Zhong (2002: table 2).

Agric./GDP; Rural/urban population: 1952: Perkins and Yusuf (1984: tables 2–1, 2–2). 1980, 2001: Ravallion et al. (2004:13). 1992–2002: Kwiecinski and Li (2002: 37). 2001–2007 ratio of rural/urban is 58/42 (World Bank, "China at a Glance," September 24, 2008).

Table C.21. *Agricultural Growth Performance – Disaggregated and By Sub-Periods (Percent per Year 1952–1987)*

Subsector	1952–78	1978–84	1984–87
Crops	2.5	5.9	1.4
Grain	2.4	4.8	−0.2
Cotton	2.0	17.7	−12.9
Animal husbandry	4.0	10.0	8.5
Fishery	19.9	12.7	18.6
Forestry	9.4	14.9	0
Sidelines	11.2	19.4	18.5
Agriculture overall	2.9	7.7	4.1

Note: In 1952, the weights (%) of the sub-sectors in 1952 were: crops, 83.1; animal husbandry, 11.5; fishery, 0.3; forestry, 0.7; sidelines, 4.4. In 1987, the weights were: crops, 60.7; animal husbandry, 22.3; fishery, 4.7; forestry, 4.8; and sidelines, 7.0. Outputs from village-run enterprises were excluded.

Source: Lin (in Chai, ed., 2000: table 1). 1987–97: 4.4% per year. 1997–2007: 3.7% (World Bank, "China at a Glance," September 24, 2008).

Table C.22. *China and the Rest of the World – Comparisons of Income Inequality (Gini Coefficient)*

Region or Country	1980s	1990s
Eastern Europe	25.0	28.9
China	28.8	38.8
High-income countries	33.2	33.8
South Asia	35.0	31.8
East Asia and Pacific	38.7	38.1
Middle East and North Africa	40.5	38.0
Sub-Saharan Africa	43.5	47.0
Latin America and the Caribbean	49.8	49.3

Source: Chai (ed., 2000: 549–53: table 1).

Indonesia

Table C.23. *Selected Economic Indicators: Growth Rates and Ratios (Annual Percent, 1966–2002)*

	1966–76, Suharto	1976–90, Suharto	1990–97, Suharto	1998–99, Financial Crisis	1999–2002, Recovery
GDP growth	6.4–6.7	6.4–6.7	6.4–6.7	–13.0	3.2
Agric. growth	4.3	3.0	2.5	–1.3	2.0
Population growth					1.3
Agric./GDP	45.5	30.7	20.1	16.9	15.9
Exports/GDP		25.6	26.5		
Agric. labor/total	70.0				40.0
Rural/urban	80/20	69/31	64/36	61/39	66/44
Poverty incidence	40.1	15.8	17.7	24.2	18.2
Rural poverty	40.4	15.7	19.9	25.7	21.1

Sources and Notes:

GDP growth: 1966–1997, Suharto era: World Bank (March 2002: table 1.1). During these three decades, population growth rate per year was 2.06%. An alternative estimate for the Suharto years, 1998–99 and after, is in Timmer (June 2005b). Post-crisis, 2001–2006: 4.8%

Agric. growth: 1960–88: real gross value added calculated from five-year averages (Van der Eng, 1996: table 2.3). 1985–90, 1990–97, 1999–2002: Timmer (June 2005b: App. 2(b), table A 2.1).

Population growth: 1998–2004: World Bank, "Indonesia at a Glance," September 15, 2005.

Agric./GDP: 1970, 1980, 1990, 1998, 2002: Timmer (2005b: App. 2(b), table A 2.2). Another estimate for the 1960s, 35%, and for 2001, 17% (Mangara, 1998: table 1; World Bank, 2003a: 110).

Exports/GDP; Exports of goods and services/GDP: World Bank, "Indonesia at a Glance," September 19, 2005. Estimates are for 1984, 1994, 2003 (30.7%); 2004 (30.9%).

Agric. labor/total: 1970, 2000, World Bank (January 2003: fig.1)

Rural/urban population; poverty incidence; rural poverty incidence: 1976, 1990, 1996, 1998, 2002, Timmer (2005b: App. table A 4). Poverty incidence in 1970 was 60%. The estimation of poverty used a different methodology in 1990 and a different basket starting in 1996. These led to higher estimates of incidence than in the previous years. Poverty rate in 2006 was 17.8%.

Table C.24. *Contribution of Agricultural Growth to Poverty Reduction, 1984–96*

	Urban	Rural	Total
Poverty head count:			
Observed change in poverty (% point)	−22.14	−41.82	−39.24
Impact of agricultural growth (% point)	−12.16	−31.12	−25.74
Contribution of agricultural growth (%)	54.94	74.40	65.58

Source: Timmer (June 2005b: table 4).

Malaysia

Table C.25. *Selected Growth Rates and Ratios (1960s– 2000s)*

	1960s	1970s	1980s	1990s	2000s
Agric. GDP/total	31.2	27.4	20.3	13.1	4.0
Agric. GDP growth	6.0	5.2	3.5	0.2	3.7
Export growth	6.0	8.2	9.2	12.7	6.9
GDP growth	6.5	7.7	5.9	7.2	5.6
GDP per capita growth	3.5	5.2	3.1	4.5	3.6
Agric. empl./total			31.6	20.4	15.5
Population growth	2.9	2.4	2.7	2.6	1.9

Source: World Development Indicators.

Appendix C

Tunisia

Table C.26. *Selected Economic Indicators (Average Annual Percent, 1960s–2000)*

Indicator	1960s	1970s	1986–90	1991–95	1996–2000
GDP growth	4.7	7.6	2.9	3.9	5.6
Agric./GDP	24.0	16			14.0
Exports/GDP			33.0	44.9	
Agric. Labor/total	56.0	35.0			16.0
Rural pop./total	64		48	40	33
Agric. Growth	1.6	4.4	8.6	2.1	3.5
Population growth					1.2
Rural/urban	64/36		48/52	40/60	33/67
Poverty incidence	40.0		11.2	7.9	4.1
Rural poverty	17.0	14.6	19.1	14.8	8.3

Sources and Notes:

GDP growth: 1960s, 1970s: World Bank, 1982: para.2.06.; 1986–2000: Joint World Bank–Islamic Development Bank (2005: table 1.2). In 1984, Tunisia had food riots. 1997–2007: 4.8% annual growth (World Bank, "Tunisia at a Glance," September 24, 2008).

Agric./GDP: 1960s, 1970s: World Bank, 1982:para 2.05. 1996–2000: World Bank (2004b: para 2). It is noteworthy that the agric./GDP has remained fairly constant for three decades! In "Tunisia at a Glance" (August 25, 2005), the ratio of agric./GDP is 12.6% (2004). 2007: 10.9 % (World Bank, "Tunisia at a Glance," September 24, 2008).

Rural pop./total: World Development Indicators.

Exports/GDP: Exports of goods and services/GDP: World Bank, "Tunisia at a Glance," August 25, 2005. Estimates are for 1984, 1994, 2003 (43.1%), 2004 (43.8%). The ratio of imports of goods and services to GDP for the late 1990s to early 2000s is just slightly higher.

Agric. labor/total labor: 1960s, 1970s: World Bank, 1982: para 2.05 1996–2000: World Bank, June 2006a: Executive Summary, pp v.

Agric. growth: 1960s, 1970s: World Bank, 1982: Para 2.06. 1986–90: agriculture value added: World Bank, June 2006a: paras 17–18. Another source: data for only 1989–90: growth of value added fluctuated from 10 to 30% during that short period. 1991–1998: year-to-year fluctuations from –10 to + 30.3%. World Bank, June 2000: 8, paras 1–3. 1997–2007: 2.5% (World Bank, "Tunisia at a Glance," September 24, 2008).

Population growth: World Bank, "Tunisia at a Glance," August 25, 2005. 1998–2004: average estimate. 2000–07: 1% (World Bank, "Tunisia at a Glance," September 24, 2008).

Rural/urban ratio: 1960s, 1980s: World Bank, 1982: para. 2.16. 1991–95: World Bank (August 1995: para 2.11). 1996–2000: World Bank, "Tunisia at a Glance," September. The fast rate of urbanization is indicated by the 73:27 urban:rural ratio of 1997–2003 period (World Bank, "Tunisia at a Glance," June 2004: Annex A 1).

Poverty incidence, rural poverty: 1960s, 1970s: percentage living below absolute poverty (World Bank, 1982: para 2.14). Headcount index, 1991–2000: Joint World Bank–Islamic Development Bank (2005: table 1.3).

Table C.27. *Selected Economic Indicators*

WDI Data	1960s	1970s	1980s	1990s	2000s
Agriculture, value added (% of GDP)	17.7	17.7	13.8	14.0	11.4
Agriculture, value added (annual % growth)	−0.2	6.3	3.2	6.7	2.0
Exports of goods and services (annual % growth)	5.8	12.0	4.9	4.8	4.9
GDP growth (annual %)	5.4	7.2	3.6	5.1	4.9
GDP per capita growth (annual %)	3.3	4.9	1.0	3.3	3.8
Population growth (annual %)	1.9	2.1	2.5	1.7	1.0

Table C.28. *Comparison of Human Development Indicators: Tunisia (1970–75, 2000–2001) versus Lower-Middle-Income Countries (2000–2001)*

Indicator	Tunisia, 1970–75	Tunisia, 2000–2001	Lower-Middle-Income Countries, 2000–2001
Life expectancy (years)	55	72	69
Total fertility rate (births per woman)	5	2	2
Infant mortality (per 1,000 births)	94	26	33
Gross primary enrollment (% of school population)			
Male	79	123	107
Female	65	116	107
Adult illiteracy (% of population 15 years and older)			
Male	51	18	9
Female	77	39	21

Source: Joint World Bank–Islamic Development Bank (2005: table 1.4).

Brazil

Table C.29. *Selected Quality of Life Indicators (1980–2000)*

	1980	1990	2000
Poverty incidence (% of households)	40.0	40.7	33.6
Poverty incidence (% of individuals)			
Indigence R$65.07	32.8		25.7
Poverty R$131.97	60.9		51.4
Ratio of average income 10% richest/40% poorest	21.5	26.7	23.6
Infant mortality (per 1,000 births)	79.2	48.0	29.6
Northeast	112.8	72.9	44.2
Access to improved water source	60.7	74.2	87.3
(% of households)			
Northeast	30.8	43.3	67.0
Northeast rural	4.9	10.6	22.8
Access to sanitation	51.3	63.2	71.3
(% of households)			
Northeast	30.9	41.2	54.2

Sources and Notes: World Bank (January 2004: table 9).

Poverty incidence: Two lines are used (both in 1996 R$): indigence – R$38/month per person, or USD 12; poverty level at R$ 269, or USD 86. World Bank (2004a: figs. 1, 14). The two lines correspond roughly to the core poor and the two dollar/day poor. Population below national poverty line is 22% for 2001–2007 (World Bank, "Brazil at a Glance," September 24, 2008). Using the World Bank's definition of poverty as "less than one dollar per day," poverty headcount ratio fell from 14 to 8% between 1990 and 2004 (World Bank and International Finance Corporation, 2007).

Table C.30. *Selected Income and Non-income Dimensions of Underdevelopment (Percent)*

	1970	1980	1990	2000
Income distribution				
Top decile	46.36	47.67	48.70	
Lowest quintile	3.83	3.39	2.60	
Gini coefficient		58.40	61.60	59.60[a]
Land distribution				
Gini coefficient		0.85		
Poverty				
National[b]		40.0	40.7	33.6
Northeast		66.8	68.6	57.4
Northeast rural			84.9	72.6
Illiteracy				
Adult (population age 15 and older)		22.8	18.7	12.4
Northeast		41.6	36.4	24.3
Youth population, 15–24 age group		12.0	9.8	4.2
Northeast		27.0	22.7	9.6

[a] For rural incomes, it is also 0.59 (2000) (Byerlee, Xinshen Diao, and Jackson, 2005).
[b] Refers to poverty rate of households, not individuals.

Sources:
Top decile: 1970, 1980, 1990: Baer (2001: tables 6.9, 9.7).

Lowest quintile: 1970, 1980, 1990: Baer (2001: tables 6.9, 9.7)

Gini coefficient: World Bank (January 2004: table 9).

Gini coefficient for land: World Bank (July 2002: fig. 2.2b). In Latin America, only Venezuela has a higher Gini coefficient, at around 0.9.

Poverty rate of households, national, northeast, and northeast rural: World Bank (January 2004: table 9). The World Bank's poverty rate is USD 2 per day. In terms of poverty incidence of individuals, World Bank, "Brazil at a Glance," April 14, 2006. 1998–2004: 22% below the poverty line.

Illiteracy: World Bank (January 2004: table 9).

Table C.31. *Selected Growth Rates and Structural Ratios (Percent per Year or Ratios, 1920–2002)*

	1920–29	1933–39	1939–45	1950–73	1974–80	1981–94	1995–99	2002
GDP	3.9	4.9	3.2	7.5	6.8	1.9	2.3	1.5
Industry	2.8	11.3	5.4	8.0	9.39	1.17	1.4	1.5
Agriculture	4.1	1.7	1.7	4.5	4.82	2.47	3.5	5.8
Population	1.5	1.5	2.3–3.0	3.1	2.5	2.0		1.2
Inflation				29.3	41.6	507.2	16.6	8.3
Agric./GDP		57.0	28.0	22.0	19.2	9.0		6.1
Exports/GDP						13.5	9.5	
Rural pop./total			70	44			22	16
Rural/urban pop.			70/30	44/56			22/78	16/84
Primary commodity exp./ total commodity exp.				99.0 (52.0)	64.0 (35.0)	43.0 (24.0)	31.0 (15.7)	

Note. Per capita GDP is estimated to have grown by 3.3% per year since 1930! (Angus Maddison and Assoc. 1992).

Sources:

GDP: 1920–45: Baer (2001: 39) 1950–2002: World Bank (January 2004: table 1). For the sub-period 1968–74, the annual growth averaged 11.3%.

Industry: 1920–45: Baer (2001:39). 1950–73: an arithmetical average of 1964–73 (Abreu, Bevilaqua, and Pinho (1997). 1971–94, 1995–99: Baer (2001: table A.1). 2002: World Bank, "Brazil at a Glance," September 3, 2003.

Agriculture: 1920–45: Baer (2001: 39); 1950–73, 1971–94: Baer (2001: table A.1); 1995–99, 2002: World Bank, "Brazil at a Glance," September 3, 2003. *Population:* 1920–45: Schuh and Alves (1970: 27); 1950s to 1980s: Baer (2001:66, 8): 8); 1998–2004: World Bank, "Brazil at a Glance," March 14, 2006.

Inflation: CPI, 1950–2002: World Bank (January 2004: table 1), World Bank "Brazil at a Glance," March 14, 2006: GDP implicit deflator, in annual percent: 2003, 15.2; 2004, 8.2.

Agric./GDP: 1933–39, 1939–45: Baer (2001: 39, 47). 1966 (in 1953 constant prices): Baer (2001: table 4.5). 1974–80: Baer (2001: table A.1). 1982, 2002: World Bank, "Brazil at a Glance," September 3, 2003.

Exports/GDP: Exports of goods and services/GDP: World Bank, "Brazil at a Glance," March 14, 2006. The estimates are for 1984, 1994, 2003 (0.164) and 2004 (0.18).

Rural pop./total: WDI Development Indicators.

Rural/urban pop. ratio: 1939–99: Baer (2001: 3). 2001–2002: World Bank, (2006a: 7). *Primary commodity exp.:* 1955–96: Baer (2001: table 11.1). These numbers include non-agricultural exports. The numbers in parentheses refer to only major agricultural commodities of coffee, sugar, soybeans, and their derivatives.

Table C.32. *Importance, Structure, and Growth of Brazilian Agriculture: Selected Indicators (Percent per Year, 1920–2002)*

	1920/22–1930/32	1930/32–1940/42	1940/42–1950/52	1950/52–1960/62	1967–70	1977–81	1981–86	1993–96	2002
Agric.labor/total labor		65.7	59.8	53.5	40	29	29	25	20.6
Agric./GDP		57.0	28.0	22.0		19.0	9.0	6.8	6.1
Total growth	2.9	6.3[a]	1.4	4.7	4.7	5.0	1.8		5.8
Exports	2.1	0.1	4.1	2.3					
Internal	5.1	-0.4	1.0	5.4					
Animal	1.4	0.6	2.6	4.2	2.3	5.1	-0.9	0.9	
Extractive plant products	4.8	23.1	0.5	5.9					

[a] This rate would be much lower at only 1% if the growth of extractive plant products were excluded.

Sources:

Agric. labor/total labor: 1930–1962: Schuh and Alves (1970: table 22). 1967–96: World Bank (2001/02) World Bank (2006a: 6) *Agric./GDP:* 1930–52: Baer (2001: 39, 47). 1966 (in 1953 constant prices): Baer (2001: table 4.5). 1974–80: Baer (2001: table A.1). 1982, 2002: World Bank, "Brazil at a Glance," September 3, 2003. 2007: 4.9%; World Bank, "Brazil at a Glance," September 24, 2008.

Total growth (of agricultural production): 1920–62: Schuh and Alves (1970: table 31). 1967–96: Baer (2001: table 31). 2002: World Bank, "Brazil at a Glance," September 3, 2003; "Country at a Glance," September 24, 2008: 1987–97: 2.1%; 1997–2007: 4.2%.

Export, internal, animal, and extractive plant products: growth rates of major components of total agricultural production: Schuh and Alves (1970: table 31). Extractive plant products are firewood and vegetable charcoal as replacements of liquid combustibles. 1977–1996 livestock: Baer (2001: table 15.1).

Table C.33. *Post-WWII Brazilian Agriculture: Relative Importance and Performance Indicators (Percent, 1950–85)*

	1950–60	1960–70	1970–80	1985
Sector shares in total output				
Agriculture	24	18	12	10
Industry	24	32	36	35
Services	52	50	52	55
Sector growth rates (annual averages)				
Agriculture	4.5	4.0	4.2	2.2
Industry	9.0	6.0	8.9	
Services	6.1	5.1	8.7	
Total	6.7	5.3	8.2	
Sector shares in employment				
Agriculture	60	54	44	29
Industry	14	13	18	22
Services	26	33	38	49
Sector share in total exports				
Agriculture	88	87	71	43

Sources: World Bank (July 1990: tables 1.1, 1.2, 1.3, 1.6). For the post 1985 years, in annual percent (World Bank, "Brazil at a Glance," March 14, 2006): 1984–94: 2.2%; 1994–2002: 4.1%; 2003: 5.5%; 2004: 5.3%. For more recent years, the average yearly growth rate for 1987–97 was 2.1%; that for 1997–2007 was 4.2%. However, as of the mid-1990s, Agric./GDP declined to around 5% (World Bank, "Brazil at a Glance," September 24, 2008).

Table C.34. *Evolution of Productivity Ratings, 1987–98*

Year	Crops	Livestock	Agriculture
1987	100	100	100
1992	103.6	110.0	105.7
1998	122.4	123.6	122.8

Source: Baumann (2002: table 6.6).

Chile

Table C.35. *Selected Socio-Economic Indicators, 1940–2001*

	1940s	1950s	1960s	1970s	1980s	1990s	2001
Growth (% per year)							
GDP		2.5	4.4	0.9	6.8	5.0	2.8
Agriculture	1.72	1.72	1.72	9.0[a]	7.4	1.8	6.5
Inflation		32.2	32.2	32.2	20.5	2.5	1.5
Population						1.2	
GDP per capita	2.0	0.3	2.3		5.0	3.6	1.5
Exports				9.0[b]	9.7	8.8	9.7
Structure (% of total)							
Agric./GDP	15.5	15.6	10.5	8.5	5.5	9.5	8.5
Rural/total			32.0	25.0	19.0	18.0	14.0
Exports/GDP					13.7	24.1	
Copper exports/total			70.5	70.5	47.3	40.1	37.0
Agric. exports /total			5.1	3.7	10.1	12.6	33.9
Human development indicators							
Poverty incidence (%)							
Lower					40	17	
Upper					47	21	
Infant mortality (per 1,000)			120	79.3	19.4		

[a] This high rate of 9% for the 1970s is somewhat misleading. It is very different from the rate given by another source, which puts it at roughly 3.2%, if one excludes the depressed growth of the 1970–73 years (Valdes et al., 1990: table 1–1B).
[b] Growth of only noncopper exports. The growth rate was negative for 1971–73.

Sources and Notes:
GDP growth rate: 1940s, 1937–52, 1970s: Valdes et al. (1990: 4, 5); 1950s–1960s: World Bank (January 1980: table I-5); 1980s–2001: World Bank, "Chile at a Glance," August 26, 2003. Total factor productivity growth for the 1986–2000 period is estimated to be 1.9% per year. The other two major factors accounting for the sustained and high growth are physical capital accumulation, growing at 2.5% per year, and labor and human capital at 2.% (World Bank, January 2002: table 2). 1997–2007: 3.8%; 2006: 4.3%; 2007: 5.1% (World Bank, "Chile at a Glance," September 24, 2008).
Agriculture growth rate: 1940s–1960s: Castillo and Lehman (1982: 3); 1973–1978: World Bank (January 1980: 184). The 1970–73 period had negative growth. 1980s–2001: World Bank, "Chile at a Glance," August 26, 2003. 1997–2007: 5.6%; World Bank, "Chile at a Glance," September 24, 2008.
Inflation rate: 1950s–1970s: These are estimates of the average compound annual rate for the period; World Bank (January 1980: 12–14). 1980s: Calvo and Mendoza (1999: 28); 1990s: the decline was gradual to single digits down to low levels. Zahler (1999: 56); 2001: World Bank (2003a: 63).
Population growth: World Bank, "Chile at a Glance," August 25, 2005; 1998–2004: in average annual percent.
GDP per capita: 1950s–1960s: World Bank (January 1980: table I-5); 1980s–2001: World Bank, "Chile at a Glance," August 26, 2003.
Exports: 1970s: World Bank (January 1980): table III-8. 1980s–2001: World Bank, "Chile at a Glance," August 26, 2003 and August 25, 2005. In annual percent, for 2003: 8.8; 2004: 8.9. 1997–2007: 2.6; 2006: 3.5; 2007: 4.1 (World Bank, "Chile at a Glance," September 24, 2008).
Agric./GDP: 1940s–1970s: World Bank (January 1980: table I-7); 1970s: Valdes et al. (1990: table 1–2) 1980s–2001: World Bank, "Chile at a Glance," August 26, 2003; 2006: 4.1%; World Bank, "Chile at a Glance," September 24, 2008.
Rural population/total population: 1960s–1980s: Valdes et al. (1990: table 1–1.A). 1991: Krueger et al. (eds., 2001: 101); World Bank, "Chile at a Glance," August 26, 2003.
Exports/GDP; exports of goods and services/GDP: World Bank "Chile at a Glance," August 25, 2005. Data are: for 1984, 1994, 2003, 0.24; for 2004, 0.23.
Copper exports/total exports: 1960s–1970s: World Bank (January 1980: 104); 1980s–1990s: World Bank (1998: box 4.5. "The returns from bold reforms: The case of Chile. 2001"
Agriculture exports/total exports: 1960s: Valdes et al. (1990: table 1–2); 1970s, 2001: World Bank (January 23, 2002); 1980s, 1990s: World Bank (1998. box 4.5). "The returns from bold reforms: The case of Chile; 2001": World Bank (January 2002: 3).
Poverty incidence: "Lower" refers to the extreme poor; "upper" to the less poor (World Bank, January 2002); World Bank (2002b: table 8).
Infant mortality: Valdes et al. (1990).

Table C.36. *Selected Indicators: Annual Growth and Protection Rates (1940–92)*

	Unit	1940–60	1960–70	1970–80	1975–80	1980–83	1983–89	1989–92
Agric. Growth	%	1.72	1.80	1.90	2.2	-1.0	5.1	3.0
GDP	%		4.2	2.5	7.5	-3.4	6.2	6.1
Rates of protection			60-64	65-69	70-74		75-79	80-84
Wheat	EPC		-0.37	-0.14	0.93		0.77	0.02
Cattle	EPC		-0.54	-0.47	-0.33		-0.16	0.03
Milk	EPC		0.00	-0.42	-0.25		0.28	0.01
Apples	EPC		-0.36	0.03	0.39		0.32	-0.20
Grapes	EPC		-0.37	-0.05	0.47		0.47	-0.10

Sources and Notes:

Agric. GDP growth rate: 1940–60: Castillo and Lehman (1982: 3). 1960–92: World Bank (August 1994: table 1). These agriculture GDP growth rates include forestry and fishing. For more recent years, in average annual percent: World Bank, "Chile at a Glance," August 25, 2005; 1984–94: 6.1; 1994–2004: 3.0; 2003: 3.3; 2004: 6.1.

GDP growth rate: 1960–92: World Bank (August 1994: table 1).

Effective protection coefficients (EPC) for wheat, cattle, milk, apples, grapes: 1960–1979: Valdes et al. (1990: table 3–8). These commodities account for around 43% of total value of crop production in 1969. In the later years, there was an increase in the share of fruit production. These are the most important commodities and representative of the policy regime.

Select Bibliography

Abdul Aziz Abdul Rahman. 1998. "Economic Reforms and Agricultural Development in Malaysia." *ASEAN Economic Bulletin* (Singapore) 15 (April): 59–76.

ABRARE. 2006. Ministry of Agriculture and Fisheries.

2007. Australian Commodity Statistics. http://www.nff.org.au/farm-facts.html.

2009. "Productivity Movements in Australian Agriculture." *Australian Commodities* 16 (1, March Quarter). http://www.abare.gov.au/interactive/09ac_mar/htm/a1.htm.

Abreu, Marcelo de P., Afonso S. Bevilaqua, and Demosthenes M.Pinho. 1997. "Import Substitution and Growth in Brazil, 1890s–1970s." Revised paper presented at a meeting in Paipa, Colombia, May 2–3, "Industrialisation and the State in Latin America," part of the IDB Project on the Economic History of Latin America in the 20th Century. http://www.econ.puc-rio.br/mpabreu/pdf/td366.pdf.

Acemoglu, Daron, Simon Johnson, and James A. Robinson. 2003. "An African Success Story: Botswana." In Dani Rodrik, ed., *In Search of Prosperity: Analytic Narratives on Economic Growth*, pp. 80–119, Princeton, NJ: Princeton University Press.

Acharya, S. S. 1997a. "Input subsidies in Indian Agriculture: Some Issues." In V. S Vyas and P. Bhargava, eds., *Policies for Agricultural Development*, pp. 87–119, Jaipur: Rawat Publications.

1997b. "Agricultural Price Policy and Development: Some Facts and Emerging Issues." Presidential address, 57th Annual Conference of Indian Society of Agricultural Economics, Thrissur, January 2–4,

Agenor, Pierre-Richard, and Karim El Aynaoui. July 2003. *Labor Market Policies and Unemployment in Morocco: A Quantitative Analysis*. World Bank Policy Research Working Paper No. 3091. Washington, D.C.: World Bank.

Agriculture and Agri-Food, Canada, 2007. "Profile of a Canadian farm family income in 2004". Research and Analysis Directorate, Strategic Policy Branch. December 2006. http://www4.agr.gc.ca/resources/prod/doc/pol/pub/2004tx_prfl/pdf/prof-04-fam_e.pdf

Ahluwalia, Deepak. March 2003. "Orissa Structural Adjustment Loan: Note on Agriculture Growth Issues." Draft. Washington, D.C.: World Bank.

Akiyama, Takimasa, and Donald F. Larson, eds. 2004. *Rural Development and Agricultural Growth in Indonesia, the Philippines and Thailand*. Canberra: Asia Pacific Press/ World Bank.

Ali, Muhammed. 2000. "Eradicating Corruption: The Singapore Experience." Paper presented at the Seminar on International Experiences on Good Governance and Fighting Corruption, Bangkok, February.

Allcott, Hunt, Daniel Lederman, and Ramon Lopez. April 2006. "Public Institutions, Inequality and Agricultural Growth: The Public Expenditure Connection." World Bank Research Working Paper No. 3902. Washington, D.C.: World Bank.

Alston, Julian, and Philip Pardey. 1996. *Making Science Pay: The Economics of Agricultural R&D Policy*. Washington, D.C.: American Enterprise Institute.

Anderson, Kym, and Alberto Valdes, eds. 2008a. *Distortions to Agricultural Incentives in Latin America*. Washington, D.C.: World Bank.

2008b. *Distortions to Agricultural Incentives in Latin America*. Washington, D.C.: World Bank.

Anderson, Kym, Ralph Lattimore, Peter Lloyd, and Donald Maclaren. September 2008. *Distortions to Agricultural Incentives in Australia and New Zealand*. World Bank Agricultural Distortions Working Paper No. 9. http://siteresources.worldbank.

org/INTTRADERESEARCH/Resources/544824–1163022714097/Australia_
NZ_0908.pdf.

Angus Maddison and Associates. 1992. *The Political Economy of Poverty, Equity, and Growth: Brazil and Mexico.* Oxford: Oxford University Press for the World Bank.

Anwar, Talat, Sarfraz K.Qureshi, and Hammad Ali. 2003. "Landlessness and Rural Poverty in Pakistan." http://www.pide.org.pk/pdf/psde20AGM/Landlessness%20 and%20Rural%20Poverty%20in%20Pakistan.pdf.

Armington, Paul, S. 1969. "A Theory of Demand for Products Distinguished by Place of Production." *International Monetary Fund Staff Papers,* XVI, (1969), 159–76.

Ashley, Caroline, and Maxwell Simon. 2001. "Rethinking Rural Development." *Development Policy Review* 19 (4): 395–425.

Asian Legal Resource Centre. February 27, 2009. "Violations of Rights under Failing Land Reforms." http://www.alrc.net/doc/mainfile.php/alrc_st2009/540/.

Aubert, Claude, and Li, Xiande. 2002. "'Peasant Burden': Taxes and Levies Imposed on Chinese Farmers." In *China in the Global Economy – Agricultural Policies in China after the WTO Accession.* OECD.

Australian Government, Department of Agriculture, Fisheries and Forestry. 2005. *Australian Agriculture and the Food Sector: Stocktake.* Canberra.

Australian Government, Department of the Treasury. 2002. *Australia's Century since the Federation at a Glance.* Parkes.

Australian Government Productivity Commission. 2005. *Trends in Australian Agriculture: Productivity Commission Research Paper.* http://www.pc.gov.au/__data/assets/pdf_ file/0018/8361/agriculture.pdf.

Australian Government, Department of Agriculture, Fisheries and Forestry. 2005, 2008. http://www.daff.gov.au/

Au Yeung, Jean. 2000. "Fighting Corruption: The Hong Kong Experience." Paper presented at the Seminar on International Experiences on Good Governance and Fighting Corruption, Bangkok, February.

Avillez, Francisco. 1993. "Portuguese Agriculture and the Common Agricultural Policy." In Jose Da Silva Lopes, ed., *Portugal and EC Membership Evaluated,* pp. 30–50, London: Pinter Publishers / New York: St. Martin's Press.

Avillez, Francisco, Timothy J. Finan, and Timothy Josling. 1988. *Trade, Exchange Rates and Agricultural Pricing in Portugal.* World Bank Comparative Studies: the Political Economy of Agricultural Pricing Policy. Washington, D.C.: World Bank.

Baer, Werner. 2001. *The Brazilian Economy: Growth and Development,* 5th ed. New York: Praeger.

Baer, Werner, and Antonio Nogeira Leite. 2003. "The Economy of Portugal Within the European Union: 1990–2002." *Quarterly Review of Economics and Finance,* 43: 738–54.

Baganha, Maria Oannis B. 1998. "From Close to Open Doors: Portuguese Emigration under the Corporative Regime." Universidades de Coimbra. http://ies.berkeley.edu/ research/files/CP02/CP02-Close_to_Open_Doors.pdf.

Baioa, Manuel, Paulo Jorge Fernandes, and Filipe Ribeiro de Meneses. 2003. "The Political History of Twentieth Century Portugal." *E-Journal of Portuguese History* 1(2). http:// www.brown.edu/Departments/Portuguese_Brazilian_Studies/ejph/html/issue2/pdf/ baioa.pdf.

Balisacan, Arsenio M., and Hal Hill. 2003. "An Introduction to the Key Issues." In Arsenio M. Balisacan and Hal Hill, eds., *The Philippine Economy: Development Policies, and Challenges,* 1–44. Oxford: Oxford University Press.

Ban, Sung Hwan. 1979. "Agricultural Growth in Korea, 1918–1971." In Yujiro Hayami, Vernon M. Ruttan, and Herman M. Southworth, eds., *Agricultural Growth in Japan, Taiwan, Korea, and the Philippines*, pp. 90–116, Honolulu: University Press of Hawaii for the East–West Center.

Ban, Sung Hwan, Pal Yong Moon, and Dwight H Perkins. 1980. *Studies in the Modernization of Republic of Korea: 1945–1975, Rural Development.* Cambridge, MA: Harvard University, Council on East Asian Studies.

Bandarra, Nelly Jazra. 2002. "Les perspectives de développement rural au Portugal." *Revue du Marche Commun et de l'Union Européenne*, No. 454: 44–54.

Baran, Paul. 1952. *The Political Economy of Underdevelopment.* Manchester School. Manchester: Manchester University Press.

Barton, Glen T., and Martin Cooper. 1948. "Relation of Agricultural Production to Inputs." *Review of Economics and Statistics* 30 (May): 117–26.

Bateman, Merill J., Alexander Meeraus, David M. Newberry, William Asenso Okyere, and Gerald T. O'Mara. June 1990. *Ghana's Cocoa Pricing Policy.* Agriculture and Rural Development Department, WPS 429. Washington, D.C.: World Bank.

Bates, Robert H. 1998. "The Political Framework of Agricultural Policy Decisions." In Carl K. Eicher and John M. Staatz, eds., *International Agricultural Development*, 3d ed., 234–39. Baltimore: Johns Hopkins University Press. Originally titled "The Political Framework for Price Policy Decisions." In Charles Mann and Barbara Huddleston, eds., 1985 *Food Policy Frameworks for Analysis and Action*, Terra Haute: Indiana State University Press.

Baulch, Robert and Neil McCulloch. 2000. "Tracking pro-poor growth." ID21 insights No. 31. Sussex: Institute of Development Studies.

Baumann, Renato. 2002. *Brazil in the 1990s: An Economy in Transition.* London: Palgrave in association with St. Anthony's College, Oxford.

Beesly, Timothy, Robin Burgess, and Berta Esteve-Volart. September 2004. "Operationalizing Pro-poor Growth: India Case Study." Study prepared for the World Bank Pro-Poor Growth Project.

Berkson, William. 1989. "Testability in the Social Sciences." *Philosophy of Social Sciences* 19: 157–71.

Besancon, Marie. 2003. "Good Governance Rankings: The Art of Measurement." World Peace Foundation, WPF Program on Intrastate Conflict and Conflict Resolution, John F. Kennedy School of Government, Harvard University, Cambridge, MA. http://belfercenter.ksg.harvard.edu/files/wpf36governance.pdf.

Bhalla, G. S. 1995. "Agricultural Growth and Industrial Development in Punjab." In John W. Mellor, ed., *Agriculture on the Road to Industrialization*, pp. 67–112, Baltimore: Johns Hopkins University Press for the International Food Policy Research Institute.

Bielenberg, N. P. October 22, 2002. "The Irish Land Commission and the Evolution of Land Law in Ireland and Its Impact on the Agricultural Economy." Stewart's Limited Farm Management Consultants, Property Valuers and Compensation Consultants. http://www.everysite.co.uk/sources/4000104/4000747/4029478/Eire. pdf?id=4029478.

Binswanger, Hans P. 1994. "Agricultural and Rural Development: Painful Lessons." Simon Brandt Address, delivered September 21, 1994, at the 32d annual meeting of the Agricultural Economics Association of South Africa, Pretoria. Reprinted in Carl K. Eicher and John M. Staatz, eds., *International Agricultural Development*, 3d ed. Baltimore: Johns Hopkins University Press, 1998.

Binswanger, Hans P., and Klaus Deininger. 1997. "Explaining Agricultural and Agrarian Policies in Developing Countries." *Journal of Economic Literature* 35 (4): 1958–2005.

Binswanger-Mkhize, Hans, P., and Alex F. McCalla. 2010. "The Changing Context and Prospects for Agricultural and Rural Development in Africa." In Prabhu Pingali and Robert Evenson, eds., *Handbook of Agricultural Economics*, Vol. 4, pp. 3571–3712. Amsterdam: Elsevier.

Blair, David. November 2008. "Somalia: Analysis of a Failed State." http://www.telegraph.co.uk/news/worldnews/africaandindianocean/somalia/3479010/Somalia-Analysis-of-a-failed-state.html.

Blanco, Luisa, and Robin Grier. 2007. "Long Live Democracy: The Determinants of Political Instability in Latin America." http://www.ou.edu/cas/econ/wppdf/instabili-tyinla%20rg.pdf.

Blaug, Mark. 1997. *Economic Theory in Retrospect*, 5th ed. Cambridge: Cambridge University Press.

Bloome, Peter. 1993. "Privatization Lessons for U.S. Extension from New Zealand and Tasmania." *Journal of Extension* (International ed.) 31 (1). http://www.joe.org/joe/1993spring/intl1.php.

Brandao, Antonio Salazar T., and Jose L. Carvalho. November 1991. *Trade, Exchange, and Agricultural Pricing Policies in Brazil*, Vol. 1. World Bank Country Study. Washington, D.C.: World Bank.

Brandt, Loren. 1993. "Interwar Japanese agriculture: Revisionist Views on the Impact of Colonial Rice Policy and the Labor-Surplus Hypothesis." *Explorations in Economic History*, 30: 259–93.

Bravo-Ortega, Claudio, and Daniel Lederman. 2005. "Agriculture and National Welfare around the World: Causality and Heterogeneity since 1960." Policy Research Working Paper No. 3499. Washington, D.C.: World Bank.

Brookfield, Harold, ed. 1994. *Transformation with Industrialization in Peninsular Malaysia*. Oxford: Oxford University Press.

Brotherhood of St. Laurence. July 2002. "Poverty: Facts, Figures, and Suggestions for the Future: Australia." http://www.bsl.org.au/pdfs/poverty.pdf.

Byerlee, Derek, Xinshen Diao, and Chris Jackson. 2005. *Agriculture, Rural Development and Pro-Poor Growth: Country Experiences in the Post-Reform Era*. Agriculture and Rural Development (ARD) Discussion Paper, 21, Report No. 37058. Washington, D.C.: World Bank.

Cairns Group, 2005. http://cairnsgroup.org/Pages/050706_g8.aspx.

Calkins, Peter, Wen S. Chern, and Francis C. Tuan, eds. 1992. *Rural Development in Taiwan and Mainland China*. Boulder, CO: Westview Press.

Calvo, Guillermo, and Enrique G. Mendoza. 1999. "Empirical Puzzles of Chilean Stabilization Policy." In Guillermo Perry and Danny M. Leipziger, eds., *Chile: Recent Policy Lessons and Emerging Challenges*, 25–54. Washington, D.C.: World Bank Institute.

Canadian Encyclopedia: Agriculture Research and Development. 2011 Historica Dominion. Agricultural Research and Development. Article by Bertrand Forest. http://www.thecanadianencyclopedia.com/index.cfm?PgNm=TCE&Params=A1SE C815710).

Canadian Encyclopedia Historica. The article is entitled "Agricultural Research and Development" Article by Bertrand Forest The Canadian Encyclopedia © 2011 Historica-Dominion http://www.thecanadianencyclopedia.com/index.cfm?PgNm=TCE&Params=A1ARTA0000070.

Canadian Federation of Agriculture. September 1, 2008. "Impact of Agriculture." http://www.cfa-fca.ca/pages/index.php?main_id=72.

Canadian Government. November 2006. *The Next Generation of Agriculture and Agri-Food Policy, Federal, Provincial and Territorial Initiative – Economic Background: Changing Structure of Primary Agriculture.* http://www4.agr.gc.ca/AAFC-AAC/display-afficher.do?id=1201189157429&lang=eng

Castillo, Leonardo, and David Lehmann. January 1982. "Agrarian Reform and Structural Change in Chile: 1965–79." In "Rural Employment Policy Research Program," Working Paper WEP 10–6/WP53:1–30. International Labor Office, Geneva. Central Intelligence Agency. The WorldFactbook. https://www.cia.gov/library/publications/the-world-factbook/rankorder/2172rank.html

Chacko, K. C. 1997. *Economic Development of India and the Experiences from Other Major Economically Developed Countries.* New Delhi: Vikas.

Chai, Joseph, C. H. 1992. "Consumption and Living Standards in China." In *The China Quarterly*, No. 131, Special Issue: The Chinese Economy in the 1990s (September 1992), pp. 721–749.

Chambers, J. D., and G. E. Mingay. 1966. *The Agricultural Revolution, 1650–1880.* London: B. T. Batsford.

Chance, Hon. Kim. February 2003. "Managing Climate Risk in Agriculture." Freemantle, Australia. http://www.aares.info/files/2003_chance.pdf.

Chapman, Graham. 1982. "The Green Revolution Game: A Gaming Simulation." The Green Revolution Partnership. grahampchapman@googlemail.com.

Chapman, Graham, and Isabelle Tsakok. 1989. *Exaction: A Gaming Simulation of National Development.* Lancaster: Development Policy.

Chenery H., and T. N. Srinivasan, eds. 1988. *Handbook of Development Economics*, Vol. 1, pp. 276–331 Amsterdam: Elsevier.

Chu, Henry, and Jerry Hirsch. 2005. "Brazil's Rise as Farming Giant Has Price Tag." *Los Angeles Times*, August 21, http://articles.latimes.com/2005/aug/21/world/fg-brazag21.

Chu, Ke-young, Hamid Davoodi, and Sanjeev Gupta. 2000. "Income Distribution and Tax and Government Social Spending Policies in Developing Countries." International Monetary Fund Working Paper WP/00/62.

Chung, Yung Il. 1990. "The Agricultural Foundation of Korean Industrial Development." In H. Lee Chung and Yamazawa, Ippei, eds., *The Economic Development of Japan and Korea: A Parallel with Lessons.* Westport, CT: Praeger.

Clark, Gregory. 2005. "The Condition of the Working Class in England, 1209–2004." *Journal of Political Economy* 113 (6): 1307–40.

Clark, Sally H. 1994. *Regulation and the Revolution in United States Farm Productivity.* New York: Cambridge University Press.

Cleaver, Kevin. January 1982. *The Agricultural Development Experience of Algeria, Morocco and Tunisia.* Staff Working Paper, # 552. Washington, D.C.: the World Bank.

Cochrane, Willard W., and Mary E. Ryan. 1976. *American Farm Policy, 1948–1973.* Minneapolis: University of Minnesota Press.

Cockcroft, James D. 1998. *Mexico's Hope: An Encounter with Politics and History.* New York: Monthly Review Press.

Coelli, T. J., and D. S. Prasada Rao. 2003. *Total Factor Productivity Growth in Agriculture: A Malmquist Index Analysis for 93 Countries, 1980–2000.* Working Paper No. 02/2003, Centre for Efficiency and Productivity Analysis, School of Economics, University of Queensland.

Collier, Paul. 2007. *The Bottom Billion: Why the Poorest Countries Are Failing and What Can Be Done About It*. Oxford: Oxford University Press.

Collyer, Michael. 2004. *The Development Impact of International Labour Migration on Southern Mediterranean Sending Countries: Contrasting Examples of Morocco and Egypt*. Working Paper T6. Sussex Centre for Migration Research. http://www.files. emigration.gov.eg/Upload/Publications/English/16/temporatyintenrationalmigra-tionegyptmorocco.pdf.

Connolly, L. A. Kinsella, G. Quinlan, and B. Moran. December 2008. "Farm Incomes, 2007." *Situation and Outlook in Agriculture, 2008/09*, pp. 1–12. Compiled by Marian Moloney, Teagasc, Rural Economy Research Centre. http://www.agresearch.teagasc. ie/rerc/downloads/SitOutl_2008_Proceedings_a.pdf.

Corkill, David. 1993. *The Portuguese Economy since 1974*. Edinburgh: Edinburgh University Press.

1999. *The Development of the Portuguese Economy: A Case of Europeanization*. Contemporary Economic History of Europe Series. London: Routledge.

Cortbridge, Stuart, and Gareth A. Jones. 2006. "The Continuing Debate About Urban Bias: The Thesis, Its Critics, Its Influence and Implications for Poverty Reduction." London School of Economics and Political Science, Department of Geography and Environment. http://www2.lse.ac.uk/geographyAndEnvironment/research/ researchpapers/99%20corbridge%20jones.pdf.

Cuddihy, William. April 1980. *Agricultural Price Management in Egypt*. Agriculture and Rural Development Department. Staff Working Paper No. 388. Washington, D.C.: World Bank.

Curtin, Chris, Trutz Haase, and Hillary Tovey, eds. 1996. *Poverty in Rural Ireland: A Political Economy Perspective*. Dublin: Oak Tree Press in association with the Combat Poverty Agency Report Series. http://www.nationsencyclopedia.com/Europe/Ireland-ECONOMY.html.

Dalziel, Paul. July 1999. "New Zealand's Economic Reform Programme Was a Failure." http://jtc.blogs.com/dalziel-1999.pdf.

Danbom, David B. 1979. *The Resisted Revolution: Urban America and the Industrialization of Agriculture, 1900–1930*. Ames: Iowa State University Press.

Dasgupta, Ajit K. 1978. *Agriculture and Economic Development in India*. New Delhi: Associated Publishing House.

Da Silva Lopes, Jose, ed. 1993. *Portugal and EC membership Evaluated*. London: Pinter Publishers.

Day, Richard H. 1967. "The Economics of Technological Change and the Demise of the Sharecropper." *American Economic Review* 67 (June): 427–49.

Debatisse, Michel, Isabelle Tsakok, Dina Umali, Stijn Claessens, and Kutlu Somel. November 1993. "Risk Management in Liberalizing Economies: Issues of Access to Food and Agricultural Futures and Options Markets." Europe and Central Asia Regional Office. Middle East and North Africa Regional Office. Technical Department Report No. 12220 ECA. Washington, D.C.: World Bank.

Deininger, Klaus. 2003. *Land Policies for Growth and Poverty Reduction*. World Bank Policy Research Report. Washington, D.C.: World Bank / Oxford: Oxford University Press.

Deininger, Klaus, and Gershon Feder. 2001. "Land Institutions and Land Rights." In Bruce L. Gardner and Gordon C. Rausser, eds. *Handbook of Agricultural Economics*. Vol. 1A: *Agricultural Production*, pp. 287–331. Amsterdam: Elsevier.

De Gorter, Harry, and Johan Swinnen. 2002. "Political Economy of Agricultural Policy." In Bruce L. Gardner and Gordon C. Rausser, eds., *Handbook of Agricultural Economics*. Vol. 2B: *Agricultural and Food Policy*: 1893–1943. Amsterdam: Elsevier.

De Janvry, Alain, and Elizabeth Sadoulet. June 2002. "Land Reforms in Latin America: Ten Lessons Towards a Contemporary Agenda." University of California at Berkeley. http://are.berkeley.edu/~sadoulet/papers/Land_Reform_in_LA_10_lesson.pdf.

De Mesquita, Bruce Bueno, and Hilton L. Root, eds. 2000. *Governing for Prosperity*. New Haven, CT: Yale University Press.

Dernberger, Robert F. 1999. "The People's Republic of China at 50: The Economy." In Richard Louis Edmonds, ed., *The People's Republic after 50 Years*, pp. 44–53, Oxford: Oxford University Press.

Dethier, Jean-Jacques. 1989. *Trade, Exchange Rate and Agricultural Pricing Policies in Egypt*. Vol. 1: *Country Study. The Political Economy of Agricultural Pricing Policies*. Report No. 9802. World Bank Comparative Studies. Washington, D.C.: World Bank.

Dorward, Andrew, Jonathan Kydd, and Colin Poulton. 2006. "Traditional Domestic Markets and Marketing Systems for Agricultural Products." Background paper # 41359 to World Development Report 2008.

Drabble, John H. 2000. *An Economic History of Malaysia, c.1800–1990 – The Transition to Modern Economic Growth*. London: MacMillan Press/New York: St. Martin's Press in association with the Australian National University.

Easterly, William. 2001. *The Elusive Quest for Growth: Economists' Adventures and Misadventures in the Tropics*. Cambridge, MA: MIT Press.

Ebel, Beth. 1991. *Patterns of Government Expenditure in Developing Countries During the 1980s: The Impact on Social Services*. UNICEF International Child Development Centre, Innocenti Occasional Papers, Economic Policy Series, No. 18. Florence: Spedale degli Innocenti.

Eberstadt, Nicholas. 1996. "Material Progress in Korea since Partition." In Ramon H. Myers, ed., *The Wealth of Nations: The Policies and Institutional Determinants of Economic Development*, pp. 131–163, Stanford, CA: Hoover Institution Press.

Economicexpert.com. 2003. "Agriculture in Australia, Agriculture Marketing Act." http://www.economicexpert.com/s/agriculture:in:australia.html.

Economist. 2005. "China's Land Disputes: Turning Ploughshares into Staves." June 23.

Econtech. 2005. *Australia's Farm-Dependent Economy: Analysis of the Role of Agriculture in the Australian Economy*. Farm Institute, Surry Hills.

Edwards, Sebastian, Gerardo Esquivel, and Graciela Marquez, eds., 2007. *The Decline of Latin American Economies: Growth, Institutions, and Crises*. Chicago: University of Chicago Press.

Eicher, Carl K., and John M. Staatz, eds. 1998. *International Agricultural Development*, 3d ed. Baltimore: Johns Hopkins University Press.

El-Ghomeny, Riad M., ed. 2003. *Egypt in the Twenty-First Century: Challenges for Development*. London: Routledge Curzon Taylor and Francis Group.

Essakali, Mohamed Dalil. December 2005. "Rural Access and Mobility in Pakistan: A Policy Note." Transport Note No. TRN-28. Washington, D.C.: World Bank.

European Commission, Agriculture and Rural Development. July 2009. "Turkey: Agriculture and the Enlargement." http://ec.europa.eu/agriculture/enlargement/countries/turkey/profile_en.pdf.

Fan, Shengen, ed. 2008. *Public Expenditures, Growth and Poverty: Lessons from Developing Countries*. International Food Policy Research Institute (IFPRI). Baltimore: Johns Hopkins University Press.

Fane, George, and Peter Warr. 2003. "How Economic Growth Reduces Poverty: A General Equilibrium Analysis for Indonesia." In Ralph van der Hoeven and Anthony Shorrocks, eds., *Perspectives on Growth and Poverty*, pp. 217–234, Tokyo: WIDER: United Nations University Press.

FAO. 2000. "Turkey: Country Profile." *New Agriculturalist.* http://www.new-ag.info//country/profile.php?a=878.

Farrell, Maura, JohnMcDonagh, and Marie Mahon. 2008. "Agricultural Extension Advisory Services: The Challenge of Implementing a Multifunctional Advisory Programme." Rural Economy Research Center (RERC), Teagasc, Athenry 1, Geography Department, National University of Ireland, Galway 2. Working Paper Series, Working Paper 08-WP-RE-06. http://www.teagasc.ie/advanced_search.asp.

FAS online. August 29, 2005. "Expenditures and Activities of Cairns Group Countries: Australia." http://ffas.usda.gov/cmp/com-study/1998/comp98-au.html.

Faucette, Judith. June 28, 2008. "Historic Maori Land Compensation Agreement: New Zealand Agrees to Largest Indigenous Land Settlement to Date." http://australian-indigenous-peoples.suite101.com/article.cfm/historic_maori_land_compensation_agreement.

Federico, Giovanni. 2005. *Feeding the World: An Economic History of Agriculture, 1800–2000.* Princeton, NJ: Princeton University Press.

Fei, John C. H., and Gustav Ranis. 1964. *Development of the Labor Surplus Economy: Theory and Policy.* Homewood, IL: Irwin.

Fei, John C. H., Gustav Ranis, and Shirley W. Y. Kuo, with the assistance of Bian Yu-Yuan and Julia Chang Collins. 1979. *Growth with Equity: The Taiwan Case.* Oxford: Oxford University Press for World Bank Research Publication.

Fleck, Susan. 1994. "Employment and Unemployment in Mexico's Labor Force: Cover Story." *Monthly Labor Review*, November. http://findarticles.com/p/articles/mi_m1153/is_n11_v117/ai_16040951/?tag=content;col1.

Focus Migration. 2009. *Country Profile: Morocco.* No. 16. Hamburg Institute of International Economics. http://www.focus-migration.de/typo3_upload/groups/3/focus_Migration_Publikationen/Laenderprofile/CP_16_Morocco.pdf.

Fogel, Robert William. 2004. *The Escape from Hunger and Premature Death, 1700–2100: Europe, America and the Third World.* Cambridge: Cambridge University Press.

Foster, William, and Alberto Valdes. 2008. "Structural Characteristics of Chilean Agricultural Households: A Typology of Rural Households and Income Determinants from the 2003 CASEN." Background paper to OECD. 2008. *Review of Agricultural Policies: Chile.*

Fosu, Augustin Kwasi. 2002. "Political Instability and Economic Growth: Implications of Coup Events in Sub-Saharan Africa – New Perspectives on Transition Economies: Africa." *American Journal of Economics and Sociology* (January). http://findarticles.com/p/articles/mi_m0254/is_1_61/ai_84426604/?tag=content;col1.

Frank, Jeffrey. November 2002. "Two Models of Land Reform and Development in Brazil." http://www.thirdworldtraveler.com/South_America/Land_Reform_Brazil.html.

Freedman, David A. 1991. "Statistical Models and Shoe Leather." *Sociological Methodology* 21: 291–313. http://www.wprod.rochester.edu/college/psc/clarke/204/Freedman91.pdf

Freire, Dulce, and Shawn Parkhurst. 2002. "Where Is Portuguese Agriculture Headed? An Analysis of the Common Agricultural Policy." Prepared for the conference on the European Union, Nation-States and the Quality of Democracy: Lessons from Southern Europe, University of California at Berkeley, October 31–November 2, 2002.

Fulghiniti, Lybian E., and Richard K. Perrin. 1993. "Prices and Productivity in Agriculture." *Review of Economics and Statistics* 75 (3): 471–82.

Furtado, Celso. 1976. *Economic Development of Latin America: Historical Background and Contemporary Problems.* Translated by Suzette Macedo. Cambridge Latin American Studies, No. 8. Cambridge: Cambridge University Press.

Garcia, Victor, and Laura Gonzalez Martinez. December 1999. *Guanajuatense and Other Mexican Immigrants to the United States: New Communities in Non-Metropolitan and Agricultural Regions.* Julian Samora Research Institute, Working Paper No. 47. http://www.jsri.msu.edu/RandS/research/wps/wp47.pdf.

Gardner, Bruce L. 2002. *American Agriculture in the Twentieth Century: How It Flourished and What It Cost.* Cambridge, MA: Harvard University Press.

Gardner, Bruce L., and Gordon C. Rausser, eds. 2002. *Handbook of Agricultural Economics.* Vol. 2B: *Agricultural and Food Policy.* Amsterdam: North-Holland, Elsevier.

Gillmor, Desmond A. 1987. "The Political Factor in Agricultural History: Trends in Irish Agriculture, 1922–85." *Agriculture History Review* 37 (2): 166–79. http://www.bahs.org.uk/37n2a5.pdf.

Glaeser, Edward L., and Claudia Goldin, eds. 2006. *Corruption and Reform: Lessons from America's Economic History.* Chicago: University of Chicago Press.

Glass, J. C., and D. G. McKillop. 1990. "Production Interrelationships and Productivity Measurements in Irish Agriculture." *European Journal of Agricultural Economics* 17 (3): 271–87.

Gopinath, Munisamy, and Terry L. Roe. 1997. "Source of Sectoral Growth in an Economy Wide Context: The Case of U.S. Agriculture." *Journal of Productivity Analysis* 8: 293–310.

Gordon, Thiessen. 1999. "Canadian Economic Performance at the End of the Century." Remarks by Gordon Thiessen, Governor of the Bank of Canada to the Canada Club, London, June, 2. http://www.bank-banque-canada.ca/en/speeches/1999/sp99–5.pdf.

Government of Malaysia. 2004. *Malaysia: 30 years of Poverty Reduction, Growth and Racial Harmony.* Economic Planning Unit, Prime Minister's Department. Malaysia. A Case Study from Scaling Up Poverty Reduction: A Global Learning Process and Conference. Shanghai, May 25–27. World Bank Document 30782. http://www-wds.worldbank.org/external/default/WDSContentServer/WDSP/IB/2004/12/06/0000 90341_20041206100324/Rendered/PDF/307820Malaysia01see0also0307591.pdf.

Government of Morocco. 2008. *Plan Maroc Vert.* Ministère de l'Agriculture et des Pêches Maritimes. Rabat.

Government of New Zealand. October 24. "Growing for Food." Parliamentary Commissioner for the Environment. Ke Kaitiaki, Taiao a Te Whare Paremata, Wellington. http://www.pce.govt.nz/reports/allreports/1_877274_51_8_summary.pdf.

Government of New Zealand, Ministry of Agriculture and Forestry. 2003. "New Zealand: An Agriculture and Forestry Exporting Nation." http://www.maf.govt.nz/mafnet/rural-nz/overview/nzoverview006.htm.

Government of New Zealand, Ministry of Economic Development. December 2007. "Well-being and Prosperity: Economic Development Indicators, 2007." http://www.med.govt.nz/templates/MultipageDocumentPage____32726.aspx.

Government of New Zealand, Ministry of Social Development. "The Social Report, 2008." http://www.socialreport.msd.govt.nz/economic-standard-living/income-inequality.html.

Greasley, David. 2005. "Refrigeration and Distribution: New Zealand Land Prices and Real Wages 1873–1939." *Australian Economic Review* 45: 23–44. http://www.econ.canterbury.ac.nz/personal_pages/les_oxley/pdf_files/greasley_oxley_refrigeration.pdf.

Grigg, David. 1992. *The Transformation of Agriculture in the West*. Oxford: Blackwell.

Griliches, Zvi. 1957. "Hybrid Corn: An Exploration of the Economics of Technological Change." *Econmetrica* 25: 501–22.

Grindle, Merilee S. 1988. *Searching for Rural Development: Labor Migration and Employment in Mexico*. Ithaca, NY: Cornell University Press.

Gujarati, Damodar N. 2003. *Basic Econometrics*, 4th ed. New York: McGraw-Hill.

Gulati, Ashok, and Sudha Narayanan. 2003. *The Subsidy Syndrome in Indian Agriculture*. New Delhi: Oxford University Press.

Gwartney, James, Richard Stroup, Russell Sobel, and David Macpherson. 2009. "Institutions, Policies and the Irish Miracle: Ireland's U Turn." Mason, Ohio: Thomson South-Western.

Hagen, Everett E. 1962. *On the Theory of Social Change: How Economic Growth Begins*. Homewood, IL: Dorsey Press .

Hall, Julia, and Grant Scobie. March 2006. "The Role of R&D in Productivity Growth: The Case of New Zealand Agriculture 1927–2001." New Zealand Treasury Working Paper 06/01. http://www.treasury.govt.nz/publications/research-policy/wp/2006/06–01.

Hansen, Bent. 1991. *The Political Economy of Poverty, Equity and Growth: Egypt and Turkey*. World Bank Comparative Study. Oxford: Oxford University Press for the World Bank.

Harte, L. N. 2002. "Questioning Agricultural Policy in the Modern Irish Economy." University College, Department of Agribusiness and Rural Development, Dublin. www.teagasc.ie.

Hartwell, Ronald Max, et al. 1972. *The Long Debate on Poverty: Eight Essays on Industrialization and the "Condition of England."* London: Institute of Economic Affairs.

Harvard – Stanford Poverty Team. 1992. Indonesia: The Poverty Report.

Havens, A. E., and E. M. Rogers. 1961. "Adoption of Hybrid Corn: Profitability and the Interaction Effect." *Rural Sociology* 26: 409–14.

Hayami, Y., and V. Ruttan. 1985. *Agricultural Development: An International Perspective*, rev. ed. Baltimore: Johns Hopkins University Press.

Hayami, Yujiro, Vernon M. Ruttan, and Herman M. Southworth, eds. 1979. *Agricultural Growth in Japan, Taiwan, Korea, and the Philippines*. Honolulu: University Press of Hawaii for the East–West Center.

Hayami, Yujiro, Ma. Agnes R. Quisumbing, and Lourdes S. Adriano. 1990. *Toward an Alternative Land Reform Paradigm: A Philippine Perspective*. Quezon City: Ateneo de Manila University Press.

Heckelman, Jac C., and Dennis Coates, eds. 2003. *Collective Choice: Essays in Honor of Mancur Olson*. Berlin: Springer.

Hedley, D., and L. Lu. 2004. "The Impact of the 2002–03 Drought on the Economy and Agricultural Employment." *Economic Roundup* (Autumn), The Treasury, Canberra.

Henzell, Ted. 2007. *Australian Agriculture: Its History and Challenges*. http://books. google.com/books?id=vNj-OKU4CFwC&dq=henzell++on+Australian+agricultu re&printsec=frontcover&source=bl&ots=NLe-Wdz02C&sig=Oi3_oVgF813vP-ORyOn0541YpMw&hl=zh-CN&ei=Nlv4SaPXEsWHtgeXiLHtDw&sa=X&oi=b ook_result&ct=result&resnum=1#PPP1,M1.

Hicks, Sir John. 1969. *A Theory of Economic History*. Oxford: Oxford University Press.

Hill, Hal. 2000. *The Indonesian Economy*, 2d ed. Cambridge: Cambridge University Press.

Hirschman, Albert O. 1958. *The Strategy of Economic Development*. Yale Studies in Economics, 10. New Haven, CT: Yale University Press.

Ho, Samuel P. S. 1978. *Economic Development of Taiwan, 1860–1970.* New Haven, CT: Yale University Press.

——— 1994. *Rural China in Transition: Non-Agricultural Development in Rural Jiangsu, 1978–90.* Oxford: Clarendon Press.

House, Anthony. February 28, 2001. "Terra Nullius and Australian Colonialism." History 101–01. http://ptomng.com/z2001terranullius.htm   http://www.treasury.gov.au/documents/110/PDF/round3.pdf.

Hubbard, Glenn R, and William Duggan. 2009. *The Aid Trap.* New York: Columbia University Press.

Huffman, Wallace E., and RobertEvenson. 1993. *Science for Agriculture.* Ames: Iowa State University Press.

Huppi, Monika, and Martin Ravallion. 1991. "Sectoral Structure of Poverty During an Adjustment Period: Evidence for Indonesia in the mid-1980s." *World Development* (UK) 19 (December): 1653–78.

Hurt, R. Douglas. 1994. *American Agriculture: A Brief History.* Ames: Iowa State University Press.

Iacocca, Lee. 1986. *Iacocca: An Autobiography.* New York: Bantam Books.

Intal, Ponciano S., Jr., and John H. Power. 1990. *Trade, Exchange Rate and Agricultural Pricing Policies in the Philippines.* The Political Economy of Agricultural Pricing. World Bank Comparative Studies. Washington, D.C.: World Bank.

International Finance Corporation. 2007. *Health in Africa.* Sec. III: *The Case for Investing in Private Health Care Sector in Sub-Saharan Africa.* http://www.ifc.org/ifcext/healthinafrica.nsf/AttachmentsByTitle/IFC_HealthinAfrica_Sec3/$FILE/IFC_HealthInAfrica_Sec3.pdf.

International Fund for Agricultural Development (IFAD) August 2006. *Republic of Turkey: Country Strategic Opportunities Paper.* Report no. EB 2006/88/R.12 http://www.ifad.org/gbdocs/eb/88/e/EB-2006-88-R-12.pdf

"Ireland Economy." *Encyclopaedia of Nations.* http://www.nationsencyclopedia.com/Europe/Ireland-ECONOMY.html.

Jansen, Marius B., and Gilbert Rozman, eds. 1986. *Japan in Transition: From Tokugawa to Meiji.* Princeton, NJ: Princeton University Press.

Jayne, T. S., Takashi Yamano, Michael T. Weber, David Tschirley, Rui Benfika, Antonio Chapoto, and Ballard Zulu. 2003. "Smallholder Income and Land Distribution in Africa: Implications for Poverty Reduction Strategies." *Food Policy* 28: 253–75. https://www.msu.edu/~chapotoa/Land%20Paper.pdf.

Jenkins, Glenn P., and Andrew Lai. 1989. *Trade, Exchange Rate and Agricultural Policies of Malaysia.* World Bank Comparative Studies. Washington, D.C.: World Bank.

Johnson, D. Gale. 1992. "Economic vs. Non-economic Factors in Chinese Rural Development." In Peter Calkins, Wen S. Chern, and Francis C. Tuan, eds., *Rural Development in Taiwan and Mainland China*, pp. 25–39, Westview Special Studies in Social, Political, and Economic Development. Boulder, CO: Westview Press.

Johnson, D. Gale, and Marilyn Corn Nottenburg. 1951. "A Critical Analysis of Farm Employment Estimates." *Journal of American Statistical Association* 46 (June): 191–205.

Johnson, R. W. M. 2000. "New Zealand's Agricultural Reforms and Their International Implications." http://www.iea.org.uk/files/upld-book18pdf?.pdf.

Johnston, Bruce F. 1970. "Agriculture and Structural Transformation in Developing Countries: A Survey of the Research." *Journal of Economic Literature* 8 (2): 369–404.

Johnston, Bruce F., and John W. Mellor. 1961. "The Role of Agriculture in Economic Development." *American Economic Review* 51 (September): 566–93.

Joint World Bank–Islamic Development Bank. 2005. *Tunisia: Understanding Successful Socioeconomic Development.* Joint Evaluation of Assistance. Washington D.C.: World Bank.

Jomo, K. S., ed., 1993. *Industrialising Malaysia: Policy, Performance, Prospects.* London: Routledge.

Jones, E. L. 1974. *Agriculture and the Industrial Revolution.* Oxford: Basil Blackwell.

Josling, T. 1975. "Agricultural Protection and Stabilisation Policies: a Framework of Measurement in the Context of Agricultural Adjustment." c/75/LIM/2, Food and Agriculture Organization.

Kakwani, Nanak, and E.Pernia. 2000. "What Is Pro-Poor Growth?" *Asian Development Review* 18(1): 1–16.

Kalaitzandonakes, Nicholas G. 1994. "Price Protection and Productivity Growth." *American Journal of Agricultural Economics,* 76 (November): 722–32.

Kalaitzandonakes, N. G., F. J. Spinelli, and M. Bredahl. 1993. "Market Liberalization and Productivity Growth: Lessons from the Deregulation of New Zealand Agriculture." *Economic Research Service,* RS-93-6: 77–82.

Kanbur, Ravi. 2005 "Growth, Inequality, and Poverty: Some Hard Questions." *Journal of International Affairs* 58 (2): 223–32.

Kang, Kenneth, and Ramachandran, Vijaya. 1999. "Economic Transformation in Korea: Rapid Growth without an Agricultural Transformation?" *Economic Development and Cultural Change* 47 (4): 783–801.

Kendall, M. G., and Stuart A. 1961. *The Advanced Theory of Statistics,* Vol. 2. New York: Charles Griffin, Quoted in N. Gujarati Damodar, *Basic Econometrics,* 4th ed. New York: McGraw-Hill, 2003.

Kendrick, John, and Carl Jones. 1951. "Gross National Farm Product in Constant Dollars, 1910–50." *Survey of Current Business* (U.S. Department of Commerce) 29 (August): 644–58.

Kennedy, Kieran. 1998. "The Irish Economy Transformed." www.teagasc.ie.

Kennedy, Kieran Anthony, Thomas Giblin, and Deidre McHugh. 1988. *The Economic Development of Ireland in the Twentieth Century.* London: Routledge.

Kennedy, Peter. 1998. *A Guide to Econometrics,* 4th ed.. Cambridge, MA: MIT Press.

Knight, Frank Hyneman. 1921. *Risk, Uncertainty and Profit.* Boston: Houghton Mifflin/ Cambridge, MA: Riverside Press.

Knoblauch, H. C. 1962. "Discussion." *Journal of Economic History* 19: 595–99.

Krakar, Eileen, and Kim Longtin. May 2005. *An Overview of the Canadian Agriculture and Agri-Food System.* Research and Analysis Directorate, Strategic Policy Branch, Agriculture and Agri-Food Canada. http://dsp-psd.pwgsc.gc.ca/Collection/A38-1-1-2005E.pdf.

Krooss, Herman Edward. 1966. *American Economic Development: The Progress of a Business Civilization,* 2d ed.. New York: Prentice Hall.

——— 1974. *American Economic Development: The Progress of a Business Civilization,* 3d ed. New York: Prentice Hall.

Krueger, Anne O., Maurice Schiff, and Alberto Valdes, eds. 1991. *The Political Economy of Agricultural Pricing Policy.* 3 vols. A World Bank Comparative Study. Baltimore: Johns Hopkins University Press for the World Bank.

Kuo, Shirley, W. Y., Gustav Ranis, and John C. H. Fei. 1981. *The Taiwan Success Story: Rapid Growth with Improved Distribution in the Republic of China, 1952–1979.* Boulder, CO: Westview Press.

Kuznets, Simon. 1968. *Toward a Theory of Economic Growth with Reflections on the Economic Growth of Nations.* New York: Norton.

Kwiecinski, Andrzej, and Xiande Li. 2002. "The Role of Agricultural and Other Policies in Raising Rural Incomes in China." In *China in the Global Economy – Agricultural Policies in China after the WTO Accession.* Paris: OECD.

Lains, Pedro. 2003. "New Wine in Old Bottles: Output and Productivity Trends in Portuguese Agriculture, 1850–1950." *European Review of Economic History* 7 (1): 43–82.

Lamble, Thomas. February 7, 2005. "Miracle Down Under: How New Zealand Farmers Prosper Without Subsidies and Protection." Center for Trade Policy Studies, No. 16. http://www.freetrade.org/node/110.

Langevin, Mark. S, and Peter Rosset. September 17, 1997. "Land Reform from Below: The Landless Workers Movement in Brazil," No. 287. Movimento dos Trabalhadores Rurais Sem Terra (MST). http://www.mstbrazil.org/rosset.html.

Lardy, Nicholas. 1990. "Chinese Agricultural Development under Reform and Future Prospects." In T.C. Tso, ed., *Agricultural Reform and Development in China: Achievements, Current Status, and Future Outlook.* Sixth Colloquium Proceedings, IDEALS, Inc.

Lahiff, Edward. 2009. "Land Redistribution in South Africa." In Hans P. Binswanger-Mhize, Camille Bourguignon, and Rogier Van Den Brink, eds., *Agricultural Land Distribution: Toward Greater Consensus*, pp. 169–200. Washington, D.C.: World Bank.

Lee, Teng Hui. 1995. "Strategies for Transferring Agricultural Surplus under Different Agricultural Situations in Taiwan." Data from table reprinted in Thomas P. Tomich, Peter Kilby, and Bruce, F. Johnston, eds., *Transforming Agrarian Economies: Opportunities Seized, Opportunities Missed*, p. 328, Ithaca, NY: Cornell University Press.

Lee, Teng-Hui, and Yueh-Eh Chen. 1979. "Agricultural Growth in Taiwan, 1911–1972." In Yujiro Hayami, Vernon M. Ruttan, and Herman M. Southworth, eds., *Agricultural Growth in Japan, Taiwan, Korea, and the Philippines*, pp. 59–89, Honolulu: University Press of Hawaii for the East–West Center.

Lele, Uma, ed. 1991. *Aid to African Agriculture: Lessons from Two Decades of Donors' Experience.* Baltimore: Johns Hopkins University Press for the World Bank.

Lewis, W. Arthur. 1954. "Economic Development with Unlimited Supplies of Labour." In A. N. Agarwala and S. P. Singh, eds., *The Economics of Underdevelopment*, pp. 400–449, New York: Oxford University Press.

Li, K. T., Gustav Ranis, and John C. H. Fei, 1988. *The Evolution of Policy behind Taiwan's Development Success.* New Haven, CT: Yale University Press.

Lin, Justin Yifu, Fang Cai, and Zhou Li. 1996. *The China Miracle: Development Strategy and Economic Reform.* Hong Kong: Chinese University Press of Hong Kong.

1999. *The China Miracle: Development Strategy and Economic Reform.* A Friedman Lecture Fund Monograph. Hong Kong: Chinese University Press for the Hong Kong Centre for Economic Research and the International Centre for Economic Growth.

Linehan, Denis. "Globalization: From Celtic Tiger to Celtic Snail." www.ucc.ie.

Lipton, Michael. 1977. *Why Poor People Stay Poor: Urban Bias in World Development.* London: Temple Smith.

Lofgren, Hans, and Sherman Robinson. 2008. "Public Spending, Growth, and Poverty Alleviation in Sub-Saharan Africa: A Dynamic General-Equilibrium Analysis." In Shengen Fan, ed., *Public Expenditures, Growth and Poverty: Lessons from Developing Countries.* International Food Policy Research Institute (IFPRI), pp. 184–224, Baltimore: Johns Hopkins University Press.

Lopez, Ramon. May 2005. "Why Governments Should Stop Non-social Subsidies: Measuring Their Consequences for Rural Latin America." World Bank Research Working Paper No. 3609. Washington, D.C.: World Bank.

——— January 2005. "Under-investing in Public Goods: Evidence, Causes, and Consequences for Agricultural Development, Equity and Development." *Agricultural Economics* 32, Issue Supplement (s1): 211–24.

Lopez, Ramon, and Gregmar I. Galinato. 2007. "Should Governments Stop Subsidies to Private Goods? Evidence from Rural Latin America." *Journal of Public Economics* 91 (5–6): 1071–94.

Lopez, Ramon, and Sebastian J. Miller. 2008. "Chile: The Unbearable Burden of Inequality." *World Development* 36 (12): 2679–95.

Luh, Y., and Spriro F. Stefanou. 1993. "Learning by Doing and the Sources of Productivity Growth." *Journal of Productivity Analysis* 4: 353–70.

MacSharry, Ray, and Padraic White. 2000. *The Making of the Celtic Tiger: The Inside Story of Ireland's Boom Economy.* Cork: Mercier Press.

Maddison, Angus, and Associates. 1992. *The Political Economy of Poverty, Equity and Growth: Brazil and Mexico.* Oxford: Oxford University Press for the World Bank.

Magharebia. July 25, 2008. "Morocco Promotes Rural Tourism." http://www.magharebia. com/cocoon/awi/xhtml1/en_GB/features/awi/reportage/2008/07/21/reportage-01.

Malthus, Thomas R. 1798–1826. *Essay on the Principle of Population.* The first edition was published in 1798 anonymously. Malthus published six editions.

Mangara, Tambunan. 1998. "Economic Reforms and Agricultural Development in Indonesia." *ASEAN Economic Bulletin* (April).

Martinez, Bengoa Javier, and Alvaro Diaz. 1996. *Chile: The Great Transformation.* Washington, D.C.: Brookings Institution / Geneva: United Nations Research Institute for Social Development.

Matthews, Alan, Carol Newman, and Fione Thorne. 2006. "Productivity in Irish Agriculture." Rural Economy Research Center (RERC), Teagasc. Working Paper 06-WP-RE-14. http://www.teagasc.ie/advanced_search.asp. http://www.agresearch. teagasc.ie/rerc/downloads/workingpapers/06wpre14.pdf.

McCalla, Alex F. March 2000. *Agriculture in the 21st Century.* Fourth Distinguished Economist Lecture. CIMMYT (International Maize and Wheat Improvement Center) Economics Program. Mexico City. D.F.

McCalla, Alex F., and John Nash, eds. 2007. *Reforming Agricultural Trade for Developing Countries: Key Issues for a Pro-Development Outcome of the Doha Round,* Vol. 1. Washington, D.C.: World Bank.

McCloskey, D. N., and S. T. Ziliak. 1996. "The Standard Error of Regression." *Journal of Economic Literature* 34: 97–114.

Meehl, P. E. 1978. "Theoretical Risks and Tabular Asterisks: Sir Karl, Sir Ronald, and the Slow Progress of Soft Psychology." *Journal of Consulting and Clinical Psychology* 46: 806–34.

Meenakshi, Rajiv. 2008. "Ensuring Rural Infrastructure in India: Role of the Rural Infrastructure Development Fund." Munich Personal RePEC Archive. http://mpra. ub.uni-muenchen.de/9836/1/MPRA_paper_9836.pdf.

Mellor, John W. 1966. *The Economics of Agricultural Development*. Ithaca, NY: Cornell University Press.

ed. 1995. *Agriculture on the Road to Industrialization*. Baltimore: Johns Hopkins University Press.

Meneces-Filho, Naercio and Ligia Vasconcellos. University of Sao Paolo. 2004. *Brazil: Has Economic Growth been Pro-Poor? Why?* Washington, D.C.: World Bank.

Mere, Francisco. March 1, 2007. *Rural Migration in Mexico: An Overview*. 2007 Agricultural Outlook Forum. http://www.usda.gov/oce/forum/2007_Speeches/PDF%20speeches/PalafoxF.pdf.

Mighell, Ronald L. 1955. *American Agriculture*. Census Monograph Series. New York: John Wiley.

Migot-Adholla, Shem, Peter Hazell, Benoit Blarel, and Frank Place. 1991. "Indigenous Land Rights Systems in Sub-Saharan Africa: A Constraint on Productivity?" *World Bank Economic Review* 5 (1): 155–75.

Miller, David. 1999. "Lessons from Ireland." Government of New Zealand, Ministry of Agriculture and Fisheries (MAF), *Off-Farm Income: Theory and Practice*. http://www.maf.govt.nz/mafnet/rural-nz/profitability-and-economics/employment/off-farm-income-theory-and-practice/ofincth9.htm.

Minami, Ryoshin. 1994. *The Economic Development of China: A Comparison with Japanese Experience*. New York: St. Martin's Press.

Mingay, G. E. 1972. "The Transformation of Agriculture." In *The Long Debate on Poverty: Eight Essays on Industrialization and the "Condition of England."* London: Institute of Economic Affairs.

1977. *The Agricultural Revolution: Changes in Agriculture, 1650–1880*. London: Adams & Charles Black.

1996. "Review of Agricultural Revolution in England: The Transformation of the Agrarian Economy, 1500–1850," by Overton, Professor Mark, University of Exeter. http://www.history.ac.uk/reviews/paper/mingay.html.

Monk, Paul M. 1990 *Truth and Power: Robert S. Hardie and Land Reform Debates in the Philippines, 1950–87*. Monash Paper No. 20. Monash University, Centre for Southeast Asian Studies.

Monke, Eric, et al. 1986. "Portugal on the Brink of Europe: The CAP and Portuguese Agriculture." *Journal of Agricultural Economics* 37 (3): 317–21.

Moore, Geoff. February 18, 2001 "Fact Sheet: Terra Nullius." *Australian Aborigines History and Culture Research Project*. http://www.aaa.com.au/hrh/aboriginal/factsht28.shtml.

Moreira, Manuel Belo. 1989. "The Crisis of Portuguese Agriculture in Relation to the EEC Challenge." *Agriculture and Human Values* (Winter–Spring): 70–81.

Morris, Alice Albin, and Sebastian Morris. 2003. "The Rural Infrastructure Development Fund: A Review." In Sebastian Morris, ed., *India Infrastructure Report, 2003: Public Expenditure Allocation and Accountability*, pp. 260–68. New York: Oxford University Press.

Mosher, A. T. 1966. *Getting Agriculture Moving: Essentials for Development and Modernization*. New York: Praeger.

Mullen, John. 2007. "The Importance of Productivity Growth in Australian Agriculture." Paper 20, presented at 51st annual conference of the Australian Agricultural Resource Economics Society, February 13–16, Queenstown, New Zealand.

Mundlak, Yair. 1988. "Endogenous Technical Change and the Measurement of Productivity." In Susan M. Capalbo and John M. Antle, eds., *Agricultural Productivity: Measurement and Explanation*, pp. 316–331, Washington, D.C.: Resources for the Future.

2005. "Economic Growth: Lessons from Two Centuries of American Agriculture." *Journal of Economic Literature* 43 (December): 989–1024.

Myers, Ramon H., ed. 1996. *The Wealth of Nations in the Twentieth Century: The Policies and Institutional Determinants of Economic Development*. Publication No. 437. Stanford, CA: Hoover Institution Press.

Myrdal, Gunnar. 1968. *Asian Drama: An Inquiry into the Poverty of Nations*. Hamondsworth: Penguin.

National Competitiveness Council. 2006. *Overview of Ireland's Productivity Performance, 1980–2005*. Forfas. http://www.forfas.ie/media/ncc061019_productivity_performance_overview.pdf.

Nel, Philip. 2003. "Income Inequality, Economic Growth and Political Instability in Sub-Saharan Africa." *Journal of Modern African Studies* 41 (4): 611–39.

Nelson, Edward. 2005. "Monetary Neglect and the Great Inflation in Canada, Australia and New Zealand." Munich Personal RePEc Archive (MPRA), *International Journal of Central Banking* 1 (1). http://mpra.ub.uni-muenchen.de/822/1/MPRA_paper_822.pdf.

New York Times. January 19, 1988. "New Zealand Inflation."

New Zealand Agriculture. http://www.nationsencyclopedia.com/economies/Asia-and-the-Pacific/New-Zealand-AGRICULTURE.html.

New Zealand Government's Official Statistics Agency. May 1999. "Income Distribution of New Zealand" 1999. http://www.stats.govt.nz/products-and-services/Articles/income-distrib-May99.htm.

New Zealand Government. Ministry of Agriculture and Forestry (MAF). 2003. 2008. http://www.maf.govt.nz/

Nolan, Peter. 1988. *The Political Economy of Collective Farms: An Analysis of China's Post-Mao Rural Reforms*. Boulder, CO: Westview Press.

North, Douglass Cecil. 1961. *The Economic Growth of the United States, 1790–1860*. Englewood Cliffs, NJ: Prentice Hall.

1966. *Growth and Welfare in the American Past: A New Economic History*. Englewood Cliffs, NJ: Prentice Hall.

Nyanteng, V., and Seini, A. W. 2000. "Agricultural Policy and Its Impact on Growth and Productivity, 1970–95." In E. Aryeetey, J. Harrigan, and M. Nissanke, eds., *Economic Reforms in Ghana: The Miracle and the Mirage*, pp. 267–283, Oxford: James Currey & Woeli.

Nyberg, Albert, and Scott Rozelle, 1999. *Accelerating China's Rural Transformation*. Washington, D.C.: World Bank.

O'Brien, Marc, and Thia Hennessy, eds. 2008. *An Examination of the Contribution of Off-Farm Income to the Viability and Sustainability of Farm Households and the Productivity of Farm Businesses*. RMIS 5490. National Development Plan. http://www.teagasc.ie/research/reports/ruraldevelopment/5490/eopr-5490.pdf.

OECD Observer. April 2001. "Economic Survey of Portugal: Policy Brief."

Office of the Auditor General of Canada. 2007.

O'Gorman, Colm. 2006 "Agriculture Has Always Been Our Mainstay: What Is Happening to It Now?" *Inside Ireland*. http://www.insideireland.com/sample09.htm.

Okhawa, Kazushi, and Henry Rosovksy. 1967. "The Role of Agriculture in Japan's Development." In Gerald M. Meier, ed., *Leading Issues in Development Economics*, pp. 304–15. Oxford: Oxford University Press.

Olfert, Rose M. 2006. "Future Role of Agriculture in Rural Canada." Paper presented at "Driving Growth in Your Business: Who's in Control?" Meyers Norris Penny. Canada

Rural Economy Research Lab (C-RERL). http://www.crerl.usask.ca/presentations/ Brooks_ag_days_feb_07_rev_pres.pdf.

Olson, Mancur 1971. *The Logic of Collective Action: Public Goods and the Theory of Groups.* Cambridge, MA: Harvard University Press.

O'Neill, Suzanne, Anthony Leavy, and Alan Matthews. 2000. "Measuring Productivity Change and Efficiency on Irish Farms." End of Project Report 4498, prepared for the Teagasc Rural Economy Centre. http://www.teagasc.ie/quicksearch.asp. http:// www.teagasc.ie/research/reports/ruraldevelopment/4498/eopr-4498.asp

2000a. "Measuring Productivity Change and Efficiency on Irish Farms." End of Project Report 4498, prepared for the Teagasc Rural Economy Centre. www. teagasc.ie.

Orden, David, Robert Paarlberg, and Terry Roe. 1999. *Policy Reform in American Agriculture.* Chicago: University of Chicago Press.

Organisation for Economic Co-Operation and Development (OECD). 1999. *Review of Agricultural Policies in Korea, 1979–1990.* Paris.

2002. *China in the Global Economy: Agricultural Policies in China after the WTO Accession.* "Opening Statement" by Qinglin Du, Minister of Agriculture, China.

2008a. *OECD Review of Agricultural Policies: Chile.* http://www.oecd.org/document/25/ 0,3343,en_2649_33797_40171161_1_1_1_1,00.html#Highlights.

2008b. "Agricultural Policies in OECD countries: At a Glance 2008." http://www.oecd. org/document/47/0,3343,en_2649_33773_40900655_1_1_1_37401,00.html.

June 2008. "Policy Brief: Economic Survey of Canada." OECD Observer http://www. oecd.org/dataoecd/20/27/40811541.pdf

March 2009. "Risk Management in Agriculture: A Holistic Conceptual Framework." TAD/CA/APM/WP (2008) 22 /Final. http://www.oecd.org/ dataoecd/27/46/42750215.pdf.

Organisation for Economic Co-operation and Development in Washington. August–September. 2003. "Subsidies to Agriculture: Why?" No. 46. http://www.oecdwash. org/NEWS/LOCAL/oecdwash-aug-sept2003.pdf.

Osava, Mario. March 2007. "Brazil: No Consensus on Success of Land Reform." http:// ipsnews.net/news.asp?idnews=37053.

Overton, Mark. 1998 *Agricultural Revolution in England: The Transformation of the Agrarian Economy, 1500–1850.* Cambridge Studies in Historical Geography, 23. Cambridge: Cambridge University Press.

Pardey, Philip, et al. October 2007. *Science, Technology and Skills.* University of Minnesota, Department of Applied Economics. INSTEPP. Science Council, CGIAR.

Parker, William. 1972. "Agriculture." In Lance Davis, Richard Easterlin, and William Parker, eds., *American Economic Growth*, pp. 369–417, New York: Harper & Row.

Patrick, Hugh T. 1971. "The Economic Muddle of the 1920's." In James William Morley, ed., *Dilemmas of Growth in Pre-War Japan*, pp. 211–266, Princeton, NJ: Princeton University Press.

Patrick, Hugh, and Henry Rosovsky, eds. 1976. *Asia's New Giant: How the Japanese Economy Works*, pp. 211–266, Washington, D.C.: Brookings Institution.

Pazvakavambwa, Simon, and Vincent Hungwe. 2009. "Land Redistribution in Zimbabwe." In Hans P. Binswanger- Mhize, Camille Bourguignon, and Rogier Van Den Brink, eds., *Agricultural Land Distribution: Toward Greater Consensus*, pp. 137–67. Washington, D.C.: World Bank.

Pearson R. Scott, et al. 1987. *Portuguese Agriculture in Transition.* Ithaca, NY: Cornell University Press.

Perkins, Dwight. 1986. *China: Asia's Next Economic Giant?* Seattle: University of Washington Press.

Perkins, Dwight, and Shahid Yusuf. 1984. *Rural Development in China.* A World Bank Publication. Baltimore: Johns Hopkins University Press.

Perkins, Dwight. 1994. "Completing China's Move to the Market". In Chai, Joseph, C.H., ed. 2000. *The Economic Development of Modern China. Volume III: Reforms and the Opening Up Since 1979*: Chapter 2. An Elgar Reference Collection, pp. 40–63, Cheltenham, UK. Northampton, MA, USA.

Phelan, G., J. Frawley, and M. Wallace. 2002. "Off-Farm Income and the Structure of Irish Agriculture." Teagasc. Rural economy Research Centre, Department of Agribusiness, Extension and Rural development, University College, Dublin. www.teagasc.ie.

Phelps Brown, Henry, and Sheila V. Hopkins. 1962. "Seven Centuries of Building Wages." In E. M. Carus-Wilson, ed., *Essays in Economic History*, pp. 168–178. London: St. Martin's Press.

Pintado, V. Xavier. 1964. *Structure and Growth of the Portuguese Economy.* Hammer: European Free Trade Association.

Plevin, Rich. 1999. "World Bank Subverts Land Reform in Brazil." *Economic Justice News Online* 2 (3) (1999).

Popper, Sir Karl. 1953. "The Problem of Induction." Reprinted in David Miller, ed., 1983. *A Pocket Popper*, pp. 101–17. Oxford: Fontana Paperbacks.

1961 *The Poverty of Historicism.* New York: Harper Torchbooks.

1963. *Conjectures and Refutations: The Growth of Scientific Knowledge.* London: Routledge and Kegan Paul (First Edition).

1965. *Conjectures and Refutations: The Growth of Scientific Knowledge.* London: Routledge and Kegan Paul (Second Edition).

Prebisch, Raul. 1950. *The Economic Development of Latin America and Its Principal Problems.* New York: United Nations.

1959. "Commercial Policy in the Underdeveloped Countries." *American Economic Review Papers and Proceedings* 64 (May): 251–73.

Purohit, Brijesh C., and V. Ratna Reddy. 1999. *Capital Formation in Indian Agriculture: Issues and Concerns.* National Bank of Agriculture and Rural Development, Mumbai.

Quibria, M. G. , ed. 1994. *Rural Poverty in Developing Asia.* Vol. 1: *Bangladesh, India, and Sri Lanka Asian Development Bank.* Manila: Asian Development Bank.

Radwan, Samir, Vali Jamal, and Ajit Ghose. 1991. *Tunisia: Rural Labour and Structural Transformation.* London: Routledge.

Rajkumar, Andrew Sunil, and Vinaya Swaroop. May 2002. *Public Spending and Outcomes: Does Governance Matter?* World Bank Policy Research Working Paper No. 2840. Washington, D.C.: World Bank.

Ramachandran, Vijaya. 1995. "Does Agriculture Really Matter? The Case of Korea, 1910–1970." *Journal of East Asian Economics* 6 (3): 367–84.

Ranis, Gustav. May 1996. "The Trade-Growth Nexus in Taiwan's Development." Discussion Paper 758. Economic Growth Center, Yale University. An earlier version of the paper was presented at the Cornell Conference on Government and the Market: The Relevance of the Taiwanese Performance (1945–1995) to Development Theory and Policy, May 3–4, 1996.

Rasmussen, Wayne. 1962. "The Impact of Technological Change on American Agriculture." *Journal of Economic History* 19: 578–91.

Ravallion, Martin. 2004. "Pro-Poor Growth: A Primer". World Bank, Policy Research Working Paper No. 3242. Washington, D.C.: World Bank.

Ravallion, Martin, and Chen, Shaohua. September 2004. "China's Uneven Progress against Poverty." World Bank Policy Research Working Paper No. 3408. Washington, D.C.: World Bank.

Ravallion, Martin, and Gaurav Datt. 1994. "How Important to India's Poor Is the Urban–Rural Composition of Growth? Policy Research Working Paper 399, December 1994. Reprinted in the *World Bank Economic Review* 10 (1): 1–25 (1996).

Rawski, Thomas G. 1979. "Economic Growth and Employment in China." *World Development* 7 (8/9): 769.

Reardon, Thomas. 2006. "The Rapid Rise of Supermarkets and the Use of Private Standards in Their Food Product Procurement Systems in Developing Countries." In Ruben Ruerd, Maja Slingerman, and Hans Nihoff, eds., *Agro-Food Chains and Networks for Development*, pp. 79–105 Dordrecht: Springer.

Roc, Nancy. March 2009. "Haiti: The Bitter Grapes of Corruption," FRIDE, a European Think Tank for Global Action. http://www.fride.org/publication/583/haiti-the-sour-grapes-of-corruption.

Root, Hilton L. 2006 *Capital and Collusion: The Political Logic of Global Economic Development.* Princeton, NJ: Princeton University Press.

Rosenstein-Rodan, Paul. 1943. "Problems of Industrialization of Eastern and South Eastern Europe." *Economic Journal* 53 (210/211): 202–11.

Rostow, W. W. 1999. *Theorists of Economic Growth from David Hume to the Present.* Oxford: Oxford University Press.

Rothenberg, Winifred B. 1995. "The Market and Massachusetts Farmers, 1750–1855." In R. Whaples and D. Betts, eds., *Historical Perspectives on the American Economy*, pp. 71–106, Cambridge: Cambridge University Press.

Roumani, Anna. May 2004. *Brazil: Reducing Rural Poverty through Access to Land.* Case Study presented at the Shanghai Conference on Scaling Up Poverty Reduction, May 25–27. Report No. 30836. Washington, D.C.: World Bank.

Rozelle, Scott D., and Daniel A. Sumner, eds. 2003. *Agricultural Trade and Policy in China: Issues, Analysis and Implications.* Aldershot, Hants: Ashgate.

Ryan, Bryce, and Neal C. Gross. 1943. "The Diffusion of Hybrid Seed Corn in Two Iowa Communities." *Rural Sociology* 8: 15–24.

Saito, Osamu. 1971. "The Rural Economy: Commercial Agriculture, By-employment, and Wage Work." In Marius B. Jansen and Gilbert Rozman, eds., 1986. *Japan in Transition: From Tokugawa to Meiji*, pp. 400–420, Princeton, NJ : Princeton University Press. Also reprinted in Tolliday, Steven, ed. 2001. *The Economic Development of Modern Japan, 1868–1945: From the Meiji Restoration to the Second World War.* Volume 1, 2001, pp. 179–199. Elgar Reference Collection. Cheltenham, U.K. and Northampton, Mass.: Elgar; distributed by American International Distribution Corporation, Williston, Vt.

Samuelson, Paul A. 1954. "The Pure Theory of Public Expenditure." In *Review of Economics and Statistics* 36 (4): 387–89.

Sandrey, Ron A., and Scobie, Grant M. "Changing International Competitiveness and Trade: Recent Experience in New Zealand Agriculture." *American Journal of Agricultural Economic*, No. 76: 1041–46.

Sarris, Alexander H. January 2001. "The Role of Agriculture in Economic Development and Poverty Reduction: An Empirical and Conceptual Foundation." Draft, prepared for the Rural Development Department of the World Bank.

Save the Children. March 1, 2005. "NZ's Child Poverty Levels Unacceptable." http://www.savethechildren.org.nz/new_zealand/newsroom/nz_child_poverty.html.

Sayre, Laura 2003. "Farming without Subsidies? Some Lessons from New Zealand." Rodale Institute. http://newfarm.rodaleinstitute.org/features/0303/newzealand_sub-sidies.shtml.

Scaniello, Jorge Alvarez, and Gabriel Porcille. 2006. "Institutions, the Land Market, and Income Distribution in New Zealand and Uruguay, 1870–1940." Paper presented at the 14th International Economic History Congress, Helsinki, August 21–25. http://www.helsinki.fi/iehc2006/papers2/Scaniello.pdf.

Schnepf, Randall D., Erik Dohlman, and Christine Bolling. December 2001. "Agriculture in Brazil and Argentina," Economic Research Service, U.S. Department of Agriculture, *Agriculture and Trade Report*, WRS-01-3.

Schuh, G. Edward in collaboration with Alves, Eliseu Roberto. 1970. *The Agricultural Development of Brazil*. Praeger Publishers, New York, Washington, London.

Schultz, Theodore W. 1953. *The Economic Organization of Agriculture*. New York: McGraw-Hill.

1964. *Transforming Traditional Agriculture*. New Haven, CT: Yale University Press.

1979. "On Economics and Politics in Agriculture." In Theodore W. Schultz, ed., *Distortions of Agricultural Incentives*, pp. 3–23, Bloomington: Indiana University Press.

Schwarztman, Stephan. January 27, 2000. "The World Bank and Land Reform in Brazil." Environmental Defence, MST. http://www.mstbrazil.org/LandReform.html.

Sen, Amartya. 2000. *Development as Freedom*. New York: Alfred A. Knopf.

Shah, Anwar, ed. 2005. *Public Expenditure Analysis*. Public Sector Governance and Accountability Series. Washington, D.C.: World Bank.

Sheehy, Seamus J. 1980. "The Impact of EEC Membership on Irish Agriculture." *Journal of Agricultural Economics* 31 (3): 297–310. http://www3.interscience.wiley.com/journal/120156901/abstract?CRETRY=1&SRETRY=0.

1988. "Irish Agriculture into the Nineties." *Irish Banking Review* (Autumn): 21–32.

1992. "Irish Agriculture and CAP Reform". *Irish Banking Review* (Summer): 3–13.

Shen, T. H. 1964. *Agricultural Development on Taiwan since World War II*. Ithaca, NY: Cornell University Press.

1970. *The Sino-American Joint Commission on Rural Reconstruction: Twenty Years of Cooperation for Agricultural Development*. Ithaca, NY: Cornell University Press.

Singer, Hans Wolfgang. 1950 and 1975. "The Distribution of Gains between Investing and Borrowing Countries." *American Economic Review*, May Vol. 40. Reprinted in Sir Alec Cairncross and Mohinder Puri, eds., *The Strategy of International Development: Essays in the Economics of Backwardness*, pp. 43–57, London: Macmillan, 1975.

Skogstad, Grace. 2007. "The Two Faces of Canadian Agriculture in a Post-Staples Economy." *Canadian Political Science Review* 1 (1): 26–41.

Slayton, Tom, and C. Peter Timmer. 2008. "Japan, China and Thailand Can Solve the Rice Crisis – But US Leadership Is Needed." Center for Global Development, Washington, D.C.

Slicher Van Bath, B. H. 1963. *The Agrarian History of Western Europe, A.D. 500–1850*. London: Edward Arnold.

Sparling, David, and Pamela Laughland. July 2008. "Are Canada's Large Farms Really Different?" Vista on Agri-Food Industry and the Farm Community, Ottawa, Catalog No. 21-004-X.

Spooner, Peter G. 2005. "On Squatters, Settlers and Early Surveyors: Historical Development of Country Road Reserves in Southern New South Wales." *Australian Geographer* 36 (1): 55–73.

Stevens, Robert D., and Cathy L. Jabara. 1988. *Agricultural Development Principles: Economic Theory and Empirical Evidence.* Baltimore: Johns Hopkins University Press.

Stiglitz, Joseph E., Deborah L. Spar, and J. Habib Sy. 1999. "Global Public Goods: Knowledge and Information." In Kaul Inge, Isabelle Grunberg, and Marc Stern, eds., *Global Public Goods,* pp. 306–10. United Nations Development Programme. Oxford Scholarship Online. www.oxfordscholarship.com.

Sturzenegger A. C., and B. Martinez Mosquera. 1990. *Trade, Exchange Rate and Agricultural Pricing Policies in Argentina.* A World Bank Comparative Study. Washington, D.C.: World Bank.

Sumarto, Sudarno, and Asep Suryhadi. 2003. "The Indonesian Experience on Trade Reform, Economic Growth and Poverty Reduction." Paper presented at the Trade, Growth and Poverty Conference, London, December 8–9.

Sunding, David, and David Zilberman. 2001. "The Agricultural Innovation Process: Research and Technology Adoption in a Changing Agriculture Sector." In B. Gardner and G. Rausser, eds., *Handbook of Agricultural Economics,* Vol. 1, pp. 208–261, Amsterdam: North-Holland.

Sury, M. M. 2001. *India: A Decade of Economic Reforms, 1991–2001.* Delhi: New Century Publications.

Syrett, Stephen, ed. 2002. *Contemporary Portugal: Dimensions of Economic and Political Change.* Aldershot, Hants: Ashgate.

Taleb, Nassim Nicholas. 2007. *The Black Swan: The Impact of the Highly Improbable.* New York: Random House.

Tang Zhong and Ma, Jiujie. 2003. "'*San nung' wen ti yu jing ji zeng zhang*" [Agricultural structural adjustment and farmers' income growth]. In Bocheng Ji and Ruilong Yang, eds., March 2003, *A Report on Chinese Economic Development in 2002,* pp. 255–288, Beijing: Renmin University of China Press.

TD Bank Financial Group. November 28, 2007. *Canadian Agriculture Begins a New Era: Growth Opportunities Abound.* Special Report. http://www.td.com/economics/special/db1107_agri.pdf.

Thiessen, Gordon. 1999. "Canadian Economic Performance at the End of the Twentieth Century." Remarks to the Canada Club, London, June 2. http://www.bank-banque-canada.ca/en/speeches/1999/sp99-5.pdf.

Thompson, Theresa, and Anwar Shah. March 2005. *Transparency International's Corruption Perceptions Index: Whose Perceptions Are They Anyway?* Revised discussion draft Washington, D.C.: World Bank

Timmer, C. Peter. 1988. "The Agricultural Transformation." In H. Chenery and T. N. Srinivasan, eds., *Handbook of Development Economics,* Vol. 1, pp. 276–331. Amsterdam: Elsevier.

1989. "Indonesia: Transition from Food Importer to Exporter." In Terry Sicular, ed., *Food Price Policy in Asia,* pp. 22–64, Ithaca, NY: Cornell University Press.

December 1997. "How Well do the Poor Connect to the Growth Process?" Harvard Institute for International Development for the USAID/CAER project.

2002. "Agriculture and Economic Growth." In Bruce Gardner and Gordon Rausser, eds., *The Handbook of Agricultural Economics,* Vol. IIA, pp. 1487–1546. Amsterdam: North-Holland.

September 2004. "Operationalizing Pro-Poor Growth: Indonesia." Country study done for the World Bank. Draft.

May 2005a. "Agriculture and Pro-Poor Growth: Reviewing the Issues." Center for Global Development, Washington, D.C.

June 2005b. "Operationalizing Pro-Poor Growth: Country Study for the World Bank – Indonesia." Draft.

July 2005c. "Agriculture and Pro-poor Growth: An Asian Perspective." Center for Global Development, Working Paper No. 63.

2007. *A World without Agriculture: The Structural Transformation in Historical Perspective.* Henry Wendt Lecture. Washington, D.C.: American Enterprise Institute. Same paper published in 2009.

August 27, 2010. "Behavioural Dimensions to Food Security." Proceedings of the National Academy of Sciences. www.pnas.org/cgi/doi/10.1073/pnas.0913213107 PNAS Early Edition.

Timmer, C. Peter, ed. 1991. *Agriculture and the State: Growth, Employment and Poverty in Developing Countries.* Ithaca, NY: Cornell University Press.

Tomich, Thomas P., Peter Kilby, and Bruce F. Johnston. 1995. *Transforming Agrarian Economies: Opportunities Seized, Opportunities Missed.* Ithaca, NY: Cornell University Press.

Toye, John, and Richard Toye. 2003. "The Origins and Interpretation of the Prebisch–Singer Thesis." *History of Political Economy* 35 (3): 437–67. http://exeter.openreposi-tory.com/exeter/bitstream/10036/25832/1/Toye%20HPE%20Prebisch%20Singer.pdf.

Toynbee, Arnold. 1884. *Lectures on the Industrial Revolution.* Sec. 6: *England in 1760: The Condition of the Wage Earners.* Section 14: *The Future of the Working Classes.* T. and A. Constable, Printers to her Majesty: Edinburgh University Press. Boston: Beacon.

Transparency International. 2008. Corruption Perceptions Index. http://www.transparency.org/news_room/in_focus/2008/cpi2008/cpi_2008_table.

Tsakok, Isabelle. 1990. *Agricultural Price Policy: A Practitioner's Guide to Partial- Equilibrium Analysis.* Ithaca, NY: Cornell University Press.

Tsakok, Isabelle, and Bruce Gardner. 2007. "Agriculture in Economic Development: Primary Engine of Growth or Chicken and Egg?" *American Journal of Agricultural Economics* 89 (5): 1145–51.

Tweeten, Luther. 1971. *Foundations of Farm Policy.* Lincoln: University of Nebraska Press.

UNICEF–ILO–World Bank Group. December 2006. *Child Labor in Venezuela: Children's Vulnerability to Macroeconomic Shocks.* Understanding Children's Work: An Inter-Agency Research Cooperation Project, Working Paper.

United States Department of Agriculture (USDA). 1992. *Agricultural Outlook, 1992.* USDA Economic Research Service Report.

February 2009. "Agricultural Economy and Policy Report – Brazil." http://www.fas.usda.gov/country/Brazil/Brazil%20Agricultural%20Economy%20and%20Policy.pdf.

United States Department of State. 2001. *The Economy of Chile: The World Factbook.* ttp://motherearthtravel.com/chile/economy.htm.

August 2009. "Background Note: New Zealand." http://www.state.gov/r/pa/ei/bgn/35852.htm.

Valdes, Alberto, and Esteban Jara. 2008. "Chile." In Kym Anderson and Alberto Valdes, eds., *Distortions to Agricultural Incentives in Latin America*, pp. 119–158, Washington, D.C.: World Bank.

Valdes, Alberto, and William Foster. 2005. "Reflections on the Role of Agriculture on Pro-Poor Growth." Paper prepared for the Research Workshop: The Future of Small Farms, Wye, Kent, June 26–29. Paper expanded and reprinted in *World Development*, 38(10) (October 2010): 1362–1374.

Valdes, Alberto, Eugenia Muchnik, and Hernan Hurtado. 1990. *Trade, Exchange Rate, and Agricultural Pricing Policies in Chile*. Vol. 1: *The Country Study*. World Bank Comparative Studies. Washington, D.C.: World Bank.

Van den Brink, Rogier, Glen Thomas, Hans Binswanger, John Bruce, and Frank Byamugysha, 2006. *Consensus, Confusion and Controversy: Selected Land Reform Issues in Sub-Saharan Africa*. World Bank Working Paper No. 71. Washington, D.C.: World Bank.

Van der Eng, Pierre. 1996. *Agricultural Growth in Indonesia: Productivity Change and Policy Impact since 1880*. London: MacMillan Press.

Van Zyl, Johan. 1995. *The Relationship between Farm Size and Efficiency in South African Agriculture*. Washington, D.C.: World Bank.

Verner, Dorte. April 2005. *Poverty in Rural and Semi-Urban Mexico during 1992–2002*. World Bank Policy Research Working Paper Series, No. 3576. Washington, D.C.: World Bank.

Veterinary Services, 2008. http://www.teara.govt.nz/en/veterinary-services/4

Vincent, Jeffrey R., Rozali Mohamed Ali, and Associates. 1997. *Environment and Development in a Resource-Rich Economy: Malaysia under the New Economic Policy*. Harvard Institute for International Development, Institute of Strategic and International Studies, Malaysia.

Wagner, Wieland. 2010. "The Dark Side of the Boom: Chinese Fight Property Seizures by the State," *Der Spiegel*, August 3. http://www.spiegel.de/international/world/0,1518,709691,00.html.

Ward, Tony. 2006. "The First Twenty Years of the Treaties: Aboriginal Economic Development in the New Zealand and Canada." 14th International Economic History Congress, Helsinki, August 21–25.

Warr, Peter G. February 2002. "Poverty Incidence and Sectoral Growth: Evidence from Southeast Asia." United Nations University, World Institute for the Development Economics Research, Discussion Paper 2002/20.

January 2003. "Industrialization, Trade Policy and Poverty Reduction: Evidence from Asia." *Festschrift Conference in Honour of Peter Lloyd*. Melbourne. Also Working Paper no. 2003–03 of the Department of Economics RSPAS, Australian National University, Canberra. http://rspas.anu.edu.au/economics/publish/papers/wp2003/wp-econ-2003-3.pdf

Weber, Maria, ed. 2001. *Reforming Economic Systems in Asia: A Comparative Analysis of China, Japan, South Korea, Malaysia and Thailand*. Cheltenham: Edward Edgar Publishing in Association with Instituto Per Gli Studi Di Politica Internationazionale (ISPI).

Wikipedia. January 1, 2009. Squatting (pastoral). http://en.wikipedia.org/wiki/Squatting_(pastoral).

World Bank. 1953. *The Economic Development of Mexico*. Report No. 10952-ME of the Combined Mexican Working Party. International Bank for Reconstruction and Development. Baltimore: Johns Hopkins Press for the World Bank.

1961. *The Economic Development of Venezuela.* Report No. 10111. Washington, D.C.: World Bank.

1968. *The World Bank Report on the New Zealand Economy, 1968.* Presented to the House of Representatives by Leave, Wellington, New Zealand. Washington, D.C.: World Bank.

1978. *Portugal: Agricultural Sector Survey.* World Bank Country Study. Washington, D.C.: World Bank.

1980. *Chile: An Economy in Transition.* World Bank Country Study. Washington, D.C.: World Bank.

1982. *The Agricultural Development Experience of Algeria, Morocco and Tunisia.* Staff Working Paper 552. Washington, D.C.: World Bank.

March 1989. *Portugal: Tras-os-Montes Regional Development Project – Staff Appraisal Report.* Report No. 7538-PO. Washington, D.C.: World Bank.

1990a. *Indonesia: Strategy for a Sustained Reduction in Poverty.* World Bank Country Study. Washington, D.C.: World Bank.

July 1990. *Brazil: Agriculture Sector Review: Policies and Prospects.* Report No. 7798-BR, Vol. 1. Washington, D.C.: World Bank.

May 1991a. *Ghana: National Agricultural Research Project – Staff Appraisal Report.* Report No. 9313-GH. Washington, D.C.: World Bank.

May 1991b. *Brazil: Key Policy Issues in the Livestock Sector: Towards a Framework for Efficient and Sustainable Growth.* Report No. 8570-BR. Washington, D.C.: World Bank.

1993a. *The East Asian Miracle: Economic Growth and Public Policy.* A World Bank Policy Research Report. Oxford: Oxford University Press for the World Bank.

1993b. *The Arab Republic of Egypt: An Agricultural Strategy for the 1990s.* A World Bank Country Study. Washington, D.C.: World Bank.

June 1994. *World Development Report: Infrastructure for Development.* Oxford: Oxford University Press for the World Bank.

July 1994. *Brazil: The Management of Agriculture, Rural Development and Natural Resources,* Report No. 11783-BR, Vol. 1. Washington, D.C.: World Bank.

August 1994. *Chile: Strategy for Rural Areas – Enhancing Agricultural Competitiveness and Alleviating Rural Poverty.* Report No. 12776-CH. Washington, D.C.: World Bank.

June 1995. *Brazil: A Poverty Assessment,* Report No. 14323-BR, Vols. 1 and 2. Washington, D.C.: World Bank.

August 1995. *Tunisia – Poverty Alleviation: Preserving Progress While Preparing for the Future.* Report No. 13993-TN. Washington, D.C.: World Bank.

1997a. *At China's Table: Food Security Options.* Washington, D.C.: World Bank.

1997b. "Understanding the Present." In Joseph C. H. Chai, ed., *The Economic Development of Modern China.* Vol. 3: *Reforms and the Opening up Since 1979,* pp. 512–19. An Elgar Reference Collection. Cheltenham.

1998. *The Kingdom of Morocco: Rural Development Strategy.* Report No. 16303-MOR, Vol. 1. Washington, D.C.: World Bank.

1999. *Review of Agricultural Policies in Korea, 1979–1990.* Washington, D.C.: World Bank.

February 1999. *A Productive Partnership: The World Bank and the Republic of Korea, 1962–1994.* www.worldbank.org.

May 1999. *Rural China: Transition and Development.* Report No. 19361-CHA. Washington, D.C.: World Bank.

June 1999. *India: Towards Rural Development and Poverty Reduction.* 2 vols. Report No. 18921-IN, Vol. 2. Washington, D.C.: World Bank.

August 1999. *India: Foodgrain Marketing Policies: Reforming to Meet Food Security Needs.* Report No. 18329-IN, Vol. 2. Washington, D.C.: World Bank.

1999. *Entering the 21st Century.* World Development Report 1999/2000. Washington, D.C.: World Bank.

2000a. *East Asia: Recovery and Beyond.* Washington, D.C.: World Bank.

2000b. *World Development Report* 2000/2001: Attacking Poverty. Washington, D.C.: World Bank.

June 2000. *Republic of Tunisia: Agriculture Competitiveness Study.* Report No. 20883-TN. Washington, D.C.: World Bank.

April 2001. *Rural Poverty Reduction in Brazil: Towards an Integrated Strategy.* Vol. 1: *Policy Summary.* Vol. 2: *Background Studies.* Report No. 21790-BR. Washington, D.C.: World Bank.

June 2001. *Mexico: Land Policy: A Decade after the Ejido Reform.* Report No. 22187-ME. Washington, D.C.: World Bank

August 2001. *Chile: Poverty and Income Distribution in a High-Growth Economy: The Case of Chile, 1987–98.* Report No. 22037-CH, Vol. 1. Washington, D.C.: World Bank.

2001a. China: Overcoming Rural Poverty. Washington, D.C.: World Bank.

2001b. *India: The Challenges of Development: A Country Assistance Evaluation.* Operations Evaluation Department. Washington, D.C.: World Bank.

December 2001. *Nicaragua: Public Expenditure Review: Improving the Poverty Focus of Public Spending.* Report No. 23095-NI. Washington, D.C.: World Bank.

2001c *World Development Report 2002: Building Institutions for Markets.* Washington, D.C.: World Bank.

2001/02 *Brazil: Agriculture Sector Review – Policies and Prospects.* Report no. 7798-BR. Vol. 1. Washington, D.C.: World Bank.

2002a. *India: Evaluating Bank Assistance for the Agricultural and Rural Development: A Country Assistance Evaluation.* Operations Evaluation Department Working Paper Series. Washington, D.C.: World Bank.

January 2002. *Republic of Chile: Country Assistance Strategy.* Report No. 23329-CH. Washington, D.C.: World Bank.

February 2002. *Chile: Country Assistance Evaluation.* Report No. 23627. Washington, D.C.: World Bank.

March 2002. *Determinants of Agricultural Growth in Indonesia, the Philippines and Thailand.* Policy Research Working Paper 2803. Development Research Group, Rural Development. Washington, D.C.: World Bank.

2002b. *Chile's High Growth Economy: Poverty and Income Distribution, 1987–1998.* World Bank Country Study. Washington, D.C.: World Bank.

July 2002. *Reaching the Rural Poor in the Latin American and Caribbean Region.* Washington, D.C.: World Bank.

2002c. *Reaching the Rural Poor: A Renewed Strategy for Rural Development – A Summary.* Washington, D.C.: World Bank.

2003a. *Little Data Book.* Washington, D.C.: World Bank.

2003b. *Rural Poverty Alleviation in Brazil: Towards an Integrated Strategy.* World Bank Country Study. Washington, D.C.: World Bank.

2003c. *Sustainable Development in a Dynamic World.* World Development Report. Washington, D.C.: World Bank.

July 3, 2003. *Indonesia: Water Management and Irrigation Sector Management Program.* Project Information Document, Report No. AB313. Washington, D.C. : World Bank.

July 2003 *India: Sustaining Reform, Reducing Poverty – A World Bank Policy Development Review.* Washington, D.C.: World Bank.

September 2003a. *India: Revitalizing Punjab Agriculture.* Report No. 37609. Washington, D.C.: World Bank.

September 2003b. *Orissa Economic Revival Credit/Loan.* Public Information Document. Washington, D.C.: World Bank.

October 2003a. *China: Promoting Growth with Equity.* Country Economic Memorandum. Report No. 24169-CHA. Washington, D.C.: World Bank.

October 2003b. *Economic Update: Korea Brief.* www.worldbank.org.

October 2003c. *Nicaragua Land Policy and Administration Regime: Towards a More Secure Property Rights Regime.* Report No. 26683-NI. Washington, D.C.: World Bank.

December 2003. *India Country Brief.* Washington, D.C.: World Bank.

2003d. *World Development Report 2004: Making Services Work for Poor People.* Washington, D.C.: World Bank.

2004a. *Little Data Book.* Washington, D.C.: World Bank.

January 2004. *Brazil: Country Assistance Evaluation.* Report No. 27629-BA. Washington, D.C.: World Bank.

February 2004. *Chile: New Economy Study,* Vol. 1: *Executive Summary and Policy Recommendations.* Report No. 25666-CL. Washington, D.C.: World Bank.

March 2004. *Turkey: A Review of the Impact of the Reform of Agricultural Sector Subsidization.* Report No. 34641. Washington, D.C.: World Bank.

June 2004. *Tunisia: Country Assistance Strategy.* Report no. 28791-TUN. Washington, D.C.: World Bank.

2004b. *Tunisia: Rural Development and Poverty Reduction, 1990–2003.* World Bank Operations Evaluation Department. Washington, D.C.: World Bank.

July 2004. *Inequality and Economic Development in Brazil.* A Country Study. Report No. 30114. Washington, D.C.: World Bank.

2004c. Shanghai Conference: Reducing Poverty, Sustaining Growth. Case Study of China: China's 8–7 National Poverty Reduction Program. http://info.worldbank.org/ etools/docs/reducingpoverty/case/33/summary/China-8–7PovertyReduction%20 Summary.pdf.

2005a. *Development Challenges and Poverty in Bihar.* http://siteresources.worldbank.org/ INTINDIA/Resources/chapter_1.pdf.

2005b. *Bihar: Towards a Development Strategy.* Washington, D.C.: World Bank.

2005c. *Indonesia: Support for Poor and Disadvantaged Areas Project.* Report no. 28244-ID. Washington, D.C.: World Bank.

May 2005. *Tunisia: Fourth Economic Competitiveness Development Policy Loan.* Report No. 32297-TN. Washington, D.C.: World Bank.

August 2005. *Turkey: Joint Poverty Assessment. In 2 vol. Report no. 29619-TU.* Washington, D.C.: World Bank.

February 2006. *Structural Change and Poverty Reduction in Brazil: The Impact of the Doha Round.* Staff Working Paper 3833. Washington, D.C.: World Bank.

March 2006a. *The Rise and Fall of Brazilian Inequality, 1981–2004.* Staff Working Paper 3867. Washington, D.C.: World Bank.

March 2006b. *Kingdom of Morocco: Country Economic Memorandum – Fostering Higher Growth and Employment with Productive Diversification and Competitiveness.* 2 vols. Vol. 1: *Synthesis.* Report No. 32948-MOR. Washington, D.C.: World Bank.

June 2006a. *Tunisia: Agricultural Policy Review.* Report No. 35239-TN. Washington, D.C.: World Bank.

June 2006b. *Chile: Development Policy Review.* Vol. 2: *Main Report.* Report No. 33501-CL. Washington, D.C.: World Bank.

June 2006c. *Arab Republic of Egypt – Upper Egypt: Challenges and Priorities for Rural Development – A Policy Note.* Report No. 36432-EG. Washington, D.C.: World Bank.

July 2006a. *Argentina: Agriculture and Rural Development – Selected Issues.* Report No. 32763. Washington, D.C.: World Bank.

July 2006b. *Chile: Towards Equality of Opportunity, 2006–2010 – Policy Notes.* Report No. 36583-CL. Washington, D.C.: World Bank.

2007a. *India: Land Policies for Growth and Poverty Reduction.* Report No. 32898-IN. Washington, D.C.: World Bank.

April 2007. *Chile Investment Climate Assessment.* Vol. 1: *Executive Summary and Policy Recommendations.* Report No. 39672-CL. Washington, D.C.: World Bank.

June 2007a. *Mexico: Creating the Foundations of Equitable Growth, 2006–2012.* Report No. 39993-MX. Washington, D.C.: World Bank.

June 2007b. *Kingdom of Morocco: Creating Conditions for Higher and More Equitable Growth in Morocco – Policy Notes.* Vol. 1: *Main Report.* Report No. 40197-MA. Washington, D.C.: World Bank.

July 2007. *Bangladesh: Strategy for Sustained Growth.* Bangladesh Development Series, Paper No. 18. Report No. 41245. Washington, D.C.: World Bank.

November 2007. *Ghana: Meeting the Challenge of Accelerated and Shared Growth.* Vol. 2: *Background Papers.* Report No. 40934-GH. Washington, D.C.: World Bank.

2007b. *World Development Report 2008: Agriculture for Development.* Washington, D.C.: World Bank.

January 2008. *Social Exclusion and Mobility in Brazil.* Report No. 42486. Washington, D.C.: World Bank.

April 2008. *Turkey: Country Economic Memorandum: Sustaining High Growth – Selected Issues.* Vol. 1: *Main Report.* Report No. 39194. Washington, D.C.: World Bank.

April 7, 2008. *Turkey: Land Registry and Cadastre Modernization Project.* Project Appraisal Document. Report No. 43174-TR. Washington, D.C.: World Bank.

2009a. *Global Economic Prospects: Commodities at the Crossroads.* Washington, D.C.: World Bank.

2009b. *Land Reform, Rural Development and Poverty in the Philippines: Revisiting the Agenda.* Technical Working Paper No. 49503. Washington, D.C.: World Bank.

2009c. *Africa's Infrastructure: A Time for Transformation.* Washington, D.C.: World Bank. http://web.worldbank.org/WBSITE/EXTERNAL/COUNTRIES/AFRIC AEXT/0,,?contentMDK:22047464~pagePK:146736~piPK:146830~theSitePK:258 644,00.html.

April 2009. *Brazil Country Brief.* http://web.worldbank.org/WBSITE/EXTERNAL/ COUNTRIES/LACEXT/BRAZILEXTN/0,,contentMDK:20189430~pagePK:1 41137~piPK:141127~theSitePK:322341,00.html.

March 2010. *Royaume du Maroc: Revue du Secteur Agricole: Un Agenda pour une Transformation Reussie.* Report No. 51727-MA. Washington, D.C.: World Bank.

World Bank and Agence Française de Developpement (AFD), Kreditanstalt fur Wiederaufbao Entwicklungsbank (KfW), Bunderministerium fur Wirtshafliche Zusammenarbeit und Entwickburg (BMZ), Deutsche Gessellschaft fur Technische Zusammenarbeit und Entwickburg (GTZ), and UK Department of International Development (DFID). 2005. *Pro-Poor Growth in the 1990s: Lessons and Insights for 14 Countries – Operationalizing Pro-poor Growth Research Project.*

World Bank and International Finance Corporation. 2007. *Brazil: Country Partnership Strategy, 2008–11.* Report No. 42677-BR. Washington, D.C.: World Bank and IFC.

World Bank and International Finance Corporation. 2009. Doing Business. http://www.ifc.org/ifcext/media.nsf/content/SelectedPressRelease?OpenDocument&UNID=92 6B33153090F5DE852574EC00554520

Wu, Yu-Shan. 1994. *Comparative Economic Transformations: Mainland China, Hungary, the Soviet Union, and Taiwan.* Stanford, CA: Stanford University Press.

Yamada, Saburo, and Hayami, Yujiro. 1979. "Agricultural Growth in Japan, 1880–1970." In Yujiro Hayami, Vernon M. Ruttan, and Herman M.Southworth, eds., *Agricultural Growth in Japan, Taiwan, Korea, and the Philippines*, pp. 33–53, Honolulu: University Press of Hawaii for the East–West Center.

Yamamura, Kozo. 1986. "The Meiji Land Tax Reform and Its Effects." In Marius B.Jansen and Gilbert Rozman, eds., *Japan in Transition: From Tokugawa to Meiji*, pp. 382–399, Princeton, NJ: Princeton University Press.

Yunkaporta, Yukon. June 16, 2006. "Land Rights Canada: Canadians First Nations Battle for Land Rights Against Complex Native Title Laws." http://aboriginalrights. suite101.com/article.cfm/land_rights_canada.

January 1, 2008. "Reconciliation and Colonialism: The Clash between Aboriginal Law and Western Capitalism." http://australian-indigenous-peoples.suite101.com/article.cfm/reconciliation_and_colonialism.

Zahler, Roberto. 1999. "Comment: An Alternative View of Chile's Macro Policy". In Perry Guillermo and Danny M. Leipzinger, eds. 1999. *Chile: Recent Policy Lessons and Emerging Challenges*: World Bank Institute, pp. 55–62, Washington, D.C.: World Bank.

Zhao, Shiji, Katarina Nossal, Phil Kokic, and Lisa Elliston. 2008 "Productivity Growth: Australian Broadacre and Dairy Industries." *Australian Commodities* 15 (1, March quarter). http://abareonlineshop.com/PdfFiles/ac_08_agricultural_productivity_article.pdf.

Zhu, Qiuxia. 2001. "Development of Rural Enterprises (TVEs) in China and Adjustment Policies in the light of WTO accession." In *China in the Global Economy: China's Agriculture in the International Trading System.* Paris: OECD.

Index

Printed in the United States
by Baker & Taylor Publisher Services